To Mason Carr —
With thanks,
and good wishes.
Win Griffith

HUMPHREY
A CANDID BIOGRAPHY

HUMPHREY

A CANDID
BIOGRAPHY

by Winthrop Griffith

William Morrow & Company   *New York, 1965*

for my mother
Florence Griffith

CONTENTS

AUTHOR'S NOTE AND
ACKNOWLEDGMENTS   ix

Part I *THE MAN*

  1 IMAGES AND IMPRESSIONS   3
  2 DEFEAT AND VICTORY   17
  3 A GREEN LAND   34
  4 A DARK TIME   50
  5 TEACHER   63

Part II *THE POLITICIAN*

  6 PASSION FOR POLITICS   79
  7 GRASS ROOTS   91
  8 THE PRAGMATIST   105
  9 MAYOR   117
  10 THE ILLUSIONS OF POWER   131
  11 1948   145

Part III *THE SENATOR*

  12 FIELD OF FORCE   169
  13 THE EDGE OF DIXIE   181
  14 ACCEPTANCE   196
  15 IMPORTANCE   211
  16 INFLUENCE   224
  17 1960: THE EDGE OF LIBERALISM   238

Part IV *THE LEADER*

  18 TALENT AND TECHNIQUE   255
  19 CONVICTION   269
  20 "NUMBER TWO"   286
  21 THE PRESIDENCY   301
  22 POWER AND PURPOSE   317

Index   329

Photographs appear between pages 180-181

Author's Note and Acknowledgments

This book describes, as completely and honestly as possible, an unusual man who identifies with and seeks to lead the people of the United States. It is not a conventional, chronological biography about a man who has been a pharmacist, teacher, Mayor, and Senator, and is now Vice President of the United States. It is about the personal and political development of Hubert Horatio Humphrey.

Much of the material in this book has never been published. Most has been drawn from my observation of Humphrey, from interviews with individuals who have watched him closely from some valuable perspective, and from such prime sources as the Congressional Record.

I worked as an assistant to Humphrey in his Senate office in Washington from January 1960 to February 1964. That experience was valuable for my understanding of the man and the preparation of this book. With day-to-day contact for four years, I learned to interpret his words and actions on the basis of knowledge about his habits and ambitions. With direct involvement in his office operations, I knew which statements were written or dictated by him and which were "ghosted" by others. That distinction is important in judging a man's ideas and intellectual capacity. Many of his comments quoted in this book were made informally, in the privacy of his office or in conversation with the author and others.

Initially I was concerned about the ethical problem of using material which had come to me through my privileged position on Humphrey's staff. Before I began to write this book I had made a basic decision *not* to use anything from a private situation which would embarrass him or others. But I was surprised and relieved to realize that Humphrey rarely restricts the expression of ideas, facts, or phrases to the privacy of his office; at one time or another he places them in the public domain through candid conversations with reporters or speeches in open meetings.

The period covered by this book emphasizes the years 1960

through 1964, but is not limited to them. I have traced Humphrey's life and political career from his birth through his election as Vice President—and have even projected a step into the future.

Humphrey is not portrayed here as an isolated figure against a blank background. His story is told as an integral part of the times and forces which have helped to shape him and which, in recent years, have been significantly influenced by him.

This book cannot be definitive; Humphrey and the political circumstances in which he is involved continue to change, and he is likely to remain politically powerful for many years. For that reason conventional reporting techniques and rigid academic methods are insufficient to describe him. Portions of this book are analytical, interpretive, and—in a few places—impressionistic. I have endeavored, of course, to be accurate in narration and description. Those scenes or quotations which I did not personally observe were drawn from reliable individuals, and usually I checked their accuracy with at least two direct participants.

I cannot claim that I approached the subject of this book with clinical objectivity. But I have sought to maintain the perspective of an interpretive reporter. My essential purpose has been to express clearly and to share with others my knowledge and understanding of a colorful and unusual political leader who could become President of the United States, and to be relatively detached and candid in that task. That is one reason I wrote this book *after* I had left the payroll of the United States Senate and the impressive presence of Humphrey, and why it is being published well after the campaign and election of 1964. I neither sought Humphrey's "authorization" nor checked the manuscript with him.

My understanding of Humphrey would have remained narrow and this study of him would have been shallow without personal interviews with ninety individuals who have known, watched, or competed against him at different times in his life. I was not able to interview all those who have known or worked with him closely, but I tried to achieve some balance of friends and adversaries, liberals and conservatives, Democrats and Republicans, and supporters and critics. I respected the wishes of many sources to remain anonymous because I valued openness in these interviews more than justification for footnote documentation. If appropriate at some future date when time has erased any possible political or

professional consequences for the individuals who were interviewed, my detailed notes will be made available to political scientists or historians.

I wish to express particular appreciation to the following persons
for their courtesy, time, and insights. (All titles relate to the positions these men and women held at the time of the interviews,
most of which were conducted in the spring and summer of 1964.)

In the United States Senate: Majority Leader Mike Mansfield
of Montana, Minority Leader Everett M. Dirksen of Illinois, Mi-
nority Whip Thomas H. Kuchel of California, John Stennis of Mis-
sissippi, Russell B. Long of Louisiana, Clinton P. Anderson of New
Mexico, Paul Douglas of Illinois, Jacob K. Javits of New York,
Joseph S. Clark of Pennsylvania, George S. McGovern of South
Dakota, Gaylord Nelson of Wisconsin, and Ernest Gruening of
Alaska.

In the corps of Washington political analysts and newsmen:
columnists Walter Lippmann, Rowland Evans Jr., Doris Fleeson,
and Holmes Alexander; James Reston and E. W. Kenworthy of
The New York Times; Charles W. Bailey II of the Cowles publications; William Roberts of Time-Life Broadcast; William Theis
of United Press International; Robert McCormick of the National
Broadcasting Company; and Roger Mudd of the Columbia Broadcasting System.

In the Administration: Frederick G. Dutton, Assistant Secretary
of State; Robert Lee, Deputy Assistant Secretary of State (and
former correspondent for the Ridder Publications); Thomas
Hughes, Director of the State Department's Office of Intelligence
and Research (and a former legislative assistant to Humphrey);
Lawrence O'Brien, Assistant to Presidents Kennedy and Johnson;
Harry C. McPherson, Deputy Assistant Secretary of Defense (and
a former general counsel to the Senate Democratic Policy Committee).

In a variety of Washington roles: former Senator from Minnesota
Joseph Ball (Humphrey's opponent in the 1948 election); attorneys
Max M. Kampelman (once legislative assistant to Humphrey),
James Rowe (a former White House Assistant under President
Roosevelt), and Joseph Rauh (a founder of Americans for Demo-
cratic Action); Dr. Evron Kirkpatrick, Executive Director of the
American Political Science Association; Francis R. Valeo, Secretary

to the Senate Majority; and Andrew J. Biemiller, AFL-CIO legislative director (and a former Congressman from Wisconsin).

In Humphrey's office: present or former staff assistants William Connell, John G. Stewart, Norman Sherman, David Gartner, Miss Violet Williams, Julius Cahn, Cyril King (now Government Secretary of the Virgin Islands), and Herbert J. Waters (now Assistant Administrator of the Agency for International Development).

In Minnesota: Governor Karl Rolvaag; Mayor Arthur Naftalin of Minneapolis; Mrs. Burton Joseph, Democratic national committeewoman; Ray Hemenway, former chairman of the Democratic Farmer-Labor Party; Dr. William A. Anderson, former chairman of the University of Minnesota's Political Science Department; John Cowles Sr., president of the *Minneapolis Star and Tribune;* and Ed Ryan, former Minneapolis police chief and now county sheriff.

Dozens of men and women in the South Dakota communities of Wallace, Doland, and Huron helped me to understand Humphrey's background and a part of America that I had glimpsed only briefly before my most recent visit.

I thank Humphrey himself for several private interviews and for opening many of his personal files of memoranda and correspondence to me, and the members of his family for their candid and perceptive comments, particularly his wife, Muriel Humphrey; his sister, Mrs. Frances Howard; and his uncle and aunt, Mr. and Mrs. Arthur Haugen.

I take full responsibility, of course, for all the opinions and conclusions expressed in this book, and for the accuracy of all the material.

For a variety of personal and practical reasons, I am deeply grateful to Mr. Norman Cousins of New York; Mr. and Mrs. Michael Hudson of San Francisco; Mr. Eiler Ravnholt, Assistant Senate Librarian; Mrs. Mary Lasker of New York; Mr. and Mrs. Kenneth Gray of Washington; Mr. and Mrs. Charles Bailey of Washington, Mr. and Mrs. Dean Belbas of Minneapolis; and Mr. Ray G. Delphey Jr., assistant cashier in the Loan Department of the Riggs National Bank of Washington.

Above all, my wife, Patricia, gave to me soft words of encouragement and to the manuscript a hard and talented pencil when both were desperately needed.

PART I

THE MAN

1

Images and Impressions

He is a happy man. He looks uncomfortable when he is not smiling, and his laugh is more eloquent than the best of his speeches.
He loves life and likes work. He gives himself to people and draws
strength from contact with them. His manner can be churlish and
his tongue acid, but only in moments when he is buffeted by the
demands of too many people to whom he has said yes. He is a
positive man, and there is much kindness in him. He likes a bit of
pomp once in a while, but is seldom pretentious. He wears no
masks. He is an open man.

He rarely looks back and never broods; he regards tomorrow as
a great adventure and hates to ruin it with schedules. He spends
more time worrying about the next generation than about his
appointments for next week. He is an authentic humanitarian and
an indifferent planner. He responds to the moment and rejoices in
the present. He does not just begin a workday; he attacks it. He
does not just live a day; he devours it, savoring every minute until
long after midnight, when he recognizes with disappointment and
disdain that the rest of mankind has gone to sleep.

Even in haste Hubert Horatio Humphrey does not just look at
people; he sees them. Once, running down the U. S. Capitol steps
after a lengthy committee session which made him late for his next
meeting, he saw a teen-age boy in a crowd of tourists. The boy, in
pain, was clutching his stomach. Humphrey guided him into the
building, ordered a guard to find a chair, called for Senate physician Dr. George Calver, reassured the boy with soft words and a
gentle arm, then raced to his car to be sped to his next appointment.

Throughout his life Humphrey has changed as much as any

man and grown much more than most. But his basic personal characteristics do not change. Approaching late middle age and twenty years of life and work in Washington, he is still boyish and buoyant, is still inclined to speak with the phrases of Bryan Populism and act the role of a Roosevelt New Dealer, and is still provincial in many of his tastes and fascinated by parochial projects. He has become also a man of international stature and national influence, a man with a sense of history and a concern for his own and the nation's destiny, and a man of personal power and passionate purpose.

On the day and night of his election to the Vice Presidency, November 3, 1964, Humphrey displayed the mercurial nature of his moods and the diversity of his background. He reveled in the knowledge that the election came on St. Hubert's Day and at one point proclaimed with glee, "I'm the Vice President!" In another moment his expression was almost somber as he spoke of his new responsibilities, and he modestly answered a reporter's question with the comment, "It's not for me to say; President Johnson is the leader of the country, and he'll make the programs and policies." He ate a hot dog for lunch and beef stroganoff at a post-election buffet. He spent part of the afternoon sweeping the floors of his house at Lake Waverly; in the evening he spent an hour telephoning powerful Democrats who were sweeping the election in most areas of the country. When reporters asked him what he considered the "high point" of the campaign, he answered, "The end." When the score of reporters and assistants finally left him late in the afternoon, to return to election night headquarters in Minneapolis, he and a single friend went back to the village of Waverly for "a little visit" with some of the townspeople. "I may never have another chance to chat with these good people alone again," he said. He shook hands with the proprietors and a few customers in the village grocery, the hardware store, the drug store, and the gas station. ("Hi, Frank, how's business?") For fifteen minutes he talked informally with the town's parish priest. "I just wanted to say hello," he told the owner of the hardware store; on the man's request, he phoned his mother to say hello. "That was great," he said when he finally left Waverly to drive to Minneapolis. "I love that little town. I love those people."

At 12:30 A.M. as the election returns confirmed a landslide victory for the Johnson-Humphrey ticket, he wanted to leave his private suite on the eighteenth floor of the Sheraton-Ritz Hotel "to see all my friends" at a public victory rally off the lobby of the Raddison Hotel. His advisers told him that it would be improper for him to plunge into the crowd at that point or to go in front of the television cameras before the President spoke at another victory rally in Austin, Texas. He waited, but complained, "I just want to be Humphrey, and not some damned character they've made up for me." When he finally arrived at the rally, he looked out at the crowd of Minnesotans and said that he had come "to the source of my strength, the people. . . ." At 3:30 A.M. he broke away from another victory celebration to confer with the head of a Secret Service unit which had moved in to guard him. At 4 A.M., surrounded by Secret Service men, he walked across the deserted hotel lobby and into a private room to tape a network television program. Just before he went to bed (for only two hours' sleep before departing for the President's ranch in Texas), he wished aloud, "I hope that they don't coop me up so that I can't get close to the people when I want to."

One incident, in August 1963, illustrated how he can give a variety of impressions, some of them apparently contradictory. The scene was Andrews Air Force Base, near Washington. The circumstance was his return from Moscow after the initialing of a treaty suspending atmospheric testing of nuclear weapons.

It was an important point in the history of the U.S.-U.S.S.R. relations and a dramatic moment. A Presidential jet, with THE UNITED STATES OF AMERICA boldly painted along the full length of its fuselage, roared to a stop on the airport apron. A dozen cameramen, a score of reporters, and a hundred State Department and Congressional officials respectfully stepped forward. The passenger hatch of the plane opened, and several members of the Senate Foreign Relations Committee descended with dignity.

Humphrey, who had spent seven years working to encourage a U.S. effort for a test ban treaty and deserved as much credit as any man for its achievement, emerged into the glare of the midafternoon sun, his eyes shaded by a proper diplomatic homburg. In one hand he held a leather briefcase containing a copy of the treaty. In the other he carried a paper shopping bag. "Hey," he called to the cluster of newsmen, "who's with ABC? I've got a TV film for you

from Russia!" An ABC man gratefully accepted a flat package
from Humphrey's bag. "And here's one for Movietone News,"
Humphrey shouted as he handed another film to a cameraman. A
black-jacketed motorcycle messenger stepped forward to ask,
"Anything for NBC-TV, Senator?" Obligingly Humphrey answered, "You bet!" He reached deep into his bag without looking,
pulled out a slice of cheese, stared at it, perplexed for an instant,
and apologized, "Whoops, that's my blue cheese from Copenhagen." The cheese was put back in the bag, in exchange for
NBC's film.

His mission for the news networks completed, he walked to a
bank of news microphones to offer a statesmanlike report on the
treaty, conferred for a few minutes with State Department officials,
then moved toward his waiting chauffeur and black Lincoln Con-
tinental. Abruptly he stopped, turned to face the jet, and said to
no one in particular, "I forgot my beer."

At that moment two Air Force sergeants—each carrying a case of
Danish beer—stepped out of the magnificent jet, walked with military precision to Humphrey's car, and loaded the beer into its
trunk. "Now we can go," Humphrey said decisively.

A year after the incident at the airport a few reporters scoffed at
the effect of Humphrey's work in the field of disarmament and
could remember only that he had played errand boy for censor-
bound American television newsmen in Moscow. Humphrey's
earthy exuberance and his refusal to assume the stereotyped man-
nerisms of high position often kindle a spark of ridicule in public
reports about him. For many of the years of his national prominence his reputation was cast in a mold of such words as "Glib . . .
talks too much . . . impulsive . . . lacks dignity . . . too liberal
. . . smart, but disorganized . . . a quick mind, but spreads himself
too thin . . . eloquent, but abrasive. . ."

The public image of a man begins with his superficial physical
characteristics. One television-radio newsman, with both a philo-
sophic and technical understanding of the effect of screened images, describes Humphrey's face this way:

"Humphrey loses something when he is on camera. He is a
warm, friendly, appealing man in person. But on television his
face often seems unfriendly, unpleasant, and cold. The features
are too sharp. The deep lines running diagonally from the nose to

the sides of the mouth give the whole face a downward cast. When he is not smiling, he seems to be frowning. He has good eyes; they sparkle with spirit. But the viewer's attention is drawn away from them to that massive, high-reaching forehead and to those black eyebrows of his, which rise to sharp points in the middle."

The same newsman, who personally likes Humphrey, also offers a clinical assessment of Humphrey's voice:

"It has one virtue as a radio voice: it is unusual—not like the usual well-modulated voices of announcers—so it attracts attention. But it is, generally, an amazingly unpleasant voice. It is high and rasping, and sometimes almost like a snarl. The neutral listener too quickly gets an idea that the voice belongs to a man who is superficial, angry, cocky, or afraid."

Throughout his political career Humphrey has been told often that he "does not look like" a Mayor, or a Senator, or a Vice President, or a President. Impatiently he suggests that two of the worst Presidents of the United States—Franklin Pierce and Warren Harding—were among the handsomest men to hold that office.

Rigid generalizations about Humphrey are likely to be accurate only for a fraction of time or for a fragment of his personality and appearance. His moods are mercurial, and his expressions and inflections are directly affected by his moods. The individual who has met him only in a late afternoon hour, when he is tired, harassed by a hundred obligations, and complaining about the petty pressures of political life, will sustain one view of him—probably negative. The individual who has seen him meeting with a group of students for lunch and talking informally to them about the nobility of democratic government will maintain a strongly positive attitude toward him. He is, in fact, neither handsome nor ugly. His appearance depends greatly on how much sleep he has been getting, whether his current efforts are succeeding or failing, and on such simple matters as the performance of the pen in his desk set or the air-conditioning unit in his bedroom. His voice can be warm and resonant or abrasive and cold, depending on the number of speeches he has made in the previous twenty-four hours, whether he has had to wolf down cold chicken and lukewarm coffee moments before speaking, and whether he feels stimulated or bored by the text prepared for him. The difference in reactions of people who observe him can be amusing. In the fall of

1959 both *The Saturday Evening Post* and *Pageant* magazines published articles about him. Walter Ridder wrote in the first: "His figure appears slight. . . . He seems smaller than his five feet eleven inches." Al Toffler wrote in the second: "A broad-shouldered five-eleven, Humphrey looks larger."

The one quality on which almost all observers agree is his energy. It is awesome. In his first year as Mayor of Minneapolis two of his chauffeurs retired with cases of pneumonia and a third escaped from the exhausting pace to a rest home. One *New York Times* reporter says that a breakfast interview with Humphrey "is like working an eight-hour day." At the Democratic National Convention in Atlantic City in 1964, Humphrey spent one twenty-hour day working with his staff, arbitrating a dispute between two delegations, conferring with convention and White House officials, appearing on several television programs, herding his family from one reception to another, standing in receiving lines and shaking a thousand friendly hands. He went to bed at 5 A.M. only because he could find no one awake in his hotel headquarters with whom he could have an early morning breakfast conversation or strategy meeting. When his wife and staff occasionally conspire to get him away from Washington for a weekend of rest, he merely becomes restless. ("It was awful," he said after one weekend. "I just SAT there for two days.") When his friends or doctors tell him that he should get more sleep, he answers, "Sleep? I can sleep in the hereafter!" Most reporters write knowingly about the vitamin pills former pharmacist Humphrey keeps in his office. When questioned about his energy, he does not try to trace its source. "It's just there," he says, "like Mount Everest."

Privately he admits that he often becomes "bone-tired and so weary that I can't stand up." Near the end of a grueling year of campaigning during 1959–60 he astounded old friends by sitting down to shake hands after a speech in the Moose Hall in St. Cloud, Minnesota. He still had a smile for each person he met, but his face was pale, his shoulders were slumped downward, and his right elbow barely left the table top as he reached out to shake hands. His energy is, in fact, enormous, but it is not "endless," as some writers suggest. More significant than his energy is his restlessness. "I can't relax," he often says. "I don't know how." The distinction of his furious pace is not that he is *able* to move so fast for such long periods, but that he is *compelled* to by the restlessness inside him. Senator George McGovern, who moved into the house next to Humphrey's when he first came to Washington, was awakened at two o'clock one morning by his wife calling, " Come here and look. What's the matter with Hubert?" After a day and night of hard work on Capitol Hill, Humphrey was scrubbing the kitchen walls.

He fondly remembers that in rare moments of listlessness when he was a boy his father would tap him on the shoulder and utter one word: "Activity!" His dedication to work is a strength; he has progressed from success to success, in part, because he has always been eager to work harder and for more hours of the day than any competitor or colleague. But his compulsion to and respect for activity—unadorned motion of any sort—tend to shade his judgment of people and his sense of discrimination. He once said of a pipe-smoking associate, "It makes him look too calm. I don't trust people who smoke pipes; I think they hide all their unanswered mail under the desk." To an assistant who was quietly editing a speech transcript, he hollered, "You look too serene! You ought to look hurried and harried!" One morning when he arrived in his office he was told that an assistant had been working on an article for him since 6 A.M. "That's great!" he exclaimed, not bothering to ask what the article was about or for which magazine it was being written. He often appears to respect quantity far more than quality; he would prefer to distribute ten hastily written and marginally important news releases than one perfectly composed, significant statement. Motion, volume, sound, and large numbers of people hustling around him please him. The results too often are misdirected energy, wasted talent, unresolved confusion, faulty judgments, and careless mistakes.

Humphrey's mind is as restless as his energy and body, but he uses it with greater discipline. It is quick and highly retentive. His eyes race over the headlines and key paragraphs in the gray masses of type in *The New York Times, The Washington Post,* and two or three other newspapers each morning; eight hours later he can recall scores of facts and figures. He can skim through an eighty-page report written in ponderous government style and filled with technical information and begin to ask intelligent questions before his colleagues have read a third of the way through it. His mind is enterprising and imaginative; he can spend ten minutes being briefed on a subject or problem new to him and then move into an extemporaneous debate against experts and hold his own. He is endlessly curious. "Tell me something I don't already know," he says often to his knowledgeable friends. His intelligence quickly penetrates sham, and he is impatient with wordiness in others. Often his brevity overwhelms a visitor who walks into his office with a carefully rehearsed presentation of some proposal and an armful of charts and supporting documents. After a few minutes of the visitor's introductory remarks, Humphrey asks a quick question which draws out the essence of the proposal, announces his decision of approval, instructs the visitor on what he should do next to advance his proposal, and phones an assistant with an order to "follow up."

Humphrey can—and often does—master a new, highly technical, and intricately detailed subject if he chooses to spend a dozen hours (that's almost an infinity for him) studying it. He frequently remembers the name of someone he has not seen for ten or twenty years. But he has neither total recall of printed material nor a James Farley memory for the names of individuals. In January 1963 he read a text which included the fact that 785,000 out-of-school teen-agers were unemployed in the United States. The next day, in an informal speech, he boosted the number to "more than eight hundred thousand." Two days later the figure rose to "almost one million." Finally, on a network television program, he referred to "more than one million unemployed teen-agers." A frantic assistant urged him to return to the basic, accurate figure. "Why should I?" he asked defensively. "That figure is a week old; there probably *are* more than a million unemployed teen-agers by now." In the mid 1940's he was introduced to Ray Hemenway, then a resident of Albert Lea, Minnesota, and a local Democratic Party leader. The two men next saw each other in a chance meeting on a Minneapolis street. Humphrey stammered, "Well, uh, hello there . . . er . . . buddy. How are things in North Dakota?" Hemenway, who later became state chairman of the party and a Democratic national committeeman from Minnesota, has never since been impressed with tales of Humphrey's retentive mind.

Humphrey is an independent thinker. He has an open mind which is seldom bound by dogmatic notions or rutted with rigid stereotyping attitudes. Despite his instinct to move quickly to the immediately practical, he easily qualifies as an intellectual; he enjoys ideas for their own sake. But he is not a particularly creative thinker. Many who have worked for him label him an effective "brain-picker," and he admits that most of his novel ideas (they flow out of him at the rate of about fifty a day) are blended and reshaped from the ideas of other men. He thinks best in conversation, learns best by listening to other human voices, and communicates best by speaking. He rarely takes the time to read books and seldom writes—with his own hand—more than a few words scribbled at the edge of a memorandum or at the bottom of a letter. In composing his speeches, articles, or letters, he prefers to dictate to a secretary—and likes several other people to be in the room at the same time. It took him six years to learn to relax while using what he calls "that cold little dictating monster which keeps buzzing back at me." Friends and assistants who have known him for years have never seen him touch a typewriter. One of Washington's most respected political reporters and writers agrees that Humphrey produces brilliant, quotable, and incisive phrases, but he adds, "Humphrey has always been in too much of a hurry to learn to he a good writer in the way that John F. Kennedy was a good writer. That's why Humphrey's statements are so full of clichés; he does not have the writer's discipline for economy in using words. He lacks a talent for the *memorable* phrase." A friend who has known and worked with him off and on for more than twenty years claims that he does not appreciate, and can not even recognize, a good literary style.

Most of the people in an audience for a Humphrey speech could not care less that he might lack a literary style or that they might not be able to remember any of his phrases the next day. Just before the 1964 election, *The Washington Post* reported, "He is the best speaker of the four major candidates." A power and force beyond words pour out of him when he is on a platform. It is incorrect to identify a Humphrey speech as an "appearance." It is a performance. He acts out his message with rapidly changing vocal inflections, a vast array of gestures by his hands and arms, and a variety of facial expressions which somehow convey a mood and meaning to the back row of a crowded auditorium. His words and gestures are not all contrived. One reason for the excitement he can generate in an audience is his spontaneity. Most of his audiences sense that they are listening to a man who is exploring his own mind and that he is giving them something new and exciting. Often his speech to a responsive audience is like an act of love: pain, passion, and joy are shared. Some of his greatest admirers admit that they feel overwhelmed, drained, and exhausted after a particularly effective speech.

Humphrey is generally rational and deliberate when dealing with issues and the tasks of high responsibility. But he is more naturally an emotional man. He does not attempt, as much as most public men, to hide his emotions. They flow freely, bringing tears to his eyes as quickly as laughter to his lips. Frequently he literally cries when he tells a friend or an assistant about the hunger he has seen in the slums of Chile or the pathetic loneliness of the children he has visited in an orphanage in Greece. He has trouble controlling himself when he learns of the death of a friend—and he considers tens of thousands of people his friends. In the trying hour on August 26, 1964, when he waited for a call from the White House which would summon or eliminate him as the Vice Presidential candidate, he spent ten minutes in a phone conversation with the widow of a friend who had just died. In the middle of a particularly busy day near the end of the first session of the 88th Congress, he took the time to drive to a Washington church to deliver the eulogy at the funeral of a Negro woman he hardly knew. Why, he was asked later, had he accepted that painful and awkward task? "She was the wife of my driver," he answered. "He asked me to do it." That, for Humphrey, was reason enough.

His character is basically decent and generous. He does not smile at or even tolerate jokes which include expressions or innuendos of anti-Semitism or any other form of bigotry. His language, even in private, is seldom laced with profanities much stronger than "damn" and "hell," although he uses those expletives with frequency. He boasts openly about his achievements on public projects—and sometimes grabs a bit more credit than he deserves—but he keeps silent about the fact that he helps many individual friends or even casual acquaintances with his own money. (He is far from being wealthy.) In 1951 he overheard a part-time file clerk in his Senate office speak of his problem in meeting expenses while attending Howard University in Washington. The next day his personal secretary placed an unmarked envelope with a hundred dollars in it in the clerk's box. He never mentioned the gift to anyone, and quickly changed the subject when the man tried to thank him.

He is almost incapable of vindictiveness. If a friend tells him that another politician has been knifing him or his efforts, he is likely to say, "Don't worry about it; he's just confused." He was tearful and angry for only a few hours after Adlai Stevenson pulled out of what he thought was a firm commitment to give him the Vice Presidential nomination in 1956. When Stevenson phoned him after throwing open the choice to the Democratic Convention, he bubbled over with enthusiastic expressions of support and friendship. In 1960 he met with a group of labor leaders in Madison, Wisconsin. They explained that they could not announce their support for him in the primary election, that they were afraid of making a commitment and would remain neutral. The Humphrey supporter who had arranged the meeting waited for him to demand that he be repaid for the years of favors he had done for the labor leaders. Instead Humphrey nodded his head sympathetically and said, "I know, fellows. It looks like Kennedy will win. I understand." Some of his more professional political advisers lose patience with this "lack of toughness." (When pressed to a political wall, Humphrey can be tough. He learned in 1960 that one national labor leader was about to announce for Kennedy during the primaries; his stinging complaints about "ingratitude" pushed the leader back to neutrality.)

Humphrey tends toward overstatement and exaggeration in his speech, but he is essentially an honest man, and unusually candid for a politician. "I can't lie to those people," he once told a secretary who wanted him to get rid of some office pests. "I'm a lousy liar. I tried it once, and it didn't work." There is a steady consistency between what he says in private and what he says in public. His privately expressed attitudes and ideas rarely contradict his public statements or actions. His wife and other individuals who know him best believe that this integrity accounts for a big part of his happiness; his emotional health never suffers from feelings of guilt.

Humphrey takes his convictions seriously; there is a passion and an intensity behind most of his basic beliefs and what he calls "commitments of conscience." He takes himself—as a man and an individual—far less seriously. For all his confidence, he often has flashes of a "What am I doing here?" thought in moments when he is aware that he is, as he puts it, "sitting at the table of men of power." It is not accurate to call him modest, and the suggestion of some of his friends that he underestimates himself is debatable. But he often expresses sincere amazement at his own success and prominence. When he sees his picture on the front page or cover of a major newspaper or national magazine, his eyes glitter and he says, "Isn't that something!" In early 1962 he announced to his assistants with pleasure and awe that he had been asked to address Washington's Gridiron Club. "They've asked ME to speak at the Gridiron Club," he said. "All the important men in the country will be there!" He was not being coy. His tone of voice indicated absolutely no recognition that he, Hubert Humphrey, was important and that such an invitation was normal. After a private meeting with Henry Ford II he phoned a Minnesota reporter to announce, as though it would be the biggest story of the month, "I thought you'd like to know that I just had a forty-five-minute meeting with Henry Ford, THE Henry Ford!" The reporter blandly asked what the meeting was about. Humphrey answered that he could not divulge the purpose or content of the discussion. He simply thought that the fact of a meeting between Henry Ford and Hubert Humphrey was news. Humphrey does not consciously downgrade his position and prestige; he is simply not aware of it most of the time. If Hubert Humphrey were President of the United States and he learned that the Minister of Agriculture in Nicaragua wanted to see him, he would probably be truly flattered.

There is no question about his intense ambition. That quality was evident in him from the time he passed from kindergarten to the first grade. But there is a peculiar ambivalence to his motivations and quest for success. Most of his decisions to seek higher office have not been made in precise, contrived, dramatic fashion. Often they have simply evolved, or he has made an effort to step higher without even reaching a clear decision. More than most men, he believes that one man's efforts can affect a mass of men, influence events, or help shape a nation's character. But there is a streak of humility, a touch of an inferiority complex, and a hint of fatalism in his attitude toward his own progress and aspirations. Why did he first run for public office, in 1943? "I was between jobs and waiting for the draft; I just thought I'd give it a whirl." Why did he try for the United States Senate in 1948, when Minnesota had never elected a Democrat to that body? "A lot of people were suggesting it, and it just seemed the thing to do." Did he, in June 1964, think that he would get the Democratic Vice Presidential nomination? "Well, I guess we'll soon find out. There is a time for men and politicians, as well as a time for ideas. Maybe 1964 is my year." Does he think he will ever be President? "Who knows."

Humphrey wanted to be Mayor, Senator, and Vice President, and he never hesitated to do what was necessary and prudent to achieve those positions. He would like to be President. He is a normal man with a robust ego and a normal politician with a love for the spotlight. He enjoys being powerful, and he has fun being famous. But the focus of his attention and the direction of his ambitions have always pointed more to what he wants to do than what he wants to be. Inevitably he has been accused of being an opportunist. "What's wrong with accepting opportunities?" he answers. "Is a man supposed to turn away from them?" Cynics have often suggested, derisively, that Humphrey is a "do-gooder." "What the hell am I supposed to be," he asks impatiently, "a do-BADDER?" Those who do not know him well, particularly skeptics who attach selfish motives to any human action or hope, cannot quite believe that his interest in the welfare of people in distant lands or generations and his pleas for "kindness, justice, and opportunity for all men" are anything more than platform-contrived platitudes. The opposite view is taken by a Washington newsman who has known him for years as a friend, reporter, and occasional critic. "Hubert Humphrey," he says seriously, "is too good to be true."

To those who have cut through the persistent images and fragmentary impressions which have clung to his public reputation, Hubert Humphrey is most truly a human being, both grand and imperfect. He is certainly not the demagogue or devil his enemies denounce, but he does have significant faults and definite limitations. He is not the superman or saint his most ardent admirers describe, but he is a good man.

His distinction as a man lies in his empathy with other human beings. He is a compulsive talker, but his success in communicating himself and his ideas is possible because he rivets his attention on the individual person or the group in front of him. He is also a perceptive listener, because he feels that every human being is important and he cares about what any human being wants to tell him. He gives what is in him to others. He also receives and absorbs the ideas, the aspirations, the faith, and the strength of others. He needs human contact the way a generator needs a source for the power it produces.

Few men are more vibrantly alive than Hubert Humphrey. He is like his own very big, fast-beating heart—pumping out the power of life and taking in the substance of it.

2

Defeat and Victory

Far better it is to dare mighty things, to
win glorious triumphs, even though
checkered by failure, than to take rank
with those poor spirits who neither enjoy
much nor suffer much, because they live
in the gray twilight that knows not victory
nor defeat.

—Theodore Roosevelt

The character of a man is tested, and often revealed, by defeat or
victory. Hubert Humphrey can perhaps be seen most clearly in
the moments when he has been vanquished or victorious.

He has lost three elections. The first was in 1943, when as a
young man he ran a close second in a field of nine in the Minneapolis Mayoralty election. The next loss was in April 1960, when
he placed second to John F. Kennedy in the Wisconsin Presidential primary election. In both of those elections he won far more
votes than anyone had expected, and he considered each a "moral
victory."

Defeat—unexpected, total, and humiliating—came on May 10,
1960, in West Virginia. Humphrey, the polls and politicians had
said, would win that primary election battle against Kennedy. The
people of West Virginia—simple, earthy, plain-spoken—were his
kind of "folks," Humphrey had thought. He had a solid record of
advocating the Roosevelt-Truman welfare-type programs which
were both necessary and popular in the economically depressed
state. A poll of West Virginia voters taken just after the Wisconsin
primary revealed a 64 percent to 36 percent edge for Humphrey
over Kennedy.

Humphrey lost the election, in many areas by a two-to-one margin. He lost in the cities and towns and farms. He lost in the coal counties and in the counties were local political bosses had pledged to turn out the votes for him. He lost the veterans' vote, the labor vote, the women's vote. He lost the young and the old, the educated and the uneducated, the prosperous and the hungry. He lost the small Catholic vote and the big Protestant vote.

There were many reasons for the defeat. His staff and organization were limited; in some areas they were amateurish and in others nonexistent. Emblazoned across the front of his campaign bus was a phrase which must rank as one of the all-time worst political slogans: OVER THE HUMP WITH HUMPH. He had no money. After Wisconsin his campaign was $17,000 in debt and most of his financial sources were already drained or soon closed to him. All of his expenditures in the West Virginia primary totaled less than $25,000; the Kennedy organization spent $35,000 on television alone. Franklin D. Roosevelt Jr., with a magic name in Social Security-conscious West Virginia, traveled the state to speak glowingly of Kennedy's impressive war record—which was proper —but also asked with heavy innuendo, "Where was Hubert Humphrey during the war?"—which was improper. Most West Virginians, patriotically proud of their state's record for the highest rate of armed forces volunteers, knew or were soon told that Humphrey had remained in Minneapolis throughout World War II. (F.D.R. Jr. did apologize to Humphrey—a few days after the election.)

Humphrey lost because too many voters believed what many of the Kennedy staff members sincerely believed at the time: that he was only a "front man" for a stop-Kennedy conspiracy by other candidates, and that he could not possibly win the Democratic nomination for the Presidency. Humphrey lost, above all, because a great many West Virginians did not want to be identified by the rest of the country as bigots. Columnist Joseph Alsop, clearly friendly to Kennedy, a Catholic, identified Humphrey as "the candidate of the bigots." Humphrey, who does not have a trace of bigotry in him, was defenseless against the surge of West Virginians who wanted to prove their tolerance by voting for Kennedy.

The campaign had hurt Humphrey, politically and personally. Election night devastated him. The West Virginia polls closed at 8 P.M. Forty minutes later the first precinct reported: Kennedy, 96 votes; Humphrey, 36 votes. By ten o'clock Humphrey knew he was beaten.

Kennedy was in Washington, watching a movie, and later sipping champagne with a few friends in his Georgetown home. Humphrey was in Charleston, pacing through the painful minutes in a Ruffner Hotel suite, its two rooms filled with overstuffed furniture and bordered with gaudy wallpaper. His wife, Muriel, was with him. His chief staff assistant, Herbert J. Waters, was at his side. Washington attorneys and Humphrey advisers Jim Rowe and Joe Rauh—whose political techniques were as different as their names were similar—were there. Mrs. Burton (Geri) Joseph, a friend of the Humphreys and a Minnesota party leader, stayed close to Mrs. Humphrey. A *Life* magazine photographer and a reporter, on assignment to do a story about the attractive and politically talented Mrs. Joseph and not about Hubert Humphrey, were in the suite. A few other friends and a secretary shared the experience.

Between ten o'clock and midnight none of them spoke for long periods of time. Mrs. Humphrey was nervous, but she held herself in fragile control as she listened to her husband phone old friends and advisers in Washington and Minnesota to say, "I've lost, old pal." There were a few short outbursts of anger at the Kennedy campaign tactics. Two of the men argued briefly and bitterly about the alternative methods for Humphrey to concede the election. Soon after midnight Humphrey edited and approved a wire of congratulations to be sent to Kennedy headquarters in the Kanawha Hotel.

Most in the Humphrey group remained numb or agitated. Humphrey's eyes were red and damp, his shoulders sagged, and he moved with heavy steps when he walked to a window to look out at the sprinkle of rain falling on Charleston. He was calm. When he spoke, it was to quell the furious expressions of anger or sorrow by others. He would place his hand on a trembling shoulder and say, "Now, now . . ." His outward concern was directed toward his wife, his friends, his staff. He asked for nothing and said nothing about his own feelings.

Someone called, "Hubert, come here; Kennedy's on television." Humphrey watched and listened to the man who had beaten him so decisively. Kennedy did not yet claim victory, but it was evident he was containing elation. He announced he would fly to Charleston to greet his supporters.

Humphrey clicked off the television set. Those in the room were silent for many minutes. A few started nervously when the telephone rang. A secretary answered the call, then frantically shouted, "Senator! Senator! Senator Kennedy is in the hotel! He's on his way up! Humphrey, puzzled only for an instant, said, "Take it easy. That's not possible. We just saw Senator Kennedy on television. He's in Washington . . ."

There was a moment of wonder, then all of them realized that Robert Kennedy—the opposing candidate's brother and prime strategist—was coming to the suite. In 1960, and particularly on the night of May 10–11, the people around Hubert Humphrey did not like Bobby Kennedy. A few hated him. He stirred their anger far more than did John Kennedy, or any other opponent Humphrey had ever faced.

The Humphrey group stood in the middle of the room as if frozen. For two or three minutes—to some it seemed an hour, to others a few seconds—they waited.

A soft knock sounded on the door. Fingers and faces clenched tightly. No one moved but Humphrey, who walked slowly to the door and opened it.

Bobby stood in the center of the doorway, in front of a mob of reporters and photographers. His hair was disheveled and wet with rain; his eyes red and startlingly open and eager. Mrs. Joseph, a former newspaperwoman, thought, What a fantastic scene! But the *Life* photographer behind her was too absorbed in the drama of the moment to take what would have been an exclusive picture.

Humphrey spoke first. "Hello, Bobby," he said, reaching out with his right hand. Kennedy shook it and said, "Hello, Hubert." Bobby saw Mrs. Humphrey in the back of the room, walked to her, took both of her hands, and gently kissed her on the cheek. It was an instinctive act, a gesture of kindness and concern. But some who had been watching Mrs. Humphrey were certain that she would slap him if he lingered for another moment.

Humphrey moved to her and said to Mrs. Joseph, "Geri, would you get Muriel's coat?" He told Bobby he would meet him later at Kennedy headquarters. Then he turned to his friends and said, "Let's go down to our headquarters." Even in defeat he was still in command—of himself and of others. With Humphrey leading, the room emptied quickly. He rode with his wife and Geri Joseph to his campaign headquarters on Charleston's Capitol Street. In front of the office—a converted store with a big plate glass window covered with the blue and green VOTE FOR HUMPHREY posters —Mrs. Humphrey cried openly and said, "I just can't go in." Humphrey held her hand for a second, then asked Mrs. Joseph, "Would you mind taking Muriel back to the hotel, please?"

He stepped alone into the main room of his headquarters. Its floor was littered with election night debris: a dusty, damp mixture of crumpled paper cups, soft drink bottles, cigarette butts, and torn campaign leaflets. A few hundred persons—volunteers and reporters, staff assistants and cameramen—held to the edges of the room or clustered close to one wall with a big blackboard exhibiting the election returns. Humphrey stood by himself in the center of the room, staring at the names of West Virginia's counties and the numbers of votes cast for, but mostly against, him. A reporter from a New York newspaper, who had followed Humphrey through the winter and spring of his quest for the Presidency, regarded the beaten candidate as a forlorn and pathetic figure. The reporter thought about the struggles of Humphrey's life, of his rise from obscurity and hardship, through success against the odds in Minnesota politics, to prominence and influence in the United States Senate, to this—a dreary scene in a dirty room on a rainy night in Charleston, West Virginia.

Finally, with labored steps, Humphrey moved across the room and onto a slightly raised platform. He unbuttoned his raincoat, handed it to assistant Herb Waters, and stepped before a bank of microphones and television lights.

"I am no longer a candidate for the Democratic nomination for President of the United States," he said in a husky and deliberate voice. Three Charleston girls who had worked sixteen-hour days as Humphrey volunteers pulled handkerchiefs out of their purses. An older man near the door cried audibly, and had to leave. Humphrey spoke slowly and solemnly for another minute, pledging his effort to work for "liberal and progressive" programs in the Democratic platform and emphasizing his intention to run for reelection to the Senate from Minnesota in the fall. His voice was heavy with emotion, but it did not crack.

He finished his formal statement and paused for a few seconds, head slightly bowed, eyes down. Then he raised his head, and with the pain still clearly covering his face, looked out to the men and women staring at him with anxiety and affection.

"Thank you," he said to them. "You're good people."

(Other men have acted differently in the final moment of large and painful defeat. Many have gone into hiding, simply letting their supporters drift away. Many have had the grace to say a few words about "fighting a good fight." Occasionally a man reacts to defeat as Richard Nixon did after the California gubernatorial election in 1962, with bitter complaints and sneering sarcasm. In his final moment of defeat Humphrey spoke of the future, and then looked to the campaign workers and reporters and said, "Thank you. You're good people.")

He took his raincoat back from Herb Waters and slowly buttoned it as Jimmy Wolford, a West Virginia folk singer who had joined the campaign early in the year, strummed his guitar three times. He paused to listen as Wolford twanged the melody of "Give Me that Old-Time Religion" and in his mountain accent sang the campaign lyrics which had been set to it:

> "Ah'm goin' to vote fo' Hew-but Hum-free,
> Ah'm goin' to vote fo' Hew-but Hum-free,
> Ah'm goin' to vote fo' Hew-but Hum-free,
> He's the man fo' you an' me."

(The lively rhythm was gone from the song now, and Jimmy sang it slowly and sadly. Humphrey listened patiently. Most of the women and some of the men in the room were crying; even cameramen and reporters swallowed hard as they watched Humphrey and listened to the second verse of the song.)

> "He makes evva-body happy,
> He makes evva-body happy,
> He makes evva-body happy,
> He's the man fo' . . ."

Jimmy could not finish. His voice broke on the third "He makes everybody happy," and the final line of the verse became muffled sobs as his pudgy body shook and his head lowered to rest on the strings of his guitar.

Humphrey stepped quickly to the folk singer's side, patted his shoulder, and said softly, "That's okay, Jimmy." Then he turned, nodded to Waters, said, "Let's go, Herb," and walked out of the room and into the dark, misty night.

He fulfilled what he considered his obligation to visit the opposition's headquarters in the Kanawha Hotel and congratulate John F. Kennedy on his victory. ("It was very nice of you to come over, Hubert," said the man who would be President for three years and would rely on Humphrey as a friend and ally during that too short time.) Humphrey slept a few hours, flew back to Washington early in the morning, and went immediately to his office in the New Senate Office Building. "I've got work to do," he told his personal secretary, Violet Williams, and then spent an hour dictating short notes of congratulations to Minnesotans who had received press attention for such distinctions as winning cow-milking contests or reaching fiftieth wedding anniversaries. Near noon he summoned three staff assistants, asked to be brought up to date on legislation pending in the Senate, and turned to a discussion of plans for his coming re-election campaign in Minnesota.

He struggled hard to rekindle some spark of enthusiasm in himself and his depressed aides, and for a few minutes he failed. He looked very small sitting in the high leather chair behind his big desk. His words faded into murmurs as he gazed at the green office phone to his left.

"Look at that," he whispered, pointing to the ten plastic light buttons representing the telephone lines into his office. "All of them are dark. No one is calling. No one is interested in a loser. God, I hate to lose. When you offer yourself to the people, when you stand before them and say, 'Here I am; I give myself to you,' and the people reject you . . . well, it's humiliating, that's all."

He swiveled the chair toward the window and looked out toward the brick hotel and apartment buildings, the stone hulk of Washington's Union Station and the sky of a clear spring day beyond. Slowly he spoke, to himself more than to the men in the room:

"I really thought I could win . . . maybe. I really thought I could be President . . . a *good* President."

Suddenly he bounded out of his chair, clapped his hands together to break the mood, and said, "I'm going over to the Senate; see you guys later." In a few minutes he was in the Senate chamber, smiling at reporters and tourists in the galleries, laughing at the good-humored expressions of friendship and sympathy from his colleagues, and glowing in the spontaneous stream of tributes to him by other Senators speaking on the floor. Then he plunged into a debate on a complex tax bill.

That was the way Hubert Humphrey reacted to the one major defeat of his political life.

Humphrey has enjoyed many political and legislative victories, but one of his greatest triumphs was his nomination for the Vice Presidency at the Democratic National Convention in Atlantic City. That personal victory came on August 26–27, 1964, four years, three months, and two weeks after the gloomy night and morning in Charleston, West Virginia. It was not a quick and easy triumph. Humphrey's character was tested and revealed again in the pressure and suspense preceding President Lyndon Johnson's announcement and the delegates' inevitable approval of his "recommendation" of Humphrey for the Vice Presidency.

This was to have been John Fitzgerald Kennedy's convention. He had chosen the site and approved the basic schedule. Kennedy himself had once said, "Life is unfair." Life's unfairness had removed him, and now his convention belonged to a man he had beaten for the Presidential nomination and later chosen as his Vice President in 1960, Lyndon B. Johnson. Life could also seem ironically schematic: the day Kennedy had set for his own renomination acceptance speech, August 27, 1964, was Johnson's birthday.

The luck of life and the accidents of politics had eliminated some able men (one was Robert Kennedy) and elevated others to President Johnson's consideration of a running mate. Johnson, still identified often as a Southerner and a conservative, needed an able man who could also balance the ticket. Hubert Humphrey, eminently identified as a liberal and a Northerner, was close to the top of Johnson's list of possibilities from the beginning.

But the President remained silent about his choice during the month before the convention. He also contrived through a hundred devices and comments to focus the attention of the press and the public on a convention of little intrinsic drama. Through friends, assistants, and reporters he discreetly or bluntly divulged that he had added names to his list, or had eliminated names, or had made up his mind, or had not made up his mind, or would announce his decision a week before the convention, or would wait until the last minute.

The mood of those close to Humphrey in Atlantic City ranged from confidence to confusion. In moments of exhaustion and anxiety their sense of reality sometimes faded into a feeling that all the maneuverings and speculation for the Vice Presidency were part of some grand game or weird joke, played and directed by a higher authority with the sense of humor and showmanship of a master puppeteer. The feeling was not entirely illogical.

The intrigue was baffling in the days leading up to nomination day, but there were many signs which pointed to Humphrey as the choice. The President had done little to discourage the efforts of Humphrey supporters or to stem a tide of party sentiment toward Humphrey. On the Friday before convention week Mrs. Humphrey met the President at a Washington luncheon hosted by Senator Allen Ellender. Johnson was in a good mood; he carried a pocketful of polls reporting a rise in his popularity. He said nothing directly about the Vice Presidency, but he squeezed Mrs. Humphrey's hand and said, "Everything is going to be great." On Saturday former White House Press Secretary and newly appointed California Senator Pierre Salinger phoned Humphrey after a meeting with the President. He had mentioned to the President that he wanted to make a nominating speech for Humphrey, and the President replied, "Well, why don't you write one?"

The late Sam Rayburn, Speaker of the House of Representatives, once said that in enigmatic political situations what counted was not what a man could see or hear, but what he *felt*. Humphrey felt confident. He arrived in Atlantic City, to tell reporters, "I feel very, very good about all developments." When reporter Charles Bailey asked Humphrey for his recommendation on how many picture mats a newspaper editor should make ready for the Vice Presidency story for the next few days, Humphrey smiled and said, "One." But he did not know and could not be sure.

Despite the immense question mark hanging over his political life, Humphrey was full of smiles and exuded a sense of fun and confidence throughout the pressure-packed week. To one woman who asked how it looked for him, he joked, "Like Ivory Soap—99 and 44/100ths percent sure." But he wondered and had to wait. On Sunday night, as he relaxed with his family for an hour, there was a flurry of telephone calls, each of which—they all thought—might be THE CALL. One was from New Jersey Governor Richard Hughes, who had just talked to the President. He knew nothing. Another came from Washington and White House Assistant Kenneth O'Donnell. "He just wanted to chat," Humphrey reported as he put the receiver down. Another was from Walter Jenkins, the President's top aide in Atlantic City. He just had some questions about Humphrey's efforts to work out a compromise on the seating of two competing delegations from Mississippi.

Family and friends grew tenser with each ring of the phone. "Don't worry," Humphrey said brightly. "I'm still in the ball game." Someone asked, "What inning?" Humphrey answered, "The ninth. Two men out. The bases are loaded." He laughed. The other people in the room did not. After another call, which he took in his private room, Humphrey stepped back to the center room of the suite and said with mock gravity to his nervous son-in-law, Bruce Solomonson, "Bruce, the real news has come. In the midst of this historic moment there you sit—in all your frivolity —not knowing . . . that the President has chosen . . . YOU as his running mate." Humphrey chuckled impishly. Bruce sighed.

Most others who clustered around Humphrey during the first days of convention week were far more excited than he. On his way to a reception in the Claridge Hotel on Sunday night, Humphrey was halted in the lobby by a local television interviewer who nervously waved a microphone in his face and asked in rapid-fire sequence, "Senator, do you know anything? Are you nervous? Are you anxious? How are you bearing up?" "Obviously, a lot better than you are," Humphrey answered calmly with a benign smile. He did not show any nervousness, even though he had no idea when or if he would receive word from the President. But he knew that if it came it must come soon. The deadline for decision was only three days away—Wednesday evening—when the Vice Presidential nomination would have to be announced to the convention.

He worked hard during the week to solve half a dozen convention problems, but he had announced to his staff and friends when he first arrived in the crowded city, "This is great. I'm going to have fun here." An assistant proudly informed him that a private penthouse in the Shelburne Hotel had been reserved for him and Mrs. Humphrey "to get you away from the mobs." "But I don't want privacy!" Humphrey declared. "I WANT to be with the mobs!"

He plunged into the mobs of people as if he were campaigning for a seat on the Atlantic City municipal council. After a television program for the American Broadcasting Company in Convention Hall, he spent half an hour shaking hands with ABC employees, starting with News Chief and former White House Press Secretary James Hagerty, and continuing with cameramen, directors, coffee boys, technicians, and telephone operators, while his frantic assistants tried to pull him away.

Immediately after another television program in Convention Hall, a joint appearance on NBC's "Meet the Press" with the second Vice Presidential possibility, Senator Eugene J. McCarthy, the President phoned the two men in the studio. He was full of praise, saying to Humphrey, "Hubert, teacher gives you an A-plus. Neither of you failed. You were excellent. It was wonderful." Still Humphrey did not know the final answer to the big question.

On Monday, Martin Agronsky interviewed Humphrey, Mrs. Humphrey, and two of their children for a CBS-TV program. Agronsky quoted the President as saying that he wanted a man as running mate who had tasted both victory and defeat, then he asked Humphrey, "You have known both victory and defeat. . . . What about Charleston, West Virginia, in 1960? How did that affect you?" Humphrey answered seriously, "I like to win. I don't like to lose. But I learned by losing. I think defeat can strengthen a man, can give him character." Agronsky noted that the President's most recent criteria for a running mate seemed to fit Humphrey. "Maybe," Humphrey said as he and his wife and children remembered the high hopes of four years ago. "But I've had disappointments before. And I've made up my mind that this thing won't break my heart, or the hearts of my family, if I don't get it."

On Tuesday night Humphrey and his wife had a steak dinner in the Colony Hotel suite of his old friend James Rowe, also a close associate of the President. He learned then that he would be called to Washington to see the President—probably that night. But the weather turned ugly, and it was decided not to risk a flight to

Washington. Humphrey was told he would receive instructions sometime the next day. He was told nothing more. He was now "almost sure" that the nomination would be his, but his stomach was beginning to churn. As he had guessed the previous week, the suspense would continue until the final hours before the scheduled nominating speeches on Wednesday evening.

He slept late Wednesday morning, breakfasted with his son Douglas (reporters asked later what he had eaten for breakfast, the ultimate sign that a man has achieved public importance), leisurely showered and shaved, and then met for half an hour with Senator Olin Johnston of South Carolina. The crowd of reporters and cameramen in the hallway outside his suite speculated grandly on the meaning of the meeting; Humphrey and Senator Johnston merely chatted about the weather (hot and humid), the Mississippi delegations' credentials squabble (now resolved), and the height of Senator Johnston's son-in-law. ("He's taller than any of the Humphrey boys.") Just before 1 P.M., Humphrey pushed his way through the wires, television cameras, and the bodies and questions of newsmen to get into his tenth-floor office suite in the Shelburne. Inside, he took off his coat, looked at his watch, walked to a window, and stared down at the Atlantic City boardwalk and beach. "Gene [Senator McCarthy] is down there," he said. "I wish I were down there on the beach."

The first signs of nervousness began to show. He paced the length of the long room once. Looking at the door and hearing the muffled sounds of a hundred newsmen outside, he said, "I feel locked in." At 1:18 P.M. his secretary, Pat Gray, handed him a phone message slip, and he asked his friends and assistants to clear the room. Fifteen minutes later, after completing the call, he invited them back. "Nothing," he said in answer to their questioning faces. Then he said to Mrs. Gray, "Are some of my friends outside? Let some of them come in here. I want to see some people now." They came in, one or two at a time, to give him a hug or handshake, to introduce a son or a cousin, to ask him, "How's it going?" "Great, just great," he answered, most relaxed in the moments of small talk with old friends.

During a break in the stream of visitors he stood by himself at one end of the room and muttered, "Why doesn't the man call?" At two fifteen he pointed to a solitary red telephone on a corner desk and asked with mock apprehension, "What is this—a hot line from the White House?" With rapid motions he pulled the receiver of the phone to his ear and then jammed it back onto the cradle. "It's alive!" he said with a comic grin. The men in the room laughed.

At one minute to three o'clock the call came, from Presidential Aide Jenkins. In the middle of his instructions the phone line went dead. Humphrey tapped his fingers on the phone. Mrs. Gray calmly received the call-back from Jenkins, and Humphrey continued the conversation. As he spoke, two New Jersey state policemen stepped through the doorway. A photographer assigned by the Democratic National Committee came into the room. A Federal Aviation Agency pilot appeared without announcement. Jenkins instructed Humphrey to go to the local airport and explained only that the President wanted to talk to him about his ideas and recommendations for the Vice Presidency. Humphrey answered, "Okay, I'm ready. Let me be clear on all this. Mrs. Humphrey is supposed to meet Mrs. Johnson when she arrives, right? I'll go to the airport now. Is that all?" That was all. Humphrey still did not have the final, absolute word. He beckoned to son-in-law Solomonson as he hung up. "Bruce," he whispered, "go up to my room. Go into the bathroom. In my black case on the soap dish are some pill bottles. One has green pills in it. Bring me one of the green pills. I've got an upset stomach." But he was grinning.

At Bader Airport, just outside Atlantic City, Humphrey saw Senator Thomas Dodd of Connecticut getting into the six-seat Piper Aztec waiting for him. Dodd had also been called to the White House. They asked each other identical questions and gave each other identical answers: "Did he tell you anything?" "No." On the flight south Dodd talked. Humphrey was quiet most of the time. He remembered, I've been disappointed before. . . . I will not let this thing break my heart. Then he went to sleep.

In the Rose Garden behind the President's office reporters questioned Humphrey as he waited to be called inside. A light rain began to fall, very much like the sprinkle which had fallen on Charleston on the night of May 10, 1960. One of the reporters suggested that the group move under cover because of the rain. Humphrey replied with a grin, "Oh, is it raining? I thought we were being blessed."

Shortly after 6 P.M. he entered the oval office of the President of the United States. President Johnson sat behind his desk. Secretary of State Dean Rusk, Secretary of Defense Robert McNamara, and Presidential Assistant McGeorge Bundy were in the room.

There were no words which would please historians with a sense of drama. Without prelude President Johnson said to Hubert Humphrey, "Any Senator worth his salt would have known a month ago that I was going to pick you."

This was Humphrey's moment of victory. He was relieved, but too impressed and awed to remember later exactly what he thought, said, or did. At six thirty the President placed a call to Mrs. Humphrey in her Shelburne Hotel room in Atlantic City. "Hello, Muriel," he said. "You looked real good on television this afternoon." "Thank you, Mr. President." "We're going to nominate your boy tonight. I want you to put on your best bib and tucker for him." "I'll put on my best bib and tucker for both of you." "I've got him on the phone here to talk to you; we're taking good care of him for you."

Humphrey took the phone and asked his wife, "How are you?" "Fine," she answered. "But you tell him [the President] that if he pulls any more of these I'll have to have a chair behind me all the time." Humphrey laughed, asked if she was ready for the convention session, and ended, "See you later."

They were together when Humphrey's moment of triumph came in Convention Hall at Atlantic City. At 12:27 A.M., August 27, 1964, the Democratic National Convention formally nominated Humphrey for the Vice Presidency, by acclamation.

From then on the hours moved quickly and the fruits of triumph flowed freely. Many more reporters trailed him to note every word he spoke. The people in the hallways and crowded ballrooms and on the jammed street corners waved and cheered. (A woman at the curb in front of the Shelburne Hotel on Michigan Avenue said ecstatically to a companion, "There I was. In this big crowd. All of a sudden—WHOOSH! This big black car rolls up to the curb. And there HE was. It was HUBERT HUMPHREY! Standing right next to me! I mean it. Just two feet away. And there I was! Gawd!")

Humphrey's first formal appearance after the nomination was at a reception in his honor at the Hotel Dennis. With bells clanging and a band blaring and a thousand arms waving and five hundred bodies pressing toward the slightly raised platform, he grinned, laughed, joked, and spoke joyous words of victory. He stayed at the reception—for which guests paid a thousand dollars each for the privilege of attending—for ten minutes. In the hotel kitchen on the way out he lingered for fifteen minutes, chatting with waitresses, cooks, busboys, and dishwashers.

On Thursday night the triumph reached another climax. Humphrey spoke to the convention for twenty-four minutes and was interrupted by applause thirty-five times. Above him and the platform were modest-sized portraits of Franklin Delano Roosevelt, Harry Truman, and John Fitzgerald Kennedy. Behind him, on one side, was a huge picture of the stern face of Lyndon B. Johnson. On the other side, towering just as high above him, was a giant picture of his own smiling face. At the end of his speech, as the huge Convention Hall thundered with cheers, applause, and stamping feet, Humphrey turned to the several men he had invited to the platform as his formal escort. One was Herb Waters, the former assistant who had held his coat when he spoke to a few hundred silent people in a dusty room in Charleston four years before. "My voice broke! My voice broke!" Humphrey shouted now above the happy din. Waters, his eyes filled with tears, shouted back, "It's okay. It's okay. You did great." Mrs. Humphrey stood in the President's box to the right of the platform, looking at her husband and smiling. The applause and music and cheers rolled on and on.

At nine fifteen the following morning, Friday, Humphrey was just a man again. He was asleep in his room on the ninth floor of the Shelburne when Mrs. Humphrey stepped in and nudged his shoulder. "Dad, you'd better wake up. We have to be all packed and ready by ten. The White House people called. The President wants us to leave [by limousine, helicopter, and jet for the President's ranch in Texas] by eleven o'clock."

Humphrey struggled to open his eyes. Stiffly he pulled himself to a sitting position on the edge of the bed. He was still groggy with sleep, and his voice was husky.

"It's impossible," he muttered. "Impossible . . . just impossible. . . . It's all impossible."

On the eve of his nomination Hubert Humphrey had relaxed

for half an hour on a sun deck of the Deauville West Hotel, over-
looking the Atlantic City boardwalk and beach. He was waiting to
be interviewed by William Lawrence of ABC-TV. It was warm
and clear; a soft breeze flowed in from the sea. Coatless and holding a drink, he leaned against the deck railing and looked out to
the darkening blue Atlantic. "What a beautiful day; what a beautiful evening," he said. The beach was almost deserted, but a few
convention delegates and vacationers strolled the boardwalk
twenty feet below. A teen-age boy called, "Hey, Senator Humphrey, what are you doing up there?" Humphrey answered pleasantly, "Just waiting to do a little television program." An older
man, wearing a delegate's badge, shouted, "How's the next Vice
President?" Humphrey beamed and shouted back, "I don't know,
but *I'm* fine." A sunburned man in bathing suit and yellow terry-
cloth jumper identified himself, then explained, "You remember.
We met in 1960. I sent you that shirt from California." Humphrey
held his neutral smile for a moment, then recognized the man and
replied, "Oh yes, now I remember. A green shirt. Great. I wear it
out at the lake." About thirty people on the boardwalk were now
looking up at the man in shirt sleeves at the railing, shouting their
greetings and good wishes, addressing him as "Hubert" or "Humphrey" or "Senator" or—with knowing smiles—as "Mr. Vice President." Humphrey did not look like the stereotype of a Senator or
Vice President then; he could have been a small-town Midwestern
businessman, prosperous enough to bring his family to one of the
better hotels by the seashore. But he did not have such a man's
anonymity. The people recognized him, and he responded. He
asked individuals where they were from, questioned them about
the quality of the swimming or fishing, and said he wished he
could be down there with them. At that comment the little crowd
of people applauded and a woman cried up, "We're with *you,*
Humphrey."

Humphrey was obviously touched. He was also slightly self-
conscious before the reporter's eyes of ABC newsman Lawrence, so
he said good-bye to the people and stepped back out of sight of the
boardwalk. Sitting next to Lawrence as sound men and make-up
men fussed over him, he was relaxed and reflective in the warm
glow of the summer twilight and the attention of the people.

"You know," he said quietly, nodding toward the boardwalk,

"this is one of the nice things about politics. You go a long way, and work a long time, and travel to a lot of places, and finally many people know you and recognize you and are friendly. I like that.

"I guess I haven't gotten this the easy way, this friendship of so many people. It's been sort of piecemeal, a bit at a time, and I've made a lot of mistakes. To get this friendship and maybe the respect of people takes a lot of doing, my way. It takes a lot of years."

3

A Green Land

In the late spring of a kind year South Dakota is a green and gentle land. After rain the moist earth is carpeted with the color of life. Fields of corn are dark green and glossy under the June sun. A soft spring pastel lingers in the stalks of young wheat. The yellow-green of alfalfa hints at the fullness of summer and coming harvests.

Eastern South Dakota is prairie. It is open land. Nothing restrains the flow of pleated fields and endless plain; there are few fences or trees, and no mountains. The earth is exposed and passive, waiting for whatever the turns of nature and the hands of man will do to it. The open land submits; it takes and it gives.

The town of Wallace is small and contained, as are the thousand other towns which dot the vast Dakota prairie. It nestles against the crossed arms of State Highway 20 and County Road 27, and under a protective canopy of elder and elm. From the highway little can be seen above the clump of trees: a single church spire, a water tank, a grain elevator.

Hubert Horatio Humphrey Jr. was born in Wallace, in a room over his father's drug store, in a narrow building on Main Street, on Saturday morning, May 27, 1911.

The roots of Humphrey's family tree were spread wide. His father's ancestors left Wales in 1648 to settle in the new American colonies. Humphrey's great-great-great-grandfather, Elijah Humphrey of Dudley, Massachusetts, served for three years in the Revolutionary Army. His great-grandfather, a Connecticut Yankee, moved West after the Civil War to farm near Union Lakes, Minnesota. His grandfather, John Humphrey, pioneered in Oregon and later returned to Elk River, Minnesota, to become a Master Farmer and organizer in the Grange. Humphrey's father, Hubert

Horatio Humphrey Sr., was born near Albany, Oregon. He broke from the family's farm tradition to be a pharmacist and small businessman. He first worked in a drug store in Lily, South Dakota, and in partnership with another businessman in Granite Falls, Minnesota, before opening his own store in Wallace. In 1915, when Humphrey was four, his father moved the family and business to Doland, South Dakota.

Humphrey's mother, Christine Sannes Humphrey, was born in Kristiansand, a seaport at the southern tip of Norway. Her father, Andrew Sannes, spent his early manhood at sea, working on Norwegian ships which sailed the trade routes from Scandinavia and Europe to China and Africa. He captained one of the first ships to nudge through the new Suez Canal. In the 1880's, Sannes ended his voyaging, took his family away from the cool coast of Norway, and drove a team of black horses into the hot and desolate prairie at the center of the American continent. He settled in South Dakota, to farm 360 acres of rich lowland between Lily and Wallace.

Grandfather Sannes was a meticulous pioneer. He wanted his farm to endure, and to be productive and beautiful. He gathered together the stones from his half section of land to use as foundation for house and barns, and painted the buildings often to protect the wood against the harsh extremes of the Dakota climate. His fields of wheat and corn were as neat and symmetrical as a plaid pattern. When Humphrey was a boy, he helped his grandfather mow the grasses at the edge of the roadway, swept the yard between the red barns and livestock sheds, and weeded a garden of flowers in front of the white frame house. During evening visits he lolled at the old man's feet listening to tales of the sea and proclamations about the evils of debt, the honor of labor, and the pursuit of excellence.

Childhood friends and neighbors remember Humphrey as a happy boy, eager to please, and one who "made you feel good when he was around." He was persistently curious and talkative. His massive energy and thin body, one relative suggested, "were like a Rolls Royce engine in a Model T frame." His fair skin, easily burned in the summer sun, earned him one nickname: "Pinky." Customers in his father's drug store who watched him clean the shelves and medicine jars gave him another: "Dusty."

Humphrey was helpful and hard-working as a boy. He could

also be cleverly mischievous. When he was three, and his mother caught him in a prohibited prank, he hid under a lattice-sided porch to escape punishment. At the end of the day Humphrey Sr. crawled under the porch, on his wife's instructions, to apply a switching to his son. The boy charmed him by calling from the dark, "Daddy, is Mama after you, too?" On his seventh birthday he invited every boy from miles around to a party, then organized them into a successful conspiracy to dump his mother's hired girl into a rain barrel.

Young Humphrey was adventurous. When the circus came, he followed the marching band out of town to help raise the tent and feed the elephants. When freight trains stopped at Doland's red station, he climbed aboard while the switchmen were not looking. As the train picked up speed outside town, he jumped with a jubilant yelp into a sand pit.

There was little which could restrain or embarrass him. After he broke his arm, he continued to play basketball and baseball with his arm in a cast. In the seventh grade, playing the leading role in *Jack and the Bean Stalk,* he tore open the back of his bloomer-type pants while descending a pegged and camouflaged pole. The other children on the stage and half the audience giggled with embarrassment or amusement. Humphrey faced front and completed his lines with a straight face.

One neighbor reported, "He was a born leader. Whenever Hubert joined the gang in our yard, there was always plenty of activity. He seemed to be able to get them all to do what he wanted them to and still keep them happy." He was either a "brilliant organizer" or a "bossy little brat," depending on the perspective of the follower. During the summer he organized baseball teams, which his father's store equipped. In winter he led the town's boys in games which he invented. His favorite game was "Napoleon at Waterloo," which he conceived after reading one of his father's books. On a snowy slope outside town he directed the boys to form two armies, one French and one British. A Doland lad who had been born in England was always assigned the role of the Duke of Wellington. Humphrey always appointed himself Napoleon. He had a burning ambition to beat the British; each Saturday afternoon he did. With bigger snowballs and more aggressive tactics than the nine-year-old "Duke of Wellington,"

Humphrey rewrote the history of Napoleon's final summer defeat at the hands of the British.

He was fiercely competitive. Selling copies of the St. Paul *Dispatch* on the streets of Doland each afternoon, he hollered the headlines more stridently than any other paper boy. Years later he said, "Every time a competitor would start up against me, I'd redouble my efforts. I don't say that I had a monopoly, but let's say that I cornered the market, so to speak, on the newspaper business in town."

Outside the familiar environment of Doland, Humphrey was relatively meek. He did not travel outside South Dakota until he was in the eighth grade; then he accompanied his father on a business trip to Minneapolis. He had never before seen a fire engine, and was convinced that Minneapolis was "the biggest city in the world." Spending most of the visit with his face glued to the window of his father's hotel room, he peered down on the crowded streets and waited for the sound of sirens.

Humphrey had time for boyish daydreams. His favorite flight into fantasy transformed him into a knight, on a big horse, riding into the dark woods to slay a dragon. On clear days he lived the dreams. With the precision of a child's imagination, he packed cinnamon rolls which became venison, grasped a limb which became a lance, and stalked into a clump of trees at the edge of Doland to become the brave knight Roland.

His earliest practical ambition was to be a druggist, like his father. Later his childhood goal was to be a chemist, and then a chemical engineer. A political career was not really considered when he was a child and teen-ager. He was elected junior class president in high school, but that first political campaign of his life was a relatively minor effort. He was a good student; his high school transcript records A's in every subject, except for two lonely B's in Latin and Glee Club. If he favored any subject, it was history. He starred on the debating team and most of the school's dramatic productions and was on every sports team: forward in basketball, left half or end in football, second or third base in baseball, and a half-miler in track. "I wasn't particularly good in any sport," he admits, "but I was enthusiastic and scrappy."

It was a healthy, active, and positive childhood, marred only occasionally by deep trouble or tragedy. Only one experience crushed his ebullience: the influenza epidemic of 1918, when he was seven.

He almost died. The epidemic was nationwide, but particularly virulent in the bitterly cold winter of the prairie. Humphrey was the last in his family to be infected and the first to claim recovery. When his temperature touched normal, his parents dressed him warmly and allowed him to play outside. The next day his fever shot up again; the last phase of influenza developed into pneumonia. The word spread among Doland's people that he was dying. He lay hot and still for several days, dreaming feverishly of the time when older boys had frightened him by hanging the white skull of a cow in a deserted barn in which he played. Waking, he struggled to keep his eyes open, and saw sadness and fear on the faces of his mother and father. He was afraid. He thought consciously, *I am going to die,* and he understood that this meant he must leave his parents, his home, his friends, and his town forever.

His father did not accept the pessimistic prognosis. Humphrey Sr. read in a journal of a new drug, still experimental but available in Minneapolis to pharmacists. Still too sick himself to make the trip, he asked a friend, Herb Gilbey, to go. Gilbey drove all night to Minneapolis, returning in a heavy snowstorm as Humphrey's fever climbed to a critical degree. The drug he brought back from Minneapolis broke the fever; Humphrey recovered.

Many did not. Influenza, even without the complications of pneumonia, was a killer in the days before penicillin and other antibiotics. Humphrey, his chest protected from the wind and cold by a chamois vest and his hand held tightly by his father, stood on the frozen ground of Doland's cemetery and watched the town bury children, men, and women he had known and loved.

He showed a spark of compassion when he was barely out of short pants. He occasionally expressed indignation about conditions in the "shantytown" of impoverished families and shabby boxlike dwellings outside town. His Aunt Olga tells of his crying with childish logic, "Why shouldn't the shantytown kids have shoes? They're just as good as me. I have shoes; they should have shoes, too." One Doland man recalls a winter afternoon when young Humphrey dragged a frail, wide-eyed shantytown boy into the drug store. He glared over the counter at his father and said,

"Daddy, Jonathan here doesn't have any shoes. It's cold outside. Jonathan's feet are blue. What are we going to do about it?" Humphrey Sr., half surprised and half pleased, pulled a bill from his cash register, trotted the docile Jonathan down the street to a variety store, and bought him a pair of heavy socks and tough boots.

Shantytown was a blemish on the land, a gathering of itinerants and "ne'er-do-wells" which many of the citizens of Doland ignored or sternly regarded as separate and unequal. Doland, the town in which Humphrey lived, learned, and grew from the age of four to eighteen, was a tight and tiny unit of people and buildings. They huddled together for strength and identity in the frightening loneliness and imponderable distances of the prairie. Doland's size, usually hovering around a cozy half thousand, and its isolation— the nearest towns were about twenty miles away—pushed the people and their homes close together. Doland was a true community: the whole town mourned the loss of one of its sons or daughters; the whole town rejoiced in the success of one of its own. The community atmosphere and spirit conditioned its members to be involved with one another, to care deeply about the joys and sorrows of neighbors, to live and work in close relationships. Casual human contact was rare; the doors to the homes and lives of Doland's people were open to all who lived in Spink County.

Sinclair Lewis, who was born and reared in a small prairie town and spent much of his life writing about it, mocked the rural community. In an introduction to *Main Street* he wrote:

"In America, it was almost universally known that though cities were evil and even in the farmland there existed men of wrath, our villages were approximately paradise. They were always made up of small white houses under large green trees. . . . It was Neighborliness that was the glory of the small town. In the cities, nobody knew or cared, but back home, the Neighbors were one great big jolly family."

In a 1924 visit to Sauk Centre, Minnesota, the place of his birth and the "Gopher Prairie" of his first famous novel, Lewis spoke of "this prairie village lost in immensities of wheat and naïvetés." Later he insisted, "I still felt that the ghetto-like confinement of small towns could be—not always was but could be—a respectable form of hell."

For Humphrey the prairie village of Doland, was, and to some extent still is, a marvelous miniature of heaven on earth. In his childhood he did not feel confined. He thrived on the pleasures of his youth and the simplicity of community life. He liked the informality of the neighbors, and never questioned a routine which permitted and encouraged him to walk into most homes without an announcement or knock. Privacy was neither necessary nor desired. People were important.

Humphrey rarely speaks in general or abstract terms about the places of his childhood. He remembers people more clearly than incidents. He recalls names and forgets dates: "Alice Keevan, the fifth-grade teacher—what a fine woman! . . . Irvin Herther, our coach—a big, handsome man . . . Old Doc Sherwood, our country doctor, he was a wise and warm fellow . . . Guy W. Cook, our school principal—one of the most intelligent men I've ever known." The memories of friends are distinct. "Little Ed Johnson was a wonderful friend, and he played on my baseball team," Humphrey says brightly. Then his smile fades, and he adds quickly and sadly, "He died of peritonitis . . . poor little Ed." A half century and a thousand miles have not essentially cooled the warmth he feels for individuals. At the seventy-fifth-anniversary celebration of the settlement of Wallace he looked into the eyes of an old woman and said, "I remember you; you helped take care of me when I was sick." For forty years he sent birthday messages to one of his Sunday school teachers. He still speaks proudly of the achievements of such boyhood friends as Julian Hart, now a professor of religion at the Yale Divinity School.

Doland society was uncomplicated, decent, and pure. There was no conflict of classes; almost everyone was firmly placed in what outsiders considered the middle class. Crime was rare and petty; most of the people were satisfied with what they had. Racial tensions did not exist; the town's population included only one Jewish family, and no Negroes. The major influences on a child were the school, the church, and the family.

Doland was, and is, proud of its independent school district, with its big red brick school building and staff of well-trained teachers. The school represented a huge investment for the town, and its students were expected without question to appreciate it, to study hard, to do well. The children were strongly competitive within and through the school. A motto of Humphrey's high school class of '29 was "We're out to win." It was not enough for an individual or the whole school to be good; they had to prove it to the bigger and more imposing cities of Webster, Watertown, and Sioux Falls. Doland's sports and debating teams excelled in area and state competitions. The high school relay team, including Humphrey, won its race in a state track meet. The debating team, inevitably including Humphrey, won a state tournament. The community simply assumed that its school would be a first step toward great achievements and successful careers for its children.

The church was strong. Doland's people realized they were a long way from Minneapolis or Chicago or New York, but they would be close to God. Most families of Doland attended services regularly and worked in church programs. The Humphreys were members of Doland's Methodist Church. Both parents were leaders in the church's service leagues, and their home was filled with club gatherings each Sunday evening. Humphrey was active in the choir, the Sunday school, Wednesday evening prayer meetings, and church youth groups. As a boy he often squirmed restlessly in the family pew during morning services, but he listened to and respected The Reverend Albert Hart, a conscientious minister, an eloquent preacher, and one of the town's few intellectuals. "This man, more than any other person with the single exception of my father, was a constructive influence in my life," Humphrey says.

The religious attitudes of both Humphrey and his father, who was not baptized until he was forty, were not strictly denominational. Humphrey Sr.'s library included books on the Methodist Church, Buddhism, Catholicism, and Martin Luther. Humphrey is a Christian, but he is also fond of referring to the "Judaic-Christian heritage" and seems to favor quotations from the Old Testament. He was married in a Presbyterian church, retains membership in the First Congregational Church in southeast Minneapolis, and is an affiliated member of the Chevy Chase Methodist Church near Washington. "I was brought up to believe that religion was more than a Sunday experience," he says, "and I was brought up to believe that the truly Christian man is one who understands the meaning of love, compassion, and justice, and these are standards to which one should aspire."

His religious convictions are rarely flaunted, but they are deeply rooted in his personality and affect much of what he says and does. "I can never understand how one can be a Christian and not have a sacred regard for human dignity," he says. "When the New Testament tells us that we are all one in Jesus Christ, I can see no room for segregation, bigotry, or intolerance." His lifelong effort to champion the cause of civil and human rights did not evolve, to use his phrase, "from a bunch of books or economic charts." Liberals and intellectuals often are disappointed when he indicates his motivation for a particular proposal with a shrug of his shoulders and a quick "It's just the right thing to do" or "It's only common sense, that's all." The genesis of his convictions and most of his actions cannot be traced precisely to any particular ideology: "I received my ideas from my church, from my community experience, from my family experience, and from my mother and father."

When he was a child, his family was close, but not cloying. He was the second of four children, each of whom was given an ample number of opportunities for childish pleasures, but also definite responsibilities to share in the work of the house and business. Discipline was firm, but not oppressive. Toward his older brother, Ralph, he felt competitive, and sometimes combative. Their father occasionally improvised a prize fight ring in the basement or front yard for the two brothers. Once, when Ralph traded Humphrey's phonograph ("I loved that thing; it had silver sides.") for parts to a crystal set, Humphrey took on his older and bigger brother in a fist fight. He lost, spent the next several months practicing fast footwork and boxing techniques, then outboxed Ralph in a return match supervised by their father. Toward his two younger sisters, Frances and Fern, Humphrey felt protective and responsible. He could also be impatient over their development. When Frances returned home after her first day in school, he was indignant that she had not yet learned to read. Each child tended to pursue independent interests and activities. Today they are scattered: Ralph operates the drug store in South Dakota, Frances lives in Virginia, Fern in Minnesota.

Their mother, one of twelve Sannes children, inherited a rever-

ence for family, home, and hard work from her sea captain-farmer
father. She efficiently cared for the needs of her husband and children in a time and region with few home conveniences. To Humphrey and his brothers and sisters she preached a doctrine of duty,
service, and selflessness. She was a prudent and practical wife and
mother, and impatient with waste or frivolity, but she had a quick
sense of humor and a disciplined imagination. She wrote poetry
and Norwegian-type folk stories to read to her children, and her
sweet rolls and pastries won prizes at local fairs. She cooked not by
recipe, but by taste and instinct. Mrs. Humphrey's talent for the
precise phrase and her energy were respected in Doland as extraordinary in a young woman.

Humphrey loved and honored his mother; he worshippd his
father. Humphrey Sr. was devoted to his children, and pulled
them close to him. They beamed with pride when he proclaimed
to his adult friends, "My best friends are my children, and then
my books." When Hubert Jr. was still in a crib, his father often
woke him and read to him late at night after he closed the store.
When he was a boy, his father built a small ramp and platform for
him behind the drug store counter so the two could work side by
side. His father's influence on him was immense and enduring.
"He set high standards," Humphrey says. "The one fear I've had
all my life is that I would disappoint him." Fourteen years after
Humphrey Sr.'s death his son said in answer to a magazine writer's
question, "My hero is my father. He, above all others, had the
greatest influence on my life. My father passed away in November 1949, but if ever I needed proof of immortality he has given it
to me. His mind, his spirit, his soul are ever present in my daily
life. . . ."

Older highway patrolmen still talk of the lines of cars which
stretched for miles in every direction on the day of Humphrey
Sr.'s funeral. Thousands of people came off the farms and out of
the villages that day to mourn the loss of the modest druggist and
gentle friend. They still speak of him with respect and affection.

He was a rare man. Humphrey Sr. had the businessman's normal interest in profit, but during the busiest hour of the day he
would ask one of his sons to leave his duties in the store to drive an
elderly woman home. He used modern techniques of merchandis-
ing and advertising, but when he bought radio time on the local

station to read poetry he mentioned the church, and not his store, as the sponsor. His formal education was limited to high school and a pharmacy course, but his personal library was the biggest and finest in town. As a young Republican he was converted to the Democratic Party by the oratory of William Jennings Bryan, but his real political hero was the scholarly Woodrow Wilson.

He was a romanticist. He spent precious dollars buying new books or musical recordings when the home or store needed improvements. Often he drove two hundred miles to Minneapolis to hear a performance by a symphony orchestra. He bought one house with several chimneys, over his wife's practical objections about the cold air and dust, because he liked its "atmosphere." When friends teased or skeptics scoffed at his idealism, he said, "Before the fact is the vision. Before the fact is the dream."

Humphrey Sr. was a small-town businessman, entrenched throughout his life in the middle class and fond of quoting the moralistic maxims of Harry Emerson Fosdick and Edgar A. Guest. But he was no Babbitt. His approach to life, work, and politics was neither parochial nor unsophisticated.

Most of his brothers and childhood friends left the prairie for better things in bigger cities, complaining that there was "nothing to do" or "no future for a young man" in the little towns. Humphrey Sr. stayed, and spent most of his nonbusiness efforts seeking to enrich the life and future of his community. Frequently he snagged a touring concert artist or lecturer for a side trip and appearance in Doland. He wanted his remote region to share and enjoy the fruits of sophisticated urban America and Europe. Often he spent his own money to bring artistic or educational opportunities to the narrow culture of his neighbors. Dozens of local boys who could not afford to go to college studied at home with books he bought for them.

Humphrey Sr. found pleasure in two basic avocations: talk and politics. He recognized the wealth behind printed words, but found greater joy and power in the spoken word.

He talked informally, but he talked well and most of the time. Conversation ranked close to food in importance at the Humphrey dinner table. His customers joked that in the drug store Humphrey Sr. "never sold a pill without selling an idea." When Humphrey was old enough, apparently at about age twelve, he and his father were so voluble when they were together that they were compared to "two verbal Niagara Falls facing each other." Anyone caught between the two torrents of words was likely to be overwhelmed.

Most of the talk was of politics: practical, theoretical, local, national, international, partisan, or abstract—but almost always politics. It did not matter that Humphrey Sr. was often the only Democrat or internationalist in sight in Republican, isolationist South Dakota; he welcomed and challenged conflicting viewpoints.

Humphrey's father was usually a kind and happy man, and laughed easily. When one of his deep political convictions was at stake, he could be tough and hard, as when he unsuccessfully fought a move by a private utility to buy Doland's community-owned power plant. In politics talk and conversation were not enough. He was a city councilman and then Mayor of Doland, a county chairman in Al Smith's 1928 Presidential campaign, a member of the South Dakota state legislature, and a delegate to three Democratic National Conventions.

Humphrey Sr. was involved, intellectually and emotionally, with national and international affairs. Doland may have been years behind the times in many ways, but he made his children aware of the times in which they lived and the events which helped to shape them. Humphrey can remember his father pulling out an old copy of Bryan's "Cross of Gold" speech once or twice a year, to read it aloud at the dinner table. His sister Frances remembers their father holding her and Humphrey in his lap while he recited Wilson's Fourteen Points. Humphrey Sr. often told his son after reading a news story from Washington or Moscow or Tokyo, "You should know about this, Hubert; it might affect your life someday."

The time of Humphrey's birth was a time of optimism, of hope, of pride in America. It was a time when Americans could dare the impossible, such as reaching the North Pole, or digging the Panama Canal, or making the world safe for democracy. It was a time when isolationism and political apathy were giving way to a tide of expansionism and reform.

In 1911 a hundred thousand Chinese drowned when the Yangtze River flooded. England mourned the death of King Edward VII. He had been buried in London a year before Humphrey's birth with ceremonies marked by pomp, pageantry, and Teddy Roosevelt's obvious indifference to the pomp and protocol of European royalty. The Victorian Age, the "Golden Age," the "Romantic Age" ended with that funeral, but 1911 was still one of "the good years" before the Great War. The United States exported a lively new music style in the form of "Alexander's Ragtime Band" to London. In Paris a Russian exile named Vladimir Ilich Ulyanov was embroiled in a controversy over Communist Party finances, but he continued to write and agitate against capitalism under his favored name: Lenin. In American textile factories and coal mines ten-year-old children worked fourteen-hour days, but newspapers were more concerned with the effects of King George's coronation on the social season. The portly J. P. Morgan ruled Wall Street and the American economy; a portlier William Howard Taft lived in the White House. A year, a month, and a day after Humphrey's birth the lean professor from Princeton, Woodrow Wilson, was nominated for President on the forty-sixth ballot of the Democratic National Convention.

The world was at peace on the morning Humphrey was born. Adolf Hitler was an aimless twenty-two-year-old who eked out a living by sketching post cards in Vienna. No American had ever heard of him; few knew the location of Sarajevo. Three years, a month, and a day after Humphrey's birth Austrian Archduke Francis Ferdinand was assassinated there. For America peace ended when Humphrey was six. Even then a spirit of optimism prevailed. The young men marched off to war singing about their expedition "Over there," and they looked glamorous. More than 126,000 of them did not march back. They died in the mud of Château-Thierry, on the slopes of Belleau Wood, or in the trenches at the edge of no man's land.

In the America of the two decades before and the decade after Humphrey's birth, it was a time of change, of political ferment, of a new and passionate regard for the power of the people. In the 1890's the frustrations of the nation's farmers broke through the shimmering surface of society in a tide of Populist sentiment and reform. The farmers, many of whom were deeply in debt to banking or railroad interests, revolted against the declining value of the dollar and the tight-money interests of the East. They fought for a switch from the gold standard to silver and inflation. The New

York *World* wrote: "All the silverites need is a Moses. They have the principle . . . the hustle . . . and the votes. But they are wandering in the wilderness like a lot of lost sheep because no one with the courage, the audacity, the magnetism and the wisdom to be a real leader has yet appeared among them."

William Jennings Bryan appeared out of the nowhere of the prairie, Nebraska; the silverites, the farmers, and the Populists flocked around to cling to his alpaca coat and throbbing oratory. He electrified the Democratic National Convention of 1896 with a ringing threat to the moneyed interests and the gold standard: "You shall not press down upon the brow of labor this crown of thorn. You shall not crucify mankind upon a cross of gold."

The Populist Party platform of 1892 had declared another, more general mission for their political Moses: "The powers of the government—in other words, of the people—should be expanded . . . to the end that oppression, injustice, and poverty shall eventually cease in the land." This spirit and Bryan's evangelism captured the Democratic Party. The Populists were poorly organized, and their statements were often ambiguous, but they set the goals of the reform movement and of the more practical progressives and liberal Democrats: A federal graduated income tax, woman suffrage, a farm price-support system, greater government control of the trusts, the secret ballot, and popular election of United States Senators. One by one, most of their demands were met in the decade before or after Humphrey's birth.

The moralistic Bryan, the buoyantly vigorous Theodore Roosevelt, and the idealistic Woodrow Wilson represented the steps of a progressively more mature reform movement. And the three men —so different in personality and temperament—were, in fact, linked together in a chain of political circumstance: Republican Roosevelt picked up and put into practice as President many of Bryan's proposals. Bryan, in a frenzy of antipathy toward Eastern boss support for "Champ" Clark at the 1912 Democratic Convention, pushed the nomination into underdog Wilson's hands. Roosevelt, as the Progressive "Bull Moose" candidate, split the Republican vote that November, and Wilson won the Presidency over William Howard Taft.

Humphrey was nine when the tide of reform ebbed. He absorbed his father's excitement over the Democratic nomination in

1920 of James M. Cox for President and a young aristocrat from New York, Franklin Delano Roosevelt, as his running mate. The Humphreys had been depressed by the Senate's rejection of the League of Nations and saddened by Wilson's political and physical decline, but they were heartened by the liberalism of Cox and the new Roosevelt, and by the nominees' endorsement of the League.

But after almost thirty years of political idealism and turmoil the people were tired. The Great War had helped to shatter public trust in governments and confidence in leaders who dreamed of a better world and demanded sacrifices from the people to help build it. The election of 1920 returned the nation to "normalcy." Warren Gamaliel Harding defeated Cox and Roosevelt by a wide margin. The people had been tense long enough; there had been enough change. Why not take a break? the nation seemed to say. Times were good.

"It was a good time, a good place, and a good preparation for life," a more charitable Sinclair Lewis wrote of early-century life in a small rural town. In an article titled "The Long Arm of the Small Town" he added: "It is extraordinary how deep is the impression made by the place of one's birth and rearing, and how lasting are its memories. . . ." He could have been writing about Wallace and Doland, and about Hubert Humphrey's first years.

And Humphrey might have stayed in this good place and green land. But the times changed. Lewis himself helped to stimulate an intellectual revolt against the prestige of Main Street society and the Babbittry of many small towns of the prairie. Individuals with talent, intelligence, and ambition moved out of the little towns in ever increasing numbers. Weekly newspapers of the prairie carried more and more stories on local marriages which ended with such sentences as "The groom received his degree in electrical engineering in June. The couple will reside in Los Angeles." The critical attitudes of urban America toward small towns tended to strip them of status in the system of national values. The turn-of-the-century hero and concept of Horatio Alger became schmaltz. In the vernacular of modern and sophisticated voters, the log cabin or modest frame farmhouse as a birthplace for the ambitious politician became "square."

Today Doland is different. It is still a good town, with a fine school and decent people, and they have paved Main Street. But its population is a third smaller than in Humphrey's time, and much older. The marquee of Doland's theater boasts: ALL SHOWS IN CINEMASCOPE, but the theater is closed.

Grandfather Sannes's farm, built for beauty and productivity, is in weeds. Wild broomers grass covers the roadway, yard, and fields. The farm's red barns still stand solidly on their stone foundations; the house is still sturdy and white. But inside, the rooms are empty, the doorways are veiled with spider webs, and the dusty or snowy winds of Dakota whistle through a broken window in an upstairs bedroom.

Wallace is dying. Its people, now numbering little more than a hundred, still keep their homes and gardens neat and try to give their children a good education. But few children are born in Wallace any more; the high school is closed. A few years ago the town banker died, so the bank was closed. On a stormy November night in 1960 the narrow building on Main Street in which Humphrey was born burned to the ground. It did not really matter to most of the people of Wallace. The building had been empty for years, and its wood was old and rotten.

Something happened to this land, to its people and their towns, and to the boy and man they helped to shape.

4

A Dark Time

It was a great year for America, almost everyone agreed. In 1927 prosperity fell like confetti and ticker tape over the nation's cities. Rugged individualism ruled society, the prevailing platitude suggested, and a man could do just fine by putting his nose to the grindstone. All he needed for real success was a little pluck or elbow grease.

Heroes of all types emerged in 1927. Charles A. ("Lucky Lindy") Lindbergh flew his single-engine *Spirit of St. Louis* alone from New York to Paris. Nicola Sacco and Bartolomeo Vanzetti stepped out of obscurity and into fame as they died in an electric chair in a Massachusetts prison. In Chicago, Gene Tunney got up from a controversial "long count" to beat Jack Dempsey for the heavyweight boxing title. The New York Yankees won 110 games; in the eighth inning of the last game of the season, against Washington, Babe Ruth won baseball immortality by hitting a 1–1 pitch for his sixtieth home run. New York's gaudy Mayor Jimmy Walker toured Europe with a case of champagne, a companion, and his wife. Chicago Mayor "Big Bill" Thompson appointed a committee to remove from the city's libraries all references to England. Mobster Al Capone said that prohibition was "a fine opportunity for smart young guys like myself," and raked in an estimated $105 million from his crime syndicate's operations.

The year 1927 brought amazing advances in American science and industry. Henry Ford made his last "Tin Lizzie" Model T in April; in December he unveiled the new, sleek Model A ($385 for the roadster). Warner Brothers made the first talking motion picture, which starred a singer. The first "nationwide radio hookup" linked nineteen stations for a broadcast of the Stanford-Alabama

Rose Bowl game. A new invention called "television" flashed the confident face of Commerce Secretary Herbert Hoover from Washington to New York.

The President of the United States, Calvin Coolidge, vacationed in South Dakota's Black Hills from June 15 to September 15. (He also managed a two- to four-hour nap each day while in Washington.) Local residents greeted Coolidge with signs reading: HE'S OUR PAL—IS CAL and CAL AND HIS GAL—MAY GOD BE THEIR PAL. Coolidge fished in trout streams and frolicked in cowboy outfits for newsreel cameras. For radio he reaffirmed his conviction that "the business of the country is business."

The President was keeping cool in the mountains of western South Dakota. In the hot prairie of eastern South Dakota the business of the people was survival.

In 1927 the second of Doland's two banks failed. Hubert Humphrey, sixteen, watched his father reluctantly sign the papers to sell the family's big white frame house for cash to keep his business going; then he saw his father and mother weep. The farmers around Doland, already pinched by falling prices for wheat and other grains, harvested what would be their last good crops in ten years. Two years before the stock market crash of 1929 the people of rural South Dakota and most of the Midwest were gripped by the first forces of a decade of depression and drought.

No prolonged experience moved and shaped Humphrey more than the depression-drought decade. In public statements he says positively that those years "enriched" him, that they gave him "a certain toughness," "a sort of patience," and new insights into the endurance and limitations of human beings. In many ways the decade from 1927 to 1937 did strengthen him. It burned into him a habit of struggle and a greater self-discipline for work. It added a restlessness to his energy and a determination to move out of and above any stagnant environment. It coupled his lofty idealism with an earthy pragmatism, transformed his opinions into convictions, and cloaked his ideas with a passion to put them into practice. It compelled him, always, to interpret statistics and other bland measurements of poverty and disaster into human terms.

The depression-drought decade in South Dakota also scarred him. Beneath his buoyant optimism is a small but hard seed of fatalism. Under his ebullient confidence runs a streak of insecurity, a fear that forces outside his control might, at any moment, darken his world, destroy his achievements, and depress his spirit.

The signs of insecurity, however obscured by thirty years of progress, are evident in him now. He lives and works each day as if it were his last. ("Hell, I never made any big plans during the depression; I never knew if I'd live another day.") He is propelled by unbounded natural energy, but his frenetic pace and unceasing activity seem to stem in part from some dark anxiety that if he stops, even for a moment, dust will cover his head and weeds tangle his feet. (In moments of tension he often pulls a rag from a drawer and vigorously dusts his desk and other furniture. A few weeks before his re-election as Senator in 1960, when a poll erroneously reported a 20 percent drop in his voter strength, he exhorted his campaign staff, "We've just got to get moving. I can feel the weeds growing up around me.")

The rural and national depression of the twenties and thirties, for Humphrey, is not just a memory of the past; it is a continuing threat to the present. As he talked about reports of increasing farm auctions and farm mortgage foreclosures in 1960 and 1961, his voice was edged with anxiety. National depressions, he firmly believes, begin on the farms. His proposals for government agricultural policies and programs have—at times—been conditioned as much by emotion as ideology. ("I learned more about economics from one South Dakota dust storm than I did in all my years in college," he said in the late 1950's.)

The scars of the depression-drought decade in his mind and spirit are still sore. As a positive man who rarely reflects on the past, he does not like to talk about those years. When he is challenged to remember and to relate details of the experience, a frown covers his face and his voice thickens as he mutters words which only touch on deep impressions:

"God, it was terrible . . . so hot, so terribly hot. . . . The dust, it was everywhere. . . . There was a desolation, a drabness. . . . The sky and horizon—dull and bleak. . . . Hope would leave. . . . You didn't want to stay, but there was no way to leave. . . . You felt trapped. . . ."

The memory of it now is as vivid and real to Humphrey as when the experience captured the years of his youth and dominated the life of the nation.

It started early in the prairie. Throughout the 1920's the farmers and townspeople of rural America endured a long and lonely prelude to the depression. The most respected political and financial leaders boasted of prosperity; when symptoms of weakness surged to the surface, they called for confidence, and New York Stock Exchange averages rose a dozen or so points. Farmers were more interested in the Chicago grain market quotations. In 1920 their wheat had brought $2.76 a bushel. The price was less than half of that in 1929.

World War I had boosted the demand for farm products. As the war ended and European farming resumed, the bottom fell out of America's export markets. Gross income of American farmers fell from $17.7 billion in 1919 to $10.5 billion in 1921. Thousands of farmers had taken on heavy mortgages at inflated prices to buy new land and equipment during the war; as their earnings dropped, they could not meet payments. Rural banks, reeling under waves of surrendered mortgages and defaulted loans, went under. Across the nation seven thousand banks failed between 1920 and 1929; more than half of South Dakota's banks collapsed.

In June 1929, Humphrey was graduated from Doland High School, as valedictorian of his class, and decided to enroll at the University of Minnesota in September. His father drove him the two hundred miles from Doland to Minneapolis, ending the trip near the long registration lines in front of the campus administration building. Humphrey, eighteen years old and very much aware of his small-town experience, nervously eyed the crowd, which numbered approximately three times the entire population of Doland. "There's an awful lot of people out there," he said from the security of the car. His father told him to "make the best of it."

His best was not enough, not in 1929 and 1930. National prosperity evaporated, as had rural prosperity eight years before. The economy, stretched beyond its limit and strength, snapped abruptly. One month after Humphrey entered college, prices plummeted on the New York Stock Exchange's "Black Thursday." On October 29, 1929, the show business newspaper *Variety* headlined: WALL ST. LAYS AN EGG. South Dakota farmers were soon selling eggs for five cents a dozen. The price paid for wheat in the Chicago market was halved again. December wheat earned

$1.35 a bushel at the end of 1929. A year later the price was 76 cents. Savings of wheat farmers around Doland dwindled, then were gone. Cash sales in the Humphrey drug store were rare. In February 1931, Humphrey's father drove to Minneapolis again, this time to borrow five thousand dollars from a drug wholesaler to give him a fresh start in the larger city of Huron, South Dakota. Father and son talked all one night in a downtown Minneapolis hotel about the problems of opening and establishing a new drug store in a city which already had five. At the end of the school quarter Humphrey left the university and returned to South Dakota, to help move and operate the family business.

It was a different country from that which he had known most of his life. The green and gentle land of his youth was dying.

In 1928, 1929, and 1930 rainfall in South Dakota had been far below normal. There was little snow left from each winter to nourish the hard earth during spring thaws. At first the green hues and tones faded just a bit earlier than usual, and the land languished. The sun and heat were relentless. The water which fell on the dry earth from brief showers evaporated quickly, leaving a coarse crust on top of the land. The crust cracked, then crumbled to dust. The greens were gone. The land dried to a harsh and ugly brown, then began to strangle under a lifeless gray.

America's economic system had failed. Now nature and America's farming techniques failed. For more than half a century—from the Dakotas to the Deep South—the people had used and abused the land. Cultivation had been careless. Too much had been taken from the land; too little put back. Season after season the plows had sliced into the earth, and the earth had yielded its life and abundance for a growing nation. The people and their livestock had stripped the earth of its natural net of grasses, which protected the few fragile feet of topsoil from wind and drought.

Drought came. In the summer of 1931, while the Humphreys labored to establish the new store in Huron, newspapers reported a few small dust storms in western Kansas and eastern Colorado. Rexford Tugwell, later to become one of Franklin D. Roosevelt's agricultural brain-trusters, traveled through the Midwest. He reported that the soil showed through the grass everywhere and the wheat was thin, "like the stubble on an old man's chin."

There was little rain in 1932, and less in 1933. Humphrey left

Huron for six months to complete a cram course at the Denver College of Pharmacy. He returned in May 1933, to add his pharmacist's license to the drug store's meager assets. In November the people of Huron saw the southern horizon turn gray. The sky darkened; the air was heavy with the smell of dirt. This was the first of more than ninety dust storms to cover the area in less than a year.

In Wallace and Doland and Huron the storms blanketed everything with dust, sometimes two inches deep. Street lights were left burning all day; the sun was a dead amber ball in a yellow sky. Women packed wet sheets and rags into the spaces around doors and loose windows. The people outside held damp handkerchiefs over their faces. Wheat and corn withered; roots were blown away with the dust. Cattle died from dust which turned to mud balls in their stomachs. At times cars could not be driven; vision was reduced to three feet. Halfway between Doland and Huron two children were caught in one of the worst dust storms as they left school. They wandered all afternoon and part of the night, until they dropped, exhausted, to die in the dry, gritty wind. Their bodies were found half buried in dust the next day.

Preachers in the little prairie towns turned to the Old Testament Book of Isaiah on somber Sunday mornings: "For, behold, the darkness shall cover the earth . . ." "Enter into the rock, and hide thee in the dust, for fear of the Lord . . ." "The earth mourneth and fadeth away . . ." "The mirth of the land is gone . . ." "Awake and sing, ye that dwell in dust . . ." "Behold, the Lord maketh the earth empty, and maketh it waste, and turneth it upside down, and scattereth abroad the inhabitants thereof."

The less devout found comfort in the humor of little cards which read: IF AT FIRST YOU DON'T SUCCEED . . . THE HELL WITH IT! They packed all that their cars could hold, and scattered throughout the country to join the lines of unemployed in Minneapolis and Chicago and Los Angeles.

The Humphreys remained. They had no choice, committed to stay by the indebted drug store. Humphrey Sr. approvingly watched the efforts and improvisations of Roosevelt's New Deal and tried his own experiments to save his business. The drug store's soda fountain was expanded into a restaurant; young Humphrey spent his Saturdays killing and cleaning chickens for the big weekend trade. His father taught him to inoculate hogs with a new serum. They offered other veterinary services and tied the store more completely to the fortunes or failures of the area's farmers.

It was all failure for the farmers. When they could raise any crop at all from the dusty earth, much of it was ruined by wheat rust or smut. The price of wheat dropped to a ridiculous 25 cents a bushel. Some wheat farmers sold at that price, but they were caught in an unbalanced cost-price squeeze. Income from a full acre of wheat—sixteen bushels—barely covered the cost of four-dollar shoes for a child. Some farmers did not bother to sell; they burned their wheat or corn for fuel.

The Humphrey business evolved into a profitless system of barter and loose credit. If farmers could pay at all, they brought in poultry or vegetables. (The Humphreys did, at least, eat regularly.) Most farmers simply charged their purchases. Humphrey Sr. rarely refused credit to the grim-faced men and women seeking medicine or other necessary goods. Debts to the store mounted, to almost thirteen thousand dollars. Humphrey's father shocked his family one night by announcing that he had torn up his customer account books and told his customers that they owed him nothing. Humphrey protested. His father's answer was practical: "They won't come into the store at all if they're embarrassed by a big debt. And, Son, if a revolution comes, ours would be the first store and house they would stone."

The notion of possible revolution was no exaggeration. In the winter of 1931–32 angry crowds of farmers gathered in several Midwestern towns to protest farm mortgage foreclosures and forced sales. Pickets lined highways leading to major marketing centers; outside Chicago they tore canisters from dairy farmers' trucks and spilled milk into roadside ditches. Half a dozen counties in Iowa were under marshal law.

In January 1933 the National Farm Bureau Federation's Edward A. O'Neal testified before a U. S. Senate committee, "Unless something is done for the American farmer, we will have revolution in the countryside within less than twelve months." Only three months later five hundred farmers crowded the courtroom of Judge Charles C. Bradley in Le Mars, Iowa, demanding suspension of farm foreclosure proceedings. When he refused, the mob dragged him from the bench, blindfolded him, and carried him by truck to a lonely road a mile outside of town. He was slapped, kicked, and mauled to shouts of "Get a rope! Hang him!" One end of a rope was placed around his neck, the other end over the crossbar of a telephone pole. Someone placed a hub cap over his head; others smeared his face with grease and dirt. Judge Bradley cried aloud, "O Lord, I pray thee, do justice to all men." The mob calmed, removed the rope from his neck, and wandered away.

Most of the Midwest's people were tense, but also tough and patient. Communities were stronger. Families were closer. Churches were better attended. Franklin D. Roosevelt had reported after a campaign tour of the Midwest in 1932 that there was a look of despair on the faces of the people. As President he said, after a similar tour in 1934, "They were a hopeful people. They had courage written all over their faces. They looked cheerful. They knew they were 'up against it,' but they were going to see things through."

FDR may or may not have been aware of tensions within the people. The Humphreys were: the drug store's volume in remedies for stomach ailments and constipation multiplied dramatically. Humphrey himself suffered physical symptoms of the unending work and worry. His stomach often churned with a dull ache. Sharp pains stabbed inside him. Frequently his face paled, he became nauseated, and then fainted. Several times he went to the hospital for diagnostic examinations and tests. Each time he was told, "There's nothing wrong with you."

He yearned to return to school. He longed to get away, to escape even briefly. In 1932 he pleaded with his father to let him hitchhike to the World's Fair in Chicago. His father refused to let him "travel like a bum." Humphrey screamed that he would leave home for good, and did not calm down until he had shattered a dozen glasses in the sink behind the lunch counter of the store.

The depression deepened; the drought continued. No rain at all fell in the spring of 1934. In May the winds blew more fiercely out of the Panhandle. The drought and dust storms stretched from the Alleghenies to the Rockies, and down into the Gulf states, but centered in the Dakotas. Most of the Midwest lapsed more deeply into an agricultural and economic coma. Its people struggled against hopelessness, and for survival. In the great throbbing

heartland of America life seemed to become little more than a
dull, forced murmur.

With a basement full of bartered goods and a register empty of
cash, Humphrey Sr. failed to meet the dates for payments on his
debt to the Minneapolis wholesaler. He spent desperate hours in
the evenings sitting at his desk in front of the store. Humphrey
would return to the store after dinner to see his father in the same
position he had been in an hour before: face cupped in his hands,
eyes staring down at the red figures in his account books, unmov-
ing. When the Minneapolis wholesaler demanded substantial and
regular payments, Humphrey Sr. took his account books and son
to the Twin Cities and spread the ledgers in front of the firm's
executives.

"Gentlemen, I am doing the best I can," Humphrey remembers
his father saying. "I'm getting just enough for our food and house.
Maybe you think you can get more out of this store. If you want it,
take it. I can't take your pressure anymore. I just don't have any
fight left in me. If you're going to press me, then you'd better take
the store."

The executives agreed to let Humphrey Sr. keep the store and
to leave him alone.

The family worked harder to eke out some profit, keeping the
store open later at night and diversifying its services and merchan-
dise. Humphrey had little free time. He limited his activities to
the Methodist Church's Epworth League, the local Young Democrats organization, scoutmaster duties for a Boy Scout troop, and
Wednesday and Saturday night dances. More and more frequently
he chose as his dancing partner a Huron girl, Muriel Buck. They
began dating.

(They had not seen each other for a year after their first meeting. The future Mrs. Humphrey remembers that she was not exactly swept off her feet when she first talked to Humphrey in the
drug store. "I thought he was younger than I," she recalls. "He was
a skinny boy, and he kidded and joked so much I thought he was
sort of childish.")

There was constant and lively talk about politics, and excitement over Roosevelt's New Deal programs. Muriel often met
Humphrey and his father late in the evening when the store
closed. The three took long drives over the straight roads of

Beadle County, talking and arguing about the forces of economics, the nuances of political philosophies, and the lessons of the depression. At midnight their car radio—highly receptive in the dry, flat prairie of South Dakota—picked up the news of Washington from Los Angeles Station KFI.

For Muriel, Humphrey soon became much more than a good dancer and cheerful date: "He was a frustrated boy and young man. He had so much drive; there was so much he wanted to do. There was so much inside him. He had almost too much to say. He needed someone to talk to; that was the important thing." By the summer of 1935 they were engaged.

Humphrey Sr. recognized the frustrations in his son; he and Muriel worried about Humphrey's stomach pains and fainting spells. They encouraged him to take a trip to Washington, D. C., acting as a guide for Huron's prize-winning Boy Scout troop. He left in August.

Humphrey was drawn to the Capitol. He wandered through the marble corridors and sat for hours in the public galleries of the Senate and the House of Representatives. His sister Frances, then studying at George Washington University, remembers his excitement after watching Congress. "I'm going to serve in that place someday," he told her. Then he wrote Muriel:

". . . Maybe I seem foolish to have such vain hopes and plans, but, Bucky, I can see how someday, if you and I just apply ourselves and make up our minds to work for bigger things, we can live here in Washington and probably be in government politics or service. I set my aim at Congress. Don't laugh at me. Maybe it does sound rather egotistical and beyond reason, but, Muriel, I do know others have succeeded. . . ."

His exuberance disappeared when he returned to Huron. Any ambition, any "bigger things," any success did seem beyond reason in the bleak prairie. Then, to sting the deep wounds of the depression, drought, and dust storms, another disaster swept the land.

In 1935, and again in 1936, hordes of grasshoppers devastated millions of acres of the Midwest. They swarmed over the earth with a deafening, almost metallic buzz. They chewed up the yellowed grass and weak sprouts of corn, wheat, and other grains. Even the stubble was taken; the earth was left as bare as the cement highways. The hungry hordes ate into anything made of wood; fence posts fell, the handles of pitchforks and rakes disappeared.

For some men it was the final blow, the exhaustion of hope, the end of trying. One Doland farmer remembers his father:

"He walked out of the house and into his field as the last 'hoppers moved away. He looked up at the sky for a minute—it was still filled with dust kicked up by the 'hoppers—then he dropped down on his knees. He stared at the ground for a long time. It was hard; there wasn't a sprout or root left in it. He started pounding his fist against the ground real hard. His hands were tough, but blood came running out of the knuckles. Then he moaned and started screaming, 'God damn you, land. . . . God damn you, earth.' I'll never forget his face—all covered with dust and a look of pain. Mom couldn't move; she just stood on the porch with her hands tight against her face. I was little and scared. My big brother came out. He was real good, real gentle. He took Dad over to the water pump. Dad just stood there and let my brother wash his face and hands. He didn't say anything, and got a funny smile on his face, and looked sort of relaxed—as though somebody else finally was taking care of things. The doc came out the next day. A couple of weeks later the sheriff came. Dad just smiled at him and let us guide him into the car. The sheriff drove him away to the state hospital."

The life and the land of rural America had hit bottom. After the grasshopper plagues there was nothing left to lose. The turn had to come.

A few inches of rain fell in 1936. The New Deal's alphabet agencies picked up momentum. The AAA, CWA, and WPA pumped jobs into the stagnant economy. Rain and cash trickled slowly into the Midwestern vacuum. The dust storms still raged abrasively across the land, but for some the desperate decade was nearing its end.

Humphrey and Muriel were married in September 1936. They took sixty-five dollars and his father's car for a honeymoon trip to Minneapolis and northern Minnesota. On the way back, thirty miles from Huron, the car struck and killed a cow. The young couple arrived home riding behind a tow truck and in debt to a dairy farmer. They gave all appearances of settling in Huron.

Humphrey continued to work in the drug store, rented a house, and resumed his church and scoutmaster activities. But the tensions of the depression struggle persisted, and he still suffered from the stomach pains and "blackouts." At home he and his bride talked incessantly about leaving. They pondered the practical problems of returning to the University of Minnesota, or poured over maps to make grandly impractical plans for a trip around the world.

With his son in the store as a registered pharmacist, Humphrey Sr. found time to work at—and not just talk—politics. He campaigned for and won a seat in the South Dakota Legislature. Democratic Party leaders were impressed by his work in the State Capitol at Pierre in 1937. He was urged to run for the Governorship, or possibly the United States Senate.

Humphrey Sr. longed for higher political office, but his family heatedly debated the prospect. The older Mrs. Humphrey did not want to live in Pierre, or Washington. Humphrey's brother and sisters disagreed. Humphrey sat in the library of his father's house and only listened, aware that his father's absence would obligate him to remain in Huron to tend the store.

The issue was settled later, by father and son, as they drove through the hot August night of the lonely prairie. They discussed the needs of the business, Humphrey's desire to return to school, his mother's fear that the family would split up, and his father's chances for major elective office. At the end of the long drive, in front of Humphrey's house, the older man offered his son half ownership—a full and legal partnership—in the family business.

Humphrey liked the drug store and was proud of his skills as a pharmacist. He loved his father and was afraid of hurting him. But he answered:

"I can't stay. These dust storms—I just can't take them anymore. I'm so tense I'm sick all the time. I get these pains, and I know it's because of the worry. But the depression, the dust, the drought—they're wearing me out. I want to move along, to be on my own."

A month later, in September 1937, eight years after his first unsuccessful try for a university education, Humphrey headed East again. His young wife sat next to him in the back seat of the car. His father drove. His mother looked ahead as the car ate up the miles of highway running straight away from Huron. There

was little talk. Outside, as the car approached the South Dakota-
Minnesota border, the dry, stubbled land stretched away in slight
knolls and shallow gullies to a flat horizon. No trees or buildings
marked the empty plain. At the state line only a small wood sign
stood above the dust. Its white-lettered message said: LEAVING
SOUTH DAKOTA . . . LAND OF INFINITE VARIETY.

5

Teacher

On a hot afternoon in 1938 a babble of voices drifted through the open windows of the University of Minnesota's political science offices. Department Chairman William A. Anderson, in the middle of dictating a letter, heard one voice, high-pitched and earnest, rising above the rest. He stepped to a window and looked down on a gathering of students and professors around a skinny, dark-haired young man speaking from the front steps. "Who," he asked his secretary as he pointed to the youth, "is THAT?" His secretary answered, "I think his name is Humphrey. He's from South Dakota."

Dr. Anderson listened for twenty minutes to the passionate, 225-word-a-minute voice. It raced from an angry analysis of the causes of the depression, through an incisive examination of New Deal programs, to an urgent demand that Franklin D. Roosevelt do more to spur the economy. Dr. Anderson was aware that he could neither detect any errors of fact or logic nor disagree with anything in the student's discourse. He was also amused, and wondered why the student spoke so urgently and publicly at a time when no national or student elections were imminent.

The reasons were subjective. Hubert H. Humphrey Jr., then twenty-seven, felt liberated from the confining forces of the depression and the dusty prairie. Away from family ties and the scene of frustrated ambitions, he acted like a man suddenly released from an emotional and intellectual prison. After a six-year break in his education and personal progress, he spoke like a man in a hurry to make up for lost time. As he studied or talked, the tensions left him. His stomach pains disappeared; he did not again suffer from fainting spells. He was on his own. He was doing what he wanted to do. He felt himself a man.

Humphrey and his wife arrived on the University of Minnesota campus with $670 and no purpose other than to stay and study as long as the money lasted. They rented a room on the third floor of an old house, with a kitchen the size of a small closet and a bathroom shared by another couple. At first Mrs. Humphrey could not find a job: no employer would hire a married woman. The couple agreed that she should not lie about her marital status, but that while job-hunting she would not wear her wedding ring and would sign her name only as "Muriel Humphrey." A Minneapolis investment syndicate hired her as a bookkeeper. She earned fifty-five dollars a month, their total income, while Humphrey plunged into his formal studies of political science and economics. Neither was particularly confident that he would finish work for his degree before their money was exhausted. He was determined, at first, only to get all that he could out of each academic quarter and to give his wife some chance of viewing the world outside South Dakota.

On registration day he signed for twenty-one hours of classes. The dean summoned him to his office to announce, "Eighteen units is the maximum, even for honor students. You cannot take twenty-one units." Humphrey argued, "Why not? I *paid* for twenty-one units. If someone comes into my dad's drug store wanting to buy twenty-one tubes of toothpaste, we sell them to him." The dean retorted, "This is NOT Humphrey's Drug Store. This is the University of Minnesota. We are not 'selling' education." Humphrey persisted, finally winning a compromise which allowed him to take eighteen units, on probation.

Through a combination of luck, loans, and Mrs. Humphrey's income, the couple survived financially. Humphrey excelled academically. With back credit for the year and a quarter of his academic work in 1929–31, he completed requirements for his degree in only two more years. With a straight-A average and membership in Phi Beta Kappa, he was graduated *magna cum laude* in political science in June 1939.

The Humphreys remember those two years as exciting, productive, and happy. He was a diligent student: he studied with intense concentration until ten o'clock each night. After that the Humphreys and two other couples played Monopoly and talked politics or economics until midnight or 1 A.M. Their standard meal was hamburger, but they occasionally splurged on dinner in a Minneapolis restaurant. Humphrey was jubilant when their first child, Nancy, was born in the spring of 1939. He was in the university's main library when a friend phoned the news to him. He screamed across the huge, silent room, "I've got a baby, I've got a little baby," and ran out to visit his wife and newborn child in the hospital—one of the more significant late arrivals in his hour-behind-schedule life.

He was excited as much by ideas as by babies. He was at an impressionable age in a time of national re-evaluation, social introspection, and political change. The late 1930's were years of early manhood for a new political generation, born in an age of reform and passing through adolescence in a decade of depression. Humphrey was part of a new generation of liberals, unafraid of big government and central authority, more practical than philosophical, daring to try the different and centering attention on economics. William Jennings Bryan had been one of its prophets. Franklin D. Roosevelt was its tutor. For many politically oriented intellectuals in this new generation the real hero of American society was the worker, the "little guy." Bigness in business was, *per se,* bad. The trusts should not only be busted, they should be blackened as "Wall Street moneylenders" in the public mind. For this generation of liberals the old concepts of unrestricted free enterprise and rugged individualism became passé. The idea of a powerful, compassionate central government was "in." Economics, for Humphrey's generation of liberals, was not a free-floating pattern of finance and good fortune, dominated by Eastern financial interests. Economics was a precise set of tools, to be used by government for the advancement of society and the protection of the people.

Humphrey was influenced by the tone of the time, and also by the institution in which he studied. The University of Minnesota was—and is—a respected academic institution, but it had none of the insularity of Ivy League schools. Unlike many state universities, it was not an island of intellectuals set near a village in some pastoral part of the state. Humphrey had developed a basic appreciation for "the community" through his small-town experience; it was broadened and strengthened by the University of Minnesota's atmosphere and purpose. The physical setting of the university symbolizes its position as an institution, in the center of Minnesota's political, commercial, cultural, and social center, the Twin Cities. One edge of the campus is close to the state's capital, St. Paul. The other overlooks the Mississippi River, cutting through Minneapolis. Over a main boulevard linking the two cities is a footbridge connecting two parts of the campus. The university regards itself as a central unifying force in the Minnesota community and emphasizes practical service to the state and the people as much as academic discipline and scholarly research.

In the late 1930's the university was also a center of vigorous political debate. The vital drama of the depression and New Deal sparked the clash of different social and political doctrines. On the University of Minnesota campus there were the usual preponderant masses of Republicans and Democrats, but also active and vocal cliques of socialists, Communists, Trotskyites, and Jacobins. Humphrey was stimulated by the open and constant conflict of ideas and viewpoints, but at the time he considered himself relatively nonpartisan and politically orthodox. "I was just a Midwest Populist," he says almost apologetically.

After graduation he did not want to leave the Minnesota community. But as he eyed a possible teaching career and advanced degrees, he recognized the need to earn at least one degree in another part of the country. With his wife, child, and a modest fellowship he advanced to Louisiana State University, to work for a master's degree in political science.

The year in Louisiana was a struggle. In the spring of 1939, Mrs. Humphrey had returned to South Dakota because her father suffered a heart attack. She missed Humphrey's graduation, and remained in South Dakota for the summer, to operate her father's lake resort business. Joining Humphrey in the fall, she was able to earn a few dollars typing students' theses, but that income and Humphrey's small fellowship grant were not enough. Several times, pressed by unpaid bills, the couple almost gave up to return to Minnesota or South Dakota. They were saved once by a loan from one of Humphrey's uncles. They sold their refrigerator to pay the rent one month. Mrs. Humphrey made stacks of sandwiches, which Humphrey carried to the campus each day and sold to graduate students for a dime each. The pennies of profit helped the couple pay other bills.

"It was rough, and we had to worry about money all the time," Mrs. Humphrey says. "But we were never really depressed or frightened. We had youth, health, optimism, and a dear child. We knew that even in the depression we could always get jobs of some type, and that we could survive."

They made friends in New Orleans. One was Russell Long, son of Louisiana's "Kingfish" Huey Long, former Governor and assassinated Senator. The young Long (ten years later he would be a Washington neighbor and Senate colleague of Humphrey) asked the Minnesotan to help the LSU debating team in a debate against a British team. Humphrey, Long remembers, "was a great debater, better than any we had at LSU." The young Minnesotan and a Louisiana teammate argued the negative side of the question: "Should the United States go to the aid of Great Britain in the war in Europe?" They won.

Europe was losing. In that year of debate and study for Humphrey, Hitler and Germany switched from diplomatic conspiracy to military conquest. The nations of Europe were weak and divided. Poland was invaded on September 1, 1939. The German Luftwaffe pummeled the cities of the Netherlands and Belgium. German destroyers and paratroopers took Norway. German blitzkrieg made a shambles of northern France, and the Wehrmacht ignored the old rules of warfare and the Maginot Line. Hitler taunted the French by dancing a jig after dictating surrender terms in a railroad car near Compiègne, strutted into Paris, and gazed down at the Tomb of Napoleon. President Franklin D. Roosevelt, pleading no involvement by the United States "unless attacked" but quietly proceeding to aid Great Britain, was "drafted" for an unprecedented third term.

The United States had another year of peace before the Japanese attack on Pearl Harbor. Humphrey struggled to write his master's thesis on "The Political Philosophy of the New Deal." His year at LSU was a grind, not a joy. The professors were more aloof and formal than those at Minnesota. He felt no rapport with the professor directing his thesis work. But he continued to earn A's in most of his courses, and his thesis—a carefully documented but biased study of FDR's emerging philosophy—was accepted.

The couple eagerly returned to the University of Minnesota. Humphrey hoped for a Ph.D. degree in political science and thought more seriously about a teaching career. In one year he completed all course work for his doctorate—with a straight-A record. Dr. Evron Kirkpatrick, then a young Minnesota professor and now Executive Director of the American Political Science Association, remembers Humphrey as a "good, bright student. He learned easily and quickly, and did not have to put much time into studying. He was one of the best students the department ever had."

Mrs. Humphrey worked part time in her old job with the Minneapolis investment firm, but money was still short and the couple faced a monthly crisis when the rent was due. Dr. Kirkpatrick helped Humphrey get his first professional job, instructor of a social science course sponsored by the Works Progress Administration for Minnesota teachers. The job took more and more time. Dr. William Anderson noted regretfully that Humphrey was frequently absent from one of his courses, and never completed it. Humphrey was never able to begin writing his Ph.D. dissertation.

He taught full time at the University of Minnesota through the summer of 1941. In the fall, dreading another year of financial struggle, he accepted a job as Superintendent of Teaching for the WPA's Workers Education Service in Minnesota. His status as a student ended with that job. He was thirty years old.

It was a late start and an advanced age for a man to begin a full-time professional career. He had done far more than he could have expected during the dreary days of dust storms and depressions in South Dakota. The odds had been against him, and he had had no sure goal or schedule of efforts. He had known he wanted an education. (Watching local politicians around Doland and Huron, Humphrey had thought: They are effective, but a man can do so much more if he is well educated.) His urge to complete school was unyielding, but the main force behind his effort during this period was his wife.

Muriel Humphrey's contributions to her husband's education and her impact on his career have gone far beyond the money she earned while he was in college and her sacrifice in giving up her own chance for a college degree. Her faith in him strengthened him. Quietly, and without embarrassment, she expresses her belief that "Humphrey is a great man." Hesitantly, and with an acknowledgment that "it may sound corny," she tells of her thought in 1935 "that he might be President someday." That was at a time when Humphrey was a slightly confused, incompletely educated clerk and pharmacist in his father's drug store in Huron.

She is not, however, awed by him. One friend of the couple says, "Humphrey is as thin-skinned as any politician. He doesn't like criticism. Oh, sure, he laughs it off when someone tears him down. But inside he is hurt or angered. Muriel is the only human being on earth who can really criticize Humphrey with a positive effect." Another friend adds, "Hubert Humphrey needs only one thing outside himself to make him an effective man and politician—an anchor. He's often like a cork bobbing at the top of a stormy sea. Muriel is his anchor."

At a point in marriage when many young wives begin to campaign for a new house with a "good" address, Muriel Humphrey cheerfully accepted one-room apartments and undramatic jobs to give Humphrey the freedom to pursue his education or political career. She cares little about social or formal political position; her husband is most important to her. At home, among family members, she calls him "Dad." Among close friends he is "Hubert." With most outsiders she refers to him as "Humphrey." She has rarely identified him by his progressively more impressive titles of position and political power: Mayor, Senator, Vice President. He has lost elections, and she has reacted philosophically, thinking: It's probably for the best; maybe Humphrey isn't ready for that job. After other defeats, when Humphrey has been stung, hurt, or—in her view—unfairly vanquished, she has become almost grief-stricken over "what they did to Hubert."

Almost twenty years of life in Washington and close involvement with fame and power have not corrupted her modesty and decency. Unlike many Midwestern women transplanted to the East, her tongue has not become coated with contrived accents of upper-class Philadelphia, Boston, or Richmond. Her speech is still marked by such mild expletives as "Golly," "Heck," and "Gee Whiz!" In a Washington society where one of the most polished female arts is to divulge discreetly that a dress is "Paris, of course" or "just one of Balenciaga's simpler creations," Mrs. Humphrey makes 90 percent of her own clothes. She does not try to veil her occasional surprise at finding herself in the midst of—or even influencing—men of power. When a few of her ideas and phrases on a positive effort for peace appeared in a *New York Times* report of one of Humphrey's speeches, she said, "I was just chatting with Hubert on the way home from dinner. It was scary to see my ideas in *The New York Times!*"

She has preferred to spend time with her children at home instead of working in her husband's office. Nancy, born in 1939; Hubert H. III, born in 1942; Robert, born in 1944; and Douglas, born in 1948, missed their father often during the years of his political rise, but they never lacked attention from their mother. In recent years, as the four children have moved away to marriage or school, Mrs. Humphrey has stepped more deeply into Washington life and her husband's career. She moves through the frantic scenes of conventions and campaigns with control and grace, and into the jungles of jealousy in the world of political power with perspective and a level head. Her first act after President Johnson phoned to tell her that Humphrey would be his Vice Presidential running mate in 1964 was to turn to her son Douglas and say, "Dougie, you'll probably meet the President tonight. Just remember that you address him as 'Mr. President' and not 'Mr. Johnson.' "

The Humphreys do not have a political partnership; they have a good marriage. He does not always include his wife in the major decisions of his political life. In 1959, Mrs. Humphrey learned of his final decision to run for the Presidency when she read the morning paper. She wired him: CONGRATULATIONS. LET ME KNOW IF THERE IS ANYTHING I CAN DO TO BE OF HELP. But Humphrey does respect his wife's judgment, criticism, and balanced view of his personal and political efforts, and often solicits her advice.

Her deepest respect for him—and the initial reason for her attraction to him—is based on what she calls his "instinct to educate." She sees him as a man who seeks to teach. "I was always impressed by men who could clarify complex issues or problems, men who could help the people understand those problems and could educate or enlighten them. I think this has been Humphrey's biggest contribution, in Minnesota and nationally: he has helped to educate people to greater political maturity."

Humphrey considers himself a teacher. He is, in fact, a teacher-politician (or a politician-teacher, the emphasis of role and perspective depending on the issue or audience in front of him at any given moment). He refers to himself often as a "refugee from the classroom." He proclaims that "the duty of leadership is to educate." He has often kept network television cameras or men of power waiting for an hour while he talked with a dozen students from an obscure Minnesota high school. "I can't help it," he says sheepishly later, "I just like kids." At moments when he is pressured by a hundred demands on his time, efforts, and influence, he often throws up his arms and says, "Sometimes I'd like to get out of this damn power struggle and find a nice, quiet high school to teach in." Framed in an honored spot above his desk is a white card which reads:

SOMETIMES I GROW TIRED OF:
* Dedicated People
* Community-minded People
* Things that Something
  Should be Done About

AND WHEN I GROW TIRED OF SUCH THINGS,
I LOOK WITH FONDNESS ON:
* Gentle Philosophers
* The Light of Heart
* Children

Generally Humphrey is most impressive as a speaker—and most enjoys—standing before an audience of children. He likes their "clean, fresh, eager, curious faces." Students bring out the teacher in him. In a speech or in informal remarks to a high school graduating class or a touring group of college students, he is usually less flamboyant, slower-paced, less strident, and more careful of his facts and logic.

Political scientist Kirkpatrick says "Humphrey would have made a great teacher." The spirit of the teacher has never really left him, and it is possible that if he ever retires from public life he will return to an academic setting, perhaps as a college or university president. He is rarely pedagogic, and he has had relatively few academic thoughts since leaving the University of Minnesota in 1941. But as a politician he is far more the teacher than the tactician. He would prefer to spend six days "visiting with" the people of a particular state than to spend six hours locked up with its political bosses. He would rather speak to an audience of a thousand for fifty-five minutes than to gaze for one minute into a television lens representing an audience of fifty-five million. He is not above using the techniques of propaganda and the tricks of rhetoric on a platform, and his critics suggest that his speeches sometimes verge on the demagogic, but his general purpose is to instruct and not dictate to an audience.

As a teacher-politician he is less inclined to impart knowledge than to instruct an audience to a particular viewpoint—but he can do both. Many of his public statements seem to stem from the premise: "Never underestimate the intelligence of the people—but never overestimate the knowledge they have." In a television program for Minnesota stations in 1961, at a time when most politicians were mouthing the safe cliché, "We must stand firm on Berlin," Humphrey spent three of his precious fourteen minutes describing the precise geographic location of West Berlin and another eight minutes explaining the international legal questions related to that divided city. An observer said after the program, "You wasted your time. Everybody knows where West Berlin is, and no one can understand the legal aspects of Berlin." Humphrey answered, "I think there are a lot of people scattered around who believe West Berlin is in *West* Germany. And *all* the people had better start to understand that Berlin involves more than a confrontation of guns and tanks." In 1962, preparing to speak to a labor organization, the chairman cornered Humphrey and cried, "You can't talk about Latin America and the Alliance for Progress to these guys. Why don't you damn the 'Right to Work' laws?" Humphrey retorted, "YOU damn whatever you want. I'm going to teach them a thing or two about Hemispheric survival tonight."

It is presumptuous to speculate on the deepest motivations of men in high public office. In seeking to define a man's distinction as a political leader, one can only note the salient characteristic of his public personality and try to assess the character of his conduct in office. In essence, it appears that Franklin D. Roosevelt wanted to improvise, to create. Harry S. Truman just wanted to "do his damnedest" in the job of the Presidency. Dwight D. Eisenhower wanted things to be efficient and orderly. John F. Kennedy wanted to be memorable. Lyndon B. Johnson wants a *national* identity and to be loved by the people.

Hubert H. Humphrey wants to teach, to convince the people of his own worth and the worth of his ideas and goals, to inspire the people to act toward achievement of those goals. He is not an introspective man, and when asked what basic force drives him he merely shrugs his shoulders and says, "There's just a lot of work to be done." But if the careful observer pieces together all of Humphrey's spoken or implied instincts, urges, and goals, he concludes that Humphrey dreams of the whole nation as his own classroom, with all of the people listening attentively and respectfully to teacher Humphrey, and then moving out with missionary zeal to slay the wicked dragons of evil and injustice in the world.

Humphrey enjoyed the formal role of teacher in the early 1940's, and was successful in that one, pre-political profession. Teaching, as a career, also gave him the time to flit in and out of a dozen diverse activities. After he had stuggled twelve years to complete his education, the depression ended with the advent of a wartime economy. He progressed through a series of jobs with New Deal and wartime agencies in Minnesota, first with the WPA's Workers Education Service, then as State Director for War Production Training, then as Assistant State Director of the War Manpower Commission. His friends referred to him during this period as a "government administrator." Others labeled him "a career bureaucrat." In essence, he was a teacher for three years. He liked his duties. He traveled throughout the state. He was teaching teachers or Air Force officers in programs which were considered necessary and honorable during wartime. He not only had a classroom in which to teach each day, but also an opportunity to speak or lecture to a variety of groups each night.

But the classroom, with all its satisfactions, was not enough for him. He could not be confined by four walls, he could not be restricted to the academic disciplines, he could not be fully satisfied with instructing a small group of students or challenged enough by the inquiring minds of only thirty or forty individuals. As a man he was driven to do much more. He was pushed ahead by forces within and behind him; his raw and restless physical energy, his father's high standards, his wife's contagious faith, his depression-born fears and tensions, his imprecise but rentlentless ambitions, and the power and purpose of his passionately held convictions.

His last and best formal job as a teacher was with the Political

Science Department of Macalester College in St. Paul. He was thirty-three, still skinny and pink-cheeked, but also a professor in a course titled "American Local Government" In an afternoon late in the spring semester of 1944, Professor Humphrey called the class to attention and directed the students into a discussion of a book by John Roy Carlson, on fascism. The weather outside was pleasant; a gentle wind rustled through the trees of the campus. In Washington, Franklin Delano Roosevelt was giving only minor attention to the pre-convention maneuvering which would award him a fourth-term nomination. On the foggy coast of southern England, Allied armies were marshaling for the amphibious assault on Cherbourg to begin the final conquest of Nazi Germany and Adolf Hitler. In the rocky islands of the far Pacific, American troops stepped their bloody way toward the heart of the Japanese Empire. On an isolated mesa in New Mexico scientists raced the clock and challenged the mysteries of the universe to control the power of the atom for a bomb.

In Macalester College's "Old Main" building Humphrey talked to his class of the potential strength and danger of fascism in America. He told his students to speak up with their ideas. The class session, which had begun at 4 P.M., continued past the five o'clock bell. At six fifteen professor and students recessed for a light dinner, then reassembled at six forty. The spring twilight died into darkness; the discussion continued. Humphrey debated individual students, challenged disagreeing students to debate one another, fired questions and ideas at the whole class. By eight o'clock the rest of the campus was almost deserted. Still teacher and students talked on. At eight thirty all other lights in "Old Main" were turned off. A yawning janitor waited passively outside Humphrey's classroom as the discussion raced on. The voices of some of the students became hoarse; other students were too tired to speak. But none left; all remained for another hour and ten minutes. In that time Humphrey showered his students with ideas, facts, history, economics, philosophy, clichés, questions, eloquence.

At nine forty in the evening—five hours and forty minutes after the class had been called to order—Humphrey reluctantly acknowledged the time and exhorted his students:

"What you do, what each of us does, has an effect on the community, the state, the nation, and the world. There is so much to be done, to build for a better life. Whatever your views, don't just be jeering from the bleachers. Get out and pitch for what you think is the best team. Take an interest in local government; become active, regardless of your party or viewpoint."

And then he finished the longest classroom session in the college's sixty-two-year history. Pointing a challenging finger at his students, he ended:

"Get into politics!"

PART II

THE POLITICIAN

6

Passion for Politics

Politics?

Semanticists differ on whether the word itself is singular or plural. Scholars debate the meaning of the concept. Even the dictionaries disagree. Politics is (or are), according to various sources, a science, an art, a game, a profession. One dictionary is cleverly evasive. Politics, it says, is "the science or art of political government." Political? The definition offered for that adjective is only an echo: "pertaining to or dealing with the science or art of politics." A politician, the same dictionary meekly reports, is "one who is active in politics." A politico, it concludes lamely, is "a politician."

Germany's Otto von Bismarck seemed to change his mind. "Politics," he once said, "are not an exact science." In a more exact mood he wrote: "Politics is the doctrine of the attainable." Plato suggested that the politician should be considered the ideal or perfect man. Aristotle, a bit more down-to-earth, believed, "Man is by nature a political animal." Almost twenty-two centuries later Sir John Robert Seeley offered a finely teeter-tottering definition: "History is past politics, politics present history." Perhaps most perceptively, Benjamin Disraeli said, "Finality is not the language of politics."

Many Americans tend to regard politics as something essentially corrupt or "dirty," and to dismiss politicians as fence-straddling rascals with both feet in the air, one ear to the ground and one in the gutter, and one hand over a hypocritical heart and the other in the public till. The nation reserves a special fondness for its famous public men who are "above politics." It is no longer fashionable to boost a newborn son with predictions that he will be

President fifty years hence. Even the most skilled and honorable of
American politicians usually prefer to identify themselves as
"public servants," or—more grandly—as "statesmen." Some reporters and teachers favor a precise and absurd maxim which
makes this distinction: "A politician thinks of the next election; a
statesman thinks of the next generation." Ignoring the logic that a
man is neither essentially immoral nor inconsistent if he thinks
about *both,* many Americans seem to believe that a politician can
become a statesman only when he is dead. They do allow an occasional exception: a skilled and successful politician might become
a statesman if he retires from the work of politics to issue occasional profound statements from a bench in Central Park or a
newly established library in his home town.

Americans tend to take their politics seriously; they take their
politicians less seriously. In newspaper cartoons a statesman is ten
feet tall, of lean body and straight posture, with a jaw of granite
and eyes of courage. The politician, in the American caricature, is
a plump and not very bright little fellow, with a double chin and
ostentatiously old-fashioned clothes, and a manner which is either
bumbling or conniving.

The American public attitude toward government tends to
grant respect to institutions, not individuals. The "founding fathers" are revered, but few people ever suggest that they were in
fact excellent politicians. Even the founding fathers tend to receive second billing in public estimation to the Constitution, or to
something loosely called "the sacred principles on which this
country was founded." Even today newspapers are inclined to report, "The Administration won a victory in Congress yesterday,"
instead of identifying the man or men responsible for the victory.
When Congress approved legislation to establish the Peace Corps
in 1961, few stories referred to it as "Humphrey's bill." (He had
been the first author of the legislation and remained the bill's
principal sponsor.) Most stories labeled it "the Administration's
Peace Corps program" or "the President's proposal." The people,
when they view the mighty problems and the great achievements
of their nation, cannot quite believe that individual men—human
beings like themselves—are responsible for solution or progress.
Americans want and seek out their heroes, but most often in time
of war or in such fields as sports, science, or exploration. On the

lofty plane of national achievement and big issues men become small and politicians petty in the public view.

One reason for the public's tendency to downgrade or distrust politicians is that politicians themselves are not particularly trustworthy in their public statements about themselves. The politician must, among other efforts, curry the favor of the people, fight for his votes on Election Day, and compete for his place in history. The politician craves credit when credit is due and often contrives to receive credit when it really belongs to others. A year after the Peace Corps was established and its popularity was evident, its officials joked about the number of politicians who claimed to have "fathered" the program. The total, they guessed, ranged somewhere between forty-five and sixty-eight. One of the more ludicrous scenes frequently enacted in modern Washington involves a group of men of power and position, each desperately trying to elbow his way toward the center or behind the main subject of a picture about to be taken by news photographers. Modesty and shyness are qualities rarely seen in a successful politician. When uttered by a politician, the phrase "in all humility" usually indicates that he is immensely pleased with himself.

The politician knows that he cannot continue to practice politics, and that he cannot even hope to become a "statesman," unless he can be elected and re-elected or hold a decisive influence on the election and re-election of others. The politician knows that he cannot even approach success unless he can focus wide and favorable public attention on his real or imagined talents and achievements. Many men of political skill can do just that, and do it discreetly, smoothly, and without straying from basic honesty and honor. Others are clumsy breast-beaters who love the public spotlight more than they respect personal achievement or public service. The latter type of politician tends to be more dramatic, colorful, and clever. He gives politics its prevalent image. Beneath each citizen's decision to give a man his vote is an awareness that the man, as a politician, is probably egotistical and immodest. Behind each voter's action in placing public trust in a man is a kernel of distrust. The man who seeks votes is a politician; he is thus suspect. The man who seeks re-election is involved with government, which—as many of the founding fathers said—is a "necessary evil."

Politics is not intrinsically evil, nor is it essentially honorable.

Politics does not necessarily corrupt a man, nor does it always ennoble him. Politics holds no inherent ethic or standard of human conduct.

Politics is nothing more precise than an activity, involving—in no particular order or structure—individual men and masses of people, rival interests and conflicting aspirations, the use of influence and the quest for power, the functions of the state and the techniques of government.

Politics can be the exercise of public authority for the public good or the abuse of public trust for personal aggrandizement. It can be the forging of force for a special interest or the amalgamation of authority for the common interest. It can be the rivalry of men, the cooperation of governments, or the conflict between the individual and the community. It can be the tricks of propaganda or the methods of education. It can be the effort to make laws within arbitrary boundaries of land or to establish order for artificial units of people. It can be one man seeking to convince another man, or a hundred million men.

Politics is none of these alone and more than all of them combined. Politics has no synonyms. Politics is not a doctrine, a dogma, or even a set of rules and traditions.

The successful politician fully realizes that politics—particularly in a free society and a growing nation—changes from one time to another and differs from one area to another. If there is any "rule" of politics, it is that there are no rigid formulas which apply with equal validity and effectiveness in all times and in all areas of political activity. The local official who stares out of his office at the town square of Centerville, U.S.A., and suggests that he knows the absolute elements and essential rules of politics is not a wise politician; he is bound by generalizations and precedents. The authentic politician watches the clock and knows what time it is; he listens to the people and hears their voices; he senses their current mood and understands their local or collective wants, needs, fears, and hopes. Politics, for him, is the reality of the moment and the actuality of the place. Politics, to him, is neither science nor art. He is more of a mind reader than a scientist, more of a mystic than an artist. The successful politician is both objective and subjective in his decisions and judgments. He possesses two qualities worth far more than such raw tools as money and power. He has perspicacity and empathy.

A "rule" of politics may apply to the nation for a year or two, or even a decade or two, but then it ceases to be valid as time passes and the people change. A generalization about politics might well apply to one town or even one state for a long time, but it is worthless to the politician in another town or state. The corrupt political tone of the United States in the grim years following the Civil War bears no resemblance to the political character of the United States in the two decades after World War II. The politics of Tammany Hall in New York is a world—and not just a continent—apart from the politics of the California Democratic Council. The politics of Louisiana and the politics of Minnesota are as different and far apart as the two ends of the mighty river which begins in one and ends in the other.

Politics can be compared to a river, a long, rambling, and changing river. In some locations and in some times it is dirty, ugly, noisy, and cruel; in others it is clean, beautiful, silent, and kind. It is shallow and apparently stagnant in some spots; in others it is deep and fast-flowing. It is in constant motion, but it changes course often. The seasons affect it, and the land guides it. It draws its power from a million tributaries and gives its substance to a thousand streams or a single ocean.

The river is essential to the people and the land around it. And in a society with representative, democratic government politics is essential. Politics has no particular direction, but as free people seek to resolve their conflicts, conciliate their rivalries, and to forge collective action or achievement, politics becomes a vital process.

As an amorphous activity or as a steady process, politics draws Hubert Humphrey. He has a passion for the activity of politics and a skill for the process of politics. He has exemplified many of the aspects of politics in actual scenes such as these:

With his arm draped over another man's shoulder in a corner of the U.S. Capitol he whispered in his ear, "Now look, old friend, the President really wants this bill and needs your vote for it."

In his office alone late at night, he dictated a note to somebody he had never met: "I was so pleased to read in Friday's paper that you won a prize for the best petunias at the county fair. You must really have a green thumb. Keep up the good work."

He listened to a group of angry, frustrated men from an area of the country with exhausted resources and high unemployment, telling him, "Somebody's just got to do something about things up there."

After his picture was taken with a famous baseball star, he excitedly told an assistant, "Get prints of this out to the sports editors right away."

He picked up a pencil, stared at a list of Senators, and then slowly and sadly crossed out the name of a friend who desperately wanted to be assigned to an important Senate committee.

Standing on a high, floodlit platform, he chanted a phrase about another man's voting record and heard sixteen thousand voices join his rhythmic and partisan litany.

Leaning against a store front in the cool sunlight of an October morning, he told a dozen small-town housewives and farmers that the United Nations "is the last great bulwark against war."

He was pushed, shoved, pulled, clawed, and screamed at by five hundred sweating, bellowing men and women in a fund-raising reception—and never for a moment lost his smile or showed even a hint of moisture on his forehead.

Scribbling down the name of a man who had grabbed his arm in an airport lobby to tell him that he urgently needed a loan from the Small Business Administration, he said, "I'll look into it."

Politics is Humphrey glancing—by chance—at one letter out of a thousand, in a cheap envelope from an obscure university town, typed carefully and written earnestly, and containing a good idea.

Politics is Humphrey exclaiming to a toothless, flat-chested, hungry woman outside a church in West Virginia, "My, don't you look lovely today!" It is Humphrey dancing with the plump wife of the Foreign Minister of a new African nation, sharing a mint julep with an influential columnist, pounding his fist on a table to demand help for a thousand unemployed families in a hamlet in the Appalachians. It is Humphrey quietly, patiently, tediously explaining the U.S. position to a Soviet disarmament negotiator in Geneva. It is Humphrey leaving the White House after a meeting with military leaders on a delicate international crisis and cocking his head for a moment to hear the tolling bell of St. John's Church across Lafayette Square.

Politics, for Humphrey, is work, years of it; fun, barrels of it; words, billions of them; paper, tons of it; miles, millions of them; and people—listening, demanding, denouncing, cheering, flattering, fawning, working, and voting—but always people. And once in a while politics for Humphrey is one human being, standing on a street corner and leaning low to peer into his black car as it pauses for a light, and making it all worthwhile with a shy smile and a friendly call: "Hi, Humphrey; I voted for you."

Humphrey pays the price for public attention and political power. In more than twenty years of political life he has been called repeatedly a draft-dodger, a radical, a Communist, a socialist, a fascist, a liar, a coward, a flannelmouth, a demagogue, and—worst of all—a nobody. Drinks have been thrown in his face and sugar bowls at the back of his head. He has been mocked, ridiculed, misquoted, damned, spat upon, and shot at. (All but the last touched and hurt him.) He has given up privacy, which he never really wanted or needed. He has also given up a normal family life, which he did want and the loss of which—now that his children are grown—torments him.

He often says publicly, and without embarrassment or boastfulness, "I am a politician." He has never tried to evade the identification and never thought that he might try to contrive an "above politics" image for himself. To Humphrey politics is, for the most part, a matter of relating himself to people, as individuals or in the mass. And as he must be involved at all times with people, he must be involved constantly with politics. His love of unordered activity involving people is satisfied, in part, by the unstructured activity of politics. He respects the existence of rival interests and understands the conflicting aspirations in others and in himself. He knows how to use influence and he seeks power. He identifies himself as an integral part of the community, in the political sense a homespun word for the state, and he has a quick grasp of the techniques of government.

He is clearly and almost constantly the politician, no matter what formal position he occupies or informal role he plays. He tends to see most of the problems of the United States as economic, moral, or political, with emphasis on the last. In the periodic flare-ups of crisis in Southeast Asia he sees first not a set of military or diplomatic puzzles, but rather a basic political problem. He has grown impatient at White House meetings as he has heard one man after another focus almost all attention on the military aspects of U.S. involvement in Laos or Viet Nam, and has sought to bring more attention to what he sees as a neglected need: governments in Southeast Asia which are responsive to the needs and wants of the people, and thus people who are loyal to the governments. He makes a rather crude distinction between international diplomatic and political efforts. "Diplomacy deals with diplomats," he says. "Politics deals with people."

He draws out the political nature of other men. One overlooked lesson of his eight-hour conversation with Nikita Khrushchev in Moscow in 1958 was that Khrushchev was a politician, not just a dictator. The former Soviet leader did not spend a full evening with Humphrey just because he wanted to chat, or to listen to Humphrey defend the merits of a free-enterprise economic system. Khrushchev recognized the politician in Humphrey and felt a degree of rapport with him.

The lesson of the quickly healed wounds and the fast developing friendship between Humphrey and John F. Kennedy after their bitter primary election contests in 1960 was that both were essentially political men. "Magnanimity in politics is not seldom the truest wisdom," Edmund Burke wrote, "and a great empire and little minds go ill together." The bitterness of the Wisconsin and West Virginia campaigns lingered for a long time in the minds and mouths of many of Humphrey's and Kennedy's staff assistants, but the two principals had a cordial association within a few weeks, an effective alliance within a few months, and a deep personal friendship within one year. Humphrey campaigned enthusiastically for Kennedy in Minnesota and bordering states in the fall of 1960, as the Presidential candidate knew he would. Kennedy asked Humphrey to help the campaign in such geographic areas as New York and Detroit and among such specific population groups as minorities and labor, as Humphrey knew he would. Outsiders who view politics as enduring struggles between irreconcilable forces were amazed at the close Kennedy-Humphrey relationship which flourished from late 1960 until the President's assassination in November 1963. "They fought each other intensely, and their personalities are not anything alike," one reporter said as he argued against the reality of the relationship. The answer was that Humphrey and Kennedy, for all their other differences of background and taste, found communion in their basic political instincts.

It is significant also that during Kennedy's years in the White House, Humphrey did not gravitate—either officially or socially—toward the President's stable of intellectuals, represented by Arthur Schlesinger Jr. and Theodore Sorensen. He spent most of his spare White House time and many social hours with what Kennedy jokingly referred to as his "Irish Mafia," the more politically oriented Lawrence O'Brien and Kenneth O'Donnell. O'Brien and O'Donnell speak in tough terms of what they call "the nuts and bolts" of politics, and they credit Humphrey with skill in the techniques of politics. Kennedy, according to O'Brien, often referred to Humphrey as "a damned worthy adversary" during the primary campaigns of 1960. Just as often, when he was President and needed a chore done on Capitol Hill, Kennedy would tell an assistant, "Ask Hubert to do this; he knows how."

Humphrey's effectiveness as a politician stems more from talent than skill. His political qualities are more natural and instinctive than contrived and cultivated. His characteristics as a man are reflected by his political personality. His eagerness for hard work, his empathy for people, his positiveness, his open personality, and his sense of strong conviction both strengthen and weaken his political efforts.

His will to work is most often an asset. He simply puts more energy and time into his work than most of his political colleagues or opponents. Time, in his view, is his most precious possession. He can dictate twenty letters in a half hour between meetings, when most men are inclined to sip a cup of coffee or read a newspaper. Even the most dedicated political leaders and public servants require a few hours of relaxation in the evening; Humphrey relaxes by working on his "favorite" projects. All of this tends to put him ahead of his political competitors in the sheer volume of work he turns out. But in obeying his will to work he does not often allow enough time to take stock of himself and his efforts. One adviser remembers a night in early 1960 when he was supposed to spend an hour making some basic decisions and plans for his Presidential campaign. Instead he spent the hour poking through the mail in his Senate office and answering letters which could have been handled competently by his secretaries. "I can't talk now," he told the adviser. "There's too much work to do."

His empathy for people is probably his greatest strength as a politician. His ability to place himself in the position of others gives him a quick and deep understanding of people and their problems. His audiences sense this, and respond to it with applause, support, and votes. He is, as Senator Eugene J. McCarthy and other friendly critics have suggested, "soft on people." He adapts himself to the perspective of others so completely that he has trouble saying no to any request, no matter how petty or unreasonable. It is not uncommon for him to commit himself to three or four obligations to people, all of which require his presence at the same time in different locations. His appointments secretary, responsible for his schedule, has one of the most difficult tasks in Washington, D.C.

Humphrey's positiveness gives most of his political efforts a sound and progressive tone. He is not satisfied with identifying problems; he has a determination to find solutions. The general result is that he has had a positive influence on some of the best pieces of legislation to come out of Congress since 1949. But he is less effective when the emphasis of his purpose is negative, as was often the case when he was a Democratic Senator during the years of a Republican Administration in the 1950's. In performing the legitimate functions of the opposition he more often sounded garrulous than reasonable, and his criticisms were as much partisan as constructive.

His openness as a man is, according to several reporters, a "breath of fresh air in the musty world of pompous politicians." Much of what he says and does is spontaneous; the quality is rare in an era of Madison Avenue-conditioned political campaigns, and those who see or hear him sense and appreciate his basic honesty and candor. But sometimes, his friends and political advisers say, he goes too far. In a February 1960 meeting with a group of important potential supporters for his Presidential effort, he commented, "I know I'm not the leading contender for the nomination, but I'm one of the top five being considered. And that's pretty good for a South Dakota boy, isn't it?" That was also, a frustrated friend and witness to the meeting remarked, "a hell of a way to enlist confidence and support."

Humphrey's deep and passionately expressed convictions give most of his political efforts a force and sense of purpose which most of his audiences respect. Voters may be impressed by a man's physical appearance and they may often be influenced by the tricks of propaganda, but generally they are attracted to men who clearly and sincerely *believe* in something. Even most politicians respect a hard-hitting opponent who keys his campaign to his convictions and speaks from his conscience. But politics, unfortunately, often elevates the cynic and crushes the idealist. The realities of public opinion and the maneuverings of political tacticians have, at times, left Humphrey behind as he held to a conviction on which he could not compromise. And one influential Senator has remarked, "Sometimes people are afraid of a man with intense convictions. Hubert, I must admit, is frighteningly earnest."

There is another quality in Humphrey which affects his political personality both positively and negatively. His touch of insecurity, developed primarily by his depression-decade experience in South Dakota, makes him scare easily. In a political campaign he takes nothing for granted, no matter how favorable the polls and other clues of support and probable victory. He "runs scared," a mood which most politicians consider prudent and wise. Even in the 1964 campaign he worried about voter apathy as much as he predicted victory. With Humphrey, "running scared" is not a campaign strategy consciously arrived at. It is a very real emotional state in which he finds himself as an election approaches. The result has often been an apparent lack of confidence in his public appearances. For political leadership the people want, above all others, men who radiate confidence, men who believe in themselves, and are not easily intimidated.

For all his loyalty to the traditions and policies of the Democratic Party, Humphrey is not essentially an "inner-party" politician. In at least a score of states he has been known for more than a decade as a "party workhorse," ready and eager at almost any time to hop a plane and appear as a speaker for a local fund-raising dinner or hell-raising rally on behalf of the state party organization and candidates. But his liberalism and individualism have often taken priority over his identification as a Democrat. His first training in political office was in the nonpartisan position of Mayor of Minneapolis. His success in Minnesota politics transcended party lines, and he knew it. The United States Senate divides Democrats and Republicans with a wide center aisle and a committee organization based on party membership, but strict partisanship is not of paramount influence in that body, which significantly conditioned Humphrey's political personality.

To Humphrey politics is many things. It is a science, in which he is capable of systematic study and effort. It is an art, in which he is instinctively talented. It is a game, in which he enjoys himself tremendously. It is a profession, in which he has worked and earned a living for most of his adult life. Above all, politics to Humphrey is a marvelously imprecise activity, involving people. He is not a politician of the back-room, machine-organization sort. He is a politician who draws strength and satisfaction from what he calls—sometimes reverently but most often affectionately—"the people."

For most of his political career Humphrey's people have been the people of Minnesota. They have influenced him as much as any force in his political life.

7

Grass Roots

Minnesota is not a particularly imposing state, at first glance. Its size, 84,000 square miles, is above average, but its population, about three and a half million, is less than the combined population of only two New York boroughs, Manhattan and The Bronx. There is much space and land for everyone in Minnesota, and more than eleven thousand lakes, but its people can boast of few superlatives. The state has nothing of significance which is the highest, the lowest, the biggest, or the longest in the United States. The land is graceful, beautiful, and unspectacular, with few abrupt changes of elevation.

The state does have a few modest claims to fame. It is the major producer of wild rice, carefully grown and harvested by Chippewa Indians in the marshy northern counties. It has Minnehaha Falls in the Twin Cities, the setting for Longfellow's "Hiawatha." It has the Mayo Clinic, an outstanding medical research and treatment center in the southern Minnesota city of Rochester. But wild rice is expensive stuff, with a limited market, Minnehaha Falls often dries up in the middle of the summer tourist season, and many Americans think that the Mayo Clinic is in Rochester, *New York.*

Minnesota is not the best springboard for national power or prominence. Political campaign strategists rarely consider it a "key" state; election night reporters and pundits never call it "pivotal." In the 1964 Presidential election Minnesota held only ten electoral votes, compared with forty-three for New York and forty for California. Until the Democratic Convention and President Johnson named Hubert Humphrey to the national ticket in 1964, no major political party had ever nominated a Minnesotan for the Presidency or the Vice Presidency.

But the realities of sheer size and influence are not of prime importance to Minnesotans. Perhaps most significantly, Minnesota does have the legend (and in the town of Bemidji, an immense wood statue) of Paul Bunyan. As most school children know, he was a giant of a man who—single-handed—could change the course of a mighty river or log a vast forest.

The settlement of Minnesota took Bunyanesque strength and courage; the Minnesota climate ranges from 40 degree below zero temperatures in the winter to 100 degree F. temperatures in the summer. In 1850 there were fewer than six thousand persons in the Minnesota area. But the pioneers came. First were the French-Canadian fur trappers, who worked the northern woods until fur-bearing animals dwindled to commercial insignificance. Then the woodsmen—mostly Swedes and Norwegians—came to cut the valuable timber of the forests until most of the big pine and spruce were taken. Then the miners streamed in from the industrial cities of the East until the rich ore of the great Mesabi, Vermilion, and Cuyuna ranges was exhausted.

Much of Minnesota's resources was sent to other parts of the nation, and relatively little industry grew up in the state. But there was always the land, rich land which had been smoothed by late glacial activity and nourished by centuries of idleness. The Homestead Act of 1862 and the end of the Civil War stimulated a steady and large flow of farmers into Minnesota, which had been given statehood in 1858. They were mostly Scandinavians and Germans. (Minnesota is noted as a state of Swedes, but they are outnumbered by both Norwegians and Germans.) The population remained remarkably homogeneous. Today more than 70 percent of the people are of Scandinavian or German descent. About twelve thousand Indians cling together in the north-central part of the state, and only about twenty thousand Negroes are scattered through Minnesota's cities.

The great cities of Minneapolis, St. Paul, and Duluth—linked to the rest of the country by the Mississippi River or Lake Superior—were settled and developed primarily by Yankee commercial interests, but Minnesota continued to be an agricultural state of small farms and little towns. The proportion of rural to urban population has changed—as it has throughout the United States—but today more than half of Minnesota's people are still tied to farming, and the average farm is less than two hundred acres. Minnesota farmers remain proud and independent in the face of problems created by rising production and declining prices. They think of themselves, as most Midwestern farmers do, as "the backbone of democracy," the "salt of the earth," and as men who work harder than anyone else to feed the people of the world. The wants of Minnesota farm wives are basic and simple; a University of Minnesota survey in 1950 revealed that the following were the items of greatest dissatisfaction to farm women: (1) children's job prospects; (2) savings; (3) lawns; (4) telephone service; (5) sewage-disposal system.

There is also a basic simplicity to the physical and social make-up of Minnesota. The few urban centers and most of the larger cities clutch the eastern and southern fringes of the state. The rest of the state is rural. The land in the south is rich and productive; the men who farm it tend to be prosperous, conservative, and Republican. Northward the land becomes rockier and less productive; the men who tend the marginal farms of the north are generally unprosperous, liberal, and Democratic.

Despite the differences, the people of the state speak often of "the Minnesota Community." The preponderant north European ancestry of most of the population helps to give the people a common identity. Minnesota's church membership is 41 percent Lutheran, 38 percent Catholic, and 21 percent a mixture of denominations, mostly Protestant.

It is a relatively stable state, usually lagging behind the pace of the rest of the country in social and economic changes caused by a growing and mobile population. The sense of a state community and the homogeneity of the population minimize violent social upheavals and clashes of class against class. The outsider might expect to find in Minnesota a bland, conservative, predictable political character.

The opposite is true. From the beginning Minnesota politics had an essentially flamboyant and independent tone. The agrarian revolt and the Populist movement of the last half of the nineteenth century found fertile ground in Minnesota. The National Grange—starting as a social organization for farmers but later providing the structure for a political movement—was founded by a Minnesotan, in 1867. A Minnesotan, Ignatius Donnely, fanned the sparks of an agrarian crusade against the established power of Eastern bankers and political bosses. The Non-Partisan League, the Anti-Monopoly Party, the Greenbacks, the Populists, and the Farmer-Labor Party all found shape and membership in the progressive spirit and agrarian frustrations of Minnesota's people. In 1922 the Minnesota Farmer-Labor Party elected one of its members, Henrik Shipstead, to the United States Senate. Floyd B. Olson, another Farmer-Laborite whose liberalism transcended party lines, rallied the interest of Scandinavians, Catholics, and Jews who had grown tired of being pushed around by Twin City Yankee commercial leaders. He served as Minnesota Governor in the 1930's, and ranked with such other giants of Midwestern progressivism as Robert LaFollette of Wisconsin, Burton K. Wheeler of Montana, and William "Wild Bill" Langer of North Dakota.

Generally Minnesota politics has defied precise analysis and the orthodox traditions of party organization. Members of the state legislature are not officially Democrats and Republicans; they are "Liberals" and "Conservatives." A visiting reporter from a national magazine, scratching his head in confusion over Minnesota's political structure, was told, "If you don't like our form of politics, wait a few minutes." It is axiomatic among the state's people that a Minnesota politician "would rather be unpredictable than President."

It should also be axiomatic that a large number of Minnesotans would rather be politicians than anything else. Minnesota has more government units than any other state in the nation. The units do not make much sense, except when viewed in the checkerboard pattern of counties (eighty-seven of them, compared with sixty-two in New York and fifty-eight in California) on a Minnesota state map. Around the time Minnesota achieved statehood, officials drew straight lines east and west and north and south across the map of Minnesota, arbitrarily setting off blocks of thirty-six square miles as townships, without regard to geographical barriers or population distribution. The result is that Minnesota has more than two thousand townships, each of which holds a yearly meeting to elect officers and decide such issues as whether or not to purchase a new snowplow or repair an old road grader. The number of villages, special jurisdictions, and single-project "districts" defy the imagination. It would appear that Minnesotans simply like government—the more the better.

They also like politics and politicians. Minnesotans tend to be far more politically interested and active than the people of most other states. Campaign signs cover the lawns of many private homes in the cities of Minnesota during the two or three months before an election. In the small towns it is not unusual for thousands of local residents and farmers to gather for a picnic and a full day of listening to political speeches. In the rural areas an affection for political oratory lingers from the decades when politics was as much a form of entertainment as a process for reaching collective decisions. In the agricultural doldrums of autumn and winter the people of the prairie were willing to travel miles by foot or buggy to hear a speech, and they did not mind at all if a politician needed as much as an hour "to get warmed up" in the cold air. Minnesotans still expect something special when they travel to hear a political speech, and they are not in a hurry for a politician to sum up his views in a neat, thirty-minute package. Length of a speech is not particularly important; the content and the style of delivery are. The Minnesota audience, generally, likes to hear a speech which is eloquent and entertaining, and the people are not antagonistic toward a speaker who seeks to get them "fired up." Television, radio, and the urbanizing trend of Minnesota have affected the state's politics, but the way a man speaks and what he says are still more important than how brief his speech is or how handsome his face. The Minnesota audience is, for all its love of oratory in large amounts, discriminating. The Minnesotan is more likely than the citizen of another state to remain seated and attentive for a political speech, but he is sparing in his praise. "He's SOME talker" or "Mighty fine speech" are the ultimate tributes which many rural Minnesotans bestow on a politician.

Minnesotans also tend to be impressively intelligent and sophisticated about politics, partly because of the keenness of their political interest and the caliber of their education. The excellent University of Minnesota has raised the educational level of the population, both directly and by example. The people in most areas of the state are willing to pay the costs of good schools and well-trained teaching staffs; there are almost as many independent school districts in Minnesota as there are townships. The result is

evident in the standing of the state's young men in the Armed
Forces Qualification Test. Minnesota usually ranks lowest in the
rate of its young men rejected for the armed services because of
lack of intelligence. The national average of failure in the Armed
Forces Qualification Test is usually about 16 percent; for Minnesota youths it is only 1.5 percent.

The ideological direction of Minnesota politics has been consistently progressive, and in recent years distinctly liberal. It is one
of the few states of the nation where a politician does not seek the
label "moderate"; the Minnesota politician of the past few decades
has been able to wave the banner of liberalism, and win. Until the
1940's, Minnesota tended to support isolationist policies in world
affairs, and a majority of the people—most of whose fathers or
grandfathers had settled there during a period when Lincoln was
their hero and individual freedom their prized concept—registered
Republican. But in domestic affairs even many Republicans
looked with favor on a strong, vigorous central government and
with a liberal eye on welfare-state programs.

There are many basic reasons for the intrinsic liberalism of
Minnesota politics. The Danes and Finns who pioneered in the
state brought with them the concept and practice of cooperatives,
for the marketing and distribution of farm products. Other Scandinavians, already progressive in political and economic outlook,
quickly adopted the system of cooperatives and blandly disre-
garded complaints about "socialism." Minnesotans of Scandinavian descent were never shocked when a political party or an
individual politician proposed welfare-type programs. The experiments for state-sponsored hospitals and old age programs in the
"old countries" of Sweden or Norway—soon reported through
letters by relatives "back home"—have made Minnesota's 50 percent Scandinavian population generally receptive to the welfare-
state concept.

The tone of Minnesota's predominantly Lutheran and Catholic
population has had a liberalizing effect. The Catholic Church,
usually a conservative element in many cities of the United States,
is regarded as a progressive force in such cities as St. Paul and St.
Cloud. The heavy Lutheran population contributes to both the
liberal spirit and the sense of political involvement by the people.

That denomination tends to emphasize duty to others, the idea that an individual owes a part of his life to the community.

Two institutions in the state have contributed to the quality of its politics. The University of Minnesota—partly through the active political participation of many of its professors and teachers—has lent an intellectual and idealistic mood to the substance of Minnesota politics. And the state's newspapers, dominated by the Cowles publications, have helped to nudge the people toward a liberal, internationalist viewpoint. The Cowles papers, the Minneapolis *Tribune* and the Minneapolis *Star,* fought such neo-nationalist uprisings as the America First movement of the thirties and other lingering isolationist elements of the thirties and forties.

The liberalism of Minnesota politics thus includes a generally positive attitude toward government. Politically the Minnesotan tends to accept and practice the basic idea of the individual working with others toward a common goal.

There is a significant lack of cynicism about politics or distrust of politicians among the people. The explanation, in part, is the record of clean and efficient government in the state. The people expect good government, and because they are relatively well educated and politically involved, they get it. The State Capitol has been notably free of scandal or corruption, and the state has never produced a demagogue such as the late Senator Joseph McCarthy of Wisconsin. "That State of Minnesota," said one Washington professional with an encyclopedic political knowledge of many states, "has the cleanest, most democratic, most honest, able, and efficient politics and government in the country."

Minnesota's political structures are perhaps too new and the social makeup of the state too stable to allow for a brand of "machine" politics run by autocratic political bosses. Minnesota politics is the antithesis of the boss-rule, machine-organization politics which has been common in some Eastern and Southern states. Hubert Humphrey laughed when Eastern or Southern politicians and reporters flattered him with suggestions that he controlled a well-oiled, powerful political machine in Minnesota. Humphrey could never, even if he wanted to, dominate his state party or dictate to its members; there is simply no significant political patronage power in Minnesota.

Humphrey has been liked, respected, and even adulated by the politically active citizens of Minnesota, but frequently he has been told, "We love you, Humphrey, but don't try to tell us what to do." In 1956, he and most of the other major leaders of his party supported and campaigned for Adlai Stevenson in Minnesota's Presidential primary election; the voters chose Estes Kefauver. (That was the last Democratic Presidential preference primary in Minnesota; endorsements are now made in party convention.) In 1960 state party chairman Ray Hemenway decided that he wanted to be Democratic national committeeman from Minnesota. Humphrey and other party leaders opposed him in favor of the incumbent committeeman; the party's rank and file elected Hemenway. Then Humphrey presented his candidate for party chairman, Glenn Johnson; the party convention decisively rejected Johnson in favor of George Farr. In 1964, when party leaders urged state convention delegates to vote for endorsement of a state tax amendment, one woman delegate told them, "I used to live in New York. If this were New York, I'd do what you say. But this is Minnesota. I'll vote the way I think is right. Go jump in the lake." If one of Minnesota's United States Senators or its Governor becomes too insistent on some issue, a soft-spoken farmer delegate or local county chairman might say, "Look, nobody tells me what to do. You run the country [or the state]; we'll run our county organization." After one of his requests to the party was rebuffed, Humphrey complained, "I can influence the spending of billions of federal dollars, the appointment of ambassadors, and the shape of national policy, but I can't even pick a precinct chairman in Minnesota."

That is the way Minnesotans like their politics and government; no one can "run" them or "own" them. Money has political influence in Minnesota, as it does in any other state, but it is not—as in some states—the ultimate tool of political influence. In 1958 the Democratic Farmer-Labor Party in Minnesota faced an election campaign with an almost empty treasury. Chairman Ray Hemenway was jubilant when he opened an envelope one afternoon to find a contribution of five thousand dollars. He checked the source, as was customary, to learn that the contributor represented a special interest and wanted to have a "voice" in the appointment of a state commissioner. Hemenway sadly but not at all reluctantly returned the check to the man.

The quality of Minnesota politics tends to produce an abundance of able and honest public legislators and administrators, in both political parties. Republican Harold Stassen, many national reporters have forgotten, was a skilled and effective Governor of Minnesota. National reporters also have difficulty understanding why Minnesotans seem to enjoy a prominence at national political conventions out of proportion to the size and influence of the state. In 1960, Minnesota Congressman Walter Judd was keynoter at the Republican National Convention; Minnesota Governor Orville Freeman nominated John F. Kennedy, and Minnesota Senator Eugene J. McCarthy nominated Adlai Stevenson at the Democratic National Convention. In 1964 the two apparent "finalists" for the Vice Presidential nomination at the Democratic Convention were Minnesotans McCarthy and Humphrey, and Minnesota Attorney General Walter F. Mondale (now U.S. Senator) played a key role in resolving the one major dispute at Atlantic City, a fight over seating of the Mississippi delegation.

Minnesota's political character and process seem to find uncommonly good men and to elevate them to state or national authority and prominence. One man can be immensely influential within the state (as were Floyd B. Olson, Stassen, and Humphrey), but only, apparently, if he is able, skilled, energetic, eloquent, honorable, and honest. He must also be reasonably quick on his political feet and enjoy a minimum amount of pure political luck; Minnesota voters can be as unpredictable as they are independent. Minnesotans generally demand high qualifications in a candidate, and they expect high performance and achievement once they have entrusted him with public office. They seem always to be searching for a political Paul Bunyan who will not try to dominate them. As the North-Star State, Minnesota wants its political stars to shine brightly in the national sky. Aware that their state does not have a particularly imposing posture in national affairs, Minnesotans look for extraordinary men whose talents and energies may make up for the state's modest size and considerable distance from the centers of the Eastern political and cultural establishment.

Minnesota's politics conditioned Humphrey in many ways. He arrived in the state as a man with an instinct to teach and an untapped vocation for politics. In the years he spent in Minnesota,

from approximately 1938 to 1948, he became a politician, a pecul-
iarly Minnesotan politician. He continues to reflect or exemplify
Minnesota's political character, in the manner and length of his
speeches, in his liberalism, in his independence and intellectualism, in his idealism and his efforts "to fire people up." He still
feels most comfortable when he is "out home." Often, after weeks
of power struggles and damp weather in Washington, he says, "I
need to get out of this artificial existence. I need to be refreshed.
I've got to get home and breathe clear air and be with people who
aren't all self-centered." He misses the openness of the land of his
youth and the informality of the people involved with his political
apprenticeship. On a hot summer day in 1963, riding from downtown Washington to Capitol Hill, he frowned at the heavy traffic,
the gruff sounds of trucks, and the smell of smog. "You can't
breathe here," he said. "You can't hear. Megalopolis may kill us
all yet."

He reflected the spirit of a comment by Bernard De Voto which
Minnesotans like to quote:

"I have got to have the sight of clean water and the sound of
running water. I have got to get to places where the sky-shine of
cities does not dim the stars, where you can smell land and foliage,
grasses and marshes, forest duff and aromatic plants and hot un-
derbrush turning cool. Most of all, I have to learn again what
quiet is. I believe that our culture is more likely to perish from
noise than from radioactive fallout. . . ."

Humphrey is no woodsman. He likes pheasant hunting and enjoys a sail or swim in front of his modest home at the edge of Lake
Waverly, west of Minneapolis. One of his close friends and political associates, a Minnesotan, says, "Humphrey's idea of roughing it
is to put on an old jacket and take a walk on the lawn of somebody's
estate." Whatever his inclination or indifference to formal out-
door activity, Humphrey needs the openness of Midwestern land
and people in the way that a city man needs buildings standing
high and protectively close to one another, streets teeming with
automobiles and humanity, and millions of people who provide
services and excitement but who mind their own business. Purga-
tory, for Hubert Humphrey, would be an endless ride on a New
York subway, enclosed in a dark tube and filled with human

beings who do not know him and who seem afraid of contact or conversation with one another.

For many years he reflected the Westerner's traditional antipathy toward the American East. As late as 1960 he was still denouncing "Wall Street moneylenders" and had a deep distrust of bankers, particularly *Eastern* bankers, who were, as any Populist knew, tied in with the House of Rothschild and the international munitions makers. In a bad moment of his 1960 Presidential campaign he turned to a group of his advisers, most of whom were Easterners but none of whom had attended Harvard University. "You're all a bunch of Harvard graduates," he berated them, ". . . you don't know anything about politics!"

According to the most persistent criticism about him, Humphrey talks too much. Even in the 1964 election campaign NBC News reporter Ray Scherer told television viewers, "Humphrey's speeches are too loud and too long." What the Minnesotans might consider eloquent, others in the national political arena regard as "glib." His old supporters in the upper Midwest say that his voice is "sincere and intense"; national observers often call it "abrasive." One columnist, a friend of Humphrey and a former Midwesterner, says, "Let's face it. The aura of the Midwest middle class still clings to Humphrey." Because he is so open, so ready to share all that he knows with others, and so eager to tell everyone everything about himself, he lacks—in the word of one sophisticated political reporter—"mystique." He does not mystify people, and perhaps that is what many Americans, indirectly conditioned by the European tradition of respect for reserved and austere statesmen, want in a national leader. Americans want to feel that a man who is handling the huge and unanticipated problems of the nation has a reserve wisdom, and strength and talent in depth. They are not at all eager to entrust the nation's destiny to someone who looks, speaks, and acts like the next-door neighbor. In 1960 both Humphrey and Kennedy met often with groups of local county or state party leaders in their drives for the Democratic Presidential nomination. "Humphrey would barge into the room and charge from one man to another to shake hands and introduce himself," one reporter remembers. "Kennedy, instead, would walk a few paces into the room, stop and wait for the local party leaders to *come to him*. He didn't care if they liked him or not; he wanted them to respect him."

In late 1959 one of Humphrey's top assistants ventured into the capital of an Eastern state to "sound out" possible support for the Senator for the Democratic Presidential nomination. He says that he will never forget the reaction of one old and powerful political boss who eyed him coldly and said crustily, "Why should Humphrey be President? He's from Minnesota. Where's that?"

In the view of many leaders in the Eastern political establishment—a very real force lingering from the decades when everything west of the Appalachians was regarded as wilderness—men from the Midwest and the West are not quite civilized. The election of Andy Jackson as President, according to the establishment, was a nineteenth-century fluke. Herbert Hoover was originally a Californian, but his identity was really established in New York and Europe, so he qualified. Harry Truman and Lyndon Johnson, essentially Western in background and manner, were elected President, it is argued. "Of course," reply the establishment's political leaders smugly, "but THEY first ascended to the Presidency by the accidents of Presidential deaths."

The subjective judgment of many Eastern establishment politicians and reporters that men from the Midwest or West are not truly capable of national stature has remained a very real factor in American political affairs, and it has hurt Humphrey off and on since 1948. His habit of referring to himself often as "little Hubert" or "just a country boy from South Dakota" persisted until the early 1960's, and did not enhance his stature among Eastern political leaders. In 1960, in his Presidential bid, he dreamed of becoming a political Paul Bunyan. But in the realities of national politics Paul Bunyan reverted to legend and Humphrey reverted to such comments as: "I did pretty well for a small-town boy from a little state." One reporter viewed his defeat in the West Virginia primary of 1960 as "pathetic" because "Humphrey thought by then that he had learned to survive and excel in the East, politically and socially. Then, suddenly, he was pitted against men of money, dignity, restraint, and Ivy League 'class,' and he lost. It cut down Humphrey's childlike faith in himself."

But 1960 did not destroy his confidence in himself, and in recent years the thinking of many political leaders and reporters even in the Eastern establishment has caught up with the realities of America's changed political complexion. The substance of political power in the United States—the people—has shifted westward. In early 1964, when the Census Bureau formally announced that California's population had passed New York's, many old-line political bosses in some of the Eastern states said rather defensively, "It's not the size of a state that counts." When Barry Goldwater received the Republican Presidential nomination in July 1964, establishment leaders in both political parties could only exclaim, "It's incredible; I can't believe it!" Some of them were shocked not so much by the fact that Goldwater's ideas, perhaps antithetical to theirs, guided the Republican Party as by the fact that he had won the nomination of one of the two major parties in the United States without the support of the Eastern political establishment.

The simple fact which finally dawned on many in the establishment was that the United States of America is much more than the ponderous megalopolis bounded by Boston and Baltimore, the Appalachians and the Atlantic. The years 1963 and 1964 offered many reminders of the immensity and the interrelationships in the United States. An earthquake in Alaska, racial violence in Mississippi, a population count in California, and the political ascendancy of individual men from Arizona, Texas, and Minnesota all underscored the fact that not all national problems and national power spring from Harlem or Manhattan.

Hubert Humphrey, in the words of Walter Lippmann, is "an authentic American." Humphrey's background and formative years were not significantly linked to Old World traditions which have permeated many of the political customs of the East Coast of America. His political personality was shaped in large measure by Minnesota, an open land in the center of the continent settled primarily by American pioneers. The incisive political influence on Humphrey was not English or German, Norwegian or Irish. It was American.

More than a century ago Alexis de Tocqueville described what he believed to be a part of the American character:

"They [Americans] have all a lively faith in the perfectability of man, they judge that the diffusion of knowledge must necessarily be advantageous . . . they all consider society as a body in a state of improvement, humanity as a changing scene, in which nothing is, or ought to be, permanent; and they admit that what appears to them today to be good may be superseded by something better tomorrow. . . . America is a land of wonders, in which everything is in constant motion and every change seems an improvement. . . . No natural boundary seems to be set to the efforts of man; and in his eyes what is not yet done is only what he has not yet attempted to do."

8

The Pragmatist

The politician must be reasonably adept at satisfying or conciliating the rival interests and aspirations of others. He must also learn to bridge the inevitable gap between his hopes and his resources, and to reconcile the occasional conflicts between his personal convictions and his political ambitions. It is a difficult task and a delicate process, and often results in periods of indecision.

Within Hubert Humphrey there are elements of conflict—between the man and the politician, between the idealist and the realist, between the optimist and the pragmatist. He can be maddeningly indecisive, but also understandably torn by the reality of circumstance and the intensity of his ambition. Such a time was the spring of 1943, when he was being urged to run for Mayor of Minneapolis.

Humphrey had been making what was known as "a name for himself" in the peripheral political circles of Minneapolis, as a teacher, as an administrator of New Deal programs, and as a good speaker eager to accept five-dollar fees or no-fee invitations to address local fraternal organizations. He was earning a reputation as an energetic, honest, bright young man who was "going places." At first no one—not even Humphrey—had any idea where he was or should be going. There was vague and informal chatter by his friends that he should, someday, run for political office. Some of his former fellow students and professors at the University of Minnesota spoke of an effort to win a seat in Congress. A few labor leaders suggested that he consider running for Mayor of Minneapolis. He was flattered, but noncommittal.

The talk around him became more definite, and the various suggestions turned into arguments. Many of his friends thought that the Mayor's job, a pleasant enough position requiring little more than an ability to crown the annual Aquatennial Queen and to cut ribbons opening new hardware stores, was a political dead end. Some, including Dr. Evron Kirkpatrick and Arthur Naftalin, a University of Minnesota law student and part-time reporter, argued that he could not possibly win a seat in Congress at that time. Minnesota's old Third Congressional District, considered as a possible target for Humphrey, consistently and decisively sent Republicans to Washington.

The element of timing influenced Humphrey's first, tentative step toward public office. At the moment when the urgings of his friends became more insistent, the Minneapolis Mayorality election was only a few months away; the next Congressional election would not be held for a year and a half.

Several times in March and early April 1943, Kirkpatrick, Naftalin, and others spent the evening in the Humphrey apartment, speculating on Humphrey's prospects and challenging him to make up his mind. And several times Humphrey would slap his knee and proclaim, "I'll do it. It's settled. I'll run." Then, in the cool of the following morning, he would back down, arguing, "It's impossible. It's a crazy idea. I have no money, no record, no support."

In mid-April additional support came, modest, but encouraging. Several more University of Minnesota professors told Humphrey he should run. A few municipal judges and downtown Minneapolis businessmen added their encouragement. The city's Central Labor Council offered him an endorsement (which did not include, he learned later, any significant financial or manpower help in the campaign). Humphrey phoned Naftalin to report, "A bunch of people think I ought to run for Mayor. Maybe I ought to try it. Do you think I ought to run? Do you think I'll get shot?"

The question was relevant. There had been a score of gangland-style murders in Minneapolis which matched in detail if not in numbers the bloody scenes of violence on Chicago streets during prohibition. In periods when "the heat was on" in Chicago, racketeers had spread to Minneapolis, and they stayed. National crime syndicates set up efficient branches in Minneapolis. Gambling thrived. Prostitution flourished. The twin cancers of crime and corruption strengthened each other; "the fix" was on. Municipal officials, judges, law enforcements officers, labor leaders, and others sold out the public trust for private graft. Bribery—in the form of thick wads of cash delivered in unmarked envelopes—was common. Ed Ryan, now Hennepin County sheriff, says flatly, "The city was controlled by the mobs, the racketeers, and the crime syndicates." Even after the end of prohibition gangland-style killings continued. Howard Guilford, publisher of exposé-type weekly newspapers, was murdered on September 6, 1934. Another editor, Walter Liggett, was shot to death on December 9, 1935. Patrick J. Corcoran, known in Minneapolis as the "Iron Man of Labor," was murdered on November 17, 1937. The president of the Minneapolis General Drivers Union, William S. Brown, was cut down on November 25, 1938. No arrests were made. Token police investigations were conducted, but the four murders—and several others—remained unsolved.

"Humphrey was not afraid of the two or three percent of the city's people who were dishonest or corrupt," one friend remembers. "He cared about the ninety-seven percent of the people who were good and decent citizens." Humphrey shared their frustrations over the crime and corruption which controlled City Hall and stifled the city's progress. He now considered Minneapolis his home. He was sickened by the rottenness of Minneapolis politics and government in the early 1940's.

On the evening of April 16, 1943, he listened again to the arguments of his friends that he run for Mayor. He realized that the odds were against him, but he was between jobs and had some spare time. "Okay," he finally said. "Let's give it whirl." The next morning he walked into the fortress-like Minneapolis City Hall, a dark stone, Victorian-style building, handed a precious ten-dollar bill to a clerk, and formally signed for his first candidacy for public office. He was thirty-one years old. There were nineteen days remaining before the Mayoralty primary election.

Once he had taken the first step, he ran fast and hard. He had little beyond his own will and energy and the help of such young friends as Kirkpatrick and Naftalin. They worked and campaigned twenty hours a day. Humphrey's thought to give the campaign "a whirl" turned into a determination to spend everything he and his friends had for a whirlwind of speeches, street-corner hand-shaking, press releases, and pamphlets. They were helped by William Simms, who had quit his job with the County Welfare Department to join the campaign. Simms managed the small headquarters office. Naftalin wrote speeches and press releases. Kirkpatrick gave Humphrey ideas and helped arrange his schedule, which started early in the morning and ended at only a slightly earlier hour the following morning. Humphrey packed so many extra efforts into his tight schedule that he constantly ran an hour or two late for evening meetings. Kirkpatrick and the others moved ahead of him, holding the people in a hall or living room until he arrived, breathless and exuberant. Campaign evenings often ended with appearances before local Townsend Clubs. Speech and meeting over, he danced with the old ladies and talked politics with the old men. Kirkpatrick developed a sore arm trying to pull him away; Naftalin's feet hurt after the first week of trying to keep up with him.

At midnight after one long campaign day, stopping off at his headquarters office "for just a minute," Humphrey eyed a stack of campaign literature and fired a series of questions, orders and commands: "What good are those pamphlets doing there? Put them in the car. Let's go." He and his weary assistants drove into the city's residential areas and walked the dark corridors of apartment houses until 3 A.M. to distribute pamphlets which proclaimed, always in capital letters and with many exclamation points: HUMPHREY—THE MAN FOR MINNEAPOLIS! YOUNG! HONEST! VIGOROUS!

Vigorous was not quite the word for it. When all the pamphlets were gone, Humphrey said, "Let's get something to eat, so we can talk." In an all-night restaurant on Hennepin Avenue, he reviewed the day's work, then said, "Let's talk about tomorrow." One of the exhausted men replied disconsolately, "It IS tomorrow." Ignoring the correction, Humphrey asked, "What kind of radio time do we have tomorrow night?" They explained, "None. There's no money." Humphrey, finally tired himself, snapped, "We've got to buy radio time, even if it's the cheap, late hours. I've spent all my money. Where's yours?" Kirkpatrick, Naftalin, and Simms, not quite knowing what was happening, emptied their wallets of the little money they had and agreed to buy a few minutes of time for campaign advertisements on local stations the following night.

In the May primary election Humphrey placed second in a field of nine candidates and qualified for the two-man, final election with incumbent Mayor Marvin Kline. Many residents of Minneapolis, reading the results, asked, "Who on earth is Humphrey?" Most of them learned the answer during the final month of the campaign, all of it as fast, furious, and amateurish as Humphrey's primary effort. In the June election Humphrey picked up additional votes, but not enough. He lost to Mayor Kline by less than five thousand votes, a surprisingly good showing for an unemployed, unfinanced, inexperienced young man, and considered the results a "moral victory," but he was disappointed that he had not won.

Mrs. Humphrey was not. On the morning after the election she whistled cheerfully as she mowed the lawn in front of a small apartment house the Humphreys managed in exchange for their rent-free apartment. "Why are you so cheerful?" a neighbor asked her. "Your husband just lost the election." She answered, "Maybe he wasn't quite ready for this job. Maybe he needs to know more about the city and get more experience."

After a few weeks Humphrey tended to agree. And the sting of defeat was soothed as he realized that many men of influence and authority in Minneapolis were tabbing him as "a comer." In the first month after the election he was visited twice by men of power who offered help for his political future. The first was Gideon Seymour, an editor of the Minneapolis *Star* and *Tribune*. Seymour explained that the newspapers had a Republican editorial policy, and would be likely to support him if he registered as a Republican before running for political office again. Humphrey was tempted, and asked for time to think it over. He talked with his wife about the offer that night. They realized that there was no compelling, practical reason against his registering as a Republican. The Mayor's office was nonpartisan. He did not have any official ties to the Democratic Party beyond his registration as a voter. In 1943 the Republican Party in Minnesota was the only party of power and effectiveness, and it was relatively liberal in outlook. Republican Governor Harold Stassen was an honorable, skilled, and liberal Governor, with a good record. Humphrey could easily rationalize a switch in registration and allegiance to the Republican Party.

But the next morning he told Seymour that he would remain a

Democrat. There were two personally compelling reasons. First, his father was a devoted Democrat and would be hurt and disappointed if his son deserted the party of William Jennings Bryan, Woodrow Wilson, and Franklin D. Roosevelt. Second, he "just felt" that he was, should be, and always would remain a Democrat, and he did not want such a lifelong identity to be sold so cheaply for temporary advantage.

The second offer was less honorable and not at all tempting. Humphrey was visited by an officer of an industry with major interests and investments in Minnesota. He proposed that the firm would liberally finance Humphrey's political career if Humphrey would look with favor on its corporate needs and legislative requests. It would be just an informal, quiet "arrangement," the executive explained. Humphrey smiled at this evidence of his newly won importance, and then told the man, in essence, to go to hell. "No one owns or will ever own Hubert Humphrey," he said to his wife and friends later.

The glow of his impressive election showing and the flattery of powerful men faded as he and his wife turned to their practical needs. Their bank account balance rested at a dismal total of seven dollars. Soon after the election Humphrey was sued for a thirteen-hundred-dollar printing bill which he thought some of his supporters had paid. He took several jobs to pull himself out of debt. He stoked the furnace and did repair jobs at the apartment house, worked part time in a drug store, broadcast the news nightly over Station WTCN, worked for a small public relations firm opened by Kirkpatrick and Naftalin, and continued to speak for five-dollar lecture fees. The debt was paid in six months, and the family's financial crisis eased with the steady income of his teaching job at Macalester College in St. Paul. He took that position after pledging no "open" political activity.

He studied the status of the Democratic Party in Minnesota and decided to embark on a private political project. The party was weak and ineffective. It had rarely elected major public officials in Minnesota. The Farmer-Labor Party, a third and powerful force in Minnesota politics, still enjoyed some political momentum even after the death of its leader and Governor, Floyd B. Olson. It siphoned off voter support which normally would have gone to the Democratic Party. The split of strongly liberal voters by the

Democrats and Farmer-Laborites resulted in victory after victory for Republicans in Minnesota.

Humphrey took a pragmatic attitude about his own and the party's future: a merger of the Democratic and the Farmer-Labor parties was the only key to success. He spent one evening writing a twelve-page letter to Frank Walker, chairman of the Democratic National Committee, listing the reasons for merger and asking for sanction and help. The reply from Washington was a noncommittal "Drop in and see us if you are ever in Washington."

Humphrey, too sure of himself and his plan to be brushed off, bought a train coach ticket to Washington. He worked to polish his merger plan as the train sped through a day and night to the nation's capital. If he could just talk to Democratic Chairman Walker, he thought, the National Committee would approve the proposal.

He talked briefly with the receptionist in the Democratic National Committee office, and she was not impressed. For three days he sat in the lobby outside the DNC offices, watching dozens of men move in and out of the closed doors, clutching a folder containing the written details of his merger plan, simmering with frustration and indignation that he could not even see or talk with a second-echelon staff member at the National Committee.

His money ran out and he gave up. Late one afternoon he packed his bag at his uncle's home, where he had been staying, and took a local bus back to downtown Washington. In the evening rush-hour traffic as he waited for a transfer he felt depressed and defeated. He counted his last few dollars, checked his return ticket to Minnesota, and decided to spend fifty cents on a scotch and soda in a Willard Hotel cocktail lounge. Sitting by himself and sipping the drink slowly, he felt very much alone and very unimportant as he watched the confident, smiling men of the Washington establishment come and go. He thought about home, and remembered that his father had asked him to phone a family friend, Cecil Howes, just to say hello.

Howes, a former South Dakotan, cordially asked for news of the family and then questioned Humphrey about his mission to Washington. Howes was also a former Assistant Postmaster General, and knew Frank Walker well. He told Humphrey to wait a few more minutes while he checked directly with Walker. When

Humphrey called back, he was told he had an appointment with Walker and that a car would pick him up in front of the Willard in ten minutes.

He almost panicked about the smell of liquor on his breath. He ran to a candy counter, bought three packages of peppermint drops, and chewed them all in the few minutes he waited at the curb. He was gulping down the last mouthful when "the biggest, longest, blackest car I'd ever seen" pulled up to the entrance and the driver asked, "Are you Mr. Humphrey, sir?"

"Hell, I was just little Hubert from South Dakota," Humphrey remembers. But he fought down his nervousness, and fifteen minutes later walked into "the biggest, longest, plushest room I'd ever been in," with Chairman Walker sitting at the end of it.

Walker listened carefully, asked a series of practical questions, made a few phone calls, and agreed to his plan for merger of the Democratic and the Farmer-Labor parties in Minnesota. Humphrey returned home, and was met later by two experienced organizers sent by Walker. Humphrey provided the initiative for the merger movement; he and others organized the tedious process of merger which took, in all, more than a hundred meetings. The effort began on the county level, where local officials of both parties met separately to vote on the merger proposal. Then the plan was considered, debated, and approved in separate and joint meetings at the district level. Finally, in April 1944, the two parties met in separate conventions of delegates representing all areas of the state. Both conventions approved the merger. In a final, joint convention the two parties formally became the Democratic Farmer-Labor Party.

The new DFL, grateful to Humphrey for his work, wanted to nominate him for the Governorship of Minnesota. An enthusiastic demonstration was staged for him, but he declined the nomination with these words: "I want to go in the armed forces, if I am acceptable. I want to be with these other young men and women in the armed forces, and you can't deny me that privilege."

The local draft board and the Navy recruiting office did deny him the privilege of serving. In 1940 he had first been classified 3-A and exempted from the draft because of his status as a father. Later, while teaching Air Force officers at Macalester College, he was classified 2-A and marked as an "essential civilian." In the spring of 1944 he requested and was granted a release from that classification, and applied for a Navy commission. The Navy disqualified him for a commission on physical grounds. He tried for a regular enlistment with the Navy, which would have made him an apprentice seaman, but the Navy was not then accepting volunteers. Growing more frustrated as he watched his friends and young political associates march off to war, he battled with the draft board. On September 6, 1944, he was finally classified 1-A. In midwinter he got as far as the Army induction center at Fort Snelling. With several news photographers present—he was then a political celebrity in Minneapolis—he was issued a uniform. Then, in February 1945, he was told that he had failed to satisfy the Army's physical standards; Army induction center physicians found that he had a double hernia, lung calcification (probably from his childhood case of pneumonia), and color blindness.

(In almost every election campaign of his career he has been forced to defend himself against opponents' charges that he was "a draft-dodger" or that he "didn't try very hard" to get into the armed forces during World War II. He has countered the charges or innuendos with verified documents and affidavits from draft board officials and Navy recruitment officers who were involved.)

Humphrey turned full-time to politics. He was named state campaign director for Roosevelt in 1944, after he left his teaching job at Macalester College. He had one eye on Minnesota's Third District Congressional seat, but his other eye lingered on the challenge of the Minneapolis Mayor's office, which would be up for election again in 1945. No one, not even the leaders of the merger, were quite sure how strong the new DFL would be in the 1944 election. The party picked a political newcomer, William Gallagher, to run in the Third District race. "He had no money and no strong support," one merger leader remembers. "He just made speeches. But thanks to the merger, he won the election. We bought him a new set of teeth and some new clothes, and sent him to Washington." (Gallagher served in Congress until his death, in 1948.)

Inevitably the DFL could help Humphrey no matter what the office he sought. But it was not of direct or official advantage to him for the Minneapolis Mayoralty campaign, which tradition decreed should remain nonpartisan. He continued to appear two

or three times a day as a speaker before civic and fraternal groups
and on radio. In the spring of 1945 he filed again to run against
Mayor Kline. Kirkpatrick, Naftalin, and Simms rejoined his
campaign effort. Many of the city's business leaders were anxious
about his labor support, but he won substantial backing and endorsements from various community leaders. And although he was
still a registered Democrat, the Minneapolis *Tribune* and the
Minneapolis *Star* endorsed his candidacy.

He campaigned full time, on a score of issues. His ideas for
improving the city drew praise. The *Tribune* editorialized: "He is
the type of honest, fighting liberal on whom the future of democratic government depends." Humphrey knew the city now. He
campaigned against a municipal pattern of anti-Semitism and
against lethargy in solving the city's housing and school problems.
Above all, he campaigned for leadership to "make this community
act like a community" and to "clean up this town and make it a
decent city in which to raise our children." With three children of
his own, he stressed his role as a family man and hit again and
again at "the leeches of crime, vice, and corruption."

By 1945 he was far better known by the people of Minneapolis,
and he was clearly identified as an honest, uncorruptible young
man at a time when organized crime still held many of the city's
officials in its grip. The people had become angry and reform-
minded as prostitution, gambling, bribery, and a dozen different
rackets continued to flourish. After the night of January 21, 1945,
they became determined to vote a change in City Hall.

Shortly before midnight a forty-three-year-old publisher of a
scandal sheet called *The Public Press*, Arthur Kasherman, walked
out of Hannah's Cafe near 15th and Chicago streets in Minneapolis and climbed into his car, parked across the street. His companion, Pearl von Waald, noticed that the air had been let out of
the car's tires. Kasherman nervously rolled up the window of the
car door on his side. He turned, to see a black sedan approaching
from behind; two guns emerged from its windows. The first shot
shattered glass in his car, but missed him. He pushed Miss von
Waald down, jumped out of the car, and ran east on 15th Street,
toward Chicago. "Don't shoot! . . . For God's sake, don't shoot!" he
screamed. Two more shots were fired; one bullet hit Kasherman in
the face, the other tore through his chest and into his heart. He

staggered a few feet, collapsed, and died as the black sedan roared down the street and disappeared in the dark.

Newspapers the next day identified Kasherman as a "convicted extortionist and former convict," and reported that he was "killed in a manner reminiscent of gangland executions during the prohibition era." The sheriff's office disclosed that Kasherman had come in that morning to boast and bet twenty-five dollars that he would get the police to raid a prosperous crap game operation on Nicollet Avenue that night. He told sheriffs' deputies that the game was taking in seventy-five thousand dollars a month for a Chicago-based gambling syndicate. Policeman Ed Ryan revealed that Kasherman, two weeks earlier, had talked vaguely about giving him three names to check out "if anything happens to me," but that he kept the names to himself until it was too late. The last issue of Kasherman's weekly *The Public Press,* published in December 1944, had headlined: KLINE ADMINISTRATION THE MOST CORRUPT REGIME IN HISTORY OF THE CITY. MAYOR KLINE IS A HYPOCRITE AND A LIAR.

No one linked the murder to Kline, but the city's police department failed to link the murder to anyone. No arrests were made. The murder and all the seedy aspects surrounding it remained unsolved. The people, Ryan remembers, were fed up with the criminal elements in Minneapolis and sickened by the murder. "Humphrey probably would have won the election no matter what happened," Ryan says, "but the Kasherman murder helped."

Humphrey beat Kline by 31,114 votes—a landslide in Minneapolis. He was thirty-four, had been in practical politics for only two years, and was only four years out of school and seven years away from his father's drug store in South Dakota. He was Mayor of Minneapolis, at half a million population the biggest city in Minnesota and the fourteenth-largest city in the United States.

The people had high hopes for Mayor Humphrey. But critics dubbed Humphrey and his youthful assistants "the diaper brigade." Conservative businessmen feared that he was "a captive of labor." The gamblers, the pimps, the crooks, and the corrupt police and city officials called him "the little guy," and made bets on how much money it would take to bribe him. Even the reformers and some of his friends wondered whether he would be able to do anything significant as Mayor; the city charter had set up the Mayor as little more than a figurehead and had vested the real power in the City Council. The only real authority the position carried was the appointment of the city's police chief.

9

Mayor

Everything about Ed Ryan is big. He seems to tower above men who are six feet tall. His hands are huge. His ears, nose, and jaw would seem immense if they were not attached to a head the size of a boulder. When he smiles, the arc of his mouth is like a lazy crescent moon, low and big in a twilight horizon. Ed Ryan also has the toughness of a big-city policeman, which he was in Minneapolis for twenty-one years. Even at an advanced age he puts in a long day of hard work as Hennepin County sheriff. His body is still erect and muscular, and he speaks bluntly, with the graphic phrases of men who must be involved with human violence, greed, and cruelty.

But Ed Ryan does not fit any image of a hardened and bitter cop. His voice is gentle and his eyes express both sadness and kindness. He is an intelligent, cultured man who speaks fluent French and takes an educated view of society. He is also one of the most dedicated and effective law enforcement officers in the United States.

Ed Ryan was Mayor Hubert Humphrey's choice for Minneapolis police chief in 1945.

The two men had first met when Humphrey was a University of Minnesota student and Police Detective Ryan was a neighbor. Humphrey often sat on the porch of Ryan's home and listened to his talk about the Minneapolis underworld: "You can't have rackets without a pay-off. Any Mayor with guts can put them out of business overnight if he has the right police chief. . . . If I ever get to be chief, I'll show these mugs what a clean town looks like." They worked together in the early 1940's, when Humphrey was a WPA administrator and Ryan, as head of the Police Department's

Internal Security Division, had to check the record of WPA workers under Humphrey's direction.

When Humphrey was elected Mayor, he thought first of Ryan to fill the one and only significant appointment he could make, but he wanted to be sure about the "right" man for the job of cleaning crime out of Minneapolis. The young Mayor asked Bradshaw Mintener, a Republican and a vice president of Pillsbury Mills, to serve as chairman of a new law enforcement committee. Mintener said he would accept only if Humphrey agreed to appoint an FBI-trained man as police chief. Ryan, who had attended the FBI Academy in 1942, was the only man on the Minneapolis force with such training.

The choice was obvious, but the appointment was not easy. Ryan was controversial. He had once defended the right of hate-monger Gerald L. K. Smith to rent the Minneapolis Auditorium for a speech. He personally detested all that Smith stood for, but told the City Council, "If we really have free speech here, what are we afraid of?" Some Council members called Ryan a "fascist" and "bigot"; a few days later he was "busted" from the Internal Security Division and sent to the city's Eastside Precinct. Back on a beat, Ryan ticketed a limousine owned by a prosperous bootlegger; the next day Ryan's captain gave him a scathing dressing down for his lack of "discretion." Ryan had openly supported Humphrey for Mayor in the 1943 election; entrenched police and city officials treated him coolly from then on. A powerful labor block in the City Council strongly opposed Ryan for the post of police chief, and told the man they had supported for Mayor that they would not "accept" him.

Humphrey told the labor leaders that he was not their captive. He told old-line city officials that they had had their chance to fight crime, and had done little. He rejected the argument that Ryan was "too controversial." After Mintener's law enforcement committee submitted its recommendation, Humphrey called Ryan into his office and said:

"You've been sounding off about what to do to clean up this town. Don't look now, but you're the new police chief." Then he added, "I'll take care of politics and my reputation; you take care of the Police Department and your reputation. This is going to be an honest administration of responsible men. But I want both of us to take care of the crime. I want this town cleaned up—now. I want the hoods moved out—now."

Humphrey and Ryan began by simply posting an order telling the police to crack down and by announcing that crime syndicate operations and rackets would not be tolerated. Most of the mobsters, racketeers, gamblers, and prostitutes felt the heat quickly. They knew enough about Ryan and Humphrey to realize that the order was not a bluff. Within twenty-four hours, they left town.

A few lingered. A whorehouse at Second Avenue and Eleventh Street continued its lively operations after the Humphrey-Ryan order was issued. The chief sent five of his morals squad men to close the place. The next morning the house's procurer strolled into the Police Department, pulled out a thick roll of bills, and asked, "Who do I see now?" Ryan told him, "You'd better not be seen. Get out." Ryan's men raided a Hennepin Avenue bar with a thriving back-room gambling operation. Its owner, clutching a newspaper story about the raid, walked up to Ryan and said, "Hi, chiefy. Maybe you don't know that I don't like publicity." Ryan told the man he would get more publicity and fire axes if gambling resumed in his bar.

Both Humphrey and Ryan received threatening letters and crude warnings that they would be shot unless the town was opened again. They took the warnings seriously, but neither was intimidated. Ryan's FBI friends suggested that he cease his late evening walks near his home; Ryan continued them. Humphrey was shot at late one night as he stood in front of his house; he told Ryan the next day, "The order stands."

The Mayor and his police chief would not even tolerate any pattern of petty crime, if they heard about it. As World War II ended and veterans returned home with their pockets filled with mustering-out pay, the area around the Minneapolis train station became a center for pickpockets and "clip joints," Humphrey learned that many veterans were being drugged in the bars around the station and then "rolled" of their cash in back alleys. He ordered Ryan to send a dozen of the department's biggest, toughest, and strongest men into the area and "beat the hell out of anyone who so much as looks cross-eyed at a veteran." After a few nights of activity by the rather informal force, returning veterans were no longer molested. Humphrey was adamant and unwavering in his effort to clean up the city. When there was a conflict between the crusade against crime or the preservation of a principle of civil liberty, Humphrey chose the role of crime buster.

He remembers, "The hardest job was not to beat down the hoodlums, but to overcome the cynicism of my friends and sideline critics who told me it couldn't be done."

Humphrey paid little attention to orthodox methods or to timid officials who told him repeatedly, "It can't be done." As Mayor he was an ex-officio member of most municipal boards and commissions. He surprised their members by attending. At one meeting he demanded that a school building which he considered structurally unsafe be repaired or closed. When the officials refused to act, he personally nailed boards across the entrances to the school. The building remained closed until city officials found the money for repairs.

In the period immediately after World War II, Minneapolis suffered a critical housing shortage, particularly among young veterans who enrolled at the University of Minnesota. Many of them were jammed into shacks; some young families were living in tents. Local officials told Humphrey there was no housing available, no money for a new housing program, and there were no materials available for the construction of new houses or apartment buildings. Humphrey began with an appeal, through newspapers and radio stations, for a "Shelter a Vet" program in which local residents were asked to give up spare rooms for veterans. Several hundred men were housed through that voluntary program. Then the Mayor organized a nonprofit corporation which "panhandled" fifty-six thousand dollars for a housing program. He sent his top assistant, William Simms, to an Army surplus depot in Lima, Ohio, to wangle a few hundred surplus house trailers. He bought a stack of prefabricated housing units from another surplus depot. Sheriff Ryan remembers a phone call from the Mayor which began, "Ed, you've got to help me get some soil pipe." Ryan explained that he had no idea where he could find soil pipe. "I don't care WHERE you get it," Humphrey retorted. "You've got friends. Just get me some soil pipe. I've got to have soil pipe by the end of the month." For a solid month Humphrey hounded every individual he knew to find soil pipe. "It was crazy," Ryan says, "but many of us found soil pipe—which wasn't even supposed to exist in

1946." Humphrey talked the building trades unions into helping, the prefabricated units and trailers were fitted with proper plumbing, and several thousand veterans and their families were modestly but properly housed. Later, on his urging, the City Council authorized two million dollars in bonds for a bigger housing program.

Humphrey also assumed the role of arbitrator in the city's labor-management disputes. Some of his policies were known as prolabor, but businessmen credited him with fairness, toughness, and objectivity in his efforts to avert major strikes. When power company workers stalled negotiations with management by demanding retroactive pay, Humphrey told them, "Let's forget about this retroactive pay stuff. Everybody is sick of it by now. Why not ask for a bonus or premium payment instead?" Union and company officials agreed to the new approach, and a strike was avoided. In May 1946, Humphrey charged into labor-management negotiations which were just about to break up into a strike which would close the city's ten hospitals. He told the negotiators, "If you think I am going to let the hospitals of Minneapolis close down because of a few stubborn people, you are just plain crazy. These aren't beer parlors or candy factories. These are hospitals, where some of your neighbors are sick or dying, and they are going to be kept open. Now let's start all over again and see what we can agree on." An agreement was reached just as pickets were beginning to form around the hospitals.

The Mayor refused to be bound by the extremely limited jurisdiction of his office, or to be intimidated by any special group within the city. "I am my own boss," he proclaimed often. "I am not tied to anyone's apron strings." He proved it by defying labor in an effort to reform the city's eighty-year-old charter. Humphrey wanted reform; he aligned himself with the more conservative and attainable reform plan and was bitterly opposed by the city's labor leaders, as well as by twenty-four of the twenty-six members of the City Council. He campaigned hard for the charter reform plan, but it was killed by what he called a "technicality" when the State Supreme Court forced a postponement of the special charter election.

He considered no project or problem in the city too small for his personal attention. One morning, as he prepared to leave home for his office, the milkman told him about a woman who was about to be evicted from her home for nonpayment of rent. Humphrey sped to the other side of the city, to find the woman tearfully arguing with her landlord on a sidewalk covered with her furniture. Her husband was still in the service, she explained to Humphrey, and her government support check was late that month. Humphrey turned to the landlord and said, "I'm the Mayor of Minneapolis. I'll guarantee this woman's rent payment." The landlord relented, and the woman moved back into her home.

Humphrey's leadership was challenged most critically by a polio epidemic which struck Minneapolis in 1946. In the first few months of the epidemic more than two thousand individuals were hit by the crippling and often fatal disease. Facilities were limited and treatment was still experimental. As Humphrey returned home late one night during the first week of the outbreak, he found the street jammed with cars and his front yard filled with people. They were frustrated and angry at the hopelessness of the disease and the apparent lack of attention given to the epidemic by city officials. Several mothers and fathers, carrying feverish children in their arms, stepped out of the dark and demanded of Humphrey, "Look at this, Mr. Mayor. What are you going to do about it?" Humphrey looked at the children, and had trouble forcing back the tears as he told the parents what he was doing.

Essentially he was trying to resolve the strained relations between the National Foundation for Infantile Paralysis and Sister Kenny, a strong-willed Australian who had come to Minneapolis in 1940 and attracted world-wide attention for her unusual and new methods of treating polio. Foundation officials in Minneapolis and Sister Kenny at one point refused to talk to each other. When one problem became critical, Sister Kenny said that unless the Mayor sided with her she would leave immediately and return to her home in Australia.

"Very well, Sister," Humphrey replied coolly, but cordially. "If you have made up your mind, I shall be glad to help with your travel arrangements. What day do you plan to leave?" The Sister's iron will melted; a dozen more times during the fear-filled summer she and Foundation officials acknowledged that Humphrey was "the boss."

New polio cases streamed into Minneapolis each day from all

parts of the state. City schools were closed in an effort to halt the epidemic, and Mayor Humphrey read comic strips over the radio to help keep children at home. He appealed directly to the White House after he hit a bureaucratic wall in his attempts to utilize federal facilities for the emergency; the government released Army barracks at the Twin Cities' Fort Snelling for the overflow of polio victims. Humphrey personally begged and borrowed hospital beds, and helped recruit volunteer nurses and hospital attendants. Sister Kenny angrily demanded one morning that several patients at Fort Snelling be returned to her treatment center. Humphrey snapped, "Listen here, those patients are going to stay right where they are. We're running a hospital for these people, not a bus service." The relationship between the strong-willed Mayor and the nurse was often strained, but it blossomed into a lasting friendship. Between fights Humphrey sent Sister Kenny small gifts. When she returned from one short trip, he sent a dozen red roses to her at the airport.

When the epidemic finally subsided, Humphrey was determined that Minneapolis should contribute significantly to a polio prevention and research effort. Minneapolis was the first city in the nation to sponsor free chest X-rays. Humphrey talked the City Council into putting up fifty thousand dollars and raised another fifty thousand from labor unions and business organizations to help start the Minnesota Polio Research Commission, which worked in cooperation with the University of Minnesota and the National Foundation for several years. The Foundation was impressed enough with the Commission program to award it a half-million-dollar research grant.

Humphrey fought a subtler disease which had crept into Minneapolis over the years: anti-Semitism, and a firm pattern of discrimination against Negroes and other minority groups. Soon after his election he established a Mayor's Council on Human Relations. He enlisted the sympathy and the help of dozens of community leaders in what he called "an education campaign." He spoke often and he spoke bluntly about "this evil, decaying thing in our community," and quoted Carey McWilliams' statement that in the early 1940's Minneapolis had become "the capital of anti-Semitism." He ordered a new training program for the Police Department to handle race relations problems and initiated a "community self-survey," in which citizens investigated major tension areas with the help of professional interviewers. In January 1947, after months of lobbying by the Mayor and his Human Relations group, the City Council enacted a Fair Employment Practice ordinance—the first municipal FEP legislation in the United States. It was—and is—a tough ordinance, providing for a commission to administer its regulations, and jail terms and fines for violations. Humphrey persuaded George M. Jensen, a respected business executive, to head the commission, and urged him to seek informal settlement of discrimination complaints before sending the cases to court. In the first year of the ordinance job discrimination declined noticeably in Minneapolis; the city's two biggest department stores began to hire Negro clerks for the first time.

Humphrey was hindered but not halted by the absence of legal power in the Mayor's office and by the conservative City Council, which held the formal municipal authority. "I had a voice," he says of that period. "The people had elected me. I was their Mayor. That may not be power, but it was enough."

By 1947 few citizens were inclined to ridicule him as "the little guy." Despite his frequent defiance of demands by union leaders, he easily retained the campaign support of organized labor. He also won over a large segment of the previously skeptical or downright hostile business community. His campaign re-election committee included such men as the president of the Minneapolis Chamber of Commerce and such business executives as Samuel C. Gale, vice president of General Mills; Alfred Wilson, vice president of Minneapolis-Honeywell Company; Bradshaw Mintener of Pillsbury Mills, Inc.; and David J. Winton, a lumber industry leader. In the election of 1947, Humphrey carried every ward in the city and won re-election by a record-breaking fifty thousand votes.

A variety of community leaders, including conservatives, Republicans, and businessmen, said without qualification that Humphrey "was the best Mayor Minneapolis ever had." One editor described his years as Mayor as "the most exhilarating in the city's political history, with more roller-coaster dips and turns than in any other six administrations." Bradley L. Morrison, editorial page editor of the old Minneapolis *Times,* wrote a summing up in June 1948:

"Humphrey has not transformed Minneapolis into Utopia, by any means. The city's archaic weak-mayor charter would prevent that. And it can be said that he scatters his energies over too wide an area; that he talks too much; that he often jumps to superficial judgments and conclusions which he afterwards regrets; and that he is sometimes guilty of political double talk which distresses even his most ardent admirers.

"But when the evidence is impartially weighed, the scales tip far toward Humphrey as an honest, progressive and efficient mayor. He has given the city a first-rate police administration; he has made Minneapolis soberly conscious of its human relations problems as it had never been before; and he has sweated more earnestly over the city's bad financial situation and impoverished schools than half a dozen previous mayors. Perhaps his most important contribution has been the great popular interest he had created in city government and his success in dramatizing the charter fight. Humphrey has aroused Minneapolis from a great lethargy. He has taken the city's problems down from dusty shelves and polished them with his oratory until they shine with a new interest. He has enlisted hundreds of previously dormant citizens in his fight for a new deal in city government."

Others agreed, more formally. The FBI gave Humphrey its top award for effective municipal law enforcement. A public committee honored him as the "First Citizen of Minneapolis" in both 1945 and 1947. A state-wide vote of the Junior Chamber of Commerce in 1946 named Humphrey "Outstanding Young Man of Minnesota."

Humphrey liked the accouterments of public office. He was proud of his office suite, his limousine, and his title. At least a dozen times a day he proclaimed—sometimes defiantly and sometimes pleasantly—"I'm the MAYOR." Apparently he forgot the fact only once. Driving himself home late one night, he violated a traffic regulation and was stopped by a policeman. Automatically and silently he handed the officer his driver's license. "But you're the Mayor!" the policeman exclaimed when he noticed the familiar name. Humphrey, sleepy at that late hour and only a few years away from being a struggling student, looked surprised for a moment, then replied, "I'll be damned. I AM the Mayor, aren't I?"

In his crusade to clean up and reform Minneapolis he did not forget or disdain the simple figurehead functions of the office. He

thoroughly enjoyed cutting ribbons to open new stores, crowning
Aquatennial queens, riding in open cars at the head of downtown
parades, and being mobbed by children seeking his autograph. It
was said in the city that he was ready to make a speech at the drop
of a hat, and "for lack of any ready provocation, has frequently
been known to drop the hat himself." His assistants estimated that
he gave more than two thousand speeches in his first two years as
Mayor and addressed the people by radio more than four hundred
times.

He said frequently and passionately, "I love this city." He
loved its parks and people, its tree-lined streets and beach-fringed
lakes, its bustling shopping centers and endlessly pleasant neigh-
borhoods of big homes. For all its record of crime and corruption,
Minneapolis was—and is—a remarkably sophisticated, cultured,
and progressive Midwestern metropolis. Its symphony orchestra, its
museums, and its repertory theater are among the finest in the
nation. Minneapolis broadened Humphrey's outlook as a man, in
addition to developing him as a politician. The city rounded off
some of the rough edges of his rural perspective and erased some of
the provincialism of the prairie from his outlook. In the words
of one friend, "Minneapolis shook much of the Dakota dust off of
Humphrey. It taught him to shine his shoes. He arrived as a country boy; there was very little of the hick left in him by the time he
left."

Humphrey's affection for Minneapolis, his gratitude for the
support of its people, and his pride in his terms as Mayor tend to
border on nostalgia. Even in 1964 he said without qualification,
"Being Mayor of Minneapolis was the best job I've ever had."
He still appears to favor the company of Minneapolis acquaintances and supporters. Even after sixteen years of involvement with
national politics he still leans on Minnesotans—most of them from
the Twin Cities—for practical help. More than half of the men he
called to assist him at the Democratic National Convention in
1964 were Minnesotans. He spent election night, 1964, in Minneapolis. He has thousands of friends (his Christmas card list totals
thirteen thousand names), but there are very few men with whom
he relaxes completely or trusts fully; most of these are from Minneapolis. He has close and warm relationships with many men of
fame and power, but when his personal secretary once asked him
who his *best* friend was, he answered, "Freddie."

"Freddie" is Frederick J. Gates, who in the 1940's operated penny arcades and leased pinball machines in Minneapolis. Today he owns and operates several bowling alleys in the Twin Cities where he lives. Freddie's speech might make an English teacher wince, and his appearance could be compared to some of the more colorful characters in *Guys and Dolls* or *The Last Hurrah*. For many years, as Humphrey rose to higher levels of Minnesota or national political prominence and respectability, some of the professionals around him wondered why he remained so close to Freddie. A few received tongue lashings from him when they suggested that he "get rid of that man."

Freddie (few people call him "Mr. Gates") may give the appearance of a political hanger-on, and some sophisticates suggest unkindly, "He looks like a bookie." But he has a considerable array of impressive qualities which men of political power and position prize, and he is scrupulously honest. He is totally loyal and wants nothing from Humphrey except the privilege of serving him. He has no formal position on Humphrey's staff and receives no pay, but he serves him with incredible efficiency whenever and wherever he is asked to help. He has mastered the process of solving such critical problems of the fast-moving politician as getting a shirt laundered in twenty minutes or a suit pressed in ten minutes. He knows how to talk a local police department into providing a motorcycle escort or an airline into holding a plane when Humphrey is running late. Freddie has often worked himself to the point of exhaustion for Humphrey, and sometimes into hospital confinement.

Fred Gates is also a warm, immensely generous, and intelligent man. He has a sharp political instinct, and has helped to train Humphrey in some of the more delicate aspects of political life. In 1943 he voted against Humphrey for Mayor. When he became convinced that Humphrey was determined to "make Minneapolis a clean town to raise our kids in," he made several contributions to his 1945 campaign. During the race the two men got to know each other, and after the election he walked into Humphrey's office, displayed the canceled checks and said he wanted Humphrey to appoint Ed Ryan police chief. The new Mayor made it clear that he did not like this type of "pressure." Freddie then carefully tore up the checks, dropped them into a wastebasket and said he was only making the point that it had been naïve of Humphrey to endorse *personally* the checks contributed to his campaign. Humphrey was unaware of some of the dangers involving acceptance of contributions. From then on he placed most campaign-financing responsibilities in Freddie's hands.

In more than twenty years Freddie never asked Humphrey for anything for himself. When Humphrey arranged an appointment for him to a U. S. Post Office citizens' advisory board, Freddie almost burst with surprise and pleasure. (The position required a stringent check by the FBI, which "cleared" Freddie and killed any remaining charges by Humphrey's enemies that his friend had a "shady record.")

Cicero wrote: "There is no greater bane to friendship than adulation, fawning, and flattery." Men of political fame and power often attract associates and assistants who are skilled in flattering their bosses without appearing to be yes men. Freddie shows a rare willingness to tell Humphrey exactly what he thinks about Humphrey. (Once Humphrey, immensely pleased with a picture of himself in a newspaper, wordlessly accepted Freddie's verdict: "It makes you look like a jerk.") Of the tens of thousands of individuals who address Humphrey as "Hubert," Freddie is one of the very few who are justified in claiming a first-name relationship.

"Who is Freddie?" Humphrey is often asked when he tells men of political prestige or professionalism to "clear" a problem or project with the stocky, middle-aged Minnesotan. He answers simply, "Freddie is my friend."

Humphrey, as Mayor, won lifelong friends, cultural polish, political experience, and local tributes. Yet there was a bigger prize for his performance in Minneapolis: National attention. John Gunther, author of *Inside U.S.A.,* wrote that Humphrey was "one of the best mayors in the nation." Eleanor Roosevelt said, "People have learned to believe and trust in this young, vigorous Mayor." Labor Leader Walter Reuther called Humphrey "outstanding among the young and forceful progressives on the American political scene." Leon Henderson, a Roosevelt and Truman administrator, and several others suggested that he should be considered a Vice Presidential possibility. Chester Bowles spoke of Humphrey as one of several possibilities for the Presidential nomination. All of these comments and suggestions were made before

Humphrey was even elected to the Senate in 1948. The praises were lofty and the predictions premature, and Humphrey knew it. But he enjoyed them. After addressing an Atlantic City meeting of the American Association of School Administrators in 1947, he received requests to speak from educational groups in more than thirty states.

During his second term as Mayor he was also attracting the attention of newspapers in other areas of the country. He received innumerable requests for interviews, and said yes to most of them. One came from a Louisville *Courier-Journal* reporter, Tarleton Collier, who called Humphrey at home one evening in 1948 to ask for an appointment. The Mayor set ten o'clock the next morning for the interview. Collier wrote later:

"It was eleven thirty when he showed up. The office had been steadily filling. Long-distance calls had been pouring in. Messengers came and went in a stream with handfuls of telegrams. Two secretaries kept scribbling away on memoranda of numbers that had to be called without delay, names that simply demanded seeing at once. When I was admitted to the big office, the Mayor arose briskly with his right hand outstretched while his left hand held a telephone receiver to his ear and he kept talking cheerily and without haste to somebody or other in Detroit. . . .

"The conversation with Detroit ended. The telephone began ringing for another call, but Humphrey let it ring while he apologized for being late for our appointment. 'When I talked to you last night,' he said, 'I'd forgotten that I had to do some canvassing this morning with a block committee in my church membership campaign. It sort of held me up.'

"He was fresh and chipper, as if his midnight labors, his morning rounds for the First Congregational Church, had never been. He was bouncy and boyishly happy to be at it, to be here, to be receiving a new acquaintance from Louisville. Dark-haired and slender, he looks younger than his years, with a mobile gleam of impishness that helps the impression. It is when you see his mouth as the oddly interlocking lips go together firmly under pressure of a nutcrackerish chin that you realize here is no man to belittle and that his youth is beside the point."

Despite the long delay and rather frantic pace of the interview, Collier concluded his articles on Humphrey with references to "his magnetism," "this Humphrey political genius," and "the mark of the authentic leader of men."

To such descriptions and others in 1948, Humphrey responded with a coy smile, a meaningful twinkle in his eye, and the comment:

"If the papers keep talking about my political ambitions, they may give me some ideas."

In the legally impotent office of Mayor, Humphrey had won a reputation as a man of political power.

10

The Illusions of Power

Power is, initially, a latent quality or ability. It is nothing until it is captured, used, realized, seen, or imagined.

In America the people and the press seem to regard basic political power as something of substance and shape; they speak or write about it as though it were a round of cheese, with slices of varying sizes being cut out and held by different men and different institutions. The struggle for political power is compared often to a game of chess, as though it were a clear and mathematically precise series of maneuvers.

But political power has an amoebic quality; its origins are obscure and its directions shift constantly under the pressure of amorphous forces.

In the American system political power is potential. It is nothing until it is released by effort, related to people, and realized through their awareness and acceptance of it. For a politician power is partly personal, partly a matter of position, and partly a combination of achievement and audacity. A successful politician is one who can capture the potential of power within himself and can realize it through a position related to the people. He has an aggressive talent for making people aware of both his personal power and public position.

A man can become politically powerful quickly, even though his personal power is untested and his public position holds modest legal authority. But he must know how to create impressions of power, and he must learn to utilize the illusions of power which the public visualizes. People may think that a man is politically powerful when, in the reality of one moment, he is not. But if the politician detects and understands the basis for such illusions about himself and adroitly capitalizes on them, the illusions of power can become real elements of his power. The position of Vice President of the United States holds little intrinsic power, but if the people think it does, or if influential individuals think it is a sure step toward power, it does in fact become powerful.

Hubert Humphrey has said many times, "In politics it is not so much what you are that counts; it's what people think you are." And, it might be added, it is not so much what people think a man is that counts for political power as what they think he might become. Politicians tend to look at other politicians with a view toward their current position or influence; they also wonder: Is he a comer? A politician's age and adaptability can be more important for his political success than a formal power base.

In early 1963, at a Washington cocktail party and buffet supper hosted by Ridder Publications, California Assembly Speaker Jesse Unruh mingled quietly with guests at one end of a private Georgetown dining room. At the other end a woman glanced toward him and asked her husband, "Who's that?" In a tone of great respect he answered, "That's Jesse Unruh." She wanted more detail. "Who is he? What does he do?" He answered, "Unruh's the boss out there. He'll probably *run* California someday." The woman then gazed at the then heavy-set political leader with an awe indicating that she now believed he had California's 159,000 square miles jammed into one pocket and would soon have its eighteen million people tucked into his other pockets. Unruh at the time was already a man of considerable political weight in California, developed in part because he had never publicly denied the extra, imagined power which many of its people and leaders were always adding to his reputation as "Big Daddy."

Americans tend to visualize their political leaders in the lines and shapes of cartoon caricatures. If a politician's nose and chin are slightly larger than normal, the editorial cartoonist will give him a nose the size of the Rock of Gibraltar and a chin resembling the bow of a battleship. If his eyes appear to be just a bit smaller than normal, they become beady. The tendency to exaggerate affects the public's attitude toward the character as well as the stature of political leaders. Harry Truman enjoyed an occasional game of poker and admitted he liked to sip a scotch before dinner. He was also a decisive and resourceful President who liked to read history books, characteristics which many Americans ignored. Sherman Adams, a White House Assistant in the 1950's, accepted a vicuna coat and some home furnishings from a New England industrialist. He was a frugal man, and an efficient and honorable public servant, but he became suspect of conflicts of interest, graft, and corruption, and the President of the United States was compelled by public pressure to terminate Adams' political career.

The American inclination toward political overstatement works in the other direction. If a political leader is seen in a single dramatic display of courage or wisdom which attracts the attention of the press and the people, he is on his way to becoming a saintly statesman for all time. If a political leader is successful in wielding power on one issue, he is soon reported to be "one of the most powerful men in Washington," and the public may shortly regard him as "the second most powerful man in Washington." (First spot always belongs to the President.)

Lyndon B. Johnson, when he was Majority Leader of the United States Senate, was considered by many to be in such total control of that legislative body that he was often compared with a circus ringmaster. Johnson, indeed, showed rare skills as a legislative leader and political strategist. In the 1950's his successes in guiding or directing the Senate toward legislative achievement were numerous and substantial. There were many reasons for his distinction as one of the best Majority Leaders in the history of the Senate, some of which were his own talents and energies. But he also understood the effect of the illusions of power which were created by a people and a press who like the heroes of political dramas to be bigger than life. Majority Leader Johnson also knew how to use the illusions of power. If a new Senator believed that Johnson completely dominated and controlled Democrats in the Senate, the Majority Leader did not turn away modestly from the face of such exaggeration. He simply asked for the man's vote, and usually got it. Majority Leader Johnson also understood the truth which has become a cliché: "Nothing succeeds like success." He moved quickly from one success to another because he knew that people expected him to and believed him capable of doing anything. He never rested after a single success. He never changed direction, and rarely moved off course from the attainable into some new and uncharted area of vain effort. He fully understood the immense value of sustaining the momentum of political and legislative success.

Hubert Humphrey has been far less inclined to create or utilize the illusions of power or to work at sustaining momentum in one direction. He wants people to like him rather than to bend to his will. Exaggeration of his own role or position of power is a significant but peripheral part of his political personality. He is too often too self-effacing to permit images of omnipotence. He can smile with satisfaction if someone describes him as an expert in the field of disarmament or as a deeply compassionate man because he believes both to be true. But if an admirer gushingly tells him, "You're the greatest politician in America today," he is likely to say, "Now let's not get carried away." In front of groups of reporters, meetings of politicians, or large crowds of people he frequently pokes fun at himself. Self-directed humor is a sign of an emotionally healthy or even humble man, but it does not help to create illusions of power. When Humphrey was in the Senate, an acquaintance suggested that he was "the greatest Senator since Daniel Webster." He smiled, but answered, "Oh, come now." If the same compliment had been offered to Lyndon Johnson, he might have said, "Thank you very much." And there are some members of the Senate who might, in answer to such a remark, respond, "Well now, actually I think that in some ways I might even be a *greater* Senator than Daniel Webster."

Humphrey has often been criticized for lacking direction, or momentum. In truth, his problem of appearance stems more from the fact that he cannot restrict himself to a single direction or to a single area of activity. Of course he wants to sustain a momentum of success and an upward direction for his own political career, but there are many goals or issues outside his self-interest which frequently command his attention. "Hubert Humphrey has as many causes as stars in the sky," one reporter wrote. Why, he was once asked, was he involved in so many subjects? "I LIKE all subjects," he answered. In 1961 he was requested to name the single subject he might choose if he ever took the time to write a book. He thought for only a few seconds, shrugged his shoulders, and answered, "The universe." In recent years he has not adopted quite so many causes as his own, and he has managed to give priority to such geographic areas as Latin America and such substantive issues as disarmament. But as late as 1963, when he was asked by an editor to list his "prime" areas of interest for a one-paragraph biographical sketch, he suggested civil rights, conservation, education, agriculture, disarmament, the effects of technology on the economy, drug legislation, the European Common Market, the Soviet economic offensive, Latin-American affairs, Soviet-Chinese relations, food for peace, urban affairs, small business, et cetera. Such a variety of interests can lead to excellent training for high administrative responsibility, but it does not lend itself to a reputation for a record of sustained success, or momentum. One of Washington's most thoughtful reporters says of him, "Humphrey's power has been episodic. He has it in two or three areas of activity and has exhibited power in particular years. But then he seems to disappear from view for two or three years before he emerges as a powerful man again in a particular situation or on a particular issue." The reason, frequently, was that Humphrey often moved on after obvious political successes—cutting the momentum of his public image—to explore some new fields or pioneer in a difficult area requiring years to produce results of interest to the press and public.

He is not, of course, dense about the techniques of creating illusions of power; he proved that as Mayor of Minneapolis. For all his spontaneity and action by instinct, he cares deeply about his public image as a man and as a politician.

In the winter of 1962 he called two assistants into his office to discuss "a few ideas I had coming in this morning." He spoke long and eloquently about the need for the United States to clarify its national identity and purpose. He suggested that the government needed to begin planning to achieve its long-range purpose, adding, "We must know where this country is going, where we want it to go, and what the best ways are to get there." He offered some definite ideas of his own and urged his two assistants to come up with their ideas for the practical aspects of the grand goals of America. He generated an excitement and sense of importance for the project, and an extra spark of personal loyalty in his assistants when he said, "I'm over fifty years old. A man at that age starts to think about what his final contribution will be. I want to *do* something good and important and enduring for the people of the

nation and the world before I keel over and leave. Maybe we
ought to think about this in terms of what my public image should
be. Not just what we think would win favor or affection from the
people, but what we think would be an image of quality, a true
image of worth which merits the respect of the people. It's great to
have people like me. But I want them to respect me. If we try to
create a certain image, let it be a good one. And maybe I will then
try to live up to it, to become a bit better than I really am. A
man's greatest goals and his best public image can influence him.
Now you guys do some serious thinking about this. Get to work on
this, right now. It's very important."

Thirty minutes later he inundated both men with instructions
for half a dozen immediate tasks of no greater consequence than
the preparation of a statement and press release advocating the
proclamation of a "Leif Ericson Day" in the United States. He
had indicated during the lofty discussion with his assistants the
strength of his urge to create an image not only of power but of
quality. He had been thinking deeply about his enduring contribution and what view the next generation might take of him.
He had shown his qualities of statesmanship. And then, half an
hour later he was consumed with the present moment again. Leif
Ericson, every Minnesota voter of Scandinavian descent knew, was
a Scandinavian. In the immediate tasks of his political and legislative workday Humphrey was the politician.

As a politician he has tended to be less concerned with his overall image than with the narrow view of him held by particular
groups of the population. A proclamation for Leif Ericson, a statement on Polish Independence Day, a telegram to the Friendly
Sons of St. Patrick, an article for a labor newspaper, and a speech
to South Dakota pharmacists have been as important to him as
whether the public as a whole thinks of him as a statesman or as a
politician. He is often impatient with the advanced techniques of
professional public relations, and has said, "Let's not worry about
my image. If I just do what's right and work hard, the image will
take care of itself." Through much of his career he has tended to
think of "the people" as, first, individuals, and second, as groups
with particular nationalistic, professional, or geographic identity.
At least through 1960 he tended to visualize the public as seg-
mented. He is still inclined to view "the people" in their separate
parts, and not as a single entity.

One result is that he shows amazing versatility in communicating effectively with a wide variety of types of people. Part of his personal and political appeal stems from the fact that he does not generalize himself or his audiences. He tailors his vocabulary and his manner to the particular group before him. Without deserting his basic convictions he can shift smoothly to many groups which are different in temperament, education, and viewpoint. In a single hour in the summer of 1963 he spoke to and received enthusiastic responses from a delegation of conservative Minnesota businessmen and a score of ladies from the Teamsters Auxiliary. His message to both groups—an informal discussion of his work and his beliefs—was essentially the same and completely honest for each. But there was an abrupt and subtle change in his method and manner during the few minutes between each meeting. With the Teamsters group he used metaphors based on bowling or trucking terms; with the businessmen he spoke with the phrases and statistics of the world of finance. On a single evening in early 1964 he amazed one of his assistants, Norman Sherman, by adapting himself to four distinctly different political situations in the Twin Cities area. He first offered a partisan exhortation to three hundred Anoka County Democrats. Then he offered a sound and thoughtful discourse on the nation's economic problems to a convention meeting of fifteen hundred small-town bankers. Next, he spoke informally and danced with a dozen women at a twenty-fifth-anniversary celebration for a labor leader and his wife. Finally, at midnight, he spoke quietly about the weighty and legal aspects of the Civil Rights Bill for a private gathering of intellectuals. Gaylord Nelson, when he was Governor of Wisconsin, noticed in 1960 that Humphrey was equally effective dealing with marginal farmers and Milwaukee industrialists. Minnesota Governor Karl Rolvaag remembers a 1956 joint campaign tour through southern Minnesota in which Presidential candidate Adlai Stevenson was noticeably uncomfortable and awkward meeting rural farm hands, and a candidate for state office was distinctly nervous in the presence of scientists at Rochester's Mayo Clinic. Humphrey, traveling with them, established rapport with both groups.

By both instinct and effort Humphrey develops a series of individual images, not a universal public image. He is less effective on television than he is in person partly because he cannot quite relax as he stares into the face of the three-lensed camera. He cannot, intellectually or emotionally, grasp that there are human beings "out there" behind the glass eye and red light. Before the taping of a national television interview in 1962 a New York network executive advised him to relax, to imagine that he would "just be speaking to a friend of average intelligence, education, and income." "That's fine," Humphrey said, "but what about the unfriendly people, the dumb ones, the geniuses, the plumbers, the philosophers, the slum dwellers, and the fat cats in the audience?"

Human beings, to Humphrey, are real; they cannot be turned into artificial "consumer types" or abstractions called "audiovisual response" by Madison Avenue statisticians. Because they are real, they become individuals of distinct backgrounds or identities. People are people, Humphrey thinks first, so he tends to be a warm and responsive human being when he speaks directly to them. People are also Americans, he thinks second, so he expresses his own sense of national identity and his concern for national problems in front of any audience. But quite often he thinks of people as bankers, farmers, carpenters, New Yorkers, Minnesotans, liberals, conservatives, young, old, men, or women. He simply individualizes people in his political perspective.

As his own view and political involvement have been broadened, he has, in recent years, become more effective on television and more willing to aim his remarks to a collective audience. His national identity inevitably increased the longer he was in Washington. But as late as 1960 he still tended to chop up his political personality and record and hand a different piece to each different group. In his unsuccessful effort to win the 1960 Democratic Presidential nomination he appealed to the voters of Wisconsin as a neighbor, or as a Midwesterner, or as an advocate of the workingman, or as a friend of the farmer. He sought to depict John F. Kennedy as an Easterner. In West Virginia he appealed to the voters as a New Dealer, as a hard-working antagonist of poverty, as a man of humble origins, as a poor man. He sought to identify Kennedy as a rich man. In both primary campaigns Kennedy and his aides were well aware of the need to make special appeals to special groups, but essentially John F. Kennedy appealed to the voters as John F. Kennedy, a whole man. One hour after he announced his candidacy for the Presidency in December 1959, Humphrey expressed incredibly poor political judgment when he told one newsman, "I'm going to campaign for the Presidency as if I were campaigning for county sheriff."

He would never make such a statement today. In his Vice Presidential campaign of 1964 he often spoke to businessmen as a former businessman, to Midwesterners as a Midwesterner, to farmers as a product of rural America. But he spoke more often in a manner befitting his national identity and befitting the office of the Vice Presidency. He learned too much about national politics from his defeat in the spring of 1960 to sustain a county sheriff's perspective toward campaigning or public service. He does hold on to some old political traits in the same way that he holds on to old friends; he is still, in part, the small-town country boy, the gregarious Midwesterner, and, in some ways, "one of the boys" in the Senate chamber. But his elevation to the Vice Presidency added another dimension to his political personality; he can now smile at the cold and ugly face of a television camera without appearing to sneer.

One problem in the image-making process has persisted for him. It is expressed in the frequent criticism that he talks too much, too long, or too emotionally. For many speeches he appears to prefer the length of a William Jennings Bryan oration, the evangelistic fire of a Billy Graham appeal, and the pace of a Walter Winchell newscast. Age and experience have slowed his pace somewhat. There is no compelling reason why he should become coolly rational in his manner; he is often at his best when he is evangelizing his audience toward his own convictions. But the length of many of his speeches ruins his schedules, infuriates his more professional advisers, and exhausts many of his listeners.

He and many of his friends defend the length of his speeches on several grounds. First, that he *learns* by speaking; the masses of information he has absorbed from reading or listening and the shapeless notions which spring from his conscience and experience tend to become crystallized into convictions or useful ideas in the process of communicating with other human beings. Second, that he has much to say and needs time to say it; even those aides who are most critical after he has spoken for an hour and a half often admit that, personally, they were not once bored during the course of his address. Third, that people cannot be "educated" with slogans or fifteen-minute summaries of national and world problems;

the demands for brevity and capsule comments, Humphrey suggests, are an invitation to "political demagoguery."

There are two other less rational motivations for the length of many of Humphrey's speeches. First, if he is effective and an audience obviously likes his speech, he simply enjoys speaking; after an hour of exchanging eloquence for applause his attitude seems to be, Why end a good thing? Second, if he is not effective and an audience is not "with" him, he refuses to admit failure; after an hour of clichés and listlessness he persists in trying to reach or convince the audience. He does not often fail as a public speaker. When he does, the scene is painfully pathetic; with a third of his audience gone and the rest squirming in their seats, he finally shrugs his shoulders and walks as quickly as possible out of the auditorium.

From experience he has learned to pace himself for the ten-second television "spot," the one-minute comment, and even a rigidly set period for a formal address. He will tolerate commands for brevity or half-hour restrictions, but he does not like them. His suggestion of a good compromise between a two-hour oration and a half-hour address is the one-hour lecture, a time period which he probably adapted himself to when he was a teacher. In 1960, on a campaign tour through Oregon, adviser Jim Rowe urged him to limit his remarks before a student group to thirty minutes. Humphrey contended, "Nothing worthwhile can be said in thirty minutes." Rowe persisted, offering him a ten-dollar bet that he could not limit his remarks to even forty-five minutes. Rowe watched the clock that night while Humphrey spoke. As the forty-fourth minute passed, he leaned back with the satisfied smile of a man who has won his bet. At exactly forty-four minutes and fifty seconds, Humphrey stopped abruptly, thanked his audience, walked over to Rowe and said unhappily, "Where's my ten dollars?"

As a campaigner Humphrey delights in sheer numbers of people. In the rural areas of Minnesota, where people are not particularly abundant, he was willing to drive a hundred miles out of his way for the opportunity of attending a meeting of fifty farmers or to stay up all night for the chance to shake hands with the 6 A.M. breakfast trade in a small-town restaurant. Nationally he deals with groups in the thousands or tens of thousands, but is never satisfied and never really stops campaigning. During a formal political campaign he wants the massive audience, but also the individual contact. He is one of the best hand-shaking politicians in America; he invariably greets a new friend with a firm grasp and a direct eye-to-eye gaze. He does not, as do many quick-moving politicians, shake a hand, look at his watch, and eye the next person in line all at the same moment. He keeps to a schedule only because two or three assistants are usually pushing him through and out of a crowd by digging their fists into the small of his back. A few observers have suggested, distastefully, that he is "the last of the baby-kissing politicians." He does kiss babies often on the campaign trail. He also kisses babies in the privacy of his own or his friends' homes. He likes babies.

In an interview in the summer of 1964 he expressed one of his basic attitudes about political campaigning:

"You have to give to people. I don't just *make* a speech. I *give* a speech; I try to give the people a bit of knowledge or perhaps a useful idea. And when the speech is over, I get mad when these guys keep tugging at me and saying 'Gotta get to your next appointment,' as though the next appointment were the Second Coming. I know that at many of these political meetings there are always a lot of families who have taken the trouble to pack the kids into the car and drive into town to hear me and maybe meet me. So I give them a speech, and I want it to be a good one. When it's over and I see a fine family with kids just sort of standing there, I've got to go down and meet them and talk to them just for a few minutes. The kids usually get excited, and as they walk away they shout, 'Gee, hooray, we met Humphrey.'

"Look at Dewey and Truman, in 1948. Dewey is a fine man. He's a good speaker. He has an intelligent mind. He was always on time and always well organized in that campaign. Truman? He's a terrible speaker, technically. He was always late. But he always had a little time to go down and pat the kids on the head and say a few nice words to Mama. He always took a few minutes to say hello. That's why he won—he gave to people.

"Even in Washington, I stop and talk to the kids. Sure, maybe I take ten minutes to do it, and time is precious. But I want to do it. Around this city you're always battling power, talking power, worrying about power. So when I see a child, scrubbed and bright and friendly, I just want to talk to him. It nourishes my soul. It refreshes me. Spending five minutes with a kid is like going to the beach. It helps me that much; it really does. You get as much as you give."

He often grows frustrated because he cannot talk more, give more, and be more convincing with more people. If he had the time, he would happily and personally shake every hand, see every face, try to convince every mind, and exchange the gifts of friendship with every person in every farm, town, village, city, state, and territory of the United States. And then he would take on the rest of the world.

The politician wants and must have contact with people; his awareness that the mathematics of masses of people and the tininess of his time will prohibit personal contact with most of the people frustrates him. He must turn to the press as the only alternative link with all the people.

Humphrey has a cordial relationship with most newsmen. But when he or his efforts are not receiving the press attention he thinks is deserved, he (and most other politicians) broodingly mutters complaints about a "conspiracy," as though the editors and publishers of every newspaper from Sleepy Eye, Minnesota, to New York City meet in some secret spot in the center of the continent at each full moon to plot their strategy. The notion is, of course, absurd, but the frustration is understandable. Many national politicians, including Humphrey, have at some time been "spoiled" by constant and favorable treatment in the press. In earlier stages of their careers they tend to receive more press attention because they are more colorful and less stodgy, more candid and less careful than in their mature years. Most politicians begin their careers at the local level, as mayors or state officials, and they thus tend to draw more attention because of the emphasis in news columns on local news. And a public executive, by the nature of his position at the center of policy or controversy, draws more attention than the legislator, who is only one out of many. As the politician matures, moves away to Washington, and becomes one of many important men, the press tends to give him less space in its columns. The politician, believing almost always that he and his work should command page-one importance, is disappointed and disdainful when he finds his greatest achievements and most eloquent statements used as filler material on the obituary or comic pages.

Frequently a politician's anger toward the press in general is justified. During his two terms as Mayor, Humphrey received both page-one attention and editorial-page endorsements from most of the newspapers in the Twin Cities and surrounding areas. He was supported almost unanimously when he ran for re-election as Mayor in 1947. But in 1948, when he ran for the Senate as a Democrat, his press support vanished as quickly as the support of businessmen who said, "He's great as Mayor, but that's a non-partisan office, and we've got enough Democrats in Washington as it is." Of almost five hundred daily and weekly newspapers in Minnesota in 1948, less than thirty supported Humphrey in his Senate race. None of the general-circulation newspapers in his own city of Minneapolis endorsed him.

He remembered that, and remained sensitive to the careless or intentional lapses of editorial fairness in handling his significant statements and achievements. In the years he served in the Senate it was not uncommon for him to place an angry phone call to an innocent assistant city editor who happened to be on duty at the time Humphrey erupted over the absence or play of a story about him. Reporters who were fond of quoting an ancient city room rule that the only way for newsmen to look upon politicians is "down" did not help to ease his frustrations.

Most reporters like him; he is a likable man, is reasonably candid, and is talented in coining the neat, four- or five-word phrases which sum up a situation and fit well into a brief lead paragraph. Through the years he has also become a valuable source, if not a center, of news. And through the years, as he has sought to enlarge his audience and increase his support at the national level, the press has become increasingly important to him as the main channel for reaching many people.

The politician knows that without the press his real achievements would not be reported to the people and the voters. And without the press the illusions of political power would never develop or be realized among the people.

In politics, while the illusions of power and the momentum of success are valuable elements in a man's total effectiveness and progress, they can also warp a man's view of himself and his power or blind him to the realities of political circumstances closest to him. In his terms as Mayor, Humphrey utilized the illusions of power while he was in an office of little intrinsic power. He sustained a momentum of success through his two terms, rarely leaving the front pages of newspapers, never very long out of public view, and generally credited with an ability to do anything. He looked hopefully toward greater power, national power, and he knew he had the image and the momentum to get him there in a hurry. If he had been less of an open man, if he had allowed the illusions of power to narrow his perspective with vanity, he might have overlooked a stumbling block which appeared under his fast-moving feet.

Between 1945 and 1948 the Democratic Farmer-Labor Party—Humphrey's party in Minnesota—was gradually infiltrated and finally dominated by Communists.

11

1948

In 1948 the political tide through much of the world and in most of America surged to the left. In time the tide would slow in some places and ebb in others, but in that year governments were being carried away from a comfortable conservatism or a war-enforced status quo. Nations and states were being changed by choice, conspiracy, or force. In 1945 the people of Great Britain had rejected the party of their World War II hero and leader, Winston Churchill, and chosen a Labour government. On March 15, 1946, at Fulton, Missouri, Churchill had spoken of "these anxious and baffling times." He noted that an "iron curtain" had descended on Europe, and he commented:

"A shadow has fallen upon the scenes so lately lighted by the Allied victory. Nobody knows what Soviet Russia and its Communist international organization intend to do in the immediate future or what are the limits, if any, to their expansive proselytizing tendencies."

In February 1948, Communists seized control of Czechoslovakia; the end of that country's freedom was symbolized by the mysterious death two weeks later of Czech patriot Jan Masaryk. In March, Communists won additional seats in the Italian parliament; their leader, Moscow-trained Palmiro Togliatti, became a major force in that nation's politics. In April, the Soviet Union imposed a blockade on West Berlin; the Soviet deputy military governor, General Dratvin, ignored Allied demands to open traffic to the city. In December, Madame Chiang Kai-shek flew to Washington to warn that China was about to fall into Communist hands; a month later, Nationalist General Fu Tso-yi surrendered Peiping to Red forces.

At the beginning of 1948, Communists controlled the Democratic Farmer-Labor Party in Minnesota. The new party had been loosely organized and badly split after its merger in 1944. Far-left elements of the old Farmer-Labor Party retained major influence in the new party. Communists first infiltrated and then controlled the leadership of the Young DFL Organization. They then moved into official positions in county and district divisions of the parent party. From there hard-core Communists stepped up to hold strategic positions in the state DFL Organization. By 1946, DFL leadership was dominated by Communists. Mayor Hubert Humphrey, the "father of the DFL," required police protection to attend the state convention in 1946. He walked into the auditorium to be greeted with jeers and screaming denunciations. Some of the delegates closest to the aisle spit at him or tried to trip him as he moved toward the platform. Party leaders had been obliged to ask him to speak before the convention. But when he stood on the rostrum, hundreds of delegates screamed viciously, "Facist! Warmonger! Capitalistic pig!" He was not able to complete his address. The delegates booed him off the platform and out of the auditorium.

Humphrey was identified in the community and by the press as the leader of the "right wing of the DFL." He had fought Communist attempts to control Minnesota teachers' unions and Twin Cities labor organizations. As Mayor he often ended his day and evening of work by joining bull sessions at the homes of such university professors as Max Kampelman and William Kubicek. The group considered itself liberal and anti-totalitarian in viewpoint. A few who joined were Norman Thomas-type Socialists, but all were strongly anti-Communist. They held lively, informal debates and discussions on the weaknesses, strengths, and dangers of Marxism, communism and socialism. It was all very informal and mostly academic, and the professors assumed that Humphrey came for what they called "intellectual nourishment" after a hard day at City Hall. "Humphrey's convictions were already set," Kampelman remembers. "They were strongly liberal and strongly anti-Communist. But he profited from the intellectual stimulation of those discussions. And we profited by his presence and participation. He was the practical politician; he brought that to the group."

As a practical politician Humphrey was compelled to do more than just discuss and debate the dangers of communism. He and Kampelman, who later became a top assistant and remains a close friend and adviser, went to others to weigh the extent of Communist penetration of the DFL and to formulate a plan to recapture control of the party. They were joined by men and women who were politically experienced and talented: Arthur Naftalin, who had helped Humphrey in the Mayoralty campaigns of 1943 and 1945 and who would be elected Mayor of Minneapolis in 1961; Orville Freeman, who had been a fellow student at the university and an assistant in the Mayor's office and would go on to become a three-term Governor of Minnesota and Secretary of Agriculture in the Kennedy and Johnson Administrations; Mrs. Eugenie Anderson, a political volunteer who later became Ambassador to Denmark and Minister to Bulgaria.

Humphrey also went outside Minnesota for help. In early 1947 he traveled East to help establish Americans for Democratic Action, an organization intended to be ideologically liberal, politically practical, and strongly anti-Communist in its policies and work. (The ADA has been monotonously and inaccurately branded with charges and innuendos of Communist sympathies through the years.) At a regional meeting of the ADA in Chicago in January 1947, Humphrey and Naftalin asked for help in beating down the Communists in the Minnesota DFL. They told ADA officers that they needed both organizational help and the prestige of such ADA figures as Mrs. Franklin D. Roosevelt. "Humphrey was a great idealist," ADA official Joseph Rauh remembers, "but he was immensely practical. He and Naftalin had a sound, detailed plan to boot the Commies out of the party. The national ADA backed him with all the help that it could give."

The Communists in the DFL utilized a group called the "Farmer-Labor Association" to provide them with a state-wide organization and source of funds. Its members paid dues, and the funds went into the hands of Communist leaders to help them keep a tight rein on the DFL. The liberal, anti-Communist DFL members, led by Humphrey, utilized the ADA's facilities to counter the Farmer-Labor Association's organization.

Humphrey and the others began the anti-Communist effort in essentially the same way as they had nursed the merger of the two old parties in 1944, starting at the precinct level and working through the county and district levels.

"We just outmaneuvered, outworked, and outvoted the Communists," Humphrey remembers. "We'd get forty or fifty people together and walk into a local DFL meeting run by the Communists, and just vote the old officers out and our people in. The Communists fought back hard. But if they stayed up until midnight, we stayed up until 3 A.M. If they issued five press releases, we put out ten. If they staged a local rally for support, we organized two rallies. If was tough, and sometimes the fight got dirty. But we were just as tough as the Commies were—and sometimes just as mean."

(Some of the leaders of the anti-Communist effort still argue, in retrospect, about their tactics. A few complain that Humphrey "was not tough enough," and add, "He wanted to play by the rules and be fair. You couldn't beat the Commies that way. You had to forget fair play and political morality during the duration of the fight." Humphrey replies, "I was plenty tough, and often willing to fight the Commies with their own tactics: infiltration and threats. The hardest part of the fight was that many people were still sympathetic to the Soviet Union because of the wartime alliance, and many others took the extreme view that we should 'get' anyone who even looked like a leftist. In the Commie fight I always made a distinction between the hard-core, card-carrying Communists and the people who were just naïve or confused. There is a man who today is a respected and effective civic leader in Minneapolis whom others wanted to 'get' and ruin in the forties.")

The Humphrey group enlisted support from friends in all parts of the state. In late 1947, Ray Hemenway (later state party chairman) joined others in urging Humphrey to run for the Senate. "Not until you clean the Commies out of your district and help us to purge them from the state DFL," Humphrey answered.

Two developments strengthened the anti-Communist group. Humphrey, as Mayor, managed to get copies of FBI files which identified most of the leading or subversive Communists in Minnesota. And at one state DFL meeting the Humphrey group was able to elect Eugenie Anderson treasurer and Orville Freeman secretary of the party. That put the funds and records of the DFL in the hands of the party's liberal, anti-Communist element.

Humphrey, Naftalin, Kampelman, Freeman, Mrs. Anderson, Kubicek, and others took to the road in the winter and spring of 1948 to push the final stage of their plan to purge the Communists from the DFL. For several weeks many of them drove all night and talked or organized all day. At county and district conventions they worked with local supporters to screen potential delegates to the upcoming DFL State Convention. Whenever possible, they eliminated as a candidate anyone they knew or suspected to be Communist. The final fight would have to be resolved on the convention floor. They needed delegate votes to rid the party of Communists who still held leadership positions.

Their work and organization paid off. In vote after vote at the DFL State Convention in the summer of 1948, Humphrey's forces beat down the outnumbered Communist delegates and elected their own officers. The Communists left the DFL to form their own "People's Party," an impotent element in Minnesota politics which soon died.

Humphrey had been one of many who spearheaded the anti-Communist drive, but he emerged the hero of Minnesota liberalism. He was still credited with ending the confusion and division of Democrats and liberals through his merger plan of 1944. He was honored for ridding the Twin Cities of crooks and racketeers in his three years as Mayor. He was praised for purging the Communists from the party in 1948. The new and "clean" Democratic Farmer-Labor Party nominated him for the United States Senate.

The DFL Convention also approved a resolution which commended—but did not endorse—President Harry S. Truman, who faced a definite lack of enthusiasm for his renomination at the Democratic National Convention in Philadelphia. In the international area Truman had been directing his own bold fight against communism. In March 1947, as the Soviet Union cast a threatening shadow over the fringes of the Middle East, the President enunciated the "Truman Doctrine" of military and economic aid for Greece and Turkey. In June 1947, as Communist domination of Eastern Europe threatened to spread to Western Europe, Secretary of State George C. Marshall announced details of a European Recovery Program—later known as the Marshall Plan—in an address at Harvard University. In June 1948, Truman challenged the Soviet blockade of Berlin with orders for a full-scale airlift of food and supplies which would eventually force the Russians to back down.

Domestically Truman was in trouble. Republicans controlled Congress, and had passed the Taft-Hartley labor control act, which Truman bitterly opposed. Southerners were angry with Truman for urging strong civil rights legislation. (A reporter reminded South Carolina's J. Strom Thurmond that Truman was only following the civil rights proposals advanced by Roosevelt. Thurmond responded, "I agree, but Truman really *means* it.") Conservatives thought Truman was too liberal and liberals thought he was too conservative. Even the ADA and Humphrey made noises about bypassing Truman and handing the nomination to a more dramatic and colorful figure, General Dwight D. Eisenhower, or to a former Minnesotan, Supreme Court Justice William Douglas. The people—and particularly vote-hungry Democrats—remembered the imposing manner of F.D.R., and could not get used to the idea that the stocky, plain-spoken, piano-playing, poker-loving Missourian was President of the United States.

On July 4, 1948, a week before the Democratic National Convention, Wallace Mitchell wrote in the Minneapolis *Star:* "Youthful Hubert Humphrey this week tests his political muscles in the national arena." Another story in the same edition was headlined: DEMOCRATS' HOPES DIM FOR '48, FIGURES SHOW, and stated ominously: "The fact remains, and is shown by the polls, that with the American voter Mr. Truman is no Roosevelt." Humphrey, leaving early for Philadelphia to take up his duties as a member of the convention's Platform Committee, said, "I don't think the Democratic Party ought to get panicky. Elections aren't won by Presidential candidates alone."

Elections, Humphrey and most of the other delegates knew, are also won or lost on issues. The big issue at the Philadelphia convention was civil rights, and the controversy which swirled around it centered on a single paragraph to be written by the Platform Committee and approved by the delegates.

Humphrey's entry into the national arena was not, at first, auspicious. He was one of 119 members of the convention Platform Committee, and at thirty-seven distinctly junior to most of the other members. At a public hearing of the committee on the Friday before the convention convened, Humphrey tangled with Senator Scott Lucas of Illinois, Democratic leader in the Senate, a member of the Foreign Relations Committee, and a chief spokesman for the Truman Administration at the convention. Lucas, at one point defending the Administration's foreign policy against criticism by a witness, was interrupted by the young Mayor of Minneapolis, who argued heatedly, "We need to go on the offensive instead of coming along late, like an ambulance chaser. We definitely came out second best in the last exchange of notes between this nation and Russia, and furthermore, I do not think that the State Department should dictate a foreign policy without letting the people know what the facts of our international relationships may be." Committee Chairman Francis Myers of Pennsylvania broke up the heated argument between the Mayor and the Senator. Later Lucas muttered to other members of the committee, "Who does that pipsqueak think he is?"

On Sunday, Humphrey complained to reporters that a seventeen-man subcommittee appointed to draft the civil rights and other planks was bypassing "the people who carried the ball in an attempt to obtain a clear-cut platform." By "clear-cut" he meant a civil rights plank pledging the party to enactment of the President's civil rights program, including a National Fair Employment Practices program and other legislation.

Truman, who really did "mean it" when he urged such legislation (as J. Strom Thurmond had suggested), did not, however, want to cut his political throat with a clear-cut civil rights plank. He expected a convention "walkout" by Southern delegates, according to his memoirs, but he wanted to minimize its chances or size. Scott Lucas and other Administration spokesmen at the Platform Committee meetings urged adoption of a civil rights plank similar to the one in the 1944 platform. It was a strong statement, but quite general:

"The Democratic Party is responsible for the great civil rights gains made in recent years in eliminating unfair and illegal discrimination based on race, creed or color.

"The Democratic Party commits itself to continuing its efforts to eradicate all racial, religious and economic discrimination.

"We again state our belief that racial and religious minorities must have the right to work, the right to vote, the full and equal protection by the Constitution.

"We again call upon the Congress to exert its full authority to the limit of its Constitutional powers to protect these rights."

On Monday, as the convention formally opened, that draft was presented to the Platform Committee. Humphrey and Andrew J. Biemiller, a Wisconsin Congressman and labor leader, battled Lucas and other Administration spokesmen for a stronger commitment in the plank to the specific civil rights proposals before Congress. Their discussions were not distinguished by tact or courtesy, and tempers flared in the hot, humid weather. In private sessions of the committee Humphrey and Biemiller denounced the plank draft as "a bunch of generalities" and a "sellout to states' rights over human rights." Lucas, at times, sputtered with rage. Pointing a challenging finger at the thirty-seven-year-old Mayor and glaring at the other committee members, he asked, "Who is this pipsqueak who wants to redo Franklin D. Roosevelt's work and deny the wishes of the present President of the United States? Biemiller remembers vividly that Lucas kept using the word "pipsqueak" in reference to Humphrey. Joe Rauh, the ADA official who was working outside the committee room for a strong plank, saw an Administration spokesman in a hallway on Monday night. "You ADA bastards aren't going to tell us what to do," he warned Rauh. Biemiller added fuel to the emotional fire by warning that he, at least, would submit a strong plank in a minority report to the convention, if necessary, and fight out the issue on the floor and in front of the press.

Humphrey, as chairman of the Minnesota delegation, called a caucus. The Minnesotans, proud of his record for civil rights as Mayor and trained in part by him to take strong stands on the issue in the past, instructed Humphrey to continue the fight in committee for a stronger and more detailed plank. On Tuesday the Platform Committee met all day for final agreement on the civil rights plank and others to be submitted to the convention. Late in the day the committee rejected Humphrey's pleas and agreed by an approximate vote of 70 to 30 to the moderate plank. Biemiller announced angrily that he would bring out a minority report. He and Rauh set to work writing a single paragraph to replace the final, bland paragraph in the committee's plank. In retrospect their language seems mild when compared with such civil rights proposals as the ones approved by Congress in 1964. It read:

"We call upon Congress to support our President in guaranteeing these basic and fundamental rights: (1) the right of full and equal political participation, (2) the right to equal opportunity of employment, (3) the right of security of person, and (4) the right of equal treatment in the service and defense of our nation."

That, in 1948, was regarded as the "extreme" and "strong" civil rights position. Humphrey, believing in those civil rights proposals and many more, was urged by Biemiller, Rauh, and others to continue their fight before the full convention. But he had his doubts. Rauh remembers two meetings of the liberal group, the first in Humphrey's hotel room and the second in the ADA's convention headquarters. "He was not at all sure what to do," Rauh says. "He was reluctant to make a big fight and speech on the floor." Biemiller guessed that Humphrey felt somewhat bound, as a formal member of the Platform Committee, to go along with its final recommendation and report. Both friends saw him as a man torn by his conviction about civil rights and his instinct to be practical. All through Monday night and early Tuesday morning other men reminded him of the practical aspects of the issue. None of them—not even Biemiller or Rauh—believed then that they had any chance of winning the fight before the full convention. Lucas and other emissaries from the Administration told Humphrey, "You'll split the party wide open if you do this. You'll kill any chances we have of winning the election in November." Humphrey turned to his father, a delegate to the convention from South Dakota. "Do what you think is right," Humphrey Sr. told his son, "but try not to do anything that will hurt the party." Many of his friends and some of the party's old pros warned him that he would ruin his own, then bright political future if he agreed to speak for the minority report.

He and the others talked and argued all night. At 4 A.M. he still had not made up his mind. They were almost exhausted from the strain of the committee fight, the humidity and the heat, and the tensions of the long, sleepless night. Biemiller argued that Humphrey owed it to his "conscience" to join the renewed fight, and stressed that the group needed his oratory to give them a chance of doing well on the convention floor. Finally, just before 5 A.M., Minnesota's Eugenie Anderson proposed that one short line be added to the paragraph suggested in the minority report: "We highly commend President Harry Truman for his courageous stand on the issue of civil rights." Humphrey said, "That's it. I'll do it." The others suspected that the insertion satisfied his desire to retain at least some link with the establishment of the formal party leaders and the Truman Administration. The group quickly divided responsibilities in trying to line up delegate votes for their minority report. Humphrey went to work to write his speech. With his participation assured, the others plunged into their tasks. They had less than ten hours before the convention was due to take up the civil rights plank of the platform.

Biemiller, who despite his liberalism had become close to Speaker Sam Rayburn in the House of Representatives, phoned the crusty convention chairman in midmorning. "How the hell did you get my private number?" was Rayburn's first comment. Biemiller said, "Never mind. I got it. And I've got a minority report." "On civil rights?" asked Rayburn. "What else?" answered Biemiller. "Oh, hell," sighed Rayburn, who then explained that he had just received a call from Dan Moody of Texas saying that Southerners would submit another minority report representing the states' rights view. Rayburn, loyal to the Administration but scrupulously fair, agreed to recognize Biemiller so that he could present his report and Humphrey so that he could speak for it at the afternoon session. But he suggested that he knew the convention would beat down the Southern minority report and that the impetus of that defeat would help swing the convention to support of the moderate plank.

But the young, liberal, idealistic civil rights advocates were joined by a powerful element of the party, a small number of men known as the "Northern bosses." John Bailey, then Democratic chairman in Connecticut (who would become Democratic National Chairman in 1961) tentatively asked Biemiller, "Are you guys just trying to raise a little hell for the ADA or are you really trying to get votes for the Democratic ticket?" Biemiller assured Bailey of his serious intentions, and the Connecticut party chairman agreed to support the minority report. One big city boss told Biemiller, "You kids are dead right. This is the only way we can win the election, by stirring up the minorities and capturing the cities." And then he added, "And besides, I'd also like to kick those Southern bastards in the teeth for what they did to Al Smith in 1928."

It was not easy for the party to kick the Southerners in the teeth. Most of the Democratic veterans remembered that the South had provided the only real basis of support for the party during the lean years after the Civil War. The "solid South" had remained solidly loyal through most elections as other states and areas of the country swung back and forth between Republican and Democratic Presidential candidates. But some of the Southern states voted against Catholic and Democrat Al Smith and for Republican Herbert Hoover in 1928. In 1936, on Roosevelt's powerful urging, the party abandoned the convention rule requiring a two-third vote for any candidate or convention question, an old principle worshipped by Southern politicians. A simple majority was needed to win a nomination or a contested platform issue after that change.

The Bronx's Ed Flynn, according to Biemiller, went to some of the other bosses, including Ed Kelly and Jake Arvey of Chicago, Frank Hague of New Jersey and David Lawrence of Pennsylvania. The delegations from the big, populous Northern states, worried about the dim prospects for Democrats in the 1948 elections, saw the potential of the civil rights issue among big-city voters. One by one they agreed to support a strong civil rights position for the Democratic Party. The liberal group needed 617 delegate votes—a majority—to win convention adoption of their civil rights plank. The vote was due Wednesday afternoon. On Wednesday morning the most optimistic predictions were that they could muster 150 votes. But after the Northern party leaders joined with the "kids," Humphrey, Biemiller, and the others figured that they had a chance.

Powerful men were still advising against the effort. A White House Staff Assistant told Rauh that the liberals could not possibly win, and in reference to Humphrey, added, "You'll ruin the chances of the best new talent to come along on the political road in years." Others continued to tell Humphrey directly that he was "ruining the party," or "killing your own future." Reporters and pundits insisted, "You're crazy. You kids will get slaughtered when this comes to a vote." But his mind made up, Humphrey refused to be swayed. He worked to polish the speech he would give, phoned delegates he knew, and roamed the hotel corridors to grab anyone with a delegate's badge to urge support for the minority report.

In midafternoon the convention took up the civil rights plank. Chairman Rayburn first recognized Platform Chairman Myers, representing the Administration and offering the moderate, majority-supported plank. Alabama Governor Chauncey Sparks, representing the South, spoke for a states' rights plank. Rayburn, as he had promised, recognized Biemiller, who read the liberal minority report. Humphrey sat near the rear of the platform, making final changes in the pages of his speech, typed in capital letters and being rushed to him by a secretary. Biemiller concluded, "If we adopt this minority report, we are standing by President Truman's courageous stand on civil rights."

Humphrey, wearing a big yellow TRUMAN button on his right lapel, stepped forward. He appeared tired and thin (he had lost eighteen pounds during the week of the last Democratic Convention to be held in an un-air-conditioned auditorium), but eager to begin speaking. He then gave, in high, earnest voice, the shortest and best speech of his career, and what some national leaders still call "the greatest and most effective speech in politics in this century." One reporter stressed later that Humphrey was interrupted more than twenty times by applause—and a scattering of boos. Another reporter, from Minnesota and not usually impressed by Humphrey's oratory, wrote: "He steered clear of any rabble-rousing." Most reporters and delegates, aware of the strong conflicts involved, agreed that the speech "electrified" the convention.

Humphrey looked out over the packed auditorium for a few seconds, and then spoke:

"I realize that I am dealing with a charged issue—with an issue which has been confused by emotionalism on all sides. I realize that there are those here—friends and colleagues of mine, many of them—who feel as deeply as I do about this issue and who are yet in complete disagreement with me.

"My respect and admiration for these men and their views was great when I came here.

"It is now far greater because of the sincerity, the courtesy, and the forthrightness with which they have argued in their discussions.

"Because of this very respect—because of my profound belief that we have a challenging task to do here—because good conscience demands it—I feel I must rise at this time to support this report—a report that spells out our democracy, a report that the people will understand and enthusiastically acclaim.

"Let me say at the outset that this proposal is made with no single region, no single class, no single racial or religious group in mind.

"All regions and all states have shared in the precious heritage of American freedom. All states and all regions have at least some infringements on that freedom—all people, all groups have been the victims of discrimination.

"The masterly statement of our keynote speaker, the distinguished United States Senator from Kentucky, Alben Barkley, made that point with great force. Speaking of the founder of our party, Thomas Jefferson, he said:

" 'He did not proclaim that all white, or black, or red, or yellow men are equal; that all Christian or Jewish men are equal; that all Protestant and Catholic men are equal; that all rich or poor men are equal; that all good or bad men are equal.

" 'What he declared was that all men are equal, and the equality which he proclaimed was equality in the right to enjoy the blessings of free government in which they may participate and to which they have given their consent.'

"We are here as Democrats. But more important, as Americans—and I firmly believe that as men concerned with our country's future we must specify in our platform the guarantee which I have mentioned.

"Yes, this is far more than a party matter. Every citizen has a stake in the emergence of the United States as the leader of the free world. That world is being challenged by the world of slavery. For us to play our part effectively we must be in a morally sound position.

"We cannot use a double standard for measuring our own and other people's policies. Our demands for democratic practices in other lands will be no more effective than the guarantees of those practiced in our own country.

"We are God-fearing men and women. We place our faith in the brotherhood of man under the fatherhood of God.

"I do not believe that there can be any compromise on the guarantee of civil rights which I have mentioned.

"In spite of my desire for unanimous agreement on the platform there are some matters which I think must be stated without qualification. There can be no hedging—no watering down.

"There are those who say to you—we are rushing this issue of civil rights. I say we are a hundred and seventy-two years late.

"There are those who say—this issue of civil rights is an infringement on states' rights. The time has arrived for the Democratic Party to get out of the shadow of states' rights and walk forthrightly into the bright sunshine of human rights.

"People—human beings—this is the issue of the twentieth century. People—all kinds and sorts of people—look to America for leadership—for help—for guidance.

"My friends—my fellow Democrats—I ask you for a calm consideration of our historic opportunity. Let us forget the evil passions, the blindness of the past. In these times of world economic, political, and spiritual—above all, spiritual—crisis, we cannot—we must not, turn from the path so plainly before us.

"That path has already led us through many valleys of the shadow of death. Now is the time to recall those who were left on that path of American freedom.

"For all of us here, for the millions who have sent us, for the whole two billion members of the human family—our land is now, more than ever, the last best hope on earth. I know that we can—I know that we shall—begin here the fuller and richer realization of that hope—that promise of a land where all men are free and equal, and each man uses his freedom wisely and well."

The speech was less than three hundred words and took less than ten minutes to give, including time for applause. There was not a single exclamation point in it; the speech did not need them. Its power came from a blending of Humphrey's responsiveness to the reality of the moment and the passion of his conviction.

The Minnesota delegates jumped to their feet. They were surrounded by Southern delegations: Georgia to their left, Louisiana on the right, Virginia behind them, Kentucky in front of them. The California delegation, in front of the hall, stood up and cheered. In the Illinois delegation, directly behind California, Paul Douglas, a white-haired economics professor soon to be elected to the Senate, turned to Chicago's Ed Kelly, delegation chairman, and said, "I think we should lead the parade for this." Kelly hesitated for several seconds, glanced over the auditorium of cheering, applauding, standing delegates, and then answered, "Yes." Douglas grabbed the Illinois standard and led the delegation into the aisle. California followed Illinois. Wisconsin, New York, New Jersey, Ohio fell into the cheering line. The standards of Massachusetts, Michigan, Indiana, Connecticut, North Dakota, Indiana, Kansas, West Virginia, Vermont bobbed above the parade. One of the insiders in the liberal group screamed indignantly at the convention band to play: he had bribed the bandmaster. But Rayburn shouted "No music!" and refused to open the microphones which would have amplified even more loudly the cheering demonstration. His gavel pounded, but the demonstration lasted for eight minutes.

With the auditorium finally stilled, the delegates voted first on the states' rights minority report. It was overwhelmed, 925 to 309 votes.

Then the roll was called on the Humphrey-Biemiller minority report. It was close, and the edge wavered back and forth as the states announced their votes. Hubert H. Humphrey Sr. reported South Dakota's eight votes: "Aye!" Biemiller's delegation announced "Wisconsin casts its twenty-four votes aye." A majority was achieved. Humphrey jumped to his feet as the auditorium filled with applause and cheers. He clasped his hands together over his head in the classic gesture of victory and grinned.

As the final vote was announced—651½ for the liberal plank and 582½ against—the Mississippi delegation, half the Alabama delegation, and a scattering of other Southern delegates rose to their feet and frowned. A walkout was expected, but Rayburn declared the convention recessed. The dissident Southerners fumed for two hours, and then waited for the moment when Rayburn ordered the roll call for the Presidential nomination to stride out of the hall. The thirty-five Southern delegates left the auditorium to a chorus of booing and stepped into a heavy rainfall outside. They were led by South Carolina Governor J. Strom Thurmond. In November he would pick up thirty-eight electoral votes from South Carolina, Mississippi, Alabama, and Louisiana as the "Dixiecrat" candidate for President. (And in September 1964 he would, as a Senator, move to the Republican Party.)

The convention, on the first ballot, gave Truman 947½ votes for the nomination. Senator Richard Russell, remaining in the hall and loyal to the party, received 263 votes from Southern delegates who refused to join the walkout. Alben Barkley, whose fiery keynote speech had sparked the only convention enthusiasm other than the civil rights fight, was nominated for Vice President.

At 2 A.M., July 15, 1948, Harry Truman stood on the rostrum, peered over his rimless spectacles, and brought the delegates to their feet as he snapped out the first sentence of his acceptance speech: "Senator Barkley and I will win this election and make these Republicans like it—don't you forget that." No one in that hall and few American politicians or pollsters ever will.

Humphrey, elated by his triumph and determined to campaign on his liberal record and in support of Truman's policies, returned to Minnesota to face incumbent Republican Senator Joseph Ball, a young, conscientious man who had served in the Senate since 1940. Ball had been appointed to an interim term by Governor Harold Stassen, and was decisively re-elected to a full six-year term in 1942. At that time Republicans held a modest minority of Congressional seats; Ball moved quickly up the Senate GOP hierarchy. He worked hard, won the admiration of such GOP Senate giants as Robert Taft and Eugene Millikin, and was appointed to such influential committees as Appropriations and Labor. Later he was Chairman of the Senate Appropriations Subcommittee responsible for the budgets of the Departments of Justice, State, and Commerce, and took a frugal delight in chopping their budgets "way down." He focused his attention and legislative efforts in the fields of foreign relations and labor legislation. He became increasingly concerned about "the growth of the federal bureaucracy" and the "salting of more and more power in Washington." He worried about the effect of big government on "individual responsibility, freedom, and dignity." Organized labor, he believed, was becoming almost as powerful and dangerous. Ball, as a member of the Senate Labor Committee, organized the hearings for the Taft-Hartley Act and clearly identified himself as one of the Senate leaders who pushed it through the 80th

Congress. He was deeply disturbed also by the Truman Administration's new spending programs overseas. In 1948 some political
scientists and politicians believed isolationism still lingered in the
United States, particularly in the Midwestern states. In Washington the more conservative Congressional leaders believed that the
people were not at all eager to assume additional tax burdens for
the benefit of an ungrateful, spendthrift Europe. But in March
1948 the Senate approved the Marshall Plan's European Recovery
program, including $5.3 billion in aid to Europe. Ball was one of
only seventeen Senators who voted against it.

When Ball first went to Washington to represent Minnesota in
the Senate, he had been identified generally as a liberal in a state
where even the Republican Party was considered liberal. He also
was comforted by the fact that Minnesota had never elected a
Democrat to the Senate. But in his own words, he had "become
quite conservative" while in Washington. He was moving to the
right.

In the summer and fall of 1948, Minnesota's political tide was
running to the left. Hubert Humphrey was running with it, all
over the state. As a state WPA administrator, as a political organizer and campaigner for Roosevelt, and as a Mayor, he had
already traveled to and spoken in all of Minnesota's counties. As
head of the WPA's Teacher Education program he had issued and
signed his name to thousands of impressively scripted "diplomas,"
many of which were proudly hung over the mantels in the homes
of Minnesotans. As his formal campaign against Ball began in the
late summer of 1948, he tended to his Mayoralty duties early in
the morning and late at night and moved to the campaign trail in
the hours between. By September he was campaigning full time.
On Labor Day he gave three major speeches, one in Faribault near
the Twin Cities, one in Rochester at the southern end of the state,
and one in Duluth 226 miles north. He gulped hot dogs and
gushed ideas at more than fifty local fairs or carnivals. In Orton-
ville he entered a sweet-corn-eating contest and consumed twenty-
five ears. Politics, he suggested, was "like running a drug store.
When people come in, you've got to do something for them." He
ignored complaints that his methods of campaigning were "not
dignified." He visited again in all but three of the state's counties,
traveled more than 31,000 miles, and made 691 speeches. (Tru-

man, by comparison, traveled 31,700 miles and made 356 speeches campaigning across the entire nation for the Presidency.)

Humphrey's campaign pamphlets presented him as a family man and boasted of his achievements as Mayor. They proclaimed—in consecutive paragraphs—that he wanted "to continue and expand the strong points of the New Deal program" and that he believed in "decentralized government," which to him meant, "Federal aid money should be spent and largely controlled by the localities for which it is intended." The campaign literature proclaimed breathlessly, "Liberals up and down the State of Minnesota are beating the drums to elect Mayor Hubert H. Humphrey to the Senate." Humphrey beat the drums for his small-town background, his big-city achievements, and his national stature. But he focused his attention on the issues. He centered his attack on two Senate votes by Ball: *for* the Taft-Hartley Act and *against* the Marshall Plan. Positively he said again and again that the United States should "get off the diplomatic defensive and go on the political and economic offensive throughout the world."

On November 2, 1948, Hubert Humphrey won election to the United States Senate, beating Joseph Ball by more than 243,000 votes, almost 60 percent of the total number cast in Minnesota. The Democratic Party nationally captured control of Congress from the Republicans. Despite the Democratic support siphoned off by Dixiecrat Strom Thurmond and Progressive Henry Wallace (each received close to a million votes), Harry S. Truman beat Republican Thomas Dewey by more than two million votes.

"The party proved," a jubilant Humphrey said a few days after the election, "that it fits the American pattern as made up of a hundred and forty million parts. It gave positive assurances to every group, each with equal rights to opportunity and protection."

Fifteen years later, in the spring of 1964, Joseph Ball recalled details of the 1948 campaign and reflected on the changing mood of American politics. He sat in the study of a farmhouse built near the banks of Virginia's Shenandoah River around 1750, "probably the oldest building around here, and the only one the Union forces didn't burn down during the Civil War." The dark wood walls of the study were covered with old maps and old photographs showing Ball as a young Senator with men of political power in the 1940's.

"It's been a long time since I thought much about politics," he said to open the interview. Retired from his post-Senate career as an executive with a New York shipping line, he was dressed in a heavy, expensive-looking tweed which suited his ruggedly handsome face and tall figure. His manner was quiet and soft-spoken, which suited the pastoral setting of his six-hundred-acre cattle farm nestled in a narrow valley of the Blue Ridge Mountains. He thought carefully and deliberately, and in a deep, pleasant voice answered questions slowly, often pausing many seconds between questions and answers. Candidly, and without any apparent bitterness, he spoke about the fall of 1948:

"Humphrey was no giant killer; I was the incumbent Senator, but I was no giant. He was the Mayor of the biggest city in the state. He had engineered the amalgamation of the Democratic and Farmer-Labor parties. He was all over the state, and he was a good campaigner.

"The techniques of campaigning changed. The news media are so ample; the communications media are so fast. I debated with Humphrey once, over radio, at some woman's club. He spoke so fast, and I think maybe he manufactured a few figures on me. You can't check those in the fast pace of a live radio debate. And I get too emotionally involved in the issues—that made me not a good debater. Humphrey beat me in the debate. His personality helped him, too.

"There are so many news media and reporters around politics today that they have to do all these personality feature things, to fill a column of type or a half-hour broadcast. The emphasis in politics today is on the image a man creates rather than on what the man is. There are too many polls and too many men who find out what the majority thinks from the polls, and then move to that.

"And there's no time lag in the news. You have to be quick, and fast, and glib, and you have to have a strong personality that shows through quickly. I need time to think things out, and I was never very strong on personality.

"Labor was strong in 1948, really strong in the Twin Cities and in Duluth. They went after me because of my role in working for the Taft-Hartley Act. That was a big factor in my defeat. Humphrey's liberalism was not new in the state. The Non-Partisan League had been strong in northern Minnesota. The Farmer-Labor Party had elected two men to the Senate. There was a lingering effect on that state from Floyd Olson's terms as Governor.

"The Republican strength had been in the rural areas. The small town was the backbone of the Republican Party. Then there was this population shift away from the small towns and farms into the cities. That hurt me and helped Humphrey.

"I figured that the sources of my support were the businessmen and the prosperous farmers. I pitched my 1948 campaign on the dangers of inflation and the trend toward state socialism. I had become a conservative. The people, I guess, were further left than I was. And Humphrey was to the left.

"I like the classic liberal idea—the emphasis on belief in the individual. But there are so few real individualists around today. There are fewer great individualists in politics, the men with color and distinction—George Norris, LaFollette, Cotton Ed Smith, Hiram Johnson. It's harder to be an individualist in politics and government now. The government has become so big; all this pork-barrel stuff started when I was in Washington. That cuts down on a man's independence and individualism in government and politics.

"Liberals today are so damn sure they have all the answers. That's the basic difference between Humphrey and me. He goes to the federal government all the time for solution of ills. There are a hundred and twenty farmers in Warren County here [Virginia]. There are twelve government agriculture people, federal, state, and local. That's one for ten. It's silly.

"Politics and people seem to be moving to the left all the time. They were, certainly, in 1948. Humphrey was much further to the left than I was. I guess that's it."

Ball walked outside, talking about the vegetable garden next to his house and pointing to a herd of cattle grazing on a field which sloped down toward the Shenandoah. Then he added a final comment: "I haven't talked about politics for a long time. It's really changed, I guess. I missed it for a while. I saw Humphrey a few times, in the fifties; he was friendly and helpful when I checked a few things with him for the company. But I like it here, where I am."

Ball said good-bye, started to go back into his house, then came back to the edge of the driveway. He pointed south down the little valley and said, "There's a short cut you can take by the bridge. It's a gravel road that hooks up with the road to Washington. It will save you about eight miles."

In December 1948, Hubert Humphrey left for Washington. The political roads he had traveled led inevitably to the national capital. He had taken many short cuts, some of them rocky; he was only thirty-seven. He was leaving the city he loved, Minneapolis, for a city he hardly knew, Washington. He was an experienced, successful public executive who was about to become a legislator. He was accustomed to the openness of Minnesota and the Midwest and was stepping into the political nucleus of the nation. At least in his own area of the country he had mastered the art, science, game, or profession of politics. He was a politician, about to become a Senator.

One long-time observer of him has said, "He is far more effective with people than with institutions." As 1948 ended, he faced one of the most solid and austere institutions of American government—the United States Senate.

PART III

THE SENATOR

12

Field of Force

The United States Senate is—first of all—an idea, rooted in Rome and revised by American revolutionists. It is seven paragraphs and several phrases in the Constitution. It is a complex of parliamentary traditions, Jeffersonian rules, and political precedents. It is a representative legislative body, a vortex of laws and men. It is a continuing council of changing men and moods. It is a force, an atmosphere, a forum, a mirror. It is—most clearly—a place: a thing of location, physical dimensions, and substance.

For more than a century the Senate has filled the north wing of the white-domed Capitol. Its east steps directly face the Corinthian dignity of the Supreme Court, less than two hundred yards away. The two white structures, representing two corners of the triangle of government functions, stand in isolated splendor at the top of Washington's Capitol Hill. To the west the Senate wing looks down on the third: a tide of executive office buildings, lapping at the foot of the Hill and flowing down Pennsylvania Avenue in waves of sandstone to an eighteen-acre island of magnolias and oaks shading the White House.

In an alcove outside the east entrance to the Senate chamber a pedestaled Benjamin Franklin stands, ten feet high, in marble muteness. Franklin did not like the idea of a Senate; in 1789 he favored a single house for the national legislature. Today his stone face frowns toward the swinging double doors of the chamber.

Inside, the high-ceilinged rectangular chamber offers a grand image of mellowed conflict—a blending of the present and the past, the practical and the symbolic, the sturdy and the fragile.

The rostrum and Vice President's chair, both of modern design, face curving, terraced rows of a hundred mahogany desks, their style dating to the time and taste of Henry Clay and Daniel Webster.

The recessed off-white ceiling surrounds a softly colored Seal of the United States. The carpeting, colored with hard reds and blacks, has an intricate design resembling nothing, except perhaps the patterned rugs favored in small-town theaters.

Busts of twenty former Vice Presidents pose majestically in niches behind the upper galleries. Discreetly placed beneath several desks below are dented brass cuspidors.

Guarding the rostrum and three of the exists are pairs of Levant red marble columns, solid and strong. The cream-colored walls, made of thin plasterboard, tremble when Senate aides lean against them.

There are no windows or skylights in the chamber. The Senate's home is shielded from the heat, cold, and world outside by a ring of rococo corridors, a circle of private offices and public hearing rooms, and the thick stone walls of the Capitol.

Several Senators protested this architectural isolation when the chamber was first occupied in January 1859. One introduced a resolution to extend the chamber to the outer walls to permit windows. He said, "I think it is the most unhealthy, uncomfortable, ill-contrived place I was ever in in my life; and my health is suffering daily from the atmosphere." Almost thirty years later Senator Orville Platt agreed: "Here the sunlight never enters; here we never breathe the pure air of heaven . . . While we remain we must live in a dungeon."

Facing the rostrum, Democrats sit on the left of the center aisle, Republicans on the right. Above the Democrats' west exit is a white bas-relief of a man righteously strangling a serpent and the motto *Novus Ordo Seclorum* (A New Order of the Ages); above the Republicans' east exit, in the same style, a man reclines against a plow and points to an eagle which appears to move ahead, under the motto *Annuit Coeptis* (God Has Favored Our Undertakings).

The contrast of attitudes of the Senate's critics and advocates has been more distinct. Patrick Henry read the provision establishing equal representation in the Senate for each state, large or small, and called it "the rotten part of this Constitution." Senator David I. Walsh reverently described the Senate as "the last citadel of minority rights, and the protector of the weaker States." Senator

William Maclay, a Pennsylvanian who served in the first session of the Senate, wrote in 1789:

"With the Senate I am certainly disgusted. I came here expecting every man to act the part of a god; that the most delicate honor, the most exalted wisdom, the most refined generosity, was to govern every act and be seen in every deed. What must my feelings be in finding rough and rude manners, glaring folly, and the basest selfishness apparent in almost every public transaction. . . . Our government is a mere system of jockeying opinions. 'Vote this way for me, and I will vote that way for you. . . .' "

Fifteen years later Vice President Aaron Burr brought tears to the eyes of some members when he said in his farewell speech:

"This house is a sanctuary, a citadel of law, of order, and of liberty; and it is here, in this exalted refuge, here, if anywhere, will resistance be made to the storms of political phrensy [frenzy] and the silent arts of corruption; and, if the Constitution be destined ever to perish by the sacrilegious hands of the demagogue or the usurper, which God avert, its expiring agonies will be witnessed on this floor. . . ."

A century and a half later Senators still disagreed, but with metaphors less lofty. Senator Everett M. Dirksen compared the Senate, with affection and respect, to "an old, waterlogged river scow. It isn't much to look at. It never moves fast. But it never sinks." A younger Senator, momentarily impatient, but still prudent enough to request anonymity, complained:

"The Senate is an institution, all right. A guy who is crazy enough to want to come here is sentenced to six years of hard labor by the people. He spends that time in a snake pit of petty jealousies, run by a bunch of rigid old men."

Views differ, and the Senate itself changes. American political leaders boast that theirs is a "government of laws, not men." Common sense suggests that the nation has a government, and a Senate, of both laws *and* men. Men are imperfect; they change. Every two years one third of the Senate's members face the judgment and votes of the people. Every two years the people reject at least a few, replacing old men with young, or conservatives with liberals, or statesmen with political hacks. In the election of 1946 the people of Wisconsin, Indiana, and Nevada sent to the Senate conservative Republicans Joseph McCarthy, William Jenner, and

George "Molly" Malone. Only two years later the neighboring
states of Minnesota, Illinois, and New Mexico chose liberal Democrats Hubert Humphrey, Paul Douglas, and Clinton Anderson.
The Senate has soared through "golden ages" of collective courage, wisdom, and eloquence. It has sunk also into periods tarnished
by cowardice, corruption, and indifference.

While the face of the Senate may be transformed by different
men and different times, its deeper character has been marked by
unchanging elements. They run through the fabric of its long
history like tough, unbroken threads. The toughest is the concept
and spirit of compromise.

The Senate was born as a compromise. Almost every Constitutional detail relating to the Senate was the result of what historians call the "anxious compromising" of delegates to the Federal
Convention in 1787. The founding fathers envisioned the Senate
as much more than a forum: they gave it the power to forge or
modify a national consensus out of the disagreements or demands
of the states. Ratification of the Constitution, John Adams reported, was "extorted from a reluctant people by grinding necessity."

"Grinding necessity" frequently compels most Senators to give
up some appendage or fragment of personal conviction to preserve
the heart of that conviction, or to translate that conviction into
practice, or simply to survive politically. "Half a loaf is better than
none" is a favorite aphorism among Senators who see the necessity
for compromise. "If you want to get along, go along," young Senators are told by their pragmatic seniors. "The oil can is mightier
than the sword," says Senator Everett Dirksen, reflecting on the
crusading manners of uncompromising Senators.

On a narrow ledge of the Senate chamber's north wall is an
obscure symbol of the spirit of compromise: a pair of tiny black
lacquered snuffboxes. A custodian periodically empties, cleans, and
dusts the boxes, then pours a fresh supply of snuff into each. The
two boxes are the result of a long and only partly facetious debate
on plans to remodel the chamber years ago. "Traditionalists"
among the members wanted to preserve the Senate snuff status
quo: an individual snuffbox on each desk in the chamber. The
"modernists" argued, with reasonable logic, that no Senator had

sniffed snuff for several decades; they demanded that all snuffboxes be removed from the chamber.

No one won; no one lost. But a decision was made: two, but *only* two, snuffboxes would always remain in the chamber. It was a compromise.

The spirit of compromise is matched by another essential element of the Senate's character which tends to quell passions and smooth its operations: a sense of dignity, involving both courtesy and ceremony. Visitors in the Senate galleries often are confused when they hear two members, of obviously antagonistic views, refer to each other as "my distinguished colleague" or "my good friend" in the dialogues of bitter debate. Such courtesy is not hypocritical. It is required by a formal Senate rule (adopted after two Southern Senators interrupted an angry debate to pummel each other) which prohibits language impugning the motives or personal character of any member.

The Senate's sense of dignity is ever present, but sometimes outraged. John Adams, America's first Vice President and the Senate's first Presiding Officer, indignantly reported on a debate in which a Senator's "statements were so wild and so brutally expressed as to be explained only by recognizing that the member was inflamed by drink." Senator Sam Houston of Texas took his seat in the chamber wearing a big Mexican sombrero, a blue coat with brass buttons, and a bright red vest; he enjoyed carving hearts and other pleasant designs on his desk top.

Today the Senate tends to be more conscious and demanding of dignity than during its first century. Liquor is not permitted—at least officially—in the Capitol. At those rare moments when every Senator is present, the pit of the chamber is a sea of conservatively tailored gray, black, and dark blue suits. When Senators Strom Thurmond and Ralph Yarborough wrestled each other to the floor outside a committee room in July 1964, the scene was dramatic not for its violence ("A lousy fight," commented a Capitol guard later) but because it was exceptional. The most common physical gesture of respect or persuasion in the Senate is not a hearty back-slapping, but rather a gentle tapping of a few fingers on the shoulder or coat lapel.

Dignity is a surface indication of a deeper element of the Senate's character: restraint. The traditions, rules, and operating procedures of the Senate favor containment, not creation. Throughout its history the Senate has more often been a limiting force in the government than a positive initiator of new ideas, policies, and programs. Many of the founding fathers stressed that the prime role of the Senate would be to modify and amend; they hoped that its membership would represent a conservative elite or aristocracy capable of curbing the "excesses" of the popularly elected House of Representatives. The Senate, Federalist leaders suggested, should check the "changeableness and precipitation" of the new "centralized power" and protect the people against the "turbulency of democracy."

The Senate normally has been a center of calm in the midst of any political turbulence or social turmoil. During periods of frantic pleas for action by Presidents, the press, or the people, the Senate's pace and mood have remained leisurely. For its first session the Senate was scheduled to begin deliberations on March 4, 1789. On that day only eight of the members already elected (eighteen) took their seats. A full month passed before a quorum was present and the Senate could organize. In 1963 the Senate ignored the fiscal calendar, and did not act on some essential appropriations bills until December.

James Madison stressed the value of restraint when he wrote: "The use of the Senate is to consist in its proceeding with more coolness, with more system, and with more wisdom than the popular branch."

A sculpture titled Wisdom caps the center exit at the south side of the chamber. Perhaps in quest of that quality, the Senate has etched another elemental characteristic into its history: deliberateness. Immodest Senators enjoy the distinct and usually prevalent image of the Senate as "the greatest deliberative body in the world." The phrase suggests that the whole Senate is engaged in an uninterrupted series of debates, each of them important and meaningful, eloquent and productive. That connotation is incorrectly applied. The image is a myth. A visitor to the Senate chamber, on a normal day, will likely witness a dreary scene, with only four Senators present: one sits in the Vice President's chair, signing his office mail; a second mumbles through a prepared speech about the glories of Winnigooga Park, in the northern part of his home state; the other two, reading newspapers, wait their turn to exchange friendly remarks about the merits of a new federal courthouse building in the major city of their state. The Senate is capable of an occasional "great debate," but it is not in fact "the greatest deliberative body in the world."

This is no fault. If Senators spent most of their time in lofty debate, they might see themselves more often the subjects of dramatic productions, but they simply would not get their work done. Responsible attention to the mass of intricate legislative problems they face requires their presence in committee rooms.

Though the Senate as a whole is not particularly deliberative, it *is* deliberate. It is cautious, careful, and unhurried in considering and weighing alternative decisions, or even the decision to take any action at all.

The nation's first President learned how deliberate the Senate could be in August 1789. George Washington became impatient with delay in approval of a treaty involving southern Indian tribes, then personally appeared before the Senate in an attempt to hasten action. In his presence the members dawdled with demands that every provision of the treaty be read again, and then insisted on more time to study it. The President finally withdrew, according to one member, "with sullen dignity." One of Washington's Cabinet officers reported later that the President said "he would be damned if he ever went there again." (He did not, nor did any other President step into the Senate to present a treaty until 1919, when Woodrow Wilson offered the draft Treaty of Versailles and its plan for the League of Nations.)

Washington also was stung by the first ramification of another essential Senate characteristic: independence, with a coating of self-esteem. During the first session he submitted a list of nominations for federal appointments. Despite his immense popularity, Washington was rebuffed by rejection of a gentleman named Benjamin Fishbourn, nominated for the post of Naval Officer for the Port of Savannah. Georgia's two Senators did not approve of Mr. Fishbourn. The Senate sided with them, and against the "Father of the Country."

More than a century later two other Presidents complained of the Senate's independence and self-esteem. Theodore Roosevelt commented, "Individual Senators evidently consider the prerogative of the Senate as far more important than the welfare of the country." And Wilson wrote: "A member of long standing in the Senate feels that he is the professional, the President an amateur."

These are the essential, unchanging elements of the Senate character: compromise, dignity, restraint, deliberateness, independence. They bind Senate episodes into an integrated history. They transform the Senate from a group of men into a political institution.

Looking down into the pit of the chamber from the press or the public galleries, the observer tends to see members of the Senate as smaller men than they really are. Part of the reason is the abrupt, high angle of view from the gallery to the floor of the chamber; Senators seem to be all head, chest, and feet.

Another reason may be a vague understanding of the power of the institutional Senate over its individual member. The history of the Senate is long; time has strengthened its essential characteristics. The tenure of a single member is relatively short; he is only one man within an institution built by the large number of men who have served it. The Senate does not necessarily change a man, but its elemental characteristics and its atmosphere often profoundly reshape his career and methods.

The Senate attracts—and gets—effective and successful politicians, men who are adaptable and who understand the techniques and uses of influence. It also tends to draw many men whose private and political personalities are contrary to the elements which characterize and dominate the institution.

Acceptance and effectiveness do not come easily to the new Senator with deep and passionately expressed convictions (vs. the element of compromise), who is earthy and uncontrived (vs. the element of dignity), who is impulsive and positive (vs. the element of restraint), who is trained as an executive and oriented as a man to act quickly and to be impatient with delay (vs. the element of deliberateness), and who is wedded to a cause and allied with a President (vs. the element of Senate independence from the executive branch).

The new Senator whose personality runs contrary to the institution can choose the role of Senate critic. He foregoes any prospect for significant influence within the body and proceeds to cultivate only his convictions and constituents. If he seeks influence, leadership, and effectiveness in the Senate, he may be oppressed by the Senate's basic and enduring characteristics, along with the rigid seniority system of the body. Unless he changes his personal manners and political methods, the Senate can become a prison of his ambitions.

But the United States Senate—and herein lies its real distinction and greatness—elevates the individual, offering him the opportunity to couple personal integrity with legislative and political excellence. Daniel Webster touched on the distinction when he said, "This is a Senate of equals, of men of individual honor . . . and absolute independence. We know no masters; we acknowledge no dictators."

The House of Representatives has known dictators; Speaker "Uncle Joe" Cannon ruled that body with iron discipline for two decades. The size of the House (435 members) requires tight discipline and intricately formal procedure. Power in the House slides to the Speaker, to several senior members, and to only a few outstanding young members. The Senate's relatively small size (100 members) permits a less formal organization and prohibits a tight form of discipline. Essentially the real power of the Senate is diffused.

No one man can "run" the Senate, despite the inclination of the press and the people to create images of all-powerful political masters. It is mere melodrama to identify *one* member as the "uncrowned king of the Senate," as was the late Senator Robert Kerr in the early 1960's. It is superficial to credit *one* leader with all of the Senate's triumphs, as Lyndon B. Johnson, then Majority Leader, was credited in the 1950's. It was a shock to many Senate "experts" when Richard Russell, often acclaimed as the man who "runs the Senate," lost his battle against the Civil Rights Act in 1964. Each of these men was a skilled leader and all held substantial shares of power in the Senate, but none could dictate the Senate's actions on all issues. The positions of Majority and Minority Leader are not even mentioned in the Senate rules. The seniority system clearly places extra power in the hands of committee chairmen—but only in the limited substantive areas of committee jurisdiction. The Vice President, as Presiding Officer of the Senate, has negligible formal authority.

"Who are the real leaders of the Senate?" a reporter once asked Humphrey. "There are a hundred of them," he answered without a smile.

The Senate, as a whole, might be compared to the mathematician's vector field: a field of force, each point of which possesses a definite value, magnitude, and direction. A British historian might look at the Senate and be reminded of the House of Lords in the sixteenth and seventeenth centuries. Each member of that august body was a public figure in his own right, independent of the throne.

The Senate is permitted to operate from hour to hour and day to day not so much on the basis of the formal rules of the body as by the grace of the power vested in each member by one rule: unanimous consent. Those two words appear through the pages of the Congressional Record like links in a chain binding the Senate to unanimity: "On request of Mr. ——, and by *unanimous consent,* the reading of the Journal was dispensed with." "On request of Mr. ——, and by *unanimous consent,* the following committees and subcommittees were authorized to meet. . . ." "Mr. President, I ask *unanimous consent* that the Foreign Relations Committee be authorized to file a report. . . ." Again and again the Presiding Officer utters the phrase which permits the Senate's life and work to continue: "Without objection, it is so ordered."

One man, one voice, one quick cry of "I object" is all that is necessary to bring the Senate and its thousand activities to a halt. A single individual can, without any obligation to explain or justify his objection, wreck the plans and progress of ninety-nine men.

This immense prerogative of the individual Senator is rarely employed and only occasionally threatened. But it hovers over the heads of Senate leaders at all times. The least influential member, with the most parochial of motives, may be accommodated by the members of power, position, and responsibility because the words "I object" might be hurled across the chamber.

The individual Senator holds definite power whether he exerts any effort or not. A Senator may speak not at all, or for fifteen hours, as he wishes. He may choose to spend his morning hitting a golf ball or pounding his fist on a committee table. He can decide to use his vote only to serve his conscience or a favored constituent, or as a barganing point in a delicately balanced legislative conflict. The individual Senator is a full one percent of the total power of the Senate, at the moment of truth when the whole body approaches a decision. His weight can often tip the scale of evenly matched, conflicting camps. It is no wonder that the youngest, newest, lowest-ranking member of the Senate tends to walk and speak with an aura of importance.

The individual Senator can rise in power in the Senate without any formal or sizable "power base." Many of the "giants" of the Senate, including Henry Clay of Kentucky, George Norris of Nebraska, Burton Wheeler of Montana, and Robert LaFollette of Wisconsin, came from relatively small states. In 1964 one of the most influential, effective, and respected members within the Senate was John Pastore, who also happened to be one of the shortest men in the Senate, was ranked twenty-ninth in seniority, and came from the smallest state geographically, Rhode Island.

Carved into stone above the Vice President's chair is the motto E PLURIBUS UNUM. The motto formally applies to the nation, and was adopted from the idea: "Out of many states, one nation." But the pamphlet handed to Senate visitors translates the Latin to: "One out of many." Its spirit, in the Senate, applies to each man who serves in this chamber. The Senate is, with the exception of the Presidency and the Vice Presidency, the pinnacle of political power in the United States—or at least is so regarded by the men who aspire to it. Out of the town meetings, the county councils, the city halls, the state assemblies, and the Governors' mansions, the American political process picks up and pushes forward individual men who stand out among all others. Out of millions of Americans the patchwork of state authority and the pattern of representative democracy elect a hundred individuals to ride or guide the nation's political moods.

Before he was President, Woodrow Wilson wrote:

"The Senate is in fact nothing more than a part, though a considerable part, of the public service, and if the general conditions of that service be such as to starve statesmen and foster demagogues, the Senate itself will be full of the latter kind, simply because there are no others available. There cannot be a separate breed of public men reared especially for the Senate. It contains the most perfect product of our politics, whatever that product may be."

From the high public and press galleries of the Senate the perceptive observer sees more than a chamber of marble columns and mahogany desks. He notices the symbols of conflict and elements of consistency. Through an ear of the imagination he may hear echoes of a thousand voices: statesmen and demagogues, saintly men and mean men, teachers of the people and statisticians of public opinion. The years of crisis and decision pass through his conscious thoughts: 1789, 1860, 1919, 1933, 1941, 1964. He is aware of the mottoes, the traditions, the general character and abstract assessments of the Senate. Then—at noon—a long, harsh signal buzzes through the Capitol corridors, jolting the chamber into reality and life. A clerk at the rostrum base scribbles the words: "The Senate met at 12 o'clock meridian and was called to order. . . ." Seven sets of doors swing open; from every direction men of imperfect human qualities and polished political skills stride into the field of force which is the United States Senate.

For some the Senate may be a stifling dungeon, for others a protective citadel, for a few an elevating pinnacle.

It depends on the man. It depends on the time.

Humphrey's parents, Hubert Horatio Humphrey Sr. and Christine Sannes Humphrey, emphasized the tenets of hard work and service to the community. This picture was taken a few years before the family moved from Granite Falls, Minnesota, to Wallace, South Dakota, where Hubert Horatio Humphrey Jr. was born.

Humphrey at age three. "He was a happy child," the neighbors said, "and he made you feel good when he was around." Here he holds a picture book version of *Uncle Tom's Cabin*.

The prairie town of Wallace, South Dakota, around the time Humphrey was born in 1911. His father operated a drugstore on the ground level of the building at the left; the family lived upstairs. Humphrey was born on a Saturday morning in the upstairs bedroom facing Main Street.

The railroad station at Doland, South Dakota, the town in which Humphrey grew up. When he was a boy, he dreamed of "getting on a train and riding away from the flat prairie to exciting places."

On left: He left for the University of Minnesota in 1929, but the Depression forced him to return home to help his father in the drugstore. *On right:* Minneapolis, in 1947. Humphrey revered FDR and won a reputation as the hardest working Mayor in the city's history.

A new Senator from Minnesota, a new house in Washington and a growing family. *Left to right:* Humphrey, his wife Muriel, and children Nancy, Hubert Horatio III, Robert and Douglas in 1950.

Above: Senators John F. Kennedy and Hubert H. Humphrey in January, 1960, soon after they announced their candidacies for President of the United States.

Below: Humphrey campaigned in the Wisconsin and West Virginia Presidential primary elections, lost both to Kennedy and withdrew from the race before the Democratic Convention of 1960.

Genack Studio

Above: Some people complain that Humphrey "lacks dignity," but others call him "the best unofficial ambassador we have." In 1961, in Venezuela on a mission for the Senate, Humphrey paused to play baseball with the boys of a slum near Caracas. He hit a home run.

Below: Humphrey spent more than six years in the Senate working—often alone—for a U.S. effort to secure disarmament and arms control agreements. In September, 1963, President Kennedy signed the treaty suspending testing of nuclear weapons in the atmosphere. For list of those pictured see page 327.

Yes, This is a wonderful ~~for~~ time in which to live. It challenges the best in us. It calls for doing the impossible performing ~~miracles~~. Mediocrity must give way to excellence; ~~timidity~~ to daring; fear to courage.

We dream of sending a man to the moon in this decade. We know that dream will be fulfilled only with sacrifice, a commitment a plan and program. But we shall do it.

Our greater responsibility—an even more ~~~~ demanding challenge ~~~~

Humphrey rarely writes more than a few words with his own hand; he prefers to dictate. This is a rare example of his own writing, two pages of notes for a speech is to achieve mankinds dream and hope of ~~those~~ a better world through sacrifice & commitment, a plan and a program.

Our strength is not to be measured only by our ~~strength military~~ our industry, our technology; the ~~real~~ strength of a free society is in its people — ~~their desire~~ and their commitment to freedom and social justice.

With such standards our nation will be ~~remembered known~~ not for the power of our weapons, but for the power of our compassion, and the strength of our dedication to human welfare.

he made in 1962. They sum up many of the basic elements of his personal and political philosophy. For text see page 327.

Marty Nordstrom

Above: Humphrey and President Kennedy developed a warm and deep friendship—as well as a political alliance—from 1961 until the President's death. Humphrey was grief-stricken but on the day after the assassination, November 23, 1963, he said positively, "I want to remember President Kennedy as a vital, active, creative, living human being...."

Below: Humphrey's relationship with President Johnson has been more formal than with Kennedy. But ultimately, Johnson brought Humphrey closer to the Presidency by naming him as his choice for Vice President.

13

The Edge of Dixie

Hubert Humphrey arrived in Washington in December 1948 with a shallow national reputation based on little more than his civil rights speech at the Democratic Convention. The new Senator from Minnesota, a St. Louis *Post-Dispatch* correspondent wrote, "will inevitably become known as 'The Voice.'" *Time* magazine portrayed Humphrey on its front cover as the product of a cyclonic wind out of the Midwest, and described him as "a glib, jaunty spellbinder with a 'listen-you-guys' approach." In its own jaunty style, *Time* said: "Hustling Hubert Humphrey doesn't fit the usual conception of a U. S. Senator . . . He talks and looks more like a high-school science teacher who coaches basketball on the side." Reporter Joseph Driscoll noted, "Nature gifted young Humphrey with a superb larynx, an agile mind and an inexhaustible supply of steam." In his first few weeks in Washington his voluble manner strengthened the superficial impression that he was more voice than man.

Henry James said that Washington "is a city of conversation." Humphrey did not converse; he lectured, giving the impression that he regarded the nation's capital as another county fair and that he expected to dazzle its leading personalities with his eloquence and knowledge. A Minnesota businessman with influential contacts in Washington hosted an informal dinner at the exclusive Cosmos Club for Humphrey and a variety of V.I.P.'s. The dinner was intended to be a simple get-acquainted session of relaxed conversation. Humphrey talked without pause for an hour and a half, and in the memory of one participant "hurt himself with these men by acting as though he knew more about everything than anybody." At an equally informal luncheon in the Metropolitan

Club sponsored by two Administration officials, he grabbed the center of attention and would not let go. One guest, a liberal and a top White House Aide, recalls his reaction: "I had looked forward to meeting Humphrey, but I had a terrible first impression of him from that lunch. He was all blather. He was ready to take over Washington; I had seen many Washington novices like that. He bragged endlessly about what he had done as Mayor, and boasted about some of the tough things he had done with the Minneapolis police. I was shocked by the stories this great 'liberal' told about how he had ignored all the civil liberties to get things done. He came in with the idea of taking over Washington. He acted as though he knew it all."

Humphrey, young and impatient, was nervous in the stuffy atmosphere and formal society of Washington, and sensed that he was not making a good first impression. He admitted fifteen years later, "Back in Minneapolis, I was a successful Mayor and a respected politician, and everybody liked me. In that first period in Washington, I was out of it. I was miserable. I felt like going home." Mrs. Humphrey, reeling under the responsibilities of managing four young children, a new home, and dozens of unexpected social obligations, told a reporter two weeks after she arrived, "I had no idea it would be so awful."

There were, of course, moments of pleasure, excitement, and respectful attention. Humphrey made a down payment on a new house in suburban Chevy Chase, Maryland. With his higher salary as a Senator, he could afford two cars, a Dodge sedan for himself and a Plymouth station wagon for his wife. In the two months between his election and installation as a Senator he reveled in the flow of twelve thousand letters and hundreds of invitations.

The new Senator concluded that he had a right to make at least one request of the White House. When his parents arrived from South Dakota, he phoned White House Appointments Secretary Matt Connelly to ask if he could bring them in to meet President Truman. "Sure," Connelly answered, "how about this afternoon?" Humphrey, a bit overwhelmed, suggested that they wait until his mother and father had a chance to unpack. On the afternoon before New Year's Day he and Connelly escorted the Humphrey Sr.'s into the President's office. "Dad had never been in the White House before, and it was the high point of his life," he remembers.

"President Truman was kind and gracious, particularly to Mom." Mrs. Humphrey Sr., awed by her presence in the President's private office, nervously said to Truman, "I'm just scared to death to come in here." The President gave her a gentle hug, and answered, "Oh, we're just folks here." Then he personally conducted them on a tour through the White House.

On January 3, 1949, Humphrey stood in the back of the Senate chamber and heard Chief Clerk Edward Mansur call his name. Minnesota's Senior Senator, Edward Thye, escorted him to the edge of the rostrum, where he was formally sworn in with New Jersey's Robert C. Hendrickson, Wyoming's Lester C. Hunt, and Colorado's Edwin C. Johnson. The new Junior Senator from Minnesota walked back to his desk, the tenth to the right of the center aisle in the rear row of the Democratic side. He gulped hard as he looked at the new brass plate bearing his name on the desk top, and then searched the gallery above for his wife and parents. Humphrey Sr., "with a glow around his head like one of those medieval religious paintings," dabbed at his eyes with a handkerchief. The proud father said later, "He's going to be a great Senator. Maybe he's going to be something else, too."

Humphrey was impressed by the automatic boost in stature conferred on him by Senate membership, and a bit confused by some of the mechanics and protocol of his new job. Columnist Drew Pearson invited him to a party. Radio commentator Edward R. Murrow asked him to appear on a network program. Two speaking invitations offered the amazing fees of twenty and twenty-five dollars. (In Minnesota the standard fee had been five dollars; by 1961, Humphrey's worth as a guest speaker would rise to a thousand dollars.) For the President's State of the Union Message to Congress he first sat by mistake in a row reserved for Cabinet members. He had to ask his assistant, William Simms, to find out "when in hell do we get paid." Oklahoma's new Senator, Robert Kerr, explained to him that a Senator had the privilege of summoning an elevator with three quick rings of the bell. Humphrey met other freshmen members of the Senate during the first week. At one reception for members of Congress he pulled a tall, lanky man across the room to meet his wife. "Muriel," he said enthusiastically, "this is that new liberal Democratic Senator from Texas, Lyndon Johnson. He and I are friends."

Contrary to myth, Humphrey did not irritate tradition-minded
Senators with a stream of Senate speeches in his first days and
weeks in the chamber. Aware of an unwritten rule that freshmen
Senators, like children, should be seen and not heard, he waited
almost three months before uttering his first words other than
"Aye" or "No" on votes. In March, on the urging of Montana
Senator James Murray, he made his maiden Senate address, a brief
and reasoned argument for a bill to establish a Missouri Valley
Authority comparable to TVA. "I speak for our citizens," he said,
"who live amidst great potential wealth, surrounded by wealth
that is locked up and going unused." That basic theme of his first
Senate speech—the untapped resources and energies of the United
States—would become central to many of his statements and policies through the years.

His first speech unlocked what one reporter called "a torrent of
words cascading from Humphrey's velvet tongue." But not all of
the opinion leaders and pace-setters in Washington frowned upon
or ridiculed his free and fast voice. One veteran Congressional
reporter remembers that he thought "Humphrey was a breath of
fresh air in the stuffy atmosphere of the Senate." Blair Moody, a
reporter for the Detroit *News* (and later a Senator himself), wrote
on April 8, 1949:

"For weeks, all through the civil rights row, all through the
Marshall Plan 'slowdown,' the upper hand in Senate debates has
generally been held by Republicans.

"Majority Leader Lucas is so full of verbal needles, flicked
across the aisle by Minority Leader [Kenneth] Wherry, that he
must feel a little like a porcupine. Senator [Tom] Connally of
Texas, the Foreign Affairs Chairman, gets caught off base by a
quick question . . . Republicans [Arthur] Vandenberg, [William]
Knowland and [Henry Cabot] Lodge have repeatedly had to gal-
lop to his rescue.

"But nobody had to rescue Democratic Senator Hubert Humphrey, the Minnesota freshman, when a whole bevy of Republican
isolationists took after him. Within a few minutes he was taking
after them. And before a hot hour's debate was over, even some of
the Republicans were laughing openly over what Humphrey had
done to their isolationist colleagues . . .

"He launched into an attack on everything the GOP isolationists had been arguing for for a fortnight. He lectured them for not realizing that American aid to Europe is a keynote of our drive for peace. He quoted Scriptures and said that if it would help bring peace, the United States should do not less, but more."

During that debate isolationist Senators jabbed at Humphrey about his association with the ADA, the ADA's association with a program to send American students to England, and England's association with "socialism." Humphrey answered:

"The place we hear all this talk of socialism is right here on the Senate floor. What they are thinking about and boasting about in Britain is their effort to meet human needs."

New Hampshire Senator Styles Bridges defiantly asked, "What have the British got that we haven't got?" Bridges' question was barely completed when Humphrey snapped back, "Westminster Abbey!" Reporters and visitors in the galleries laughed, Bridges blushed, and liberal Senators stepped over to congratulate Humphrey on his quick mind and debating skill.

But a quick mind, an agile tongue, and youthful energy were not enough to win respect and effectiveness in the United States Senate of 1949 and the early 1950's. Humphrey was a fervid New Dealer in a period when many Congressional leaders believed that the New Deal was dead, and good riddance. He was clearly identified as a Truman Democrat during an Administration when the President's Gallup-rated popularity often dipped below 40 percent. He was the voice of Bryan, Wilson, Roosevelt, and Truman in a time when the American people elected a Republican President, Dwight Eisenhower, and a Republican majority in both houses of Congress. He was a man who seemed too sure of himself in what Churchill had called "These anxious and baffling times." He was a left-wing, ADA officer in a period when right-wingers Joseph McCarthy, William Jenner, and other Communist-hunters filled Washington with fear and dominated the headlines of the nation's newspapers. He was, above all, a liberal in a time of what historian Richard Hofstadter described as "the rudderless and demoralized state of American liberalism" in the years after Roosevelt's death. The tide to the left of 1948 eddied into a muddy political pool in the early 1950's.

It was not an easy time for a liberal, or for any freshman Senator. The divisions of the people and their political leaders were sharp and tightly drawn. Debates in Congress were often bitter. No conscientious Senator could stay out of the hard-fought battles over foreign aid, the Taft-Hartley Act, the McCarran-Walter Immigration Act, the spread of international communism, the Korean War, the control of atomic energy, McCarthyism, and civil rights. The task of building a respectable image and a new political career was particularly delicate for a young man whose public image went no deeper than the sound of his high-pitched "glib" voice, and almost impossible when he spoke out aggressively on the issues. Humphrey stood by Truman when many were denouncing the President for indifference to domestic scandal and "softness" on communism. He defended Secretary of State Dean Acheson, who defended Alger Hiss, who was later branded by most of the public as a Communist sympathizer and was convicted in the courts of perjury. He publicly debated John Foster Dulles when that Secretary of State was being lauded for the new Republican Administration's policies of "massive retaliation," "hurling back the Iron Curtain," and "unleashing Chiang."

In his first years in Washington, Humphrey was often labeled a "pipsqueak" or "whippersnapper" and ridiculed as "the gabbiest freshman in the Senate." Mrs. Humphrey, upset by the snide paragraphs in newspaper stories and the sarcastic comments on the cocktail circuit about her husband (and oppressed by Washington's heavy, damp climate), remembers, "It was rough." Humphrey, thinking back to the tensions of the time and his conflicts with the more powerful political elders of Washington, says in rhyme to his wife's words, "It was tough."

Already depressed by his shaky beginning in Washington, he was almost devastated by the death of his father in November 1949. At the beginning of that year Humphrey Sr. had sat in the master bedroom of the Chevy Chase home and told his son, "I don't think I'll be here a year from now. I want to discuss some of your mother's needs and some of the problems at the drug store which will probably come up." Humphrey, surprised and shocked, responded, "Why do you talk that way? Don't you feel good?" His father said he felt fine, but that he had a "premonition" that he would not live out the year. His son listened patiently to his practical instructions about how he wanted his will executed. Humphrey Sr. spoke quietly, as always, and without fear.

The older man went back to his regular schedule of work after his visit to Washington. Humphrey was consumed with his legislative and political duties. He did not think about the conversation until the fall, when his father suffered a stroke. Humphrey Sr. held on for three weeks. (Doctors said he had "the strong heart of a young man.") He died of a massive cerebral hemorrhage at the age of sixty-seven, in a Minneapolis hospital.

("I didn't know where to turn," Humphrey said a decade and a half later. "I often went to Dad for advice. He was so wise and good. I still miss my Dad.")

In January, he returned to Washington for the second session of the 81st Congress. In February 1950 he made what still ranks as the worst mistake of his sixteen-year legislative career. He attacked the purpose and disputed the worth of the favorite project of the Senate's patriarch of power: a small committee with the ponderous title of "The Joint Committee on the Reduction of Nonessential Federal Expenditures," chaired by Senator Harry Flood Byrd of Virginia. Above all other elements in Humphrey's personal and political reputation in 1950, his identification as a Northerner and civil rights advocate was the most vivid. School children and federal bureaucrats at that time may have believed that Washington was, truly, a national capital and the cradle of Abraham Lincoln's Union, but it was, in 1949 and 1950, a Southern city. It was Southern in appearance, with the magnolia blossoms of short springtimes giving way to the humidity of long, hot summers; in taste, with white linen suits and frilly cotton dresses seen often on the people in downtown restaurants, which featured black-eyed peas and hush puppies; in atmosphere, with the slow pace of a small town at the edge of a lazy river running through nearby orchard and grazing lands. It was southern in its physical makeup, with grand public buildings and palatial private residences a stone's throw from grim and crowded Negro slums; in its municipal legal and social character, with Negroes excluded from downtown restaurants, lunch counters, theaters and hotels, from "white only" schools, recreation facilities, and—of course—cemeteries, from "decent" churches, "good" jobs, and such professional groups as the District of Columbia Medical Society and the D.C. Bar Association. Today Washington is a Northern-oriented city with no legal segregation, but in 1949 and 1950 it was a little piece of Dixie wedged into a cozy corner of Maryland.

The Senate was the citadel of the South in a changing capital and nation. It was dominated by Southerners; most of them considered themeslves to be ambassadors from their states and not officials of the federal government. By seniority Southerners held the chairmanships of most Senate committees. Because of their long presence and comfortable electability in one-party states, they had the time to set the tone and preserve the traditions of a chamber through which most Northerners passed for only one or two terms. Through their political skill in forging coalitions with Republican conservatives, Southern Democrats managed often to make the states' rights view prevail over the civil rights position of Presidents and Congressional majorities. The Democratic Party may have abandoned the two-thirds vote rule for its national conventions, but that rule remained sacred in the Senate.

No two men could have been more different politically and personally than Hubert Horatio Humphrey and Harry Flood Byrd, the reigning monarch of the Senate's Southern lions in 1950. Humphrey was a "grass roots" politician; Byrd controlled his state party "machine." Byrd was sixty-two, Humphrey thirty-eight. The young Minnesotan's voice and physical features were sharp; the old Virginian's voice was soft, and his face had the rounded contours of an aged cherub. Humphrey lived in a modest corner house in a residential suburb in Maryland. Byrd's Virginia estate, surrounded by dogwood trees and rolling hills of apple orchards, was almost as magnificent as Jefferson's Monticello, a hundred miles to the south, and only slightly less steeped in tradition than the Trappist monastery ten miles west of Byrd's home town of Berryville. (Most of Berryville's conservative residents, favoring Richard Nixon, were not at all pleased when eighty monks left the monastery for the first time in 1960 to come into town and vote for John F. Kennedy for President.)

Senator Byrd is a kindly, generous man. He would have ignored or tolerated criticism of his Joint Committee's work from the young and eager Humphrey—if it had been properly advanced. William White, writing about the Senate in his 1957 book *Citadel,* said that Southerners could forgive Humphrey for what he had done at the Democratic Convention "because that happened before he was a Senator" and because he was young. But White also wrote: "The Senate type . . . is in many senses more an institutional man than a public man." Harry Byrd epitomized the proper Senate type of 1950. And Hubert Humphrey violated every institutional propriety of the Senate in his speech attacking Byrd's Joint Committee.

Humphrey stood up in the Senate chamber on February 24 to deliver his speech. It was not long—less than two thousand words— and he did not attack Byrd personally or directly. But that did not matter. By attacking the merit and motivation of the Joint Committee he might as well have driven a dagger into Byrd's fiscal and legislative soul. The committee represented the heart of Byrd's thinking as an advocate of economy in government and symbolized his role as a budget cutter. Humphrey also violated Senate propriety number one by speaking on the subject without Byrd's presence in the chamber. If he had checked, he would have learned that Byrd was not present because his mother was seriously ill and he was staying near her bedside that day. Humphrey also made the mistake of delivering his speech in the middle of a debate on a bill for cotton and peanut acreage allotments involving Senators John Stennis and James Eastland of Mississippi and Spessard Holland of Florida.

Humphrey proclaimed, "The continued existence of the Joint Committee on the Reduction of Nonessential Federal Expenditures is a violation of the spirit of the Legislative Reorganization Act, as well as a waste of the taxpayers' dollars . . ."

The Southerners, incredulous that anyone could dare to suggest that Harry Byrd would intentionally waste the taxpayers' dollars, slapped their hands to their foreheads in dismay. A few reporters, generally friendly to Humphrey, shook their heads sadly at what they considered his political and legislative blunder.

Humphrey garrulously repeated the phrase "I charge." He charged that the very existence of the committee was a "wanton waste and extravagance." He charged that the hundred thousand dollars appropriated for the committee staff and printing costs "stands as the number one waste of the taxpayers' dollars." He charged that the committee "serves no useful purpose, and is merely used as a publicity medium." He charged that the committee's reports on the growth of federal bureaucracy were "undocumented." He charged that the committee "deals only in generalities and violates the purpose for which it was created by wasting public funds." He referred frequently to the Joint Committee as "the Byrd committee," and then introduced a bill (S. 1116) to abolish it.

Contrary to later reports, he did not realize after that first speech that he had made a mistake. He had simply delivered one of many speeches prepared for him by liberal friends. He had given the issue little thought beforehand, but had delivered the statement with his usual intensity. He ignored the cool stares of other Senators and almost forgot about the whole thing.

But Byrd felt wounded, or at least scratched, and rose on the Senate floor the following Thursday (March 2) to reply to the charges. He began quietly, "While I was absent from the floor of the Senate because of serious illness in my family, the Junior Senator from Minnesota attacked the Joint Committee on the Reduction of Nonessential Federal Expenditures." Other Senators on the floor nodded their heads with sympathy for Byrd and disgust for the carelessness of Humphrey.

Byrd calmly ripped into Humphrey's speech. With a tone of great logic and reason he proceeded step by step to "correct" what he called "nine misstatements."

Misstatement number one, Byrd explained, was Humphrey's charge that the appropriation for his committee was the number one example of waste. "This is not only a misstatement," Byrd said. "Even in this atomic age of superlatives it must go down as a superexaggeration." Byrd also noted, "While condemning an expenditure of $127,000 the Junior Senator from Minnesota seeks [in a bill he introduced the day before] a $250,000 appropriation for an examination of the coal industry."

Byrd referred to Humphrey's "misstatement" that the committee was a publicity medium, and commented with icy sarcasm, "As the Senator from Minnesota is a publicity expert himself . . . his statement should be regarded as a compliment."

Humphrey slumped in his chair and listened somberly as Byrd continued, "I have mentioned nine misstatements in two thousand words. This is an average misstatement in every two hundred and fifty words, and the Senator speaks like the wind." The Virginian waited for a ripple of chuckling by other Senators to subside, then he listed fifty committee efforts which he said resulted at least indirectly in savings of almost two and a half billion dollars through cuts made in the federal budget.

Byrd finally dropped a trump card by noting that the original suggestion to establish the committee had come from Roosevelt's Secretary of the Treasury, Henry Morgenthau. He concluded his formal statement in humble voice: "I have offered several times to resign [as Chairman of the Joint Committee]. I offered to resign when the Republicans took charge. I am perfectly willing to re-sign at any time." The Senate, he suggested, could abolish the Joint Committee if it wished, "but I do not want it done as a result of misinformation such as that which has been presented to the Senate."

Southern Democrats and conservative Republicans, loyal to the coalition and its leader, heeded the cue. Georgia's Walter George said resolutely that Byrd was "doing a magnificent job" as Chair-man of the Joint Committee. Others chanted the same theme, not mentioning Humphrey but simply lauding Byrd and defending the work of his committee. Butler of Maryland, Eastland of Missis-sippi, Wherry of Nebraska, and Stennis of Mississippi joined the chorus for the defense. As Stennis finished his remarks, both Hum-phrey and Williams of Delaware sought recognition from the Chair to speak. Fulbright of Arkansas, the Presiding Officer at that moment, recognized Byrd instead, who then yielded the floor to Williams. Humphrey glowered as Williams, Cain of Washington, and McKellar of Tennessee joined in the praises of the smiling Senior Senator from Virginia. Mundt of South Dakota was recog-nized, and Humphrey hopped up again to call to the Chair, "Mr. President, a parliamentary inquiry." Byrd snapped, "I yielded to the Senator from South Dakota." Mundt tried to begin his com-ment, but Humphrey cried, "Mr. President, a point of order." Humphrey challenged Byrd's process of yielding to other Senators for comments and not questions. Byrd won a unanimous consent ruling from the Chair that he could yield to whomever he wished. Humphrey complained sharply, "I contend that the rules of the Senate are being violated flagrantly." (He was right.) The Chair ignored him and recognized Ferguson of Michigan, Tobey of New Hampshire, and finally Styles Bridges of New Hampshire. All milked the moment for the last possible element of praise for Byrd and, indirectly, to jab the last possible needle into Humphrey.

Byrd, standing triumphant and surrounded by his allies, ended with a sly smile and a wry reference to Humphrey's protest about the rules: "Are there any further *questions?*" Senators on the floor and visitors in the galleries burst into laughter as Humphrey, alone and frowning, glanced around the pit of the Senate. "If not," Byrd concluded, "I yield the floor."

Humphrey was finally recognized. He began with heavy sarcasm, saying that he was "happy to see so many Senators on the floor" and twitting the Senate as a whole for its poor attendance the previous day for a speech by Connecticut's Brien McMahon, which he considered important. The twoscore Senators present glared silently at him, but he continued tactlessly:

"It would seem that this was testimonial day. This pleases me because I believe we should not wait until people pass to their heavenly reward before expressing our feelings about them. I think it is fine, although irrelevant to this issue, that the Senator from Virginia now knows how much some of his colleagues think of him and how much they appreciate him. It should give him a greater sense of warmth and security in his work." Byrd stared at him, not at all warmly. Humphrey awkwardly tried a touch of ironic humor:

"The Senator from Minnesota is no shrinking violet, and before the debate is over he will not be an apple blossom, either." This reference was to Byrd's business as proprietor of apple orchards near Berryville. No one laughed. Humphrey persisted:

"When I introduced the bill [to abolish Byrd's committee], I knew that I would set loose a hornets' nest, and I was advised that I'd be mowed down. There has been some lawn mowing going on today, but the shrinking violet has not been clipped." The silence in the chamber was heavy. Then in an unfortunately confusing transition of ideas and phrases, which made him sound callous and insincere, he added:

"I apologize for having introduced the bill in the Senator's [Byrd's] absence. I did not know the Senator was absent. I want to offer my sympathy and my condolences upon the illness of his beloved and dear mother . . . But I think that [Humphrey meant Byrd's absence, but to some it sounded as though he were speaking of the mother's illness] is an extraneous matter."

A single Senator, Paul Douglas of Illinois, came to Humphrey's defense. He had been in his office when he heard that "they were tearing Hubert apart," and ran to the chamber to try to help his friend in the "debate." But Humphrey was virtually alone. Reporters who were in the press gallery say that they will never forget the moment when a dozen Senators walked over to Humphrey, stood around him as if to isolate his figure, and then turned their backs on him and walked silently out of the chamber. At the end they used their ultimate weapon against the young, proud politician: indifference.

In the years since, the story of the Humphrey-Byrd fight of February 24 and March 2, 1950, has been oversimplified and embellished with reports that at the moment the Senate turned its back on him Humphrey realized the error of his ways and the need to reform himself. In truth, he stiffened his attack on the Joint Committee. Alone in the chamber except for Douglas and a few others, he ended his statement with a touching attempt to explain his basic position:

"It may not be a million dollars [which he had said the committee had cost during its existence], but, Mr. President, it is the principal of the thing that is important.

"On behalf of the people who believe in good government in America, I offered the proposal—and what a storm it has stirred up, a storm of protest not in behalf of the people or good government, but a storm of protest over the fact that anyone should dare touch the vested institutions of the vested coalition. I conclude by thanking my colleagues for the attention they have given me . . . and asking them to remember one thing—that while we are here together in a spirit of friendship in the Congress of the United States, and while it is a part of our code of ethics as gentlemen to be friendly and congenial one with another, our major responsibility is not the art of making friends—Dale Carnegie tells us how to do that; our major responsibility is to legislate."

Humphrey was hurt, but not at all contrite. His final words in the session were: "I commend my bill to abolish the Joint Committee on Reduction of Nonessential Federal Expenditures because I say the Joint Committee itself is nonessential." He did not stop there. He stubbornly made another statement denouncing the committee on May 31. He added another in June. And he inserted an article in the Congressional Record, criticizing Byrd's record of voting against proposals of the Truman Administration. All were ignored by the rest of the Senate; the committee continued its work and Byrd continued as Chairman.

It did not matter much in 1950 whether Humphrey's basic argument about the committee was right or wrong. Years later he still insisted that his substantive criticisms were correct and that he was right in bringing them to the Senate's attention. He also admitted to one of the Southern Senators, who had become a friend, "That was the worst mistake I ever made in the Senate." Gradually, and in retrospect, he learned two lessons from the painful experience. The first was that a Senator could not expect to win a fight if he did not know his subject thoroughly, did not have all the facts on his side, and did not understand "the Senate process." The second—and more important—lesson was one which he has repeated frequently to young men who have come to him for advice: "In the Senate it is not as important *what* a man says as *how* he says it."

A man, a politician, and a Senator learns from experience, and Humphrey learned from his rather grim experiences in his first year and a half in Washington. But it took time. He could not be calm or philosophical immediately after the disaster of his clash with Harry Byrd and the institution of the Senate. He had been humiliated, and he knew it.

On the night of March 2, 1950, he worked late in his office. Leaving Room 452 of the Senate Office Building, he walked to the end of a long, ornately decorated corridor and rang three times for an elevator. As he stepped out on a lower floor, he stood in the path of Senator Byrd. The old man and the young man eyed each other for a moment, and Humphrey managed to comment, "I guess I know when I've been run over by a Mack truck." Byrd drove off to his home beyond the Potomac in the rolling hills of Virginia. Humphrey got into his Dodge and drove across most of the width of Washington toward his house in Maryland. His car rolled down Capitol Hill and away from the dark grounds fringed with azaleas. He headed north, and passed block after block of crumbling slum dwellings crowded with Negro families. His car moved around buses filled with Negroes but driven by white men. He edged past segregated churches, segregated schools, segregated parks, segregated cemeteries. He drove by restaurants and hotels with little white cards on the doors warning: WHITE ONLY.

His mood in that hour can best be described by quoting a French diplomat who arrived in America from Paris in 1800, soon after the federal government had moved the capital from Philadelphia to the more Southerly location which had just been named "Washington." The French Minister, it is reported, took one look at the scene of his new assignment and cried:

"My God! What have I done to be condemned to reside in such a city?"

14

Acceptance

His first year and a half in the Senate, Hubert Humphrey told a group of teachers in 1963, "was the most miserable period of my life." The main reason was that he was outside the circle of socially acceptable, politically effective men in the institution of the Senate and the city of Washington. He came with a reputation as an uncompromising, undignified, unrestrained, impulsive man who was more loyal to the President and personal principle than to the Congressional establishment. His clash with the essential elements of the Senate institution was inevitable. As a man with a driving urge to be politically effective and personally popular, he was inevitably unhappy during the 81st Congress. In his first bow on the Washington stage he fell on his face.

He is not, however, a man who runs away from trouble or is inhibited by ridicule. The boy who had continued to play baseball with a broken arm and could finish his lines in a school play despite a torn costume had become a man who refused to be sidelined or embarrassed by the painful results of his clash with Senator Harry Byrd in March 1950. He made many mistakes, but he learned from them. Woodrow Wilson had said that new Senators tended either "to grow or to swell." Humphrey grew.

Max Kampelman, who followed him to Washington as his legislative assistant, remembers that Humphrey became "obsessed" with a desire to "master the Senate process." He had no intention of abandoning his convictions or assuming the role of a silent errand boy for constituents and a subservient member of the Senate establishment. But he was determined to understand the Senate and its rules, to heed its proprieties, and to learn how to move through its field of force. He was also less inclined, after the clash

with Byrd, to tackle subjects on which he had not prepared himself or to begin orating from ghosted speeches to which he had
only given a cursory glance. "Give me the facts," he ordered his
staff before a Senate debate or preparation of a floor statement. "I
want the facts, ALL of them."

On August 29, 1950, after several days of study on federal tax
law, he introduced twelve amendments to that year's tax bill. His
intention, he had advised Senate friends, was to close "loopholes"
in the law which he claimed cost the government billions of dollars of tax revenue each year. In contrast to his speech against the
Byrd committee in March, his words and manner were positively
humble when he rose in the Senate to deliver his first speech on
the tax bill.

"This subject," he said, "is one of the most complex to face
the Congress of the United States . . . In addressing the Senate
now, Mr. President—and I say this in particular to the very
distinguished and able Chairman of the [Finance] committee
[Walter George, of Georgia]—I do not do so with confidence of
mastery of tax law, because this is a new experience for me, but
rather with a desire to know more about this important subject."

Then he criticized a provision in the federal tax law, "often
abused" by businessmen, which permitted a one-year-old child to
be made a corporation partner, for tax purposes. Senator Eugene
Millikin, the senior Republican on the Finance Committee, was
not impressed with either Humphrey's humility or his interpretation of the law.

"I have never seen," Millikin retorted, "and I have never heard
such a perversion of clear-cut language of an amendment as we
have just witnessed." Several other Senators sought recognition to
speak. Humphrey, concerned about the time his statement would
consume, said, "There are going to be ten more amendments."
Millikin snapped, "Then there will be ten more perversions, if
that is the Senator's pattern." Later in the debate on Humphrey's
amendments the discussion lapsed into an exchange of mockery by
Millikin and humor by Humphrey.

Millikin: "The distinguished Junior Senator from Minnesota
[is] suspicious that there is a devil in corporations, that the devil
must be flogged, and that the sin must be beaten out of him . . ."

Humphrey: "I never have . . ."

Millikin: "I am delighted to hear this confession of repentance."

Humphrey: "Repentance? It is merely a reaffirmation of faith. A man cannot repent unless he is with sin."

Millikin: "Unless he cannot distinguish between virtue and vice."

The debate continued, with frequent and lengthy interruptions of Humphrey's prepared statement advocating his tax loophole amendments. He had begun at 2 P.M. At 7 P.M., Senator Williams of Delaware complained, "We started at two o'clock to listen to a one-hour speech. I never heard of a one-hour speech stretching into five hours." Humphrey responded pleasantly, "I should like to ask that the Senator from Minnesota be allowed to take care of himself. The Senator from Minnesota feels fine, and he will continue his address." He finished his address, and the Senate finished all twelve of his amendments with lop-sided, negative votes.

But he continued his study, convinced, according to Kampelman, that the key to political power was fiscal policy and that the key to fiscal policy was tax legislation. Humphrey assigned his research assistants to spend more of their time on tax law. Kampelman met for lunch with Charles Davis, a professional staff member of the House Ways and Means Committee, to talk taxes. He told Davis that Humphrey wanted to work toward closing tax loopholes, as did many of the members of the House committee. "Does he know anything about taxes?" Davis asked. "Not much," Kampelman admitted. "Is he smart?" Davis asked. "Yes," said Kampelman. The two men called in a group of federal tax law experts for an informal and unofficial meeting with Humphrey. The experts, including some from the Treasury Department, began by stressing that tax law was a highly complex subject and very difficult to master, particularly for someone without formal legal or economic training. Humphrey rubbed his hands eagerly. "I'm *magna cum laude.* I'll learn. Teach me."

They did, in long day-and-night sessions over several weeks. The initial group of tax experts called in other tax law specialists. They briefed Humphrey, answered his questions, and repeatedly questioned him to test his quickly increasing knowledge. Kampelman remembers, "They were amazed. The subject had taken them years to learn. Humphrey mastered the essence, plus immense detail, of tax law in a few months." In the end Humphrey ordered the experts to prepare twenty amendments which he would introduce to the 1951 tax bill which had been prepared and approved by the Senate Finance Committee. He asked his old liberal friend (and a former economics professor) Senator Paul Douglas to help.

On September 20, 1951, he introduced his twenty amendments to close tax loopholes and opened a debate which lasted for a week. "Mr. President," he said, "I rise to discuss the tax bill and at the same time to serve notice that I intend to join with a number of my colleagues in offering a large number of amendments which we believe will improve the bill."

According to Kampelman, Walter George and Eugene Millikin —the two powers of the Finance Committee—sneered with disdain. No Senator had ever seriously challenged their committee's recommendation. Through the years the Senate had all but automatically rubber-stamped tax bills as originated in the House and amended by the Senate Finance Committee. The committee's ten weeks of hearings, its senior members believed, were more than enough to satisfy the need for public and private discussion on the bill, and they fully expected the committee's 349-page report on the bill to be approved quickly and decisively by the Senate.

Humphrey spoke for less than two minutes, then Oklahoma Senator Robert Kerr broke in to question his qualifications for discussing the intricacies of tax law. Several Senators implied that Humphrey was simply reading a prepared speech on a subject about which he knew nothing. He answered, "I have spent two months in arduous labor preparing myself for this moment."

Senators George and Millikin, at first peremptory and brusque with him, interrupted his address with detailed and technical questions to challenge his knowledge. Humphrey, politely and respectfully, answered them. Once he followed an answer with a deferential question of his own: "May I respectfully ask the distinguished Chairman of the Finance Committee, who knows far more about this subject than the Junior Senator from Minnesota, if I am correct on this point?" George grudgingly responded, "Yes. Apparently you have your facts right."

Humphrey proceeded to claim "shocking abuses" of the tax law's split-income provisions for married couples. Kerr, a tall and physically powerful man with a cordially cutting debate technique, rose to ask:

"The Senator from Minnesota realizes, does he not, that the split-income provision is available to every husband and wife?"

Humprey: "Yes, and that kind of equality is something like the equality of which Anatole France spoke when he said that the rich and the poor alike can sleep under a bridge."

Kerr: "Does the Senator mean that the husband and the wife can sleep in the same bed?"

Humphrey: "I wish to keep away from marital problems."

Kerr: "Does the Senator from Minnesota regard that as a marital problem?"

Humphrcy: "I do not know about that, but it could be."

Humphrey smiled at the exchange, but he refused to be rattled or agitated by Kerr's good-natured needling. He stuck to the serious issues involving his tax bill amendments.

The Senate, usually two thirds empty during the periodic and normally perfunctory tax debates, was interested and aroused. Humphrey, Douglas, and a few others were challenging the powerful Finance Committee, and they were doing it seriously and ably. George, Millikin, and Kerr knew that they would win the fight, but they also realized as the debate progressed that they were dealing with a worthy and well-trained opponent. In the Senate such an attitude is reflected by little extra courtesies. After standing in one spot for several hours Humphrey was able to leave the debate and the chamber for a few minutes to gulp down a sandwich when Kerr asked for a quorum call, a parliamentary device to suspend debate for short periods. Humphrey returned to resume his address, after first saying, "I thank my friend, the Senator from Oklahoma, for giving me the benefit of a quorum call. It is very much appreciated."

The debate continued the next day, Friday, and through all the following week. As it neared the end, Humphrey, Douglas, and their few allies realized that they could not possibly win on their amendments. Tempers occasionally flared. At one point Douglas said on the floor, "I hope . . . we will not allow this bill to be jammed down our throats." Majority Leader Ernest McFarland of Arizona (Scott Lucas had been defeated in his Illinois re-election campaign in 1950) angrily refuted suggestions from a few others that he was "railroading" the bill through the Senate. Humphrey remained relatively calm. "I don't know why we are scrapping," he said, nudging the debate back to germane discussion of the amendments. Reporters noted what seemed—in contrast to the scenes of the Humphrey-Byrd clash of seven months before—a phenomenal sight: after one day of debate Walter George walked to Humphrey's back-row desk and shook his hand; Millikin stepped across the center aisle, put his arm around Humphrey's shoulder, and congratulated him on his knowledge of tax law and his debating skill.

All of Humphrey's amendments were rejected by more than two-to-one margins. His amendment to modify the oil depletion allowance was trounced, 71 to 9. On Friday, September 28, the tax bill as reported and revised by the Senate Finance Committee (H.R. 4473) was approved, 57 to 19. Humphrey and Douglas voted against final passage.

Humphrey's amendments lost, but he won new respect for his willingness to study a subject thoroughly, for his skill in debate, for the quickness of his mind, and above all, for his observance of the Senate's institutional proprieties and his recognition of the dignity and power of the Senate's patriarchs. The older members still frowned at the length of his speeches and lectured him about some of his impatient and uncompromising views, but they began to look at him more seriously, to offer him friendly advice and occasional help for an obscure bill which would be popular in Minnesota. They even began to like him, and occasionally to pull their punches in debate. September 1951 marked the beginning of the Senate's acceptance of Humphrey.

In 1954, when he was up for re-election after completing his first term, Senator George offered to campaign for him in Minnesota or write letters to its businessmen if Humphrey "thought it might help." Humphrey's improved relationships crossed party lines. Republican Millikin, who at first treated him with patronizing disdain, felt friendly enough a few years later to engage in humorous exchanges with his tax law adversary. In a debate on March 30, 1954, on a conference report on the excise tax bill (H.R. 8224), they traded good-natured barbs as Millikin defended and Humphrey criticized President Eisenhower's fiscal policies.

"No member of this body," Humphrey said of Millikin, "is

more able to divert the argument from the theme which has
been set for it. Of course, diversions are delightful; they are like
the side shows to a main performance, and sometimes the side
shows are more spectacular . . ."

He turned to the issue of the debate, arguing that the Eisenhower Administration's fiscal policies were "confused and un-
clear." Paul Douglas, sitting a few desks away, nodded his head in
agreement with the charge. After watching and listening intently
Millikin interrupted to tell a story about an attorney who sat
outside a courthouse to watch the pigeons. The attorney was asked
if he was a pigeon fancier. "No," he replied, according to Millikin's
story, "but I am learning something about my opponents. Every
time one says something, the other opponents nod their heads in
the affirmative. Notice the pigeons. They are constantly shaking
their heads in the affirmative." Millikin, turning to Humphrey
and Douglas, said, "That is the act of the Senator from Illinois and
the Senator from Minnesota."

Humphrey: "I thank the Senator for comparing us to the pigeons . . ."

Millikin: "I would not suggest that this comparison applies to
any of my colleagues . . . However, I remind the Senator from
Minnesota and the Senator from Illinois that a comparison might
be made with a monkey climbing a pole. The higher he goes, the
more he exposes his posterior."

Humphrey: "Now we have covered practically every animal.
Confused as the Administration may be on fiscal policy, it is expert
on the zoo."

Millikin: ". . . There are some politicians whose posteriors can
be seen on the dead level."

Humphrey: "Those are the ones we have been talking about."

Millikin: "Now the Senator is stealing my lines."

Humphrey: "It is a pleasure to steal the lines of the Senator
from Colorado."

Millikin: "Now may I go back [to the rear of the chamber] and
rest, to watch this scene with my torpid eyes?"

Humphrey: "The Senator may rest in peace."

The debate turned serious for about five minutes, with Humphrey, Douglas, and Russell Long of Louisiana discussing the ex-

cise tax bill. Douglas then quoted two lines from the Gilbert and Sullivan operetta *The Gondoliers:*

> "He led his regiment from behind—
> He found it less exciting."

Douglas: "Does not this describe the attitude of the Administration on this matter? . . . Would not that observation apply to our friend from Colorado, who now is preening himself with satisfaction because of the reduction in the tax on household appliances? . . ."

Humphrey: "The Senator from Colorado is so happy that he is chasing up the flagpole the monkey which he described a moment ago. He has joined the act."

Douglas: "Is it not true that the pole which he is climbing is very slippery?"

Humphrey: "Yes. The only regrettable thing is that, in chasing the monkey up the flagpole, what he desired as happening to the monkey may also happen to the Senator from Colorado."

Millikin: "Now that the Senator joins in associating me with these invidious animals—"

Humphrey: "A monkey is a delightful animal."

Millikin: "I was just hinting. The Senator from Illinois called me [the previous week] an alligator—"

Douglas: "A crocodile."

Millikin: "A crocodile, basking in the mud, keeping a torpid eye open, and occasionally becoming aroused and flailing his tail around . . . I am willing to bring the zoo tour to an end, although . . . there are some other animals I could mention. However, I do not think it would add much to the debate."

Humphrey: "I think we have done adequate honor to the zoo. I prefer to return to the consideration of the tax bill . . ."

Such colloquies may appear, to the outsider, to be frivolous and time-wasting. But they represent, along with the language of super-courtesy required by rules and tradition, a part of the Senate's ability to function as a legislative body. The Senate can be a cauldron of national conflicts, and the heat of debate could easily erupt into violence without the tension-breaking device of humor. The Japanese diet and the Italian parliament may, in their deliberations, be marked by greater seriousness than the United States

Senate. They also have more fist fights. "A sense of humor is more important in this place than intelligence," one veteran Senator says. "If you can't kid around or laugh in the Senate," says another, "you'll go crazy."

Humphrey's sense of humor served him well in the gradual process of acceptance by the Senate and has strengthened him in politics and life generally. In an address to a group of high school students in Arlington, Virginia, in June 1963, he said, "In a world full of conflict, tensions, and nuclear terror you have to work and laugh. The only other thing left is to be bitter and hate."

His humor is not the sophisticated wit and understatement which characterized John F. Kennedy, nor does he "tell stories" in the intricately detailed manner of Lyndon B. Johnson. In the middle of the 1964 election campaign E. W. Kenworthy wrote in *The New York Times:* "Of the four candidates for national office, [Humphrey] alone seems to be gifted with spontaneous humor." Even Republicans smiled when Humphrey, being heckled by student supporters of Barry Goldwater, said, "I don't care if you study ancient history, but don't *vote* for it."

Humphrey employs sarcasm, irony, and even slapstick, but his humor is more good-natured than malicious. He was the first person to describe the weekly report on Congress by Republicans Everett Dirksen and Charles Halleck (often called the "Ev and Charlie show") as "The Twilight Zone." At one dinner meeting of a Jewish organization in San Francisco he listened politely as a local Republican leader boasted about the bar mitzvahs he had recently attended. When Humphrey was introduced, he rose and without a word placed a yarmulke (Jewish skullcap) on his head.

Most of his joking is directed toward himself or political opponents, but he isn't afraid to tease friends. Reporters once overheard this exchange between Lyndon Johnson and Humphrey:

Johnson: "Where did you get that good-looking jacket?"

Humphrey: (Pretending to check the label of his new sportscoat) "It says here 'Neiman-Marcus, courtesy of Billie Sol Estes.' "

Humphrey's language can be amusing even when the point of his remark is serious. Complaining of the confusing organizational structure of one federal department, he once said, "It takes a ferret, two geiger counters, and three bloodhounds just to find out who's in charge." Remembering his modest financial status and the price of houses when he first arrived in Washington, he remarked, "I decided at first that we'd have to buy some sleeping bags and camp out in Rock Creek Park."

In a long debate with Everett Dirksen on the condition of Capitol Hill landscaping in the spring of 1963, he and the Senator from Illinois engaged in a half-serious, half-humorous argument about the distinction between flowers and shrubs:

Dirksen: "The Senator [Humphrey] speaks in glowing terms about the delicate shades of rhododendron. How wonderfully right he is, except that the rhododendron is a shrub. It is not a flower at all . . ."

Humphrey: ". . . We simple country folk call them flowers . . . but I take the Senator's word for it. His flowery language overwhelms me, and makes me feel he knows more about flowers than I will ever know. I will accept the statement of the Senatorial professor of horticulture."

Dirksen: "Whenever the Senator from Minnesota can convert the Senate or anyone else who is rooted in the soil to believe that a flower is a shrub, I will nominate him to the next vacant seat on the Supreme Court of the United States."

On another occasion Humphrey momentarily flustered New York's Kenneth Keating while the latter was defending the nation's folk singers against charges in a right-wing publication that their songs were Communist-inspired. To prove his point Keating was tediously reading the lyrics of one song when he was interrupted:

Humphrey: "I have examined the rules of the Senate . . . I do not recall seeing anything in the rules which would prohibit the Senator from singing, except his own good judgment."

Keating: "My voice is not of the best . . . I think it best that I do not sing [the lyrics]."

Humphrey: "Particularly without musical accompaniment."

Keating: "I would not be able to do that anyway. If I used a guitar, I would have to use a left-handed guitar."

Humphrey: "Let us not do anything 'left' around here."

Some of the more conservative Senators stiffly object to such levity in the austere chamber, but most members welcome the light interludes and humorous diversions in which Humphrey excels.

Senators lead a semi-cloistered life. They work in the same committee rooms and chamber, eat in the same private dining rooms, and—during evening debates—often sleep in the same cloakrooms while waiting for late votes. Some of them get sick of the sight of their colleagues by the end of a long Congressional session, but most develop a sense of camaraderie after a few years in the Senate. The nature and scope of their duties require most Senators to spend far more time with one another than with their families. Humphrey and Paul Douglas were both elected to the Senate in 1948. Humphrey's third son, Douglas, was born in 1948. There is no doubt that Humphrey saw much more of Senator Douglas than his son Douglas in the succeeding sixteen years.

Several Senators have suggested that Humphrey was accepted quickly in the institution because he is "a decent man you just like to have around." Humphrey's basic empathy applied as much to fellow Senators as to Minnesota voters. One apocryphal Senate story concerns a member whose mother had just broken her hip. "Everett Dirksen," the story goes, "grasped the Senator's elbow and whispered that he would offer a prayer for her. Lyndon Johnson held both of the Senator's hands and offered to pay the hospital bill. Hubert Humphrey put his head on the man's shoulder and cried."

A dozen Senators admitted in interviews in 1964 that they were irritated occasionally by Humphrey's frantic pace and long speeches, but most agreed that he was probably the only member of the Senate who did not have a personal enemy in the place. His humor and decency also appealed to most reporters.

Robert Albright wrote in the Washington *Post:* "However one rates him otherwise, he's a bright daub of color across the Senate's sepia landscape." Holmes Alexander, a columnist who said in early 1964 that his own political opinions were "to the right of Goldwater," remembers that Humphrey impressed him in their first meeting as "a good family man who talked affectionately about his sons." Alexander astounded many of his conservative readers by choosing Humphrey "Senator of the Year" in 1961. His judgment was based, in part, on Humphrey's "basic integrity and decency."

Humphrey probably spends more time on the little extra touches of human contact and courtesy than on the big and weighty substantive issues of politics and government. To one

Senator from the Deep South, with whom he battled periodically on civil rights, he sent this note:

Dear ——: You continue to be my Senatorial hero. Truly, ——, you are a remarkable man, and our country is ever indebted to you—indeed, all humanity is indebted to you—for your great leadership in the fields of [he named the man's special fields of legislation] . . . I felt this way the first year I was in the Senate, and each year my admiration and respect grow for you.

Yes, this is a fan letter. It necessitates no reply. I just wanted you to know, in the privacy of our personal lives, of my personal appreciation for what you have been doing and have done.

As ever, Your Friend
(Signed) Hubert H.

To another Senator, a Northern liberal angry with him about a specific vote, he dictated this letter in December 1963:

My dear ——: I hope you will forgive me for having asked our colleagues to vote against the Williams amendment—the so-called junk mail provision.

Like yourself, I feel that the mailing privileges extended to members of Congress have been misused in many instances . . . Having said this, you may wonder why I voted for a proposition that would permit members of the House of Representatives to send [franked mail to box-holders] throughout their districts . . . while denying Senators that privilege. I did so only because the legislative appropriation bill would never have cleared the House of Representatives unless that special privilege for House members was included. It was absolutely necessary that we have a legislative appropriation bill on the President's desk before we adjourned . . .

I have a duty as the Majority Whip to try to get action on these measures, even though at times it requires me to make compromises that I don't like. I just wanted you to know how I felt about it. If I had been in your position, I would have voted as you did.

I write this letter only because I admire you so much and respect your sense of decency and integrity.

As ever, Your Friend . . .

Such letters are not strictly necessary or expected in the Senate. Humphrey wrote them by the dozens, not just as a political tactic, but because he has a simple instinct to express his admiration for another man when he feels it and to soothe the ruffled feelings of a friend when he senses antagonism.

The same sense of fairness which has made him consistently ad- verse to racial intolerance or discrimination in any form has made him incapable of blanket condemnation of Senators from Southern states. The same sense of humanity which propelled him into leadership for the Civil Rights Act of 1964 compelled him to walk up to an Alabama Senator in the middle of the bitter debate on that legislation and say, "I hope this will all be over soon so we can be buddies again." The Southerner put his arm around Humphrey—away from the view of the press and public galleries—and answered, "Hubert, we'll always be buddies." Of the twelve Senators from the tier of Deep Southern states in 1964 (South Carolina, Georgia, Florida, Alabama, Mississippi, and Louisiana), there were only two with whom Humphrey did not have consistently cordial relationships. He could count at least six—half the group—as close and warm friends.

There were many reasons for these surprising friendships. Unlike many other highly principled, liberal Senators, Humphrey did not, after his first year and a half, stalk the corridors of the Capitol with a chip on his shoulder. At the end of a tough debate he often grabbed an opponent's arm and pulled him into the dining room off the chamber for a cup of coffee and relaxed conversation about the prospects of the latest farm bill or the collapse of the Washington baseball team.

Minnesota's essentially rural outlook and system of small farms matches those of most Southern states. It may have seemed strange to some in 1963 and 1964 that Hubert Humphrey, the liberal of Minnesota, and Herman Talmadge, the conservative of Georgia, joined their names to sponsor a major piece of legislation. But Minnesota and Georgia farmers could understand that the Humphrey-Talmadge cotton-dairy support bill was eminently logical.

Southern Senators tended to respect Humphrey for another reason. "He's an old Senate work hoss," said one privately. Often Humphrey has applied his energy to an obscure bill (such as cotton acreage allotments) of no direct value to Minnesota, but of prime interest to the South. Particularly in his work on the Senate Agriculture Committee he endeared himself to those who believed, as he did, that the "little guy," the tenant farmer in Mississippi or the marginal farmer in Minnesota, deserved a break from the federal government.

In late 1958, President Eisenhower vetoed a Democratic farm bill with liberal price support features. Near the end of the debate on the veto Humphrey derided what the Administration called "the sliding scale" of support for farm parity prices as "mostly sliding down for the small family farmer." His voice rose with evangelical ardor. "I did not come to the United States Senate," he cried, "to vote for fifty percent of a living wage for farmers." The phrase halted Georgia's Richard Russell, who had been walking toward a Senate exit. He paused to listen, then sat at a desk near Humphrey. Russell beckoned Olin Johnston of South Carolina and a few other Southerners to move closer to lend their sympathetic presence and moral support to Humphrey's fervid pleas for higher farm price supports. A Senate staff member sitting a few feet away remembers that the scene reminded him of a revival meeting. With missionary zeal Humphrey raced toward an eloquent climax to his appeal. Russell kept nodding his head up and down, mumbling aloud to Humphrey's statements, "Yes, that's right. Yes, that's absolutely right." Johnston chanted, "He's right. He's right." Another Southerner drawled again and again, "I agree. I agree." The Senate staff assistant was nervous. "I was afraid that at any moment they were all going to start shouting 'Hallelujah' and kneel down on the floor to be saved."

Humphrey's convictions on agricultural policy and his years of hard work on the Senate Agriculture Committee provided only one basis for a close working relationship with many Southern Senators. With individual Southern Senators he could usually find at least one other field of mutual interest: foreign relations, health programs, small business ("Why, Hubert's daddy was a druggist; so was mine!"), anti-trust laws or others.

In February 1962, CBS News correspondent Paul Niven asked Humphrey, "After your initial attitude on civil rights had alienated the Southerners from you, you have become quite close to them in recent years. How did this happen?" Humphrey's answer reflected some of his basic characteristics as a man and a politician, and helped to explain in part his acceptance in the Senate:

"I think we got to know each other. Somebody once said that if you want to dislike someone, don't get to know him. I think that when you get to know people, you become, in most instances, respectful—there is generally the possibility of . . . a friendship, or at least a warm acquaintanceship.

"We live together in the Senate, more so than any other group of people. We are very close physically, and we are close socially. We are close—sometimes—politically. Therefore I found that just being with my colleagues in the Senate has given me an opportunity to get to know them, and they, I think, to know me.

"I like the Southerners very, very much. They are real gentlemen. They are warmhearted people. They love politics, too. I know of no group that is more political, in the truest and the best sense of the word, than the Southern politicians. They are always filled with yarns about their family and their localities, their communities, their towns . . . They are . . . expert politicians. This I admire."

In his first term in the Senate, Humphrey was only moderately effective in dealing with the institution of the Senate. But because he was a politician, capable of relating himself to individuals of diverse opinions, he developed friendships and alliances with the men of the Senate. Southerners were not, he learned, snarling Simon Legrees with bourbon, instead of blood, in their veins and whips in their hands. And Humphrey, the Southerners discovered, was not a modern reincarnation of a Yankee abolitionist, eager to throw Molotov cocktails into the state capitols at Atlanta and Richmond. Year after year Humphrey and the Southerners battled on the basic issues of civil rights and states' rights. But they, perhaps far more than men of loose opinions or bland beliefs, could understand and respect one another.

15

Importance

In the Senate and in the broader sphere of national politics Hubert Humphrey could not be satisfied with acceptance and personal popularity in the 1950's. He wanted power and influence more than position and prestige. "I am a restless person," he once said. "When I see things that need to be done, I want to get at them. It bothers me when something isn't being done about a problem or need." He wanted to be effective, to be important.

Washington reporters and politicians disagree about the date on which he began to exert real influence. A few suggest that he assumed and held the role of an important national figure with his civil rights speech at the Democratic National Convention in 1948. One columnist believes that the point of power was not reached until he was nominated for the Vice Presidency in 1964. Another reporter thinks that his national importance ebbed and flowed in temporary tides of influence throughout that sixteen-year period.

The time of his "arrival" in the Senate cannot be dated dramatically and precisely; his identification as an important national figure evolved gradually, in the mid-1950's. One of the key elements in the process was his relationship with Lyndon B. Johnson.

On the surface there were factors which indicated that the two men were too different in background and personality to establish a political alliance and warm friendship. Johnson was from the Lone Star State; he was a Texan with a record of voting against key civil rights proposals in Congress. Humphrey was from the North-Star State; he was a Minnesotan whose whole political being seemed consumed with the crusade for civil rights. They arrived in the Senate at the same time, 1949; but Johnson moved to that body from the House of Representatives after an election victory edge of only eighty-seven votes, and Humphrey progressed to the Senate from municipal office and a landslide election victory. Johnson was at first cautious and reserved; he had to fight off the sarcastic nickname "Landslide Lyndon." Humphrey was initially cocky and voluble; he paid no attention to his most derisive nickname, "Flannelmouth."

But the similarities of background and identity were more significant. They were only three years apart in age. They were shaped in large measure by similar depression-period experiences and struggles. They grew up in modest, rural middle-class settings. Both were, briefly, teachers before entering politics. Their social and political attitudes, conditioned significantly by the depression, were essentially moralistic and economically liberal. Humphrey was almost fanatic in his advocacy of Roosevelt's New Deal; Johnson, as a Congressman, was one of the very few members of the House of Representatives who supported F.D.R.'s plan to "pack" the Supreme Court in 1937. Each was an administrator on the state level for a New Deal agency: Johnson with the National Youth Administration in Texas, and Humphrey with the Works Progress Administration in Minnesota. Each man, by 1948, had experienced both defeat and victory in campaigns for public office.

In more specific matters of style and taste they were and are alike. When they were younger, both favored flashy ties, unfiltered cigarettes, and fast cars; in middle age and the mid-1950's, they dressed conservatively, abruptly quit smoking, and became a bit more prudent behind the wheel of a car. Both men favor basic steak-and-apple-pie meals, like to go to parties, and are recognized by Washington women as unusually nimble dancers.

Above all, Lyndon B. Johnson and Hubert H. Humphrey were and are gregarious, generous, aggressive, ambitious men. In their first term in the Senate they were primarily politicians, both realizing the need for political alliances to advance their causes and themselves.

Johnson advanced more quickly in the Senate hierarchy than Humphrey. With his Southern background, his legislative experience in the House, and his quick talents as a political persuader and tactician, he was promoted—unusually early—to Senate Majority Whip under Democratic Majority Leader Earnest McFarland in 1951. (The Whip's job, at least in theory, stresses the tactical and disciplinary functions of the party leadership in the Senate.) Humphrey, eager to master "the Senate process," admired Johnson for his legislative skills. He learned from Johnson, and also good-naturedly tried to lobby the Texan into support of some of his liberal causes. "You're a big man, Lyndon," he said to Johnson in the mid-1950's. "You've got a big physique and a big talent and a big title, and you come from a big state. But when are you going to admit that you're a liberal, so you can become a *great* man?" Johnson, who has always scorned oversimplified political labels, jokingly responded, in part, by addressing Humphrey as "you Bolshevik, you."

The first substantial and more formal link between the two men was forged in 1953. In the November 1952 election Senate Majority Leader McFarland had been beaten for re-election in Arizona by a political unknown, Barry Goldwater. Johnson, as Whip, was in line for the top Democratic leadership position in the Senate. Just before Christmas he phoned Humphrey to ask for his help and vote in the Senate Democratic caucus to be held when Congress convened in January. Humphrey could not give it. He had joined a group of liberal Senators in support of James Murray of Montana for the top leadership post.

"I'll be honest with you," Humphrey told Johnson on the phone. "The liberals have been meeting. We are running someone else."

"You can't win," Johnson said.

"Maybe we can't," Humphrey replied. "But we want a show of strength. I am going to stay with the liberals."

Johnson suggested, "I might want to make you my Whip."

Humphrey was firm. "I'm sorry. I'm committed with the liberals."

Just before the January caucus Humphrey and Wyoming's Lester Hunt realized that Johnson would probably beat Murray. They went to him in an effort to bargain from what they considered to be a position of strength. Humphrey asked Johnson if he would, if elected, place such liberal Senators as Paul Douglas of Illinois and Herbert Lehman of New York on key committees. Johnson asked Humphrey and Hunt how many votes they had for Murray. Humphrey read the names of Senators whose votes he assumed were in the liberal camp. Several times Johnson said confidently and flatly, "No, you don't have him. I do." But Humphrey persisted, asking for a deal which would at least place two liberals on the Democratic Policy Committee. Johnson turned it down. "I don't have to give you anything. I have the votes."

That afternoon the Democratic Senators caucused. Humphrey thought Murray might get twenty votes. He got three. Johnson was elected Leader, and Humphrey moved to make the vote unanimous. His motive, he says, was not to weasel back into Johnson's favor. "I had to protect Jim [Murray]. I couldn't let it get out to his home state that he had received only three votes. That would have humiliated and hurt him in Montana. The only thing to do was urge a unanimous vote for Johnson, so that people outside wouldn't know that he had tried for Minority Leader and lost by such a wide margin."

Humphrey left the caucus worried about his relationship with the new Democratic Senate leader. A few hours later Johnson surprised him with a visit to his office and an unexpected offer:

"You name the man you want on the Policy Committee. I'll see that he's appointed. Name the men you want on the other major committees. I'll put them in."

Humphrey identified his candidates; Johnson scribbled down their names (and later fulfilled his pledge). As the meeting concluded, Humphrey asked, "Why are you doing this? You don't have to. You didn't make any promises." Johnson replied:

"You're one of the fellows not playing both sides of the street. [Some liberal Senators, obviously, had privately pledged their votes to both Murray and Johnson in separate conversations.] I want to work with you. I want you to help me."

Humphrey agreed. He was flattered by Johnson's attention and grateful for his assurance of support to help him get a seat on the Foreign Relations Committee. When Johnson checked with Walter George, the top-ranking Democrat on the committee, the old Southerner readily agreed to give the vacancy to Humphrey. Other leaders concurred, and the appointment was confirmed.

Some reporters have suggested that Johnson was the one and only key to Humphrey's success in the Senate. They portray the Minnesotan as a blob of political putty sculptured by the artist Johnson into a Senator of stature and influence. Johnson did, indeed, teach him much and by his help boosted him out of the positionless status of a freshman Senator. But he did not "mold" Humphrey, and his solid gesture of support after the Democratic caucus in 1953 was not mere magnanimity. Johnson needed all the help he could get. After the 1952 election Republicans held the White House and a majority in both houses of Congress. Johnson was the leader of the opposition, not a powerful lieutenant of the Administration. (Democrats regained control of the Senate in 1955, and Johnson held the Majority Leader title from then through 1960.) In the 83rd Congress he had to build a base of support.

A dozen or so liberal Democrats in the Senate took a dim view of Johnson, whom they considered a conservative Southerner and nothing more; some were not even on speaking terms with him. Johnson needed their votes. He needed someone to act as his bridge to the liberal camp. He needed Humphrey as much as or more than Humphrey needed him.

There were times when the arrangement caused tensions and problems between them. Humphrey worked hard for Johnson, as did others, through a period when Johnson earned his reputation as one of the best leaders in the history of the Senate. He rewarded Humphrey often with powerful help for pet projects or liberal legislative causes. The political alliance between the two men became stronger as some of the rough edges of Humphrey's liberalism were worn off by experience and some of Johnson's traditional states' rights views mellowed. Their friendship became stronger after countless late afternoon and evening visits for relaxed conversation. Occasionally, however, Humphrey's deep convictions and Johnson's instincts as a tactician clashed. When the Johnson-forged coalition of "moderate" Southerners and Northerners at times became shaky, Johnson demanded more from the liberal camp and Humphrey balked. Liberals sometimes accused Humphrey of "selling out" to Johnson. Southerners criticized Johnson for his conciliatory attitude toward the liberals. Once the two men had a heated argument and refused to speak to each other for several days. Johnson finally broke the ice by phoning: "Aw, come on over here and have a drink."

But the two strong-willed men weathered the legislative and personal conflicts, and resisted the efforts of other Senators to drive a wedge between them. Near the end of the 85th Congress, in August 1958, the Majority Leader wrote this note to Humphrey:

Dear Hubert: They tried on many occasions, but one thing I would never let them do was to come between us. I have too much sense.

No leader can be successful unless he has able and conscientious advisers. And I am deeply conscious of the fact that one of the ablest and most effective is a fellow from Minnesota named Hubert Humphrey.

Hubert, as I leave Washington I want you to know how grateful I am for all the help that you gave me—help without which the job could not have been done . . .

Both Johnson and Humphrey are men of strong sentiments. When Johnson suffered a major heart attack in 1955, Humphrey was one of the first men in Washington to send a get-well message, and also to pledge to "redouble my efforts" in the Senate while the Majority Leader was recuperating. Johnson was touched by his genuine expressions of concern and grateful for his loyalty during the period. When he was a patient at the Mayo Clinic in Rochester, Minnesota, Johnson asked Karl Rolvaag, then state chairman of the party, to visit him.

Johnson, Rolvaag remembers, was full of praise for Humphrey. He told Rolvaag that Humphrey had certainly "made it" as a good Senator when he succeeded in convincing Southern Senators that they should support a dairy bill. But, he stressed, "many good Senators are defeated because they just don't have time to keep up with the party work back home." He also made it clear that he expected Rolvaag and other state party leaders to protect Humphrey's political health in Minnesota.

"You can't be a statesman unless you can get re-elected," Johnson often told new Senators. Humphrey puts it another way: "There is one sure way of becoming important and influential in the Senate: just *be* here. It's sort of like squatter's rights—the longer you stay, the more important you become."

The idea is not as obvious to many Senators as it should be. The history of the Senate is littered with the records of great or near-great men whose careers were terminated abruptly by the voters back home. Some Senators who do well in their first terms become so comfortable on the pedestal of national prominence that they cannot believe the folks back in Centerville would ever vote for anyone else. They begin to forget the "little" touches which help to keep the political home fires burning. Senate Majority Leaders in this century have a frighteningly high political mortality rate. On the lofty level of Capitol Hill many men simply stop being politicians. And usually when a member of Congress ceases to be a politician, he soon ceases to be a member of Congress.

Humphrey did not let his political instincts atrophy. In his first years in the Senate he energetically joined the legislative effort against international communism; he also fought the encroachments of oleomargarine producers in dairy-minded, butter-favoring Minnesota. He enthusiastically supported the building of a NATO alliance, and never forgot the need for a federal-state-city alliance to build new port facilities in Duluth. He prodded the Truman Administration into the first large-scale grant of wheat to India's starved populace, but did not neglect to arrange loans to Minnesota wheat farmers whose crops were damaged by storms. He wrote long and idealistic letters to Presidents Truman and Eisenhower on the issues of the century, but worried more about how promptly post cards or telegrams from Minnesota were being answered by his staff.

Even in early 1964, as he faced the demanding civil rights fight in the Senate and was surrounded by speculation on his possible Vice Presidential nomination, he spent much of his time on "cases" involving Minnesota projects. On January 19 he dictated this memorandum to staff assistant Norman Sherman: "What ever happened to that special [U.S. postal] stamp for the Mayo Centennial? Have we been able to deliver? Or are we fiddling around and forgetting it? We must get this. There can be no letdown or excuses for failure." Sherman responded that he had involved Minnesota officials, the U. S. Postmaster General, and the White House in the effort. He added, in reference to his Jewish background, that he was "putting more effort into this project, per square inch, than anything since some of my deviant forebears helped build the Pyramids." Humphrey's anxiety was quieted, but he placed personal calls to the Postmaster General and the chairman of the related Senate subcommittee. The commemorative stamp was issued.

Political scientists engage in what they call "role analysis" of members of Congress. A Senator can prefer the essential role of

legislator, or public educator, or behind-the-scenes political ma-
nipulator. He can become a "megaphone" type of representative,
simply watching the polls and his mail to determine public opinion and then voting accordingly; or he can vote his conscience and
advise the voters to "take me or leave me." He can stress the role
of running errands for constituents in the federal bureaucracy, or
of initiating domestic legislation to become a national leader, or of
traveling from nation to nation to become an unofficial international diplomat. He can assume the role of leader or lieutenant in
the Senate establishment, or he can surrender a portion of his
practical influence by becoming a critic of the establishment. Most
Senators tend to stress only one role; several mix two or even three
roles in their Senate careers. Hubert Humphrey played practically
all of them. As a Senator he was politician, legislator, educator,
representative, follower, leader, diplomat, Minnesotan, American,
world citizen, an integral part of the Senate establishment, and an
almost constant critic of its rules and institutional traditions. But
his first concern was, quite logically, political survival.

As early as 1951 he considered his likely opponent in the 1954
Minnesota campaign to be Governor Luther Youngdahl, a Republican and liberal with great popularity in the state. Some of Humphrey's closest advisers figured that he would have only a fifty–fifty
chance of beating Youngdahl. In the spring of 1951 he learned,
quite indirectly, that Youngdahl was not eager to run against him,
that he considered Humphrey a good Senator from Minnesota,
but that he would probably have to run against him because of
pressure from the Minnesota Republican Party. Another indirect
report indicated that Youngdahl might refuse the Senate nomination if he received a good lifetime judicial appointment.

Humphrey, after a meeting on miscellaneous subjects with
Truman, asked the President if he knew Youngdahl and if he
would consider giving him a federal judicial appointment. Truman did remember Youngdahl; he was the only Governor and one
of the very few Republicans leaders in the country who had written him a letter of support after he fired General Douglas Mac-
Arthur midway in the Korean War. But there was no vacancy in
the federal court system in Youngdahl's area.

A few weeks later Humphrey picked up the Sunday Washington
Post and read of the death of District of Columbia Federal Judge

T. Alan Goldsborough. The next day he phoned for an appointment with the President. Truman agreed that the District of Columbia area could be considered a national one and that Youngdahl could have the appointment if he wanted it. Humphrey immediately phoned Youngdahl at a hunting lodge in northern Minnesota, and the Governor agreed to come to Washington, register at the Mayflower Hotel under the name "Smith," and meet with Humphrey and the President at the White House. (The President had insisted on secrecy until he and the Governor confirmed the appointment in person.) Humphrey and Youngdahl entered the White House through a side door. When they emerged through the front lobby after meeting with the President, Humphrey announced the appointment to reporters. That was one of the few times in Humphrey's life when he engaged in what might be described as political cloak-and-dagger intrigue. Minnesota Republican leaders were furious. They became livid when they learned that Youngdahl and Humphrey had taped a conversation about law enforcement for use in the Minnesota campaign.

In November 1954, Humphrey beat Republican opponent Val Bjornson and was returned to the Senate for a second six-year term.

Before his re-election in 1954 he—and almost every other politician in Washington—had to contend with another major problem, McCarthyism. That term recalls the shadowy political period which began on February 12, 1950, when Wisconsin Senator Joseph McCarthy addressed a meeting of the Republican Women's League in Wheeling, West Virginia. His speech, broadcast by local radio station WWVA, included this remark:

"I have here in my hand a list of two hundred and five that were known to the Secretary of State as being members of the Communist Party and who, nevertheless, are still working and shaping the policy of the State Department."

McCarthy's charge aroused deep and previously undetected fears in the nation. People were in an ambivalent mood. International communism was scoring advances in many parts of the world. The costs of anti-Communist military and economic measures were huge. The United States no longer had a monopoly of atomic weaponry. It was not enough to blame Russia's Stalin and China's Mao. Some pinned all the trouble on Roosevelt at Yalta, or Truman at Potsdam; diplomatic history, however, did not provide satisfying scapegoats for most.

But American Communists in the State Department? Microfilm in pumpkin patches? Alger Hiss? Any frustrated American reading about casualties in Korea and threats from Moscow could get his teeth into such local dangers. What if there were not really 205 Communists on the tax-supported payroll of the State Department, or 57 or 7 (McCarthy's later figures)? Obviously something fishy was going on in Washington.

McCarthy lashed the waters of national fear as if he had hooked a killer whale. Occasionally a small fish was pulled in—to offer proof to the fearful that America was about to be engulfed by a domestic Communist conspiracy.

One year after McCarthy first captured the headlines of the press and plumbed a national frustration, Senators Harley Kilgore of West Virginia, Herbert Lehman of New York, and Olin Johnston of South Carolina stood in the Senate to warn of the excesses of McCarthy's anti-Communist crusade. They reaffirmed the belief of most political leaders that investigations were proper, security programs were necessary, and the Communist conspiracy was real, but they spoke of a greater danger. Humphrey joined that Senate discussion on February 12, 1951, saying:

"It appears to me that fear and suspicion are growing throughout the country . . . American freedom cannot live in an environment filled with suspicion, and American political institutions cannot live in an environment filled with fear.

"This is a time when we need to believe in democracy. I think it is important to keep in mind not whether this kind of attack [McCarthy's] is successful politically but what it means in the long run—for the solvency, the security, and the stability of free political, economic, and cultural institutions.

"Unfortunately, there is today a psychois of fear in our nation at a time when our people need to be imaginative and creative."

There was little anyone could do about the sickness in American society until McCarthy gorged himself on headlines and the fear spent itself. A few men were brave; a few were cowardly; most simply watched the pattern of abuse of civil liberties and corrosion of national confidence. One Washington reporter literally lost sleep because he felt partly responsible for McCarthy's power.

"But what could I do?" he still asks painfully. "McCarthy would call a press conference and make some new charge against an individual or a group. He knew most of the time that the charges were nonsense; he often gave us that cynical 'Isn't this fun?' smile when he made them. We knew the charges were nonsense. But as reporters we just had to play it straight and quote his statements without interpretation. And he kept getting the headlines."

Humphrey's record during the McCarthy era was responsible, but not particularly courageous. He spoke out against McCarthy's excesses and tactics at ADA meetings or on radio and television; the Congressional Record Index, however, shows that he said nothing in the Senate directly about McCarthy or in defense of one Senator McCarthy repeatedly attacked, in 1952, 1953, and 1954. He had made the eloquent and brave statement about a "psychosis of fear" in 1951, but on May 19, 1953, he boasted in the Senate, "I bring to the attention of the Senate an editorial critical of my views appearing in the *Daily Worker* for April 14, 1953. This is not the first attack leveled against me by the Communist Party. I welcome the hostility and the opposition of the Communist Party . . ."

Humphrey was probably torn more by the conflicting forces of the McCarthy era than most politicians. He was one of the few leaders of national stature who had taken on and beaten Communists in a domestic fight (the purge of the Communists from the Minnesota DFL in 1948 described in Chapter 11, "1948"). As one of the founders and leaders of the ADA and as a distinct liberal, however, he was accused frequently and unfairly of being a "stooge" or "sympathizer" of Communist causes. In 1954 a headline in a Minnesota newspaper boldly quoted a local Red-hunter who irresponsibly tried to link him to the Communist Party. The headlines and charges upset him as he faced a campaign for re-election to the Senate.

On August 11, 1954, he introduced legislation which was subtitled "A Bill to Outlaw the Communist Party." The first paragraph of the bill stated:

"The Congress hereby finds and declares that the Communist Party of the United States, although purportedly a political party, is in fact an instrumentality of a conspiracy to overthrow the Government of the United States."

The bill then continued, more in the fashion of a political speech than a legislative document, to define the differences between the Communist Party and "regular" political parties. It identified the Communist Party as an "agency of a hostile foreign power" and provided criminal penalties for membership.

Members of the Senate almost tripped over one another in their rush to praise the bill and vote for it, despite the quietly expressed view of many Constitutional lawyers that the bill was illegal. The debate on the bill in the Senate was long on praise and short on sound discussion of its features. Senator John Sherman Cooper of Kentucky was the only member who openly voiced a solid doubt. He said, "The Humphrey [bill] . . . either duplicates many other acts on the statute books or launches out into a field of doubtful constitutionality."

"Vote! Vote!" the members of the Senate cried. And the Communist Control Act of 1954 (which has never been tested for its constitutionality) was approved unanimously, by a vote of 84 to 0. The only members of the Senate who were not formally recorded in favor of it were Estes Kefauver of Tennessee, William Langer of North Dakota, and John Sparkman of Alabama.

One close and liberal friend of Humphrey says, "That was the only time I was ever ashamed of Hubert." Another says, "It was a crummy bill, but someone had to steal McCarthy's thunder." For a time Humphrey defended his sponsorship of the bill against the criticism of civil-liberties-conscious friends. He argued that the vote of one liberal Senator for the bill "saved that man's political life" in the election that November. But he has also said that the bill was "not one of the things I'm proudest of."

McCarthy's power was spent in the spring of 1954, when millions of Americans for the first time watched him in action during the televised "Army-McCarthy" hearings. Later that year the Senate debated a proposal to censure him. Humphrey spoke once, on a procedural problem involving the censure resolution. In a preliminary vote he was one of only twelve Senators recorded against sending the censure resolution to committee. His vote on that issue was interpreted as a firm stand *for* censure; he did not feel that a study of the censure charges was necessary.

The committee, chaired by Arthur Watkins of Utah, recommended approval of a censure resolution after its investigation.

McCarthy walked into the chamber on the day of the final vote with his arm in a sling. ("Bursitis," he grumbled in answer to questions about his health.) He merely voted "Present" when the roll clerk called his name. He left the chamber before the completion of a vote which overwhelmingly condemned him.

The resolution said nothing about the cost of almost five years in which American society was blighted with fear, confusion, and hysteria. Indirectly it revealed much about the United States Senate. It read, in part:

"Resolved, that the Senator from Wisconsin, Mr. McCarthy, failed to cooperate with the Subcommittee on Privileges and Elections of the Senate Committee on Rules and Administration in clearing up matters which concerned his conduct as a Senator and affected the honor of the Senate and, instead, repeatedly abused the subcommittee and its members who were trying to carry on their assigned duties, thereby obstructing the Constitutional processes of the Senate; and that this conduct of the Senator from Wisconsin, Mr. McCarthy, is contrary to Senatorial traditions and is hereby condemned.

"The Senator from Wisconsin, Mr. McCarthy, acted contrary to Senatorial ethics and tended to bring the Senate into dishonor and disrepute, to obstruct the Constitutional processes of the Senate, and to impair its dignity . . ."

In 1955 the McCarthy era waned. Democrats recaptured majority control in both houses of Congress. Lyndon B. Johnson was Senate Majority Leader. Hubert Humphrey was beginning a new term as a Senator. The Senate had changed; he had changed. He had learned to respect Senate traditions, to observe the Senate "ethic," and to do nothing to "impair its dignity." As the 84th Congress convened, Humphrey was in the Senate establishment and on a powerful committee, Foreign Relations. He had youth, a bit of seniority, alliances, experience. Some still considered him an impractical dreamer and idealist; others thought of him as nothing more than a political hustler. But in the view of most of the Senate and much of the press, he had become, for several obvious and a thousand obscure reasons, "important."

16

Influence

In the summer of 1962, Hubert Humphrey guided a score of Peace Corps volunteers through the rooms of the Senate Committee on Foreign Relations. In Room S. 116 of the Capitol the young men and women crowded around the huge oval table used by the seventeen-member committee. Humphrey told them about the authority and structure of the committee, and explained the seating arrangement for members: Republicans at the east half of the table, Democrats at the west half, the Chairman in the middle, and each member placed in sequence away from him on the basis of seniority. Humphrey, with almost ten years of rank on the committee, first pointed to the far end of the table. "That's where I used to sit. And you know, I didn't think much of the seniority system in those days. I even attacked it a few times when I first came here." Then he patted his own chair—just two places away from the Chairman's—and with a wry smile added, "Now I don't really think the seniority system is so bad."

In sixteen years in the Senate, Humphrey never became a committee chairman or Majority Leader. At no time did he have a formal, significant power base in the Senate; his influence was largely personal. But in the judgment of many reporters and Senate insiders, his influence—at least in his last few years in the Senate—ranked in a class with such men as Walter George, Lyndon Johnson, and Robert Kerr. In the 88th Congress of 1963 and 1964, he was without question within the nucleus of Senate power—the core of half a dozen or so men who could and did wield influence on all or most legislative issues.

"Inner Club" is a misnomer for that group today; it is not all relaxed or avocational, and frequently its members are distinctly uncongenial. The nucleus of Senate power is rather an immensely hard-working, informal executive secretariat for a powerful body of independent-minded legislators. The power of the group is substantial, but never absolute; not even its members can "run" the Senate on all issues at all times. Its complexion changes with the passing of time and the changing issues facing the Senate. Harry Byrd of Virginia was in the nucleus of Senate power for a long time, on the basis of his seniority, his skill, and his chairmanship of the Senate Finance Committee, but by the 88th Congress age had reduced his activity and effectiveness and he no longer qualified. Such Senators as Fulbright of Arkansas (Foreign Relations), Magnuson of Washington (Commerce), Long of Louisiana (Finance), and even Morse of Oregon (Education) stepped in and out of the core of Senate power when their committee or subcommittee chairmanships were involved in specific issues which briefly consumed the Senate's attention.

In the 88th Congress of 1963 and 1964, the Senate group of commanding and pervading influence included only five men: Humphrey, Majority Leader Mike Mansfield of Montana, Minority Leader Everett Dirksen of Illinois, Senator Richard Russell of Georgia, and Senator John Pastore of Rhode Island. It was an unlikely mixture of men. Dirksen, of course, is a Republican; the rest are Democrats. Russell is a Southerner; the rest are Northerners. Mansfield and Dirksen are generally placid personalities, bent on conciliation; Russell, Humphrey, and Pastore are often acid-tongued in conference or debate and most eager to protect or promulgate a principle or conviction. Contact and discussion among the five men was informal but frequent. They had no staff formally assigned to them as a group, but such eager helpers as former Secretary to the Majority Bobby Baker handled chores for all of them. (Baker, who resigned under fire in October 1963 for his outside but allegedly Senate-related money-making activities, developed considerable influence within the Senate primarily because he had more direct contact with its nucleus of power and was simply "there"—in the chamber—far more than most members of the Senate. Often called "the hundred and first Senator," he also had an informal sort of seniority which dated to the time of Walter George and Lyndon Johnson in the Senate.)

The significance of Humphrey's presence in the nucleus of Senate power in the 88th Congress is that he was the only man in the group who did not hold some "number one" position. Mansfield held the top leadership position of Senate Democrats, Dirksen was top leader of the Republicans, Russell was Chairman of the Senate Committee on Armed Services, and Pastore was Chairman of the Joint Committee on Atomic Energy. Other factors qualified those men for the Senate nucleus (Russell's leadership of the bloc of eighteen or so Southern votes and Pastore's debating skill, for example), but the fact remains that each of the four qualified for the core of Senate power partly on the basis of an official and formal base of Senate authority. Humphrey's sources of influence in the Senate were more diffuse.

He rarely was bothered by comments that he was the "gabbiest" Senator or that he "doesn't have to keep any office files; he just inserts everything into the Congressional Record." On an average day in the Senate he spoke a dozen times and introduced several bills, amendments, or resolutions. He had no conscious plan to become an important Senator by being the most prolific; he looked upon each bill or speech for its individual worth or interest, and he simply liked to be heard in the Senate chamber and read in the Congressional Record. In the daily "morning hour" of each Senate session he approached his desk in the chamber with the glee of a child on Christmas morning. He opened his tan imitation-leather "floor folder" as though he were delving into a mound of presents and surprises. "What have we got for today?" he would ask an assistant eagerly. Then leafing through the stack of legislative bills or speech texts prepared at his request, he would comment, "Ah, great! Here's that speech about agricultural cooperatives in Peru. Wonderful! . . . And this is the bill for government support of the arts. . . . Good! . . . And what's this? Marvelous! . . . The revised text on overseas markets for soybean oil! Great!"

In the 1949 session—the first year of his first term—it took sixteen columns in the Congressional Record Index just to list the titles and page numbers of his legislative and oratorical activity in the Senate. In contrast, there were four columns under Senator Harry Byrd's name. In 1961—the first year of his third term— there were thirty Humphrey columns in the Index. They included almost a thousand *subjects* listed for Humphrey's Senate remarks or legislation. In his words, Humphrey did not "come to the United States Senate to become the world's greatest expert on the boll weevil."

The effect of the volume and variety of his Senate activity tended to help him form alliances. "I didn't think much of Humphrey himself or his views when he first came," one Senator says. "But he made a nice little statement about my work on the Judiciary Committee, and nobody had ever done that before." Another Senator, a Southerner, said, "I thought Humphrey was a jackass when he strutted into Washington; he'd railroaded that civil rights thing through the 'forty-eight convention, and here he was— a young squirt in the Senate for only a few weeks and his picture was on the cover of *Time*. I'd been here for several years and I don't think *Time* even *mentioned* me more than once or twice. But then Hubert put together a pretty good little bill on acreage allotments for small farmers, and—well—I agreed with him on that and worked with him on it." When Humphrey inserted articles and bills on obscure subjects into the Congressional Record, he was at least partly aware that someone, somewhere, would be pleased or impressed, perhaps another Senator.

He built influence by relating himself to all levels of the Senate hierarchy. In a sense, he also bypassed the formal Senate establishment by cultivating a source of influence outside of but affecting the Senate. He went to the people. He gave priority, of course, to the needs of Minnesotans, whom he formally represented in the Senate. But as opposed to those Senators who considered themselves "ambassadors" of their states to Washington, he regarded himself instinctively as a Senator-at-large, representing the entire United States. "I didn't come to the *United States* Senate just to serve one state or the traditions of the Senate," he said in 1962. "I came to the nation's capital to *serve the people*."

More exactly, he served specific segments of the population with which he naturally identified. He was not a slave to any special interest, but he did tend to see himself as a man with a mission to represent groups in the country whom he considered underrepresented in the formation of national policy. He was the friend of the farmer, the small businessman, and "the workingman," whose needs he considered neglected by Congress. For the first half of his Senate career he was the only Democratic Senator from the "upper

Midwest": Minnesota, Wisconsin, North Dakota, and South Dakota. He at least doubled his duties by welcoming requests for
help from "constituents" in those states. More generally, he
seemed to inherit the mantle of Western progressivism; many
looked upon him as the LaFollette (Wisconsin), or the Bryan
(Nebraska), or the Hiram Johnson (California) of the mid-
century. With particularly strong convictions born of a progressive
era and with special concerns for "America's forgotten people," he
chose to labor for the benefit of the unemployed worker, the
marginal farmer, the racial minorities, the very young and the
very old. The result, as seen in his legislative efforts, was an emphasis on liberal programs to fight falling farm income, unemployment, and abuses of civil rights, and to work for federal aid to
education and health and welfare programs.

His liberal appeal transcended geographic boundaries. He received hundreds of invitations each month to speak in such liberal
strongholds as New York City, Detroit, and California, and to such
liberal-inclined groups as Jewish organizations and labor unions.

His influence in the Senate was thus increased because he carried more than the weight of a single Senate vote or the representation of a single (and not very big) state. If a Democratic Senator
from another area of the country needed advice before he went
into the upper Midwest for a speech, he sought out Humphrey. If
a conservative Senator needed labor's support for one of his bills,
he requested Humphrey to act as an emissary. If a new Senator
wanted guidance before speaking at a Bonds for Israel dinner, he
conferred with Humphrey. If a Senator from an industrial state
wondered how the farm belt would react to a freight-rate amendment, he asked Humphrey. Hubert Humphrey not only became a
"bridge" between Lyndon Johnson and liberals in the Senate, he
also represented a dozen bridges between various other Senators
and specific groups of the population. Each year he did a thousand
favors for other Senators who needed his advice, his contacts, or
his support. In the Senate, as well as in politics generally, a man
becomes influential partly in proportion to the number of favors
he does for others.

There was another and more direct route to influence in the
Senate which Humphrey followed: involvement and effectiveness
in the field of foreign relations.

The Senate's position of power in relation to the House of Representatives has increased in this century as America's involvement in world affairs has increased. Until the turn of the century most Senators were content to orate on the lofty principles of federal vs. state authority, to amend the much too progressive proposals advanced by Presidents and to trim House-initiated tax or appropriations bills. But the Constitution granted two powers exclusively to the Senate: ratification of treaties and "advise and consent" authority over major Presidential appointments, including diplomatic officers. From the time that Teddy Roosevelt's "Great White Fleet" and Woodrow Wilson's crusade for world security ended an almost unblemished record of "fortress America," the Senate moved up in influence and into a sharing of authority with the President for the conduct of foreign relations. By the 1950's almost two thirds of federal "peacetime" budgets were directly related to foreign policy and international programs (defense, mutual security, foreign aid). The Senate became a second key necessary for the nation's conduct of foreign relations. The President, of course, held the first. As the influence of the United States in the world increased, the influence of the Senate increased. A man who aspired to influence in the Senate looked first to the field of foreign relations.

After his appointment to the Senate Committee on Foreign Relations in 1953, Humphrey turned at least half of his legislative attention to international affairs. For his Foreign Relations seat he had to give up membership on the Senate Committee on Labor and Public Welfare, which initially infuriated his friends in organized labor, and to leave, temporarily, the Senate Committee on Agriculture, a risky move for a man from a state with a 50 percent rural population. In foreign relations his interests were as diverse as in domestic affairs. In his first years on the committee he devoted significant attention to the United Nations, world food needs, world health programs, international trade, Soviet strategy, the Western alliance, European economic recovery and cooperation, Communist penetration of the Middle East, and several other major subjects. It was not until 1956 that he began to specialize in the field of disarmament, and it was not until 1961 that he showed prime interest in the geographic area of Latin America.

Beginning in 1955, he traveled overseas often; most trips were in the late fall or winter, after Congress had adjourned. Humphrey overseas was not significantly different in manner from Humphrey in Minnesota. He worked hard during fast-paced tours through Europe and the Middle East, talking with any local official who would talk with him, shaking hands with laborers and farmers, studying local economics and politics, and—on his return —filing voluminous, detailed reports and recommendations with the Department of State and the White House. But on his first overseas trips he listened far more than he talked. He learned, and his work was rewarded with appointments to Interparliamentary conferences and U.S. Delegations to UNESCO and disarmament meetings in Europe.

In 1957, President Eisenhower appointed him to the United States Delegation to the United Nations. That appointment and assignment have been among the most satisfying of his life. He was prouder of the certificate of his U.N. appointment than any of the several hundred plaques, scrolls, and honorary degrees and awards which covered the walls of his Senate office and spilled out into an adjoining hallway and reception room. His U.N. appointment was not unusual; it is traditional for the President to appoint a few members of Congress, from both parties, each year. Humphrey's work at the U.N. was unusual and impressive. He quickly adjusted to the rules and system of the General Assembly and was an effective advocate of U.S. foreign policies in the U.N.'s deliberations. Delegates of other nations, particularly from the new or smaller countries, found Humphrey accessible and sympathetic to their grievances. When the U.N. term ended, Henry Cabot Lodge, America's top U.S. representative, wrote him a warm note of gratitude for his work. Delegates of other nations often phoned him in Washington or Minnesota after he had left the U.N., to request his help in getting a proper hearing on their problems or proposals in the councils of the U.N. or the U. S. Government.

Humphrey's view of foreign affairs was broadened by his United Nations service and his overseas trips. After one meeting with Egypt's Nasser his views on the Middle East—though still strongly pro-Israel—were distinctly more flexible.

He spent little time in the bistros or on the beaches of the nations he visited—unlike some junketing members of Congress.

He was determined, as he put it, "to see the people, and not just the high government and society types."

One high State Department official, admitting that the executive branch is often anxious when a Senator announces an informal overseas trip, says flatly, "Humphrey is the best ambassador this country has." The official explains, "He always brings back useful information and good ideas, usually boosts morale with an enthusiastic speech in some lagging Embassy, makes a lot of friends for the United States among national leaders, and occasionally manages to find the solution to some foreign dispute." A former Assistant Secretary of State remembers, "Humphrey came back from some of his trips abroad steaming-mad because of a Department oversight or diplomatic snub of a foreign government or political party. He'd shake us up good, but usually we deserved it. And he had a shirt-sleeves appeal to the man on the street in other countries. His attempts to speak a phrase or two of a foreign language were usually hilarious, but he could always communicate his humanity and sincere concern to people anywhere—in the palaces or the slums."

On a typical overseas trip (he averaged one a year from 1955 on, either to Europe, the Middle East, or Latin America) he held the usual airport press conferences, observed the usual diplomatic obligations, toured the American Embassy facilities and the latest show piece of U.S. foreign aid ("There are too damn many U.S.-financed steel mills and airports rusting away in the desert," he once said), and conferred with the highest-ranking local government official the Embassy had snagged for an appointment. Then gently turning down a rigid schedule of receptions carefully arranged by an Embassy secretary ("I can drink and chitchat back in Washington"), he traveled and observed as much as possible on his own ("Just give me an interpreter, a small car, and a couple of pesos," he said in one Latin-American capital). He sought out and sounded out leaders of major opposition political parties ("Okay, so we are all buddy-buddy with the party and government in power; but what about a year from now, or five years from now, when the people throw out or vote out the government and the opposition takes over?"). He walked in on and quizzed second-echelon economic and agricultural Ministers ("Sometimes you have to get down a ways in the bureaucracy to find out what's going on"). He ordered assistants to round up local business or labor leaders and representatives of farm or student organizations ("A nation isn't just a government; it's people with powerful and special interests").

After all the formal meetings, tours, and conferences he shunned the offices, ballrooms, limousines, leaders, and opinion-makers to walk the streets, slums, and rural roads for at least several hours. He penetrated the surface generalizations and comforting myths about other nations which affected American policy and opinion. In 1956, after a walk through a slum suburb of Athens, he asked angrily, "Our reports say that Greece is 'on the road to economic recovery'? So why are so many people here hungry?" In 1961, after wandering through an economically stagnant village on the coast of South America, he said, "The trouble with our government and foreign aid people is that we're always thinking big; we can't visualize some project unless it costs ten million dollars. What about the impoverished village that just needs ten bucks for a fishing net?" In 1962, after another impromptu tour of a slum in the Middle East, he demanded, "Why do we always have to be talking about long-range foreign aid plans? Does anybody in our government mind if those people over there EAT something in the meantime?" In 1963, after he strolled along a rural road in El Salvador, he scoffed, "Everybody kept telling me about the rich soil and all the American agricultural experts in the hills outside San Salvador. So what do I see? A farmer, down on his hands and knees, using a goddamned STICK to scrape a furrow in his plot of land!" In another country visited in the same tour of Latin America, he reported, "Everybody in Washington thinks that country is friendly toward the United States. That's just jolly. Most of the students I talked to are Communists, and we haven't got a single man working to infiltrate the student organizations." And in Moscow, in August 1963, after he spent an hour shaking hands with Russians in Gorky Park, he commented gaily, "If you smile at people, they smile back."

On an earlier trip to the Soviet Union and Moscow, in the winter of 1958, he watched a performance of *Swan Lake* by the Bolshoi Ballet, visited a Russian Orthodox Church, looked in on a Soviet kindergarten class, and appeared for an interview on Moscow television and radio. "We want to know you, and we want you to know us," he said on the Moscow telecast. "We must learn to live together. You want peace, and we want peace. The only war we want to fight is the war against the ancient enemies of mankind—the war against disease, against poverty, against misery, against ignorance, and fear. . . . In this all nations can join and cooperate. The peoples of the world are tired of war and threats of war. . . .

His Moscow schedule was busy, and he met such high-ranking Soviet leaders as Foreign Minister Andrei Gromyko, Anastas Mikoyan, and Frol Kozlov. But he was not satisfied. At that time in the Soviet Union one man counted above all others: Nikita Khrushchev. Officially the prospects for a meeting with Khrushchev were bleak. Humphrey had been disappointed when only one minor U. S. Embassy secretary and no Soviet officials greeted him at the airport when he arrived Thursday night, November 27. There were no responses to his requests to meet with Khrushchev, except the matter-of-fact assurances by American diplomats that an appointment with the Chairman of the Soviet Council of Ministers was "impossible." By Monday, December 1, he felt that he was being treated like any American tourist staying at the National Hotel. In the morning he impatiently suggested cutting the Moscow visit short. "Let's get out of here," he said to assistant Julius Cahn.

But on Monday afternoon he was called to the Kremlin. He phoned Cahn and Mrs. Humphrey to report that he was scheduled to see Khrushchev in half an hour, and expressed doubt that he would have more than ten or fifteen minutes with the Soviet leader.

The Khrushchev-Humphrey meeting, which began a few minutes before 3 P.M., lasted for eight hours and twenty-five minutes. The session, in Khrushchev's Kremlin office, was unprecedented for its length and mood. The Soviet Chairman had never spent much more than an hour with any American official, and previous conferences had been generally stiff and formal. With only interpreter Oleg Troyanovsky present, Khrushchev and Humphrey at first exchanged the usual pleasantries about peace and the usual pronouncements about the need for joint cultural and artistic programs. They spoke about the proposal for an International Health Year (an idea patterned after the successful International Geophysical Year), and agreed that American and Soviet scientists could and should cooperate in fields of medical research.

Khrushchev quizzed Humphrey about American agriculture, and said that the Soviet Union suffered from a shortage of cotton. Humphrey asked, "Would you be interested in buying American cotton, possibly? What about wheat?" Khrushchev replied that his country did need wheat, but that trade with the Far East was "cheaper." (This was five years before the conclusion of a U.S.-Soviet wheat-sale agreement.)

The Soviet leader relaxed as the conversation continued. He ordered a bottle of vodka. Humphrey asked if he could take notes; Khrushchev told Troyanovsky to give the American a share of his stack of paper. Humphrey covered twenty-three sheets with notes on their discussion about trade, disarmament, the personalities of American and Russian leaders, the concept of peaceful coexistence, the Middle East, and Berlin. Khrushchev was alternately angry and affable. Humphrey challenged his interpretation of capitalism and defended the success of the American economic and political system. Khrushchev denounced U. S. Secretary of State John Foster Dulles as a "warmonger," a charge which Humphrey heatedly denied. The Russian abruptly turned reasonable, saying that he had the "deepest respect" for President Eisenhower and suggesting that the United States and the Soviet Union test their "mutual strength" through economic competition. If the two nations were on the same side, he added, "there will be no war."

Humphrey mentioned the Red Chinese system of communes, the compulsory political and production units established by Mao Tse-tung. Khrushchev astounded him by replying that the communes were "reactionary" and that the Soviet Union had tried the commune system and "it didn't work." Then he added that communes were based on the principle: "From each according to his abilities; to each according to his needs." "That won't work," Khrushchev said. "You cannot get production without incentive." Humphrey's hand raced to note the words and details of this incredible rejection of Marxist theory. (Four years later the Soviet Union and Red China finally admitted deep ideological and policy splits which Humphrey—almost alone—had predicted in the late 1950's.)

Their conversation proceeded without interruption for four

hours. In the middle of an animated discussion about German rearmament and NATO, Khrushchev said abruptly, "Let's go to the toilet." Humphrey, alone for a few minutes with Troyanovsky, asked if he had stayed too long. The interpreter told him he could remain as long as Khrushchev wanted to talk. Khrushchev returned to suggest that they continue over dinner. Trays of sandwiches, caviar, fruit, fish, beef, and poultry and a decanter of brandy were spread on a table in Khrushchev's office. There were moments when the Soviet leader was mellow; tears came to his eyes when he spoke of a son killed in World War II. At other times he slammed his fist on the table top as he talked threateningly about Soviet power. Humphrey tried to discuss "possible areas of agreement," but spoke sharply when Khrushchev "explained" Soviet policy toward Hungary, which had been crushed by Russian tanks in the 1956 uprising.

For the final three hours—at Khrushchev's request—their conversation was "off the record," and Humphrey ceased taking notes. Both men (and apparently Troyanovsky) were tireless. They delved into the details of the possible areas of agreement or cooperation between their two nations, argued about the critical areas of tension (Berlin was the big one), and shrugged their shoulders when they acknowledged that some of the issues between the two nations could never be resolved.

Finally, at eleven twenty-five, Anastas Mikoyan—who had joined them for the final hour—complained that he was tired, and announced, "It is time to go home." Khrushchev and Humphrey agreed, shook hands, and said good-bye.

Humphrey was glowing with excitement when he met aide Julius Cahn shortly after midnight in the apartment of Richard Davis, Minister Counselor of the American Embassy. Cahn and Davis urged him to dictate all he could remember, using his notes, into a tape recorder. He did so for an hour, then felt groggy and went to bed.

Humphrey was not fully aware, Cahn thought, of the immense diplomatic and political significance of his meeting with Khrushchev. He wanted to continue his scheduled tour of Europe, but was mobbed by reporters at each airport and flooded with wires to return home for a full account of his meeting. Eisenhower and Secretary of State Dulles politely asked for a personal briefing.

Wearing a fur hat, Humphrey beamed from the cover of *Life* magazine, under the headline EIGHT HOURS WITH KHRU-SHCHEV and above the caption SENATOR FROM MIN-NESOTA WITH HAT FROM RUSSIA. Some of America's most influential political leaders and reporters suggested that it would be logical for Humphrey to throw his hat into the ring for the 1960 Democratic Presidential nomination. A few remarked that the Kremlin was a peculiar place to begin a Presidential campaign.

As the 86th Congress convened in 1959, Humphrey marked the tenth anniversary of his entry into the Senate. He had moved from failure, to acceptance, to importance, to influence. One of his father's favorite authors, Ralph Waldo Emerson, had written: "An institution is the lengthened shadow of one man." The institution of the Senate is, more accurately, the lengthened shadow of *many* men. By 1959, Humphrey was tall enough in national and international affairs to cast a shadow across the Senate chamber and the American political scene. The Senate had influenced him; he was beginning to influence it.

Most veteran members of the Senate are reluctant to admit that the Senate changes. (One who does says, "Sure, there are fewer S.O.B.'s here now.") But from 1949 to 1959 almost half of the original members died or retired or were defeated for re-election. The Senate, as a body of men, was younger in 1959 than in 1949. It was less formal, less Southern in outlook and pace, and for many nostalgic members or reporters, less colorful. In May 1954 (the month of the Supreme Court's school desegregation decision), Clyde Hoey of North Carolina died; he was the last member of the Senate who wore a frock coat. (The vacancy he left on the Agriculture Committee was filled by Hubert Humphrey.) The Senate, in the words of Mike Mansfield, was becoming "more of an organization and less of an institution." Freshman Senators were no longer expected to remain silent for six months; they could make an impact on the Senate organization much more quickly. Lyndon Johnson, through his policy of giving each member at least one major committee assignment (traditionally freshmen had been assigned instead to the District of Columbia or Post Office committees), had helped to boost the opportunity for freshmen to step up the Senate hierarchy during their first terms.

Magnolias still bloomed in the brief Washington springtime, but most of the slums had been cleared out of the southwestern section of the city. The Potomac added a touch of timelessness to the Washington scene, but the federal workers who drove over its bridges each day to the sprawling Virginia suburbs tended to refer to it as "the polluted Potomac." (There was even a bit of industry on land where orchards had grown and cattle grazed ten years before.) Virginia's Harry Byrd still sat in a favored, front-row seat in the Senate chamber; so now did Hubert Humphrey.

In 1956 the State of South Carolina sent conservative Strom Thurmond (he had dropped the initial *J.* from his name sometime between then and 1948) to the Senate. But the people of Idaho, Pennsylvania, and New York sent liberals Frank Church, Joseph Clark, and Jacob Javits. In 1957, Senator Joseph McCarthy died; a special election in Wisconsin gave liberal Democrat William Proxmire that vacant seat. In November 1958 a dozen liberals were elected to the Senate, including Ernest Gruening of Alaska, Philip Hart of Michigan, Vance Hartke of Indiana, Eugene McCarthy of Minnesota, Gale McGee of Wyoming, Frank Moss of Utah, Hugh Scott of Pennsylvania, Harrison Williams of New Jersey, and Edmund Muskie of Maine. ("My God, I don't believe it!" exclaimed one old politician. "A liberal Democrat elected from MAINE!"

Humphrey, Paul Douglas, and a few other lonely liberals had been lucky in 1949 if they could muster a dozen colleagues' votes for their causes. In the 86th Congress, which began in 1959, Senate liberals approached a majority in test votes on such issues as the periodic effort to amend the filibuster rule. The Senate was no longer a citadel of Southern conservatism. Humphrey was no longer "little Hubert," talking long, loudly, and almost hourly to try to make up for the modesty of his background and the minority position of his viewpoint. He was in a position of influence, and could reasonably reach for the pinnacle of power—the Presidency. It was all very logical. The Democratic Party and the nation, his friends told him, obviously stood at the edge of liberalism.

17

1960: The Edge of Liberalism

Hubert Humphrey's liberalism is neither doctrinaire nor dogmatic. It is an imprecise blending of classic and modern liberal concepts. His liberalism rests on the premise that the individual should be as unrestricted as possible in pursuit of self-expression and self-fulfillment. He also favors a government of authority, obligated to advance practical policies of social progress and reform. He sees no conflict between the two views. In his opinion, such forces as poverty, illiteracy, hunger, and social injustice restrict individual freedom as much as the chains of a despotic government. He believes that government in a representative democracy is the proper instrument for eliminating such forces.

In the spring of 1961 he wrote in *The Midwest Quarterly*, "Liberalism is not a distinct philosophy. It is rather an *attitude*—an open approach to life and society characterized by flexibility and adaptability." He added:

"The key word which may be applied to the liberal viewpoint is 'change.' The liberal understands that life is not static, that anything—from a plant to a government—must change, or it will die . . . The liberal welcomes change. He seeks change not for its own sake, but as an inevitable force of life which must be captured and channeled toward the right direction. He is thus willing to experiment, to try the untested, to develop the new, to dare the 'impossible.'"

Change characterizes Humphrey's liberalism. The language he has employed in defining liberalism has ranged from the pedagogic to the rhetorical. An article under his name in *The American Scholar* in the fall of 1955 said: "The authors of the liberal creed are heterogeneous. There is a broad gulf between the Whig aristocrats, content with the revolutionary settlement of 1689, and the Benthamite radicals of the nineteenth century. There are profound differences among the Physiocrats, preoccupied with the problems of French agriculture, the Manchester economists of England's industrialized Midlands, the Founding Fathers and Jacksonian 'democrats' . . .'' In an article for *Think* magazine, written in 1961, he made the same basic point by simply quoting Franklin Roosevelt's answer to a question on why liberals are so often divided and conversatives generally united: "There are many ways of going forward, but there is only one way of standing still."

Time has tempered Humphrey's liberal attitudes, particularly in economics. In January 1936, when he was twenty-four, he wrote a lengthy letter to the editor of the *Evening Huronite* in South Dakota, garrulously attacking an editorial in the previous edition which criticized F.D.R.'s economic message to Congress. "I'll tell you what Mr. Roosevelt's economic policy is," the youthful Humphrey wrote. " '[It is] dollars for the masses and not dollars for the classes.' That is his new deal. Our ills are economic bondage, and our President has now given us the only legislation ever conceived or passed that can break the stranglehold of Wall Street economic slavery." By 1962 his view of big business and Wall Street had matured and mellowed. (By then he had first-name relationships with such men as U.S. Steel Corporation Chairman Roger Blough and New York Stock Exchange President Keith Funston.) In an article in the May 22, 1962, issue of *Look* magazine he urged "a growing partnership between the United States Government and business management, based on mutual respect and understanding." In contrast to his fiery Populist sentiments of 1936, he wrote soothingly: "For the most part, big corporations are a source of strength and economic vitality . . . Big business does not in fact dominate our economy."

The change in the language of his liberalism distressed many of his liberal colleagues in the Senate in the early 1960's. As he became more deeply involved with the pragmatic programs of the Administration and more firmly a part of the Senate establishment, some complained that he had "deserted the liberal cause." He, in turn, criticized what he called "professional liberals." On a television program in 1963 he said, "They glory in defeat. The hardest job for a politician today is to have the courage to be a moderate. It's easy to take the extreme position." One Senator, who describes himself as a "liberal dissident," noted unhappily early in 1964, "I'm a rebel. It's hard for me to judge Humphrey. He accommodates himself to the establishment now. He's in it. I'm against the establishment." Another liberal Senator spoke as though Humphrey had strayed from the fold: "I'm sorry Humphrey became Whip and took on responsibilities to harmonize the Senate. I liked him more as a firebrand. He has to be in on too many compromises now. He just isn't Hubert anymore . . ." The difference between Humphrey's "flexible" liberalism and the militant ideological liberalism of others was dramatized in the Senate fight over the Kennedy Administration's Communications Satellite Act in 1963. A dozen liberal Senators fought and filibustered against the plan to place Telstar under control of a private corporation. Humphrey not only voted for the bill, but helped lead the successful Administration effort for its adoption. Later a liberal Senator told a colleague that he thought Humphrey had sacrificed principle in favor of position, and he disconsolately quoted Robert Browning: "Just for a handful of silver he left us, Just for a riband to stick in his coat." Another liberal spoke more sympathetically: "It's nonsense to say that he has abandoned the liberal cause. He's both an idealist and a realist, and he balances these roles well. Without Humphrey's skill and help most of the liberals around here [the Senate] could never get anything accomplished." In *The New York Times Magazine* of August 25, 1963, Samuel Shaffer wrote: "Without Humphrey, the liberal contingent [in the Senate] would be fragmented and impotent."

In 1960, Humphrey was far more inclined to wave the banner of liberalism, to proclaim himself publicly and proudly a liberal. Riding the crest of national attention after his meeting with Nikita Khrushchev and encouraged by the results of the 1958 election, he believed that the time had arrived in America for a liberal national leader and that perhaps he was the man.

But he was slow to decide to enter the race for the Democratic Presidential nomination. On the night of June 11, 1959, he met in a Duluth hotel with his closest friends and advisers to discuss his Presidential ambitions and prospects. Minnesota Governor Orville Freeman, Senator Eugene J. McCarthy, Congressmen John Blatnik and Joseph Karth, state party leaders Gerald Heaney and Ray

Hemenway, and Mrs. Humphrey were there. They argued about whether he had any reasonable chance of winning the nomination; the meeting ended with no clear decision. Humphrey was still cautious and unsure. But the next day Freeman and McCarthy announced the formation of a Humphrey-for-President Committee.

His tentative candidacy drew the support of many "name" liberals, ranging from theologian Dr. Reinhold Niebuhr to former Brooklyn Dodger third baseman Jackie Robinson. Richard Strout wrote in the *Christian Science Monitor* on July 15: "Senator Humphrey has made it evident that he is going to base his candidacy on an uncompromising, all-out liberal appeal." During the same week Humphrey appeared as a featured speaker before the Fiftieth Anniversary Convention of the National Association for the Advancement of Colored People. He declared, "A candidate who is not a civil rights candidate cannot be elected." At the same time Senator John F. Kennedy was quietly cultivating contacts among Southern Democratic leaders, to whom the NAACP was anathema. Thomas O'Neill wrote in the Baltimore *Sun* on July 17: "While influential and highly respected in the Senate, [Humphrey] has never fully caught on with the national audience."

Humphrey moved furiously to try to attract a national audience. He stepped up his non-Washington speaking schedule and in a few months traveled to more than twenty states. In Seattle he insisted that he was not an announced candidate, but added revealingly, "I want to meet the Democratic leaders of the state and I want them to meet me and see me." At a breakfast meeting with Washington State leaders he set the basic theme of his campaign: "First of all, I am a liberal. The Democratic Party must be liberal to win the next election." In Oregon he appealed to Democrats to resist efforts to "tone down or moderate" the party and to be proud of their "New Deal-Fair Deal heritage." In Los Angeles (one reporter described him as "a weary but ever optimistic Hubert Humphrey") he demanded, "We must remake the Democratic Party into a party of liberalism."

He interrupted that Western tour and canceled several important appearances to return to Washington to cast a vote in the Senate. Throughout his informal and later formal candidacy he repeatedly left the campaign trail to fulfill his Senate obligations.

"I'm still a Senator," he reminded his staff as they tried to schedule most of his time for the campaign. "I don't care if I do have to cancel a key speech out in the country—I will *not* miss any important Senate votes."

That attitude and policy hindered his campaign effort. In contrast, Kennedy devoted almost total attention to winning the nomination. He was not upset if he missed a Senate vote occasionally or if the mail from Massachusetts to his Senate office went unanswered for a few days. Humphrey told his staff at one point, "We take care of Minnesota first; THEN we take care of the Presidential campaign." Kennedy had the luck and timing of Senate incumbency on his side. He had been elected to a full six-year term in 1958; Humphrey would be up for re-election to the Senate in 1960.

Hesitation and doubts marked Humphrey's mood as late as December 1959. Only a week before his formal announcement of his candidacy on December 30, 1959, he was still asking friends and advisers, "What do you think? Do you think I ought to run?" Kennedy, on the other hand, had made up his mind and stuck with the decision almost four years earlier, immediately after the Democratic National Convention of 1956.

The circumstances of that convention significantly affected the confidence of the two men and reflected their relative political strength within the party. Humphrey had openly sought the Vice-Presidential nomination to run with Adlai Stevenson. At a meeting with Stevenson just before the convention convened in Chicago, he and adviser Max Kampelman became convinced that the Presidential nominee would tap him. They inferred from Stevenson's remarks that he considered Humphrey the best qualified, wanted him as a running mate, and expected him to "talk up" his Vice Presidential hopes. But after his own nomination Stevenson astounded the convention and shocked Humphrey by refusing to name his choice and leaving the decision to the delegates. Kennedy, who had spoken to the full convention twice, and his able staff moved quickly in an attempt to win the Vice Presidential nomination. Many Southern delegations were for him. Humphrey, totally unprepared, did not have a chance. Lyndon Johnson, his Senate ally and friend, urged the Texas delegation to support Humphrey, but Southern delegates did not listen. Many

Northern liberal delegates leaned to Estes Kefauver, who had a campaign organization and significant support left over from his unsuccessful effort for the Presidential nomination. Humphrey's advisers urged him to drop out. He was confused and angry, and insisted that he was in the Vice Presidential race "to the bitter end." The end was bitter. In a dramatically close roll call vote Kefauver edged out Kennedy for the nomination. Humphrey was left far behind in the balloting; several reporters and politicians saw tears streaming from his eyes as the surge to Kefauver crushed his candidacy. Kennedy, after his surprising and impressive showing at the convention, was tabbed as a young, dramatic "new face" and "rising star" in national politics. Humphrey, personally hurt but still politically positive, could only say the morning after the convention, "This is all very well—IF we learn from it."

He did not learn enough from the lesson of 1956. Kennedy, who had announced his formal candidacy for the Democratic Presidential nomination in January 1960, campaigned confidently, full time and in all areas of the country, including the South. Humphrey admitted in his formal announcement that he faced an "uphill fight," spent valuable time on his Senate duties, and generally limited his appearances to the upper Midwest, a few liberal-leaning states such as California and New York, and to economically depressed West Virginia.

Liberal Democrats loved him. They cheered and stamped their feet at the eloquence of his speeches, and many told him, privately, that he was by far the best qualified. Mrs. Eleanor Roosevelt said publicly that he came the closest of any Democratic candidate to having "that spark of greatness." In California one of the state's top political professionals remembers that Humphrey "could have won a popularity contest among the party rank and file, even against Stevenson." But when he met with the money and power people of the party, he was greeted with embarrassed silence and closed checkbooks. At the beginning of his formal campaign in January 1960 he had pledges for about sixty thousand dollars, which is little more than pin money in a Presidential campaign. One reporter remembers Humphrey traveling through California in early 1960, trying to drum up support and delegate pledges: "It was pitiful. They all LIKED Humphrey. But there was no excitement or enthusiasm for him. He would have lunch with local party officials and come out beaming with smiles and optimism. But when the local party guys came out, they'd say, 'He's a great guy, but he can't win.' "

Despite his stature in the Senate and the drama of his meeting with Khrushchev, the stigma of Humphrey's 1956 convention defeat lingered. He was regarded as "one of the five serious contenders" for the nomination (Kennedy, Johnson, Symington, and Stevenson were the others), but too many powerful political leaders and influential reporters refused to take him seriously. Reporters liked him; he was quotable, accessible, and fun to cover on the campaign trail. But the old catchwords and clichés were dusted off to describe him: "ultra-liberal . . . talks too much . . . lacks dignity . . . doesn't look like a President . . . too emotional." An aura of political impotence clung to his public image. It did not matter whether the derisive phrases were fair or accurate; they had the real effect of adding to the increasingly prevalent belief that Humphrey "could not win."

The American press, even at the top national level, is made up of normal men and women whose attitudes toward the Presidency are conditioned by understandable awe for that high office. The press may regard a Senator or Governor with unqualified respect for his achievements, his political skills, and his general talents for leadership, but its judgments of him become harsh and demanding when he seeks the Presidency. One Washington reporter, a sophisticated man with ten years of experience covering national politics, once remarked, "At some point a reporter here realizes that a man he knows well—a friend—might be President. It's staggering." Familiarity does not usually breed contempt in reporters for politicians, but it does tend to make them underestimate the men who aspire to the Presidency. Humphrey, throughout the 1950's, was one of the most approachable, friendly, and unassuming political leaders in Washington; relationships between reporters and "good old Hubert" were familiar and easy. In 1960 they underestimated him as he reached for the Presidency.

Even John F. Kennedy, with his greater reserve, aura of dignity, and image of "class," was underestimated by the press in the first few months of his candidacy. One Washington reporter estimates, in retrospect, that two thirds of the capital's press corps did not believe at first that Kennedy could win the nomination, primarily because he was "too young" and because "no Catholic had ever been President." And Kennedy's formal position of power was even more modest than Humphrey's; in the Senate he was below Humphrey in seniority, and at best he stood at the periphery of influence.

Both Kennedy and Humphrey could take only one route in their struggle to win the Democratic Presidential nomination: the state primary elections. By all appearances, the first primary contest between the two men, the April election in Wisconsin, favored Humphrey. That state, a neighbor to Humphrey's Minnesota, had an off-and-on progressive pattern which seemed to be on in 1960. Wisconsin Democrats often, and with good reason, expressed gratitude to Humphrey for performing as the state's "third Senator" in Washington. The western part of the state was populated by small farm families. The center, around the capital of Madison, was distinctly liberal. Milwaukee and other cities on the shore of Lake Michigan were strong labor towns.

The familiarity of Wisconsin Democrats with Humphrey actually hurt his campaign. They knew him. They knew his wife and family background. They knew his record. Many had already seen him in person; most had been reading about him for at least a decade. There was little curiosity among the people of Wisconsin about him. He was, to paraphrase the essence of local introductions to his innumerable campaign speeches, "our old friend, our long-time neighbor, our liberal ally since 1948—good ol' Hubert."

Ironically, the progressive Humphrey's campaign often stressed old slogans and old images. He identified himself with the liberalism of the New Deal and the Fair Deal. His staff distributed thousands of pamphlets picturing him on a rostrum surrounded by chrysanthemums and backed by a huge portrait of Franklin D. Roosevelt. There were moments when he appeared more concerned about the issues of the 1930's—depression and drought—than about the challenges of the 1960's.

When he attacked the policies of the Republican Administration of President Eisenhower, he sometimes conveyed the mood and manner of a hustling pitchman. Harold Hill, the salesman of Meredith Willson's *The Music Man,* sang ominously, "You got trouble, my friends, trouble right here in River City . . . You are not aware of the caliber of the disaster . . ." Humphrey chanted the same theme, trying to jar voters from their slumbering indifference to the "stagnant economy" and the "nose dive of American prestige" under the Eisenhower Administration.

Most people in early 1960 did not really think things were that bad, and they refused to heed Humphrey's plea to "get steamed up." The Democratic Party, above all, did not want to be "remade into the party of liberalism." No one man—not even F.D.R. after his landslide victory of 1936—could succeed in reforming the party overnight. If the Democratic Party, in its collective judgment, wanted any new image, it was the image of twentieth-century youth. Hubert Humphrey did not fit it.

John Kennedy did. In 1960—particularly in Wisconsin—he was a new face and a fresh political personality. The state's voters had seen him on television and read about him in national magazines, but they wanted to know more and to see him in person. They were intrigued by his Boston accent and fascinated by the stories about his wartime heroism and his family. He was young, confident, and different. He was a celebrity.

Kennedy was also a skilled politician, who avoided firm labels such as "liberal" and tried to appeal to all voters, no matter what they called themselves. His was a total campaign in Wisconsin. Humphrey was outmaneuvered, outspent, outstaffed, outtraveled, and even outtalked. On April 9 he was out of the race for the nomination as Kennedy won 56 percent of the vote and six of ten Congressional districts.

Humphrey did not know it; he did not realize that after losing a state bordering his own the realistic, victory-hungry Democratic Party could not nominate him. The polls in Wisconsin had reported he was running behind Kennedy, and he did better in the election than expected. Winning four districts of ten was, to him, a "moral victory." Privately he said that Catholic Republicans had crossed over party lines to provide Kennedy's election win.

"On to West Virginia," some of his exultant staff members cried. "What the hell are you going to do for money?" political realist James Rowe asked them. Leaving Milwaukee for West Virginia (by way of Washington and a day's work in the Senate), Humphrey cheerfully said to reporters, "I always told you fellows politics could be fun, didn't I?"

He had neither fun nor money in West Virginia. He had to dig into his own family bank account to pay for some campaign expenses. In the month between the Wisconsin and West Virginia primaries he sensed that "the political weeds are growing up around me," and that neither his energy nor eloquence were enough to nudge the people across the edge of liberalism. He was an unhappy man, a politician bypassed by a popular tide toward an opponent. His final defeat in West Virginia and formal withdrawal from the Presidential race on May 10 left him with a sense of political desolation and a $20,000 campaign debt.

Humphrey made an enduring, positive impression on national reporters and columnists for the way he bounced back from that defeat with grace, humor, and a positive attitude of getting back to work in the Senate and Minnesota. But his confidence was shaken, at least temporarily. At the Democratic National Convention in Los Angeles in July 1960, he reached a political low point comparable to his squabble with Harry Byrd in 1950. He had a less significant role at that convention than at any since 1944, when he had been "just a delegate." As the Kennedy forces moved to lock up the nomination, he could not at first make up his mind about whom he should support. One friend who saw him at a reception on Monday of that convention week says, "I have never seen Humphrey more dejected." Humphrey knew that Kennedy would be the winner, but he, and a flood of telegrams from Minnesotans, favored Adlai Stevenson. He made his decision after a confrontation with Bobby Kennedy on Tuesday. The front runner's brother and chief campaign aide walked up to him, jabbed an index finger in his chest, and warned, "Hubert, we want your announcement and the pledge of the Minnesota delegation today —or else." Humphrey, in angry mockery of Kennedy's terse and insistent touch, jabbed a finger back at Kennedy's chest and retorted, "Bobby, go to hell."

The next day he endorsed Adlai Stevenson. As expected, the convention nominated John F. Kennedy on the first ballot and he, in turn, chose Lyndon Johnson as his running mate. At the final session in the Los Angeles Coliseum two reporters waiting for Kennedy's acceptance address watched Humphrey as he delivered a brief preliminary talk.

"Poor Hubert," said one. "He won't have a nickel's worth of power in Washington if Kennedy wins the White House—not after fighting the Kennedy clan all the way from January to July." The other reporter nodded in agreement. He glanced affectionately at the eager-voiced, sharp-featured man on the rostrum and added, "Yeah, I guess so. Humphrey's had it."

When the convention ended, the Humphreys drove north to San Francisco for a few days of rest and reappraisal. They saw Adlai Stevenson there briefly. A few weeks later Stevenson wrote this note from his Chicago office:

Dear Hubert: I have been doing one-night stands East and North since we parted on San Francisco Bay. Most of the time I have been trying to devise a suitable letter to you and Muriel—(a) to thank you for gallantry beyond understanding, and (b) to express love and loyalty in suitably masculine terms, and (c) to point out that I was honored beyond expression that you contributed so largely to my 'finest hour.'

All of the foregoing is my way of saying that I have no words with which to thank you for Los Angeles and all that you did to enliven my moribund political person.

I talked with Jack Kennedy at Hyannis Port and will help him, of course, during the campaign. If Minnesota is included on the schedule I will not be disappointed! But I hope a visit with you and Muriel does not depend on that!

With everlasting thanks and warmest regards . . .

That fine letter, it seemed at the time, was about all that Humphrey had to show for his year-long Presidential effort.

He returned to Minnesota in the fall of 1960 with two goals, one immediate and one long-range, which he expressed to his wife and staff: "First we've got to get me re-elected to the Senate. Then I'm going to become the best damned Senator who ever served in that place."

Humphrey may have misjudged the national political mood, but he understood Minnesota and was comfortable and confident with its liberalism. In speech after speech he repeated the sentence: "I am a liberal—and proud of it!" He was only mildly nervous when reminded that his opponent, Republican P. Kenneth Peterson, was a young Mayor of Minneapolis and that no United States Senator from Minnesota had ever been elected to a third term. He was confident enough to leave his own state several times to campaign for Kennedy in South Dakota, Detroit, or New York City. (In New York he impulsively suggested, "Let's go down to the United Nations; the General Assembly is in session."

Assistant Herb Waters prudently reminded him that Khrushchev was at the U.N., might conceivably throw his arms around Humphrey in a gesture of friendship, and—with the help of the wire photo services—cost him votes in Minnesota.)

Though he campaigned with his usual "running scared" instinct, he was also confident enough of his chances to risk losing votes in some areas of Minnesota by plugging hard for Kennedy. Several times old supporters came up to him and said, "Hubert, I've always been for you. But I won't vote for you this time if you keep trying to jam that Catholic down our throats." Humphrey simply turned away, ignored the warnings about anti-Catholic sentiment in some rural areas of Minnesota, and continued to devote at least one fourth of each speech to strong pleas for support for Kennedy.

On November 8, 1960, John F. Kennedy defeated Richard Nixon and won the Presidency by one of the narrowest margins in U.S. election history. He carried Minnesota by a slim twenty thousand votes. Minnesota Governor Orville Freeman was defeated for re-election by Republican Elmer Anderson by the same margin. Hubert Humphrey was re-elected to the Senate by a decisive 240,-000 vote margin. Kennedy would have been elected without Humphrey's appearances for him in New York and other cities and without Minnesota's electoral votes, but he was aware of the unqualified support Humphrey gave him and that he probably would not have won Minnesota without it. He was grateful, and phoned Humphrey soon after the election to thank him. Their conversation was warm and relaxed, without any trace of the bitterness of Wisconsin in April, West Virginia in May, and Los Angeles in July.

The election—won by Kennedy partly because of Southern support—also elevated Lyndon Johnson to the Vice Presidency. In all the post-election discussion about the broken tradition of Protestant-only Presidents, the people overlooked another significant development in 1960: the ascendancy of the Senate as a source of national leaders. Kennedy was the first man to move directly from the Senate to the White House in forty years. The campaign of 1960 represented the first time in the century that the candidates of both major parties were products of the Senate. All four men on the two 1960 tickets—Kennedy, Johnson, Nixon, and

Henry Cabot Lodge—were former Senators. And four of the five "serious" contenders for the Democratic nomination that year (Kennedy, Johnson, Humphrey, and Symington; Adlai Stevenson was the exception) had been Senators. The tradition that Governors had a much better chance for the Presidency was broken in 1960. It was one more bit of evidence of the Senate's increased influence, stature, and importance in national affairs.

Lyndon Johnson's election to the Vice Presidency put Senator Mike Mansfield of Montana in line for the post of Senate Majority Leader. Mansfield wanted Humphrey to move into the final vacancy created by the power shift of 1960, the Assistant Majority Leader position. Both Kennedy and Johnson agreed without hesitation that Humphrey should be offered the Senate Majority Whip job.

Humphrey hesitated in accepting the position. He was at his home on the edge of Minnesota's Lake Waverly when Mansfield phoned to make the offer. He was grateful, but asked for "a bit of time" to think it over.

It was winter. He put on a warm jacket and strolled down to the shore. He looked across to the little town of Waverly, where the two biggest buildings are churches and where people take their independence for granted and never worry about power struggles. Turning away from his house (and the ever ringing, ever demanding telephone), he walked a path bordering the icy fringe of the lake and weighed the disadvantages and opportunities of the Senate Majority Whip position.

It would restrict his freedom of action and expression as a Senator. It would reduce to some extent the political and legislative independence he had always enjoyed. It would make him slightly less individualistic and more responsible to the chain of leadership stretching from the White House to the offices of the legislative leaders. It would, approximately, double the scope of his work in the Senate.

But the position would give him greater influence within Congress. He would be in a better position to advance his own legislative causes. He would be able to do more to put his convictions into practice. He would speak not just to an empty chamber and through the cold pages of the Congressional Record, but directly to the men who held the greatest share of power in the nation. He would have access to the White House and a voice in central policy decisions. And finally (this *was* a significant factor affecting his decision), it would be "fun" to have breakfast at the White House every Tuesday morning with the President and other legislative leaders.

He decided to give up a bit of independence to gain a bit of power. A month later Senate Democrats voted him into the Majority Whip position. There was never any doubt. The President and Vice President supported him, but that was less important than the fact that he was regarded by his colleagues as being "of" and "with" the Senate. He had run for the Presidency, but had not abused or ignored his Senate office in that attempt. He had canceled speeches and fund-raising receptions to return to the chamber for key votes. Even though he lost his bid for the Presidency, he had emerged from the year 1960 with grace and good will; he had done nothing to "demean" the office of United States Senator. In the view of his colleagues, what he had done or failed to do outside the Senate barely mattered. It was what he had done and could do in the cloistered world of the Senate that counted. The Senate's Majority—including the Southerners—unanimously elected him to a position of leadership.

The United States Senate had not, as many had predicted twelve years before, stifled Humphrey. In the final analysis, it elevated him.

PART IV

THE LEADER

18

Talent and Technique

Political leadership, in a representative democracy, requires infinite patience and persistence. The cumbersome shape and tedious processes of democratic government depress or discard men who lack those qualities. No man in the United States can inherit or grab real leadership. To be a leader the ambitious man must spend many years cultivating his political talents and acquiring his political techniques. Time—a long time—is required for the quality of effective leadership to evolve.

Hubert Humphrey is not a particularly patient man. If he is confined to rigid programs or schedules, his temper can flare. Generally he is unable to plot a clear and precise course toward a distinct goal. In his years in the Senate he often issued finely measured proposals for "a seven-point program" to solve a national problem. More typically, he made urgent pleas for "a crash program" or "a blue-ribbon commission" to tackle a problem head-on. He is impatient with the entrapments of big government and intolerant of bureaucrats who respond to challenges with organization charts, listings of precedents, timetables, agenda, memoranda in triplicate, formal conferences, committees, subcommittees, and finally cautiously worded and expensively printed "Tentative Recommendations for Study."

"Most areas of the world," he once said, "suffer from some disease. In many regions it's dysentery. In Washington the disease of the Potomac is timidity." He scoffs at government administrators who use the expression "in the long run." "Hell," he exclaims, "in the long run we'll all be dead!" On a summer morning in 1963, when he was immersed in a dozen urgent tasks, his secretary poked her head through the doorway to his private office and asked "for a minute to check some long-range plans with you." (She needed his decisions on several important invitations for events less than a week away.) "Long-range plans?" he asked in dismay. "There ARE no long-range plans. You just get up in the morning and go to work. That's the only plan you ever make." His secretary knew that his jovial tone veiled a serious mood; she disappeared to leave him to his work of the moment.

If he is told that the Department of State needs a week to prepare a speech text he has requested, he usually turns instead to an assistant with instructions to have a draft prepared by the following morning, or in ten minutes he will personally dictate "notes" from which he will ad-lib. If an aide begins to explain the difficulties involved in an assigment, he responds, "I don't care HOW it's done; just DO it." When he is told that a problem is, at least for the moment, unsolvable, he tries to solve it anyway, and right away. On an average day he speaks the word "now" a hundred times. One of the few foreign-language words he remembered after several tours through Latin America was *"Pronto."*

Almost everything, for him, is urgent. At least half of his spoken statements, if appropriately punctuated in written transcriptions, would end in exclamation points. "Time," he once said, "is man's most precious possession. Time is meaningless unless it is used. Wasted time can never be recovered. We haven't got a minute to lose!"

When he speaks of time, one senses that he is thinking of life, with a capital *L*. In the midst of his consciousness there seems to be an awareness that in every instant human beings are dying of hunger, or succumbing to tyranny, or racing toward nuclear annihilation. He cannot, in the face of such waste or danger, be patient. Emotionally he cannot comprehend why mankind allows any of its members to be hungry, or enslaved, or passively balanced on the tip of a bomb.

In many of his speeches he reaches a mood of desperate earnestness in which his whole soul seems to call out, "Wake up, America! There can be no slumbering. You are a compassionate people with wisdom and resources. Don't waste them! There is so much to be done, so much work for you to do. And there is so little time for you to do it."

When he was a freshman at Doland High School, a teacher told him, "Hubert, if you don't throttle down, you'll be dead before you're a senior." Senator Clinton Anderson of New Mexico says of his first meeting with Humphrey in Albuquerque in 1946, "We were on a radio program together. I was impressed. He gave more force and coherence to the ideas of democracy and the needs for famine relief than I ever could—and I was a Cabinet member [Secretary of Agriculture] then and had been head of a world food program. But I was a bit sad, too. He seemed terribly intense. He seemed to want to save the world that afternoon. I would have predicted that he would die of exhaustion or a heart attack within two years." Humphrey still appears to be propelled, in part, by a fear that seconds, minutes, and hours are slipping away unfulfilled. Many friends and observers say that he lives and works each day "as if it were his last." He does not even like to take time to look at a clock or wristwatch. But at one end of the living room of his home—in an area less than twelve feet square—there are three clocks.

His depression-dust bowl experience "taught me a sort of patience," he says. The position of Assistant Majority Leader in the Senate developed a greater capacity for patience, or at least forced him to control his impatience. Essentially the Whip job in the Senate requires a man to be his party's persuader, to deal with dozens of independent and strong-willed men in a continuing effort to win agreement for a majority decision. As Majority Whip from 1961 through 1964 he could not enjoy the luxury of impatience. He was responsible not just to himself and his conscience, but to a President, to the institution of the Senate, and to some sixty-five Democratic Senators. He straddled the turbulent middle ground between the public, the Presidency, and the Congress. He did not have the authority of the Majority Leader, Mike Mansfield, but he shared the responsibility to forge agreement and decision out of the conflicting interests and forces represented in the Senate. Often he returned to the privacy of his office sputtering with indignation about politicians who were dull or deceitful or scowling with impatience over the slow and ponderous processes of the Senate. But in the chamber and in his relationships with other members he was relatively calm and almost constantly reasonable. Most members of the Senate agree that by 1964 he had learned to be tolerant of the differing views of others and patient about the

tedious detail of his job and the natural reluctance of the Senate to
act quickly and decisively.

He did not have to learn perseverance; his talent for leadership
springs in part from a natural determination to persist against any
odds for a cause in which he believes. "He's a stubborn jackass,"
says one politician who has opposed—and often lost to—him. "He
never gives up, does he?" asks a reporter who has watched the ups
and downs of his career. For Humphrey a political loss is "a temporary setback," a series of defeats is "an interlude," and a major
failure is "a moral victory" or "a good lesson from which we can
learn something."

From 1949 through 1960 he repeatedly introduced legislation in
the Senate which most experts said had no chance of being enacted. The first bill he sponsored, for a program of health insur-
ance for the elderly financed and administered through Social
Security, was introduced in 1949. Two years later it died as the 81st
Congress adjourned without acting on it. The following January
he introduced the bill again. Two years later it died again. For six
years he tried, and the bill failed. In 1955 he switched strategy and
asked Senator Anderson to introduce the bill, figuring that sponsorship by Anderson, a member of the Finance Committee, would
carry more weight. Every two years Anderson introduced the measure, which became known as "Medicare." The proposal picked up
supporters and made some headway through the committee process. By 1960 the Medicare Bill reached the full Senate for debate,
but was rejected. In the 87th Congress it was narrowly defeated,
primarily because of opposition from Robert Kerr of Oklahoma.
At the end of the 88th Congress in 1964, Humphrey refused to be
discouraged when busy, election-minded colleagues bypassed the
measure. "Back in 1949," he said, "nobody paid any attention to
it. Now it is an important issue and it has powerful sponsors in
Congress and widespread support among the people. Its time will
come."

In the period of 1961 through 1964, Humphrey's years of persistent effort were crowned with victory for a score of progressive
measures in the fields of education, conservation, welfare, civil
rights, and foreign relations. Throughout his Senate career his
staff kept a log of the bills and resolutions he sponsored. Every two
years a secretary retyped the pages almost without change and

replaced them in a black binder kept by his legislative assistant. Many of the measures remained in the log for six, eight, or even twelve years. Beginning in 1961, many were checked off with the notation "Approved" or "Signed into law." In the summer of 1964, Humprhey's legislative assistant, John Stewart, remarked, "It seems strange. The listings in the log have dwindled. Only a few of the old Humphrey proposals haven't passed."

(Even a Humphrey resolution to proclaim a national "Leif Ericson Day," which he had first introduced in 1952, was finally approved in the spring of 1964. He was disappointed in October when the election campaign kept him away from a State Department ceremony honoring the Scandinavian explorer. For twelve years he had promoted the resolution which identified the Viking as the first man to discover America. A week later he happily joined a parade in New York City for another gentleman credited with the discovery, the Italian Christopher Columbus.)

He once told a group of teachers, "It is the duty of a leader to get just a bit ahead of the people on an issue. And then it is his duty to educate the people. He can't get too far ahead, or he'll be alone, and he can't lecture to them or talk over their heads. I try to be a leader by staying just a bit ahead of prevailing public opinion at any time. And I try to get the people interested and involved in an issue, so they will educate themselves."

In 1950 he was far ahead of prevailing public opinion when he made his first formal statement in Washington on the issue of disarmament. On March 1 of that year, a month after President Truman announced his order for construction of the H-bomb, he inserted into the Congressional Record an address he had given at Washington's National Cathedral entitled "God, Man and the Hydrogen Bomb." At a time when most of the American people and almost all of the members of Congress were determined to build a bigger and more powerful nuclear arsenal, he idealistically and somewhat naïvely pleaded for "universal disarmament," a "halt to the terrifying arms race," and an "unequivocal agreement to abolish war." The substance of his 1950 address was more pacifistic than practical, but it did include hints of concern for the actual problems of arms control. "Our national interest, and not just peace," he said, "impels us to make new efforts to negotiate [with the Soviet Union]." He also warned against the concept of "unilateral disarmament," and spoke of the need for a "control system" for any disarmament agreement.

He spoke generally and hopefully about disarmament many times in the next four years; his statements rated only an occasional paragraph or two in Washington newspapers. "The people weren't exactly steamed up about the need for disarmament efforts as the cold war intensified," he remembers. He was. He saw two antagonistic nations hurling threats at each other and at the same time building weapons and missiles which "could end life and civilization for all time." In 1955 he concluded that universal disarmament was only a dream, but that some practical, realistic effort to halt the arms race had to be made. "The United States," he said in the Senate, "must begin to seek progress in those areas— no matter how limited—in which there appears some chance of agreement and progress."

To most Americans there did not appear to be any chance then for agreement or progress. Humphrey, however, sponsored a resolution to establish a Congressional Disarmament Subcommittee, at first made up of members of the Senate Foreign Relations and Armed Services Committees and the Joint Atomic Energy Committee. (Later it was placed under the Foreign Relations Committee.) At the same time President Eisenhower appointed former Minnesota Governor Harold Stassen as a disarmament adviser, with an office in the State Department but with no budget for any significant research. In January 1956, Humphrey's resolution was approved. He was offered the chairmanship of the new Disarmament Subcommittee, and eagerly accepted. Francis Valeo, the first subcommittee staff director, remembers, "It wasn't a popular subject. Most people in Washington had grave reservations that disarmament, *per se,* could be advanced by any rational argument. Humphrey didn't pay any attention to the doubters, but he learned as Chairman to move cautiously, to be restrained, and to hold back until the right time for his proposals."

Betty Goetz (now Mrs. Arthur Lal), who replaced Valeo as staff director and remained in that position to become one of the few disarmament experts in the nation, says that Humphrey was determined to become "responsible" in his new position. "I want to stop talking in generalities and get to specifics," he told her. "We've got to go into the most important aspects of this field in a responsible, practical way."

"The most important aspect," they soon determined, was un-limited nuclear weapons testing. In April, Humphrey called a sub-committee meeting to hear testimony by Atomic Energy Commis-sion Chairman Thomas Murray. The AEC chief confirmed, for some, suspicions that unrestrained testing of nuclear weapons car-ried definite risks. In the fall Presidential candidate Adlai Steven-son, using some of the material from Murray's testimony, urged a U.S. effort for a nuclear test ban agreement. President Eisenhower said the suggestion was "dangerous." Vice President Nixon called Stevenson's proposals "catastrophic nonsense." In October 1956, Humphrey's subcommittee released a report on the technical as-pects of nuclear weapons testing and urged a policy by the United States to pursue a test ban treaty among the nuclear powers. In addition he began sending letters to Secretary of State John Foster Dulles, urging "at least" a budget, program, and staff within the Department for research into the technical and scientific aspects of nuclear weapons testing. Eisenhower and Nixon were re-elected in November. The Administration ignored Humphrey's recommen-dations to the State Department.

There was indifference in Congress also. In early 1957, Hum-phrey asked the Joint Atomic Energy Committee to conduct hear-ings on radioactive fallout from nuclear tests. The Joint Commit-tee declined. He proceeded to conduct fallout hearings through his own subcommittee; they generated interest and headlines. The Joint Committee reconsidered, and conducted its own hearings in May.

Humphrey's letters to Dulles, much less polite than in 1956, needled the State Department for "fiddling" on disarmament problems and test ban possibilities. Through this period news-papers began to give prominent play to statements by Humphrey and warnings by some scientists of the possible health risks from fallout. In 1958, Humphrey endeavored to arouse and educate Congress and the public on the nuclear test ban issue. During the week before Easter he spoke on the subject in the Senate every day. On February 4 he asked the help of Majority Leader Lyndon Johnson; Johnson rounded up more than forty Democratic Sena-tors to be present for a major Senate address on the test ban issue by Humphrey. That speech lasted four hours; it prompted related statements by twenty-two other Senators. His approach by then was both idealistic and coldly practical. He urged that an efficient

system to *detect* weapons testing had to be developed before the
United States could sign any agreement, and that the government
should stand on a policy of separating the test ban issue from
other disarmament problems and proposals. Both ideas were new
concepts at the time. (The U.S. up to then had regarded a test ban
only as a political problem, and had not thoroughly investigated
the scientific aspects of a detection or control system. The
U.S.S.R., cynically, and the more vocal American peace groups,
sincerely, were wedded to the idea of "total" disarmament, and
were unwilling to discuss "phased" disarmament.)

Humphrey was encouraged in 1958 by a flood of letters favoring
his test ban proposals and by President Eisenhower's newly announced advocacy of a test ban agreement. But in 1959 and 1960,
Congressional interest in the subject waned as U.S. and Soviet
negotiators reached an apparent stalemate in disarmament conferences. President Eisenhower sustained his effort to work for a controlled test ban agreement, but he had little support from his own
lieutenants in the State Department and Congress. Humphrey,
one Senator remembers, was "the only influential member" of
Congress who was making any significant effort for a test ban. "He
was alone—all alone—on this issue," a Republican Senator says.
"Nobody else really gave a damn about disarmament or technical
studies for detection systems of nuclear testing." Humphrey struggled to keep interest alive. On March 26, 1959, he introduced a
Senate resolution to "support the efforts of the United States to
continue to negotiate for an international agreement for the suspension of nuclear weapons test . . ." The resolution was approved, by voice vote, but most Senators considered it (in the
words of one) "a harmless little thing."

He was told repeatedly, "Why do you waste your time on this?
Nobody cares." . . . "The Soviets are never going to agree to a test
ban; give up, Hubert." . . . "It's all too technical; people don't
understand all this seismic detection business." . . . "You aren't
being realistic; you've made a good try at this, but a test ban just
isn't possible." Equally irritating to him were militant pacifists
who patted him on the back with one hand and waved BAN THE
BOMB and UNILATERAL DISARMAMENT NOW signs.
"Sometimes," he sighed, "a man's biggest problem is the cynicism
of his friends and the zeal of his supporters."

On February 4, 1960, he introduced a carefully prepared, detailed bill to establish a "National Peace Agency." The bill called for a modest step: a staff and a budget for research into test ban and other disarmament problems and coordination of the government's slowly increasing disarmament studies (then split among the State Department, the Defense Department, and half a dozen other offices). The bill got nowhere, but he did push through Congress, after four years of trying, a small appropriation for disarmament research in the State Department.

He was encouraged by President Kennedy's attitude. (On June 6, 1963, Humphrey told a conference on disarmament at Racine, Wisconsin, "The President is obsessed with the prospect of proliferation of nuclear weapons. He, better than anybody else, understands the problem. He sees a barely manageable situation slipping out of control. He is frustrated, but not hopeless.") In the spring of 1961, Humphrey worked with the Kennedy Administration to polish his legislation for a separate agency to handle disarmament research. On June 29 he introduced a bill to establish a "United States Disarmament Agency." Kennedy was cautious. In early July, when Humphrey returned from a trip to Berlin, the two men spent a late morning hour discussing international affairs. Humphrey remembers:

"We were in the middle of another Berlin crisis—a bad one. The whole world looked on as if it might be plunged into war or greater tension. The United States was boosting its defense budget to meet the new and tougher threats of the Soviet Union. President Kennedy and I talked about all this.

"Then, around noon, we went down to the White House pool for a swim. And while we were swimming back and forth we were also talking about the prospects for Congressional approval of the Disarmament Agency Bill.

"We had hardly got dried off when the President asked, 'Do you really think that we have any chance on this?'

"I answered, 'Mr. President, I don't know, but I know that we can at least give it an honest effort. If we fail, we can try again.' "

At least 90 percent of Washington's legislative experts and reporters—if they cared—expected the Disarmament Agency Bill to fail. Again and again Humphrey was asked, "How can you expect Congress to vote for a bill and funds for disarmament at a time when the Berlin crisis may blow up and when we are increasing our armed forces?" Top Administration leaders concluded that the bill had no chance of Congressional approval and that the agency should be established by executive order. Humphrey, convinced that the agency needed the strength of statutory authority, persisted. For several weeks he lobbied other Senators, helped arrange for an impressive array of witnesses, including military officers, to testify in favor of the bill, and made minor concessions to pick up extra votes. (Some Senators objected to the word "disarmament," and wanted the bill to specify "Arms Control Agency." A compromise resulted in the title "Arms Control and Disarmament Agency.")

The Senate debate lasted a week. One key amendment, which would have stripped the agency of all research funds, was beaten by a 44 to 43 vote. The bill itself was approved by a substantial majority in August. After Representative Howard Smith's Rules Committee cleared the bill, the House of Representatives quickly approved it and sent it to the White House for the President's signature.

In the summer of 1962 negotiations for a test ban treaty bogged down when the Soviet Union rejected American demands for an inspection system which would include on-site surveys of suspected nuclear tests. Humphrey was satisfied that research by the Arms Control and Disarmament Agency and others had developed an efficient detection system for all but underground tests. In late July and early August he urged the United States to seek agreement for a "limited" ban, covering tests in the atmosphere, underwater, and in outer space. Congress was skeptical, but the President made the suggestion to the Soviet Union for negotiations on the "limited" test ban idea. The Russians refused to consider it.

After he participated in the continuing but unproductive test ban negotiations in Geneva in February 1963, a somber Humphrey told the Senate, "Unless some agreement can be reached within six months, the prospect of *any* test ban agreement for many years will be nil." In the spring he sensed a "softer" line by Khrushchev in Soviet-American relations, and renewed his proposal. He picked up support from Senator Thomas Dodd of Connecticut, who had been against a general nuclear test ban agreement but now favored the idea of a limited treaty. The two men worked on a draft resolution suggesting a formal U.S. offer for such a treaty. Dodd introduced the resolution in the Senate on May 27, with Humphrey as first co-sponsor. Thirty-two other Senators joined as sponsors.

On June 10, after an informal exchange of letters and meetings between U.S. and Soviet officials, President Kennedy announced that the offer had been made and that negotiations would begin in Moscow at the end of the month. In an address at American University in Washington the President pleaded for public understanding of the need for a "first step" toward control of nuclear weapons and spoke of a world made "safe for diversity." The Moscow negotiations were successful, and on July 25 representatives of the United States, Great Britain, and the Soviet Union initialed the draft treaty suspending nuclear weapons testing aboveground. Humphrey, Senate Foreign Relations Committee Chairman William Fulbright, and other Senate leaders of both parties watched as America's Averell Harriman, Russia's Andrei Gromyko, and Britain's Alec Douglas-Home initialed the one-page document.

The Americans returned to Washington in a Presidental jet to face the Senate debate on ratification of the treaty. Approval was expected, but Humphrey remembered the lessons of 1919, when Woodrow Wilson's dream for the League of Nations was shattered by angry opposition led by Republican Senator Henry Cabot Lodge Sr. In the Senate hearings and debate on the test ban treaty he stressed the need for bipartisanship to achieve the two-thirds majority required for approval. A few liberal Democrats were irritated by "all the attention Hubert and the President are paying to the Republicans," but Humphrey devoted most of his efforts to convincing Senate Republican Leader Everett Dirksen and others of the wisdom and safety of the treaty. Dirksen at first spoke of the need for "reservations" to the treaty, which at that time would have hopelessly confused its status since almost a hundred nations had approved it. But in a dramatic and eloquent speech in September, Dirksen announced his full support and called on his colleagues to vote for ratification.

On September 24, 1963, by a vote of 80 to 19, the Senate approved ratification of the first international treaty of any type to restrict the use and development of nuclear weapons.

Harriman, chief U.S. negotiator for the treaty in Moscow, appeared on the cover of *Time*. Most American newspapers stressed Dirksen's decisive influence for Senate approval. The treaty was frequently referred to in the press as "the President's triumph." Humphrey, if he was mentioned at all, was usually quoted briefly near the end of any story. In a White House ceremony at which the President signed the treaty, Humphrey stood behind Dirksen, Harriman, Fulbright, and others who had made a very real contribution to the effort. As the ceremony ended and the witnesses filed out of the President's office, Kennedy called Humphrey back for a moment. "Hubert," he said quietly, "this is your treaty." And then he added with a smile, "And it had better work."

Humphrey sums up his own attitude about the technique of leadership with these words: "As a politician—and I AM a politician—I seek the widest area of agreement. I seek to be an educator, to bring people within the scope or within the sphere of agreement. Men can disagree, argue, and debate without being personal, without being arrogant, without being insolent. I don't agree with all men. I try to lead them into an area of agreement." On June 21, 1963, in an interview on Washington television station WETA, he remarked, "As the Whip in the Senate—a title for the Assistant Majority Leader—my task is primarily to cajole and to persuade, and to be a psychoanalyst of my colleagues in the hope that by understanding what is bothering them on a particular day, or what motivates them relating to a particular piece of legislation, I [can help bring] a consensus or majority to support a program . . ."

"Sure," he once said, "you can browbeat people and threaten them and force them to do something. But that's manipulation, not leadership. I don't want artificial progress. I want people to understand what they are being asked to do. That's the only way a free people can be led."

When Humphrey is "tough" (a political colloquialism somewhat synonomous with ruthlessness), the issue involved is usually relatively minor. He can berate a reporter for failing to file a long story on a pet bill, or shout at a listless bureaucrat who has bottlenecked some obscure project. In the period from 1960 through

1964, however, his staff can recall only one occasion when he was "ruthless." That came in 1962, when he sponsored a resolution which called for nothing more earth-shaking than a commendation for the federal program of giving surplus food to schools and authorized a "National School Lunch Week." The resolution easily passed the Senate, but in the final legislative rush of the session it was overlooked at the last scheduled meeting of the House Judiciary Committee. Humphrey phoned the committee Chairman, Representative Emanuel Celler of New York, to ask for action. Celler explained that the committee had no more meetings scheduled. Humphrey became angry, and threatened to kill every private House bill (sponsored by individual Congressman, usually for local projects) that came to the Senate unless the Judiciary Committee met again and the resolution was approved. "I don't care how you get the committee together," he told Celler. "That's your problem. I just want that resolution passed." Celler relented, called the committee together, and pushed Humphrey's National School Lunch Week resolution through the House.

For most of his efforts Humphrey employs friendly persuasion, furious work, and a cultivation of the respect of other men. "I don't agree with Humphrey often," says one Southern Senator, "but I trust him. He's not a sneaky man, and he doesn't play both sides of the street. And he doesn't ask a man to do something which he knows is contrary to the man's convictions or which would be politically dangerous to him back home."

In many of his formal speeches Humphrey uses what could be called a "hard sell" technique, pounding home a point with overstatement, repetition, and rhetoric. In conferences and discussions with other men of power he is generally logical in argument, quiet in speech, and almost soft in demeanor. On a late afternoon in 1962, during the liberals' filibuster against the Communications Satellite Bill, he slid into a chair next to one petulant and uncompromising Senator and said, "Gosh, ——, I hate a fight like this. It makes me mean; it makes everybody mean. We've got to live and work together in this place. Why don't we just chat about this bill a little and see if we can't calm things down?" The liberal answered coldly, "There's nothing to talk about." Humphrey sighed, cleared his voice, and asked, "Say, have they finished putting in that new rec room out at your house?" The liberal did not abandon the filibuster attempt, but he stopped scowling at Humphrey, and a few weeks later they were cheerfully working together on another bill. "I'd rather talk to a man—about anything under the sun—than glare at him," Humphrey says.

In early 1963, in an address on arms control to a Michigan audience, he touched on a more basic element of his capacity for leadership:

"I used to be an expert on disarmament. Now, as Senate Whip, I conduct a sort of political smörgåsbord. A leader in this nation cannot confine his interest to just one or two subjects.

"And a leader cannot just be mildly interested in things. He must *believe*. If one thing characterizes my political life, it is that I have conviction. Some people call it idealism. Maybe it is, but I don't think that a man or a leader should approach things with a sterile, rational approach. A leader must have a sense of advocacy, a sense of conviction. I do. I try to be a leader. I believe."

19

Conviction

The public reputation of Hubert Humphrey has seldom been fuzzy or obscure, even in recent years, when, as he admits, he has "mellowed and matured." But his critics suggest that he "lacks direction," and even his friends are occasionally confused by his volatile personality. "I don't know how to identify Humphrey," said one Senator who was close to him for ten years. "He is so MANY things." Another complained, "He seems to flit thoughtlessly from cause to cause. The man doesn't focus on anything. I really don't think he has a clear idea of where he's going."

Such comments are understandable, considering the variety of Humphrey's interests and the mercurial shifts of his moods, but they represent shallow assessments of the man. There is a distinct consistency in the pattern of his life and career. The coherence of his identity and the force of his leadership come, in large measure, from his convictions. They are not haphazard opinions which he has pasted to the periphery of his political personality. They are deeply rooted beliefs which dominate him and direct most of his statements.

His convictions are as simple as he is complex. Reporters have trouble writing about speeches in which he states his primary beliefs. "It was corny, but nice," said one after a typical Humphrey speech. Feature stories which touch on the substance of his messages include such comments as "He gave them the Bible bit" or "he osterized a bit of the Constitution and a bushel of corn." Grudgingly one magazine writer reported, "His style was cornier than ever, but there was something affecting and appealing about it, too."

It is not superficial to suggest that Humphrey's beliefs *are* right out of the Bible or the Constitution. He often paraphrases centuries' old concepts: "We must heal the sick, feed the hungry, teach the illiterate." . . . "The pursuit of happiness, that's what America believes is the right path." . . . "What do the people of the world seek? They seek life, liberty, and happiness."

Humphrey believes—without qualification and almost reverently—in these concepts and human qualities: justice, peace, freedom, kindness, opportunity, equality, brotherhood, life, happiness.

"Those are beautiful words, positive words, powerful words," he says. "There is nothing new about them. But maybe the trouble with this country is that we have a complex about the *new*. If the Good Lord stood on Capitol Hill tomorrow and repeated the message of the Sermon on the Mount, everybody would say, 'Oh, there's no news in that; He said it already.' We're blind to the ancient but vital truths, that's our trouble.

"We need to take some of these words which represent the essence of our beliefs and shake off the dust which our dullness has coated them with. We need to use them in a meaningful way. We need to believe them, with all our hearts and souls. We need to practice them, not just for an hour on Sunday mornings, but positively, every day."

The printed word cannot fully convey the force with which Humphrey expresses his basic convictions. As he speaks, his voice throbs with emotion and his hands stretch out as if to share a great and wonderful possession with others. His passion is contagious. In the town of Herman, Minnesota, in October 1960, he generated excitement among a few score farmers with a dynamic delivery of a message which, reduced to its substance, said, "Be kind to your neighbor." In 1962, after an interview relating to a recent Latin-American trip, one reporter left his private office with the remark: "I feel like quitting my job and going down there to do volunteer work in the slums." In one Senate debate on civil rights a Humphrey speech about "justice" moved a Southern Senator to tears. (The Southerner still voted against the bill, but he later wrote Humphrey a note of respect and admiration.) Humphrey's effectiveness as a speaker is not just the result of polished oratorical techniques. He can "capture" an audience, at least temporarily, because the spirit of his total commitment to basic ideals pervades the mood of a stuffy auditorium and penetrates the intellectualism of his listeners.

The qualities of justice, peace, freedom, kindness, opportunity, equality, brotherhood, life, and happiness are, for Humphrey, "God-given rights." If any human being on earth does not enjoy them, he believes, then no human being should feel comfortable. If some men do not feel a commitment to secure these rights for all men, they lack a sense of "humanity." He is committed. The founding fathers, he says often, were not halfhearted about their beliefs. "They pledged their lives, their fortunes, and their sacred honor. They didn't pledge a few months of their lives. They didn't pledge ten percent of their fortunes. They didn't pledge just a little bit of their honor. They gave themselves to their beliefs; they committed themselves totally."

What he calls his "commitments of conscience and conviction" are total. It is not enough for him to talk about them, however eloquently. He tries to translate them into policy and program.

"Let us begin at the beginning," he told a farm organization in 1963. "Human beings have a right to live. People must eat. Millions of people in the world are not eating enough to live." In a televised debate with conservative Russell Kirk in the same year, he said , "This nation spent seven billion dollars [in 1962] trying to *stop* American production of food in a world of the hungry. We're NUTS! How do you justify from any economic, moral, or political point of view the spending of billions [soil bank and acreage reserve payments and surplus storage costs] to stop a nation from producing food when millions of God's children are hungry?"

In those statements he touched on the ultimate, senseless tragedy of the modern world: the superabundance of food in the United States and several other nations and the hunger of people in a zone of poverty around the world. "My people out in the Midwest just don't understand this," he said at a meeting of Agency for International Development officials in early 1964. "We explain to them that you can't just give food away. The economists tell them that market values would be disrupted. The bureaucrats tell them that there is no money available to transport the food overseas. But out in the Midwest, where wheat is rotting in ugly storage bins and the newspapers are filled with stories about people starving to death overseas, my neighbors just can't accept this. And neither can I."

As he could not passively accept the pattern of an unchecked nuclear arms race, he could not ignore a need to bridge at least part of the gap between American agricultural abundance and world hunger. In 1950—his second year in the Senate—he prodded the Truman Administration into grants of wheat to famine-stricken India and Pakistan. And in 1952, at a conference of the Grain Terminal Association in St. Paul, Minnesota, he first suggested the plan which has come to be known as "Food for Peace."

On February 25, 1954, he defined the proposal in a bill (S. 3020) which authorized the President "to use agricultural commodities to improve the foreign relations of the United States, to relieve famine and for other purposes." Reporters and other Senators paid little attention to the bill. When Humphrey asked for a unanimous consent agreement to give him five minutes to speak on it, one Senator expressed irritation: "I hope this will be the last request for an extension of time. I think this morning hour today has been used a little indiscriminately."

Humphrey spoke briefly, beginning, "I have studied all these proposals [for a continuing program to send U.S. food to other nations], finding merit in most of them. But none covers the entire problem . . . I believe that [my] bill combines the best of several proposals."

The bill had five provisions. The first four related to extension of Presidential authority to use food for famine relief, efforts to increase formal exports of agricultural products, and protection of American markets and prices against the "dumping" of commodities on world markets. The fifth provision was new, and it defined the core of the Food for Peace idea. It authorized the sale of surplus U.S. food and provided "for use of foreign currencies obtained through such sales for . . . loans to increase production of goods and services in friendly countries and for purchases of goods and services in friendly countries . . ." Humphrey later explained, "In other words, our American agricultural abundance will be converted into positive programs of peace and progress in underdeveloped countries. The local currencies earned by sale of our food will be loaned back to the countries for economic development, schools, hospitals, and training programs to help the people to help themselves."

The proposal was adopted by the Eisenhower Administration, whose officials regarded it more as a surplus disposal program than what Humphrey described as "the use of America's agricultural resources as a positive arm of our foreign policy." And, he added often, as a "humane but practical" effort to feed the hungry and fight poverty.

Senator George McGovern of South Dakota, who was Food for Peace director in 1961 and 1962, says flatly, "For years Humphrey was the only voice in the Senate pushing the Food for Peace concept. The idea seized him, and he could not see why it was not quickly accepted and put into action and practice. He dramatized the issue and prodded the Administration and Congress to accept it. He was the first to propose a separate and high-level government office to administer the program. Humphrey was the Congressional father of the Food for Peace program." (McGovern is a modest man. He did not mention that he played a key role when he was in the House of Representatives to complete Congressional approval of Food for Peace legislation.)

In January 1959, President Eisenhower publicly advanced the idea and formally approved of legislation to expand Food for Peace. Humphrey continued to press for a bigger and more efficiently administered program. By 1964, American food, through sales for local currencies or outright grants, was reaching a hundred million people in eighty-five nations. The nutrition of forty million children overseas was being improved through school lunch and preschool feeding programs under Food for Peace. In Latin America, U.S.-donated food reached a third of all school-age children. In 1963, $1.7 billion worth of U.S. agricultural commodities was shipped overseas. In addition, the government's Food for Peace office cooperated with such private relief agencies as CARE, Church World Service, Catholic Relief Services, and the American Jewish Joint Distribution Committee. In 1964 fifteen private agencies were distributing U.S.-donated food valued at $379 million.

Three fourths of the commodities shipped overseas under the Food for Peace program in 1963 was sold for local currencies, because the countries most in need of food were generally the least able to pay for it with American dollars. In fiscal year 1963 these local currencies paid the equivalent of $211 million of U.S. bills overseas, for such services as construction of U.S. military housing. And local currencies equaling $746 million were lent back to participating nations for the construction and staffing of hospitals and schools, and for other development programs.

The Food for Peace program, in large measure advanced and enlarged on Humphrey's initiative, demonstrates a dual-purpose motivation which characterizes most of his proposals. He believes that individuals and nations can be kind and practical at the same time. "We did this [the Food for Peace program] first because it was the morally right thing to do," he said to a group of high school students in the spring of 1963. "We did it because we are a kind and compassionate people who cannot sit back on our abundance while people are going hungry in the world. But we also did it as a part of our overall foreign policy and security program. Our food is fighting the conditions on which tyranny and totalitarianism thrive—hunger, disease, illiteracy, poverty. In this world of struggle between the 'haves' and the 'have-nots,' food is as powerful a weapon as bombs. It is *more* powerful. Because food gives life, not death. It builds instead of destroys. Food is strength, not weakness. And I want our America to be strong so that it can save lives, not conquer nations. Let history judge us as a nation of teachers and builders, not soldiers. Let us be worthy of greatness by responding positively to the challenge of peace, not by reacting negatively to the threat of war."

Humphrey believes, deeply and completely, that peace is a positive force, not just a suspended state between wars. In the middle of a loud and angry speech about communism he once digressed to say softly, *"Peace*—what a beautiful word that is! What a positive word that is! The Communists have stolen and corrupted the word and concept of peace. We're afraid to use it in this country now, for fear that we'll be called 'pacifists' or 'left-wingers.' But I'm not afraid to say I believe in peace and I'll work for peace fulltime. The Bible says, 'Blessed are the peacemakers, for they shall be called the children of God.' I believe that."

He supports the military and defense-related programs which consume more than half of the annual federal budget. But his deep belief in the "rightness" and practicality of positive programs for peace compels him to do more. His work for a treaty suspending nuclear weapons testing was one result. The Food for Peace program is another. A third is the Peace Corps.

The idea was not new in 1960, when he introduced the first bill to establish a program to send young American volunteers overseas for teaching and economic development programs. ("So what?" he said again. "There hasn't been a really *new* idea since the time of Cicero or Christ.") The late Senator Richard Neuberger of Oregon and Representative Henry Reuss of Wisconsin had suggested the idea, along with others, and introduced legislation for funds to finance a study of the feasibility of such a program. Humphrey conducted his own study. He had spoken often of a "Youth Peace Corps" idea in addresses to student groups in 1957, 1958, and 1959. In early 1960 he called in his foreign policy assistant, Peter Grothe, and said, "I've talked about this enough. Let's just do it." He assigned Grothe to survey the methods and accomplishments of private peace corps-type programs, to determine how the principle could be applied through a larger government-sponsored program, and to assess the likely official reaction to the proposal. He had no doubt from the beginning that the public generally would be enthusiastic about the idea.

The initial reaction of most Administration officials and many Congressional leaders ranged from lukewarm to hostile. Grothe interviewed six top officials of the International Cooperation Administration, the government foreign aid agency of that time. Five of them agreed that a Peace Corps was "a nice idea," but said flatly that it could not work. A State Department official exclaimed, "That's a hairbrained idea if I ever heard of one!" "Tell Humphrey to take off his rose-covered glasses," said another. "He isn't serious, is he?" asked one Senator. "I'm not about to vote for some starry-eyed scheme to send a bunch of snot-nosed kids into the jungles," a member of the House of Representatives sniffed. Administration leaders warned that a Peace Corps could become "a haven for draft-dodgers." Richard Nixon and Barry Goldwater at first echoed President Eisenhower's skepticism.

Humphrey introduced his bill on June 15, 1960, and in an accompanying statement acknowledged that it had little chance of approval that year. "But we must begin the attempt to give our young people a chance to share their skills and energies with others," he said. He realistically set a modest limit on the Peace Corps in his first legislative proposal—five hundred volunteers. "It's a start, anyway," he said at the time. In the fall Democratic Presidential candidate John F. Kennedy announced that he favored the idea, first in an informal meeting at the University of Michigan and later in an address at the Cow Palace near San Francisco.

After the election President Kennedy advanced the Peace Corps as one of the high-priority proposals of his new Administration. Humphrey introduced the Administration bill in the summer of 1961. It was far more detailed, but it differed from his 1960 measure on only two important points: women, as well as men, could serve as volunteers, and there would be no age limitation. The President established the Peace Corps at first by executive order, while Humphrey and director-designate Sargent Shriver spearheaded the successful effort for Congressional approval.

Three years later the Peace Corps was well established as the first new and clearly successful international program of the United States in more than a decade. Congress boosted its authorization from an initial corps of five hundred men and women in 1961 to fourteen thousand in 1964.

A student visiting the Capitol in the fall of 1963 asked Humphrey, "What have you ever done in the way of important legislation?" He answered, "Well, there is nothing around which everyone calls 'the Humphrey program' or 'the Humphrey Act.' But I like to think that I have had an effect on many major pieces of progressive legislation in the past several years. And there are some which I think it's fair to say I initiated. I am most proud of three: my work for the Nuclear Test Ban Treaty, the Food for Peace program, and the Peace Corps."

He added a fourth significant achievement in 1964—the strongest civil rights act approved by Congress since the Reconstruction years after the Civil War. His basic belief in civil rights, which to him means justice and equality of opportunity, has always been more a moral conviction than a legal question. He prefers the expression "human rights," and once told a television interviewer:

"I didn't really get my thoughts about civil rights or human rights out of books. I have read a lot of these books and . . . I suppose that I have had as much formal education as most people.

But I really received my ideas on this . . . from my father and mother and some of their very good friends. I am very lucky. I had parents and adult friends who were fine, noble citizens. My father was intolerant of intolerance. And he explained to me as a boy the evil of bigotry . . . I was brought up to have respect for different religions and different races, even though we lived in a very parochial community, a little rural town.

"My father's library was filled with books that told the truth about human equality. But, essentially, this was a religious conviction . . . I think if you only had an intellectual conviction about this, it [could] get warped and cynical. You have to have a deep spiritual commitment. You have to really believe that the importance of man is in his spirit, his soul, his life, his being with a capital *B*. And if you don't believe that, I think you are apt to lose this conviction. Look at today [June 1963]. I mean, you can give up if you are only looking at it intellectually, this area of civil rights or civil wrongs or human rights or the denial of human rights. You could despair. But you can't afford to despair. We must stay with it.

"The fact is we cannot lose this battle for human rights. We can't lose it because if we lose it, we lose ourselves and are throwing in the sponge. So I must believe that we are going to win, and I believe this because I truly believe that people want to survive . . . It is the realization of the importance of one's self. If you have this . . . basic belief that humanity can govern itself and can learn to live with itself, then you are going to have the motivation to keep on with your work in the field of human rights."

Humphrey has worked more bravely for the civil rights cause than for any other in his life. Age, experience, ambition, or friendship with Southern Senators did not dull his sense of commitment. In his year at Louisiana State University in 1939-40, he was revolted by examples of bigotry and discrimination he witnessed. As Mayor of Minneapolis he fought an ugly pattern of anti-Semitism by forcing the community "to pick up a mirror and look at its own dirty face." In July 1948 he risked his own political future by pleading with the Democratic National Convention to place its faith "in the brotherhood of man under the fatherhood of God." In the spring of 1949 he became the first member of the Senate to hire a Negro professional staff member and to take a Negro guest

(Cyril King, now Government Secretary of the Virgin Islands) into the private Senators' dining room in the Capitol. Year after year—sometimes alone with Paul Douglas of Illinois and sometimes with half a dozen other liberals—he fought in the Senate for legislation to break down legalized discrimination. In 1960 he gave up any chance of support for his Presidential campaign by Southern and conservative Democrats when he called himself "the civil rights candidate."

As the Administration prepared its civil rights legislative program in May 1963, he convinced the President that several provisions, including the one banning discrimination in public accommodations, should be strengthened. In June he listened with hopeful expectation as the President announced details of the Civil Rights Bill, and then felt sick when a newscast that same night reported the murder of NAACP leader Medgar Evers in Mississippi. He joined a civil rights March on Washington in August, and returned to his office brimming with excitement. "It was great —all those people together in front of the Lincoln Memorial. I was really full of pride in being an American today." In September, when he heard the news that four children were killed when a bomb exploded in a Negro church in Birmingham, Alabama, he cried.

In January 1964, when some political professionals were telling him to "lay low" to protect his chances for the Vice Presidential nomination, he eagerly agreed to take the tough assignment to act as floor leader for the Civil Rights Bill in the Senate.

It was a strong bill, with teeth. Its main provisions would outlaw racial discrimination in most hotels, restaurants, theaters, and other public accomodations; give the Attorney General power to initiate court suits on behalf of citizens with complaints about segregation; forbid racial discrimination by employers or unions; halt federal funds to state and local programs in which discrimination persisted; and prohibit local officials from applying different standards to white and Negro voter applicants.

"We'll get a bill," Humphrey told reporters soon after New Year's Day. "We'll get a good bill, a strong bill . . . yes, WITH a strong public accomodations provision." "Yeah," said one newsman, smiling at Humphrey's perennial optimism, "and I'm the King of England."

The skepticism was justified. Civil rights leaders in the Senate would have to invoke the cloture rule to cut off the inevitable Southern filibuster against the bill. Cloture requires a two-thirds majority—sixty-seven votes if all members are present. There were sixty-seven Democrats in the Senate in 1964, but at least eighteen of them were loyal to the Southern bloc led by Richard Russell of Georgia. Since 1917, when the cloture rule was adopted, civil rights advocates had tried to cut off Southern filbusters eleven times. They had never succeeded.

On January 17, in an address at Johns Hopkins University in Baltimore, Humphrey defined the problem and pointed to the only possible solution:

"Passage in the Senate will depend very greatly on the degree of bipartisan cooperation we get. There's no use kidding anybody about it. The Southern Senators are not going to vote for a civil rights bill . . . In order to get that two-thirds vote the Democratic leadership will have to call on Senator Everett Dirksen, the Minority Leader, for Republican help. We'll need a minimum of twenty-five Republican votes to end the filibuster."

In a "Meet the Press" interview he noted that the public accommodations section of the bill had "caused Senator Dirksen some concern." That was the understatement of the year. Newspapers had reported that Dirksen was against the provision, and had grave doubts about others in the bill.

On March 9 the Senate began its discussion. On March 26, by a vote of 67 to 17, the bill was formally taken up as the pending business of the Senate. Four days later Humphrey initiated the argument for the bill with a long address which mixed moral, Constitutional, and economic points. He concluded:

"The bill has a simple purpose. That purpose is to give fellow citizens—Negroes—the same rights and opportunities that white people take for granted. This is no more than what our Constitution guarantees.

"One hundred and ninety years have passed since the Declaration of Independence, and a hundred years since the Emancipation Proclamation. Surely the goals of this bill are not much to ask of the Senate of the United States."

Senator Thomas H. Kuchel of California, the Senate Republican Whip, seconded Humphrey's plea. He noted that the House of

Representatives had strengthened and approved the bill, with strong bipartisan support. He reported that Congressional committees had taken 427 pro or con statements on the bill, filled 5,792 pages of printed testimony and discussion, and consumed a total of seventy days for public hearings.

The Southerners would not budge. Senator Russell's forces argued that the bill was unconstitutional, that its provisions infringed on states' rights, and that it would grant "dictatorial police powers" to the federal government. Russell called for total defeat of the entire bill, and made it clear he would accept no compromises. He was calmly confident his team could beat down a cloture attempt, or what they called "a gag rule."

Dirksen would not be rushed, but he was willing to talk compromise. He studied the bill in detail and then announced he would introduce "a number of amendments." In the first weeks of the debate he did not say definitely whether he would vote for or against the bill.

As leader of the civil rights forces Humphrey made three essential strategy decisions. First, his side would be well organized. Second, he would endeavor to keep the debate on a high level, to avoid bitterness, and to accommodate the Southerners in procedural matters whenever possible. Third, he would focus most of his efforts on winning Dirksen's support, and through him, the Republican votes necessary to bridge the gap between liberal Democratic strength and the two-thirds majority required for cloture.

He demonstrated organizational talents most Washington reporters never suspected he had. ("The Southern Senators," a reporter said early in the year, "are the only ones who know how to organize and to follow a leader. The liberals can't organize worth a damn; with them it's 'every man for himself,' and they wouldn't follow F.D.R. if he suddenly reappeared.") Humphrey studied, planned, consulted, organized, and led. He scheduled daily conferences for key Senators, appointed "captains" to be in charge of debate on particular sections of the bill, arranged a detailed schedule to assure the presence of a quorum in the Senate at all times, supervised a daily, staff-written newsletter to keep civil rights Senators informed, and met regularly with Minority Whip Kuchel, Majority Leader Mansfield, and other leaders. The liberals surprised themselves with their unity and efficiency.

Above all, he appealed, privately and publicly, to Dirksen's sense of patriotism and statesmanship. He praised Dirksen constantly, and hammered away at the theme of "Dirksen is a responsible man" to minimize the chances of the Minority Leader "taking a negative position and locking himself in it." He calmed liberals who wanted to criticize Dirksen for his reticence about the whole bill or opposition to portions of it. In a meeting with church leaders from Dirksen's home state, Illinois, Humphrey said, "Never threaten him on this. Appeal to his reason and his sense of responsibility." He was in contact personally with Dirksen almost every day, to solicit Dirksen's recommendations, to explain his interpretation of provisions of the bill, to confirm again and again his willingness to talk about "adjustments" of sections which Dirksen did not like.

His spirit of cooperation was sometimes strained. Before one meeting on a single section of the bill Humphrey's staff expected Dirksen's aides to present one or two amendments. They unveiled more than a hundred. Several liberal Senators lost patience. One said, "To hell with Dirksen. We'll get cloture without him." Humphrey answered, "No, you won't. We've got to negotiate with him."

He worked closely with Attorney General Robert Kennedy in the negotiations with Dirksen and other reluctant Republicans. He arranged to have Deputy Attorney General Nicholas Katzenbach spend most of his time on the tedious negotiations on dozens of amendments.

As Dirksen's role became more prominent, Humphrey intentionally submerged his own. "I'm not in this to be a hero," he told his staff. "If Everett Dirksen can walk out of all this with the olive wreath in his wavy locks, that's fine with me—if it gets us a good bill."

Fellow liberals needled Humphrey about "selling out." He argued that he considered the Civil Rights Bill of 1964 the culmination of "an effort which I helped to start in 1948." "I'm not going to sell out the substance of the bill now," he added. "That would be as bad as a man committing adultery on his wedding night."

He was devious only once in the entire effort to win Dirksen's agreement and support. Before one negotiating session he arranged for a liberal Senator to stage a political tantrum in the meeting. At a critical point in the conference when Dirksen seemed about to protest that Humphrey was not conceding enough, the liberal stood up, pointed a finger at Humphrey, shouted, "This is a goddamned sellout," and stalked out of the room. Humphrey was then able to turn to Dirksen and say, "See what pressures I'm up against? I can't concede any more on this point."

In early May the Humphrey and Dirksen negotiators reached an apparent deadlock on several critical points of disagreement. One key liberal urged suspension of negotiations. Humphrey insisted that they continue. The next day Humphrey, Robert Kennedy, Katzenbach, Assistant Attorney General Burke Marshall, and several Democratic and Republican Senators met with Dirksen in his office. The main dispute involved the provision authorizing the Attorney General to intervene with court suits in cases of discrimination. Dirksen did not like the scope of authority the provision would give the federal government, and wanted the feature of the Attorney General's authority to be separated from the public accommodations section of the bill. Humphrey suggested a compromise which would permit the states and local authorities to handle *individual* discrimination complaints and the Attorney General to step in where there was evidence of a "pattern and practice" of discrimination in a particular locality. The Minority Leader acknowledged "that would be easier to swallow," but he still argued for separation of that authority from the public accommodations section. Humphrey said, "Everett, you've got to realize the situation. My people just won't give any more. We've given a lot. You've given a lot. Let's just agree tentatively. You take it to your [Republican Senate] conference, and then we'll see." Dirksen answered, "Okay, but if I run into a buzz saw, it will have to be changed." Humphrey believed that Dirksen would feel some duty to defend the agreement to which he had tentatively agreed when he went into the Republican conference.

Dirksen did defend the agreement, and the Republican conference backed the package of amendments which had been negotiated. Both sides believed that they had won—the ideal result of negotiation and compromise. Dirksen believed that he had significantly changed the bill. Humphrey believed that he had preserved the strength and substance of it. The revisions were announced as

Russell and other Southern Senators continued their filibuster against the whole bill.

Humphrey had let the debate and filibuster drone on until he was reasonably sure he had the votes to invoke cloture. With Dirksen's support for the amended bill, he set a date for the cloture vote, June 10. During the final days he and others tried to convince several undecided Senators. On the eve of the vote he was confident, but he remarked, "You can never be absolutely sure about anything in the Senate." President Johnson, who had played a limited role in the effort because he did not want to antagonize the Southerners unnecessarily, phoned him about 7:30 P.M. to ask about the prospects for the cloture vote. "I think we have enough," Humphrey said. The President's tone was harsh: "I don't want to know what you think. What's the vote going to be? How many do you have?" Humphrey, somewhat subdued and nervous, answered "Sixty-six." That was one vote short of the required two-thirds majority. He was concerned about the President's manner, but he relaxed a few hours later when two previously undecided Senators—Williams of Delaware and Hickenlooper of Iowa—announced that they would vote for cloture. That meant sixty-eight votes, one more than necessary.

He still took nothing for granted. He placed calls to two Democratic "undecided" Senators, Cannon of Nevada and Edmondson of Oklahoma. At 1 A.M., when it was too late for any more calls, he stepped onto the Senate floor for a brief and friendly exchange with Robert Byrd of West Virginia, who was delivering an all-night final argument against cloture.

At 11:10 A.M., June 10, almost sixteen years after Humphrey had delivered his civil rights speech at the Democratic National Convention and exactly a year after President Kennedy had announced details of the bill, the buzzers sounded through the corridors and offices of Capitol Hill for the cloture vote. Humphrey sat at his desk in the front row, in the second spot away from the center aisle, between Majority Leader Mike Mansfield at the first desk and Harry Byrd of Virginia at the third. Two rows behind, at a desk next to the aisle, Richard Russell of Georgia leaned forward eagerly as the roll clerk began to call the names of the hundred Senators. Each of the men held a tally sheet in one hand and a pencil in the other. Senator Clair Engle of California, dying of brain cancer, was pushed into the chamber in a wheelchair. He forced a stiff smile but could not utter the single syllable "Aye" when the clerk called his name. His vote was recorded only after he waved his arm, pointed toward his eye, and painfully nodded his head up and down. Dirksen's voice, as usual, was mellow and breathy as he called "Aye." Humphrey answered his name softly, almost shyly. "Aye," he said, lingering on the word, affectionately stretching out the sound for an extra second. Russell almost shouted his terse "No."

Seventy-one Senators voted for cloture, four more than required to set an early date to close the debate and bring the bill to a final decision. Twenty-nine voted against cloture. Of the "Aye" votes, forty-four were Democrats and twenty-seven were Republicans.

As the victory for the civil rights forces was announced, Humphrey turned to face the back rows of desks on the Democratic side, caught the eye of Paul Douglas, and nodded his head slightly in a gesture which seemed to say, "We finally did it." Russell stood up to begin the last series of arguments against the bill, using precious minutes of the single hour he had left to speak under the cloture resolution. His voice was angry, and he complained that he was "confronted with the spirit of not only the mob, but of a lynch mob in the Senate of the United States."

It was all over, except for a few minor skirmishes and the exhaustion of each Senator's alloted hour for speaking. Nine days later, at 7:40 P.M. on the eighty-third day of debate, the Senate approved the Civil Rights Bill by a vote of 73 to 27.

Humphrey, Dirksen, and other key supporters of the bill posed for news photographers in a room off the Senate chamber. An assistant told Humphrey that several hundred people who had not been able to get seats in the Senate galleries for the final vote were still waiting outside the Senate entrance to the Capitol.

He left his colleagues and a score of reporters and photographers and walked down the east front steps toward the crowd. The people recognized him and applauded. Many were Negroes. Humphrey shook hands, gazed into their faces, and said, "Isn't this fine? You're happy, aren't you?" Some of the people shouted "Freedom" as he walked among them. Others called, "God bless you." One woman whispered, "I hope you get picked to be Vice President." An old man said, "I'm from Georgia, and I want you to know a lot of us are with you." A student said, "You gave us justice, Senator. Thank you." Others cried, "Good job . . . you did a good job."

A few hours after the Civil Rights Act was approved, Senator Russell left Washington for the weekend. The Atlanta *Constitution* reported: "It had been a long, hot Friday on Capitol Hill. Senator Richard B. Russell, who'd led a historically long Senate filibuster against the civil rights bill and who'd just seen the bill pass despite his efforts, cleared his desk and hurried to the airport. Hours later his plane put down in Winder, Georgia. He was home. The enthusiastic cheers were in his honor. Some thirty-five members of the Russell clan had gathered to meet 'Uncle Dick,' the man often voted America's most powerful U.S. Senator, to crowd around and welcome him as only family can. His arrival marked the official beginning of the 1964 Russell family reunion . . ."

Humphrey flew home to Minnesota the next morning, to be with his family and—most importantly—to visit his twenty-year-old son Robert, recuperating from an operation for cancer of the lymph gland in the Mayo Clinic in Rochester. Humphrey had remained at his leadership post in the Senate despite his deep personal concern. A few days before the final vote on the Civil Rights Bill and the day after the operation, Robert phoned to say, "Dad, I guess I've had it." His father answered, "Don't be silly. I've talked with the doctors, and everything is going to be all right." But there were tears in his eyes as he finished the call and returned to the Senate chamber to continue his work.

On July 2, 1964, President Johnson signed the Civil Rights Act in a televised ceremony at the White House. His signature completed the long process which had shaped an idea into law. Many of the men who had significantly helped in the process stood around his desk. Dirksen, Kuchel, Robert Kennedy, House leaders, and others were there. Humphrey was directly behind Johnson's right shoulder as the cameras focused on the President's hand, a set of pens, and a piece of paper that finally transformed belief into reality.

20

"Number Two"

Hubert Horatio Humphrey took the oath of office as Vice President of the United States on January 20, 1965. That was a proud day for him, but he realized that the glory of the Inauguration properly belonged to the President. He was elected to the Vice Presidency on November 3, 1964. That night he was jubilant, but he understood that the election was primarily a victory for Lyndon B. Johnson.

The real point of uninhibited personal triumph for Humphrey came on the night of August 26, 1964, when the President and the Democratic National Convention chose him for the Vice Presidential nomination. Delegates and reporters focused attention on him, as Johnson intentionally remained in the background to elicit the last bit of drama from the mystery he had created over his choice of a running mate. One newsman who was aware of Humphrey's central role in several critical convention struggles said, "Johnson may be pulling a lot of the strings, but this is really Humphrey's convention. All the interest here is in what he's doing." For seventeen marvelous minutes on nomination night, as he stood on the rostrum responding to the delegates' cheers, Humphrey was in the center of the spotlight of Convention Hall and filled the screens of most of the nation's television sets. Johnson was off stage, sitting in the Presidential box and thoughtfully stroking his chin during the brief interlude to his domination of the American political drama.

It is ironic that in the moment of his elevation to national prominence Humphrey had to begin a process of submerging a part of his political identity and personality. The Vice President of the United States, though only one step away from the world's most powerful office, must serve at the will or the whim of the President.

Mrs. Humphrey realized this quickly, and pinpointed the essential change in his role less than an hour after the President phoned to tell her, "We're going to nominate your boy tonight." As Johnson and Humphrey flew toward the convention in Atlantic City on the evening of August 26, the Humphrey family gathered in a rented house on Marion Street, a half block away from the beach. His brother and sister-in-law, Ralph and Harriet Humphrey, were there from South Dakota. His sister and her children, Mrs. Frances Howard, William Ray, and Ann, had come up from their Virginia home. His children waited with them: Nancy, now twenty-five, and her husband, Bruce Solomonson; Hubert H. III, twenty-two, and his wife, Nancy Lee; Robert, twenty; and Douglas, sixteen.

At the moment when Muriel Humphrey asked them all to assemble in the living room "for a little talk," she was the only one who knew for sure of the President's decision. "Dad is going to be nominated tonight," she began.

A few in the family sighed with relief. Some of the children's faces broke into broad grins. But there were no exclamations of joy; Mrs. Humphrey's tone was serious and practical as she continued:

"Now we have to realize something. We have always been in situations where Dad got all the attention. We are used to him being at the center of a campaign or other situations. But now we have to remember that he is number two."

Quickly and brightly she added, "And that's pretty good!"

"But we all have to make adjustments now," she explained. "Personally, Dad will always be number one for us. But in this campaign and—if we win it—in the coming years, the President is number one. His family is the First Family. From now on Dad is number two to the President and we are number two to the President's family. That's pretty high, when you think of it. But don't forget: politically and socially and in a lot of other ways we are number two now. We have to stand behind the President and his family. They are first."

For most of his career Humphrey has enjoyed being the center of attention in an ever widening political circle: first in the City of Minneapolis, then in the State of Minnesota, and finally in the

Senate of the United States. But for most of his life he has seemed
to be only on the verge of primary importance. It is surprising to
note how often he occupied a "number two" position and how
often he succeeded in moving a step higher only after his second
attempt. He was named Hubert Horatio Humphrey, the second—
after his father. He was the second child and the second son born
to his parents. One of the most notable formal achievements of his
teen-age years was placing second in a state-wide oratory contest in
South Dakota. (Karl E. Mundt, then a teacher and later a Republican Senator, was one of the judges.) He won his college degree
only after his second attempt at the University of Minnesota. He
was elected Mayor of Minneapolis on his second try for that office.
He did not completely consolidate the political party in Minnesota which helped elect him to the Senate until after two organizational struggles, the DFL merger in 1944 and the purge of
Communists from its ranks in 1948. He ran second in the key
Wisconsin and West Virginia elections in 1960. In the Senate he
ultimately became, as Assistant Majority Leader, the second-
ranking Democrat. On the Foreign Relations Committee he
reached no higher than two places away from the Chairman in
seniority. Even after he led the successful fight for the Civil Rights
Act in 1964, a magazine poll of Senators and reporters placed him
second to Richard Russell as "the most effective Senator." And he
won the Democratic Vice Presidential nomination on his second
attempt. (The first had been in 1956.)

Generally he has been most impressive and effective as a political leader in those relatively few periods when he occupied a
"number one" position: Mayor of Minneapolis, Chairman of the
Senate Disarmament Subcommittee, and chief floor leader for the
Civil Rights Bill in the Senate. His capacity for leadership is demonstrated most clearly when he is given or when he grasps prime
responsibility in a political situation. But he has never held prime
authority. When he was Mayor, the legal municipal authority was
vested in the City Council. When he was Chairman of the Senate
Disarmament Subcommittee, his formal activities had to be
cleared by the full Foreign Relations Committee and its Chairman, William Fulbright. When he was floor leader for the Civil
Rights Bill in the Senate, he remained, at least nominally, under
the authority of Majority Leader Mike Mansfield.

His effectiveness as a leader has been far more the result of a willingness to accept responsibility than use of broad authority. He would like to hold greater political authority, to occupy a formal position of prime power, to be "number one." But in many ways his experience has trained him to be a follower, not just a leader; to subordinate his own role to a cause or a man above him; to accept the restrictions of a "number two" position.

As Lyndon Johnson's running mate in 1964 he could not, as he would have liked, *publicly* suggest new national policy, propose new programs, or define the Administration's thinking on current problems or challenges. Those rights were reserved for the first man on the ticket, the President. Humphrey could only attack the Republican ticket, advocate established Democratic policies, and defend the President and the Administration's programs. On the public platform he was not authorized to pursue the role which is most natural to him: that of the positive, aggressive initiator or creator of policy and program.

There were days of frustration for him during that campaign. The nation and the world were changing rapidly, and he was not free to comment on those changes in a significant way until the President had established "the line." In the critical month of October—when Presidential Aide Walter Jenkins resigned after disclosure that he had been arrested twice on morals charges, when Nikita Khrushchev was forced out of power in the Soviet Union, when the British Labour Party won control of its government for the first time in thirteen years, when Red China exploded its first atomic bomb—he was bound to generalities or silence until the President had spoken. On election night he had to delay his public appearance until after the President had spoken on television.

He could freely attack Republican Presidential candidate Barry Goldwater. As the pattern of international politics was changing as never before, the direction of the U. S. Government was challenged as never before in the fall of 1964. Goldwater represented the American antithesis to the political philosophy of Humphrey. As a Senator, Goldwater had voted against ratification of the Nuclear Test Ban Treaty. He had voted against the Civil Rights Bill. He had voted against almost every major program advocated by Humphrey in the 1950's and early 1960's. Even though he felt no personal antagonism toward Goldwater (the two men had a cordial relationship in the Senate), Humphrey was not at all inhibited in attacking, denouncing, and mocking Goldwater's policies throughout the campaign.

Through most of the campaign weeks he managed to remain essentially positive, despite the restrictions imposed by his number two ranking on the Democratic ticket and his strident opposition to the philosophy and policies which the Republican ticket represented. He named his campaign airplane *The Happy Warrior*. Almost daily he asked the reporters with him or the audiences he faced, "Isn't politics fun?" Even in Georgia, the home of Richard Russell and the heart of the old Confederacy, he proudly repeated his pro-civil rights views. Midway through the campaign, as he toured through rural Georgia, he moved reporter E. W. Kenworthy to write in *The New York Times:*

"At the outset [of the Georgia campaign trip] he was booed lustily, but before he had finished his five-minute speech, he managed to bring forth cheers when he said he was proud to come to a state that had never left the Democratic party . . .

"The Senator's day in Georgia was like every other since he set out September 5—full of seriousness but suffused with hope and shot through with laughter.

"Like any other candidate for national office, Mr. Humphrey pays deference to regional and local interests—cotton and public power in Tennessee, price supports in North Dakota, the Appalachia [anti-poverty] bill in West Virginia.

"But all this seems secondary to his main interest. Much of the time he appears to be giving an evangelical civics lesson rather than a campaign speech . . .

"What made America different at its founding from any other nation and what gave it promise of success, he says, was what John Adams called its spirit of 'public happiness.'

"This spirit, he insists, still prevails despite all surface rancor and divisions, riots in the streets and any decline in private morals. And he is confident most of the people want this spirit to prevail.

" 'We don't see our America as weak, as confused, as immoral, as bad and as indifferent,' he said in Fort Wayne, Indiana, a few nights ago.

"Standing before the county courthouse in Terre Haute as the sun was going down, he suddenly paused and said to a mixed crowd of townspeople, farmers and college students:

" 'What a blessed land we have. What a blessed people we are—divinely blessed.'

"He said this without any of the politician's sentimentality, but simply, matter-of-factly, as if he had suddenly discovered it.

"All else in his speeches flows from this basic theme of 'the public happiness.' "

No politician could speak eloquently about a "spirit of public happiness" unless he had a deep capacity for personal happiness. Humphrey does. No matter what his position, he sustains a joy for life which astounds normal men and confuses political cynics. He has said, "I really think I would be happy if I'd never been able to leave South Dakota and were still working in the drug store, guiding the Boy Scout troop, and teaching Sunday school." He had the capacity to adjust to the ultimate "number two" position in the nation—the Vice Presidency—as he has always been able, with time, to adapt himself to any circumstance or position.

The Vice Presidency of the United States is a unique office, which has frustrated most of the men who have held it. Its only significant authority is potential authority. One contemporary Senator calls it "the illegitimate child of the Constitution." Historian Clinton Rossiter calls it "a hollow shell of an office." John Adams, the nation's first Vice President, lamented that it was "the most insignificant office that ever the invention of man contrived or his imagination conceived." Thomas Jefferson, the second Vice President, called the job "honorable and easy." The seventh Vice President, John C. Calhoun, resigned the office when he was offered a seat in the Senate. Woodrow Wilson commented, "The chief embarrassment in discussing the office is that in explaining how little there is to be said about it, one has evidently said all there is to say." John Nance Garner, a two-term Vice President under Franklin D. Roosevelt, was reported to have told Lyndon Johnson in July 1960, "Lyndon, the Vice Presidency isn't worth a pitcher of warm spit." The most famous and enduring contribution of another two-term Vice President, Thomas R. Marshall, under Woodrow Wilson, was his coining of the phrase: "What this country needs is a good five-cent cigar."

The founding fathers created the office because they had no

choice; provision had to be made in the Constitution for a successor to a President who died in office. They thus added a paragraph to Article II: "In Case of the Removal of the President from Office, or of his Death, Resignation, or Inability to discharge the Powers and Duties of the said Office, the same shall devolve on the Vice President . . ." It would seem that the founding fathers then realized that the men who occupied the office of Vice President would have nothing at all to do, so they added another paragraph to Article I of the Constitution: "The Vice President of the United States shall be President of the Senate, but shall have no Vote, unless they be equally divided."

The Constitutional authority of the Vice President is thus limited to two duties. First, he technically presides over the Senate, a task which requires little more than the ability to stay awake while sitting on the Senate rostrum and to hear the whispered instructions of the Senate parliamentarian. (In recent years that task has, in fact, been shared by freshmen members of the Senate, who sit in the Presiding Officer's chair in brief shifts and use most of the time to sign their personal mail.) Second, he can break tie votes in the Senate, which, if he is lucky, occur once or twice during his four-year term.

More recent law has been a bit kinder to the Vice President. He is paid forty-three thousand dollars a year and can draw ten thousand annually for expenses. (Lyndon Johnson has been quoted as saying that he spent up to a hundred thousand dollars a year on his public obligations, such as entertaining visiting V.I.P.'s from abroad, during his three years as Vice President.) He can appoint several young men to the U. S. Military and Naval Academies. He is on the Board of Regents of the Smithsonian Institution. (One cruel joke suggests that that law simply formalized the placement of the Vice President among the other relics of the government.) The only statutory authority of any importance for the Vice President is his membership on the influential National Security Council and his chairmanship of the National Space Council and the Equal Employment Opportunity Committee.

Legally that is all the office of Vice President gives to its incumbent. The Senate, probably more out of sympathy than anything else, traditionally reserves a nice office with crystal chandeliers for him just off the chamber, and when he is gone, places a finely sculpted bust of him in some available niche of the Capitol.

From the time of Adams and Jefferson, near the end of the eighteenth century, until the mid-twentieth century, the Vice Presidency languished as a political office. With few exceptions, the men who held the office were either utterly undistinguished or had to be dragged into acceptance of the nomination. Some of them trembled with fear if the President sneezed; others damned themselves for giving up positions of influence to enter the political vacuum of the Vice Presidency. Few did any significant work.

Thanks to Presidents Truman, Eisenhower, and Kennedy, the tone of the office changed and the activity of the men who held it increased. In 1948, President Truman, who had been left completely out of the policy-making process when he was Vice President under Roosevelt, picked the able Senate Majority Leader, Alben W. Barkley, as his running mate. After their election victory and inauguration Truman utilized Vice President Barkley as an effective legislative lieutenant on Capitol Hill. From 1953 through 1960, President Eisenhower brought Vice President Nixon into many White House activities and gave him important domestic and international assignments. President Kennedy kept Vice President Johnson in intimate contact with a broad range of Presidential problems and efforts, particularly those involving national security, and assigned him to diplomatic tasks overseas and substantive reponsibilities at home in such areas as civil rights and the U.S. space exploration program. Johnson was able to grasp the duties of the White House quickly and confidently after President Kennedy was assassinated on November 22, 1963. Part of the reason was that Kennedy had respected both Johnson and the office of Vice President, and had wasted neither.

President Johnson announced soon after he chose Humphrey that he would enlarge on the example set by Truman, Eisenhower, and Kennedy. He made it clear that Vice President Humphrey would not only be given knowledge of continuing national and international problems and close contact with White House handling of them, but that he would also have important executive and diplomatic responsibilities. Johnson told reporters several months before the election that his Vice President would supervise important aspects of several Administration programs, particularly those related to Humphrey's special knowledge and experience: disarmament, civil rights, education, health and welfare. The President confided that his Vice President would assume

responsibility in the area of foreign relations, not just for ceremonial functions, but as a sort of informal but authoritative Ambassador at Large and Presidential trouble shooter in the world.

Johnson also stressed that he was determined to make a serious
effort to provide an official residence for the Vice President in the
Washington area. The effort was long overdue. Vice Presidents
have continued to live in their own private homes after elections;
both the Nixons and Johnsons soon felt compelled to move to
more spacious quarters. The house in which Humphrey lived
throughout his Senate career was inappropriate in both size and
location for official entertaining of visiting dignitaries.

(One week before he was elected Vice President, he wandered
through his home of sixteen years in Washington's suburban
Chevy Chase, realizing that he might have to leave it for a more
formal residence. The maid, Mrs. Joyce Harper, noticed him
walking from room to room and pausing to sit in each for a few
minutes. He gazed affectionately at the familiar furnishings. When
Mrs. Harper went into the "family room" to call him for breakfast, he was sitting in his favorite chair and looking into the neatly
landscaped yard. "It's unpretentious," he said, "but it's home." He
added sadly, "I'll miss this room and this house.")

In Humphrey the President can draw on a reservoir of energy,
talent, and experience for many duties beyond those he mentioned
publicly before Inauguration Day. Humphrey is equipped to contribute detailed knowledge, perceptive analysis, and useful ideas to
the Administration in a dozen or more major policy fields. He has
a knack as a peacemaker which could be put to good use in the
Administration's behind-the-scenes efforts to settle major labor-
management disputes which threaten to disrupt the economy.
After his term as a delegate to the United Nations, a score of
overseas trips, and a decade of helping to host Foreign Relations
Committee luncheons and dinners for foreign visitors, he had
great understanding of the customs and political patterns of
dozens of nations, and probably knew more foreign leaders personally than Johnson. (As of late 1964 and early 1965, Humphrey's foreign contacts ranged from the young and rising political
stars of Latin-American nations to several post-Khrushchev contenders for Soviet power.)

The Vice Presidency has one unique quality which suits

Humphrey. It is the only position which constitutionally bridges the division of power between two branches of the federal government; the man who is Vice President has one foot in the executive branch (though its place is not defined) and one foot in the legislative branch (through the duty to preside over the Senate). Humphrey is equipped by position, contacts, and temperament to act as an influential spokesman for the Administration in the Senate. Traditionally, when a Senator ascends to the Vice Presidency, the Senate regards him as an outsider, loyal to the White House and only sentimentally tied to the old institution. Lyndon Johnson's practical influence in the Senate was not significant during his three years as Vice President, even though he had been one of the most powerful Majority Leaders in history, and even though he tried, in the Senate Democratic caucus in January 1961, to retain some formal authority and leadership over the Senate majority. Vice President Humphrey cannot exercise as much influence in the body as when he was Majority Whip. But because his influence in the Senate resulted more from personal talent and relationships than a position of authority, he began with a better chance than Johnson to sustain significant influence after rising to the Vice Presidency. There was no doubt that the Johnson Administration, well aware of its need for Congressional support, would utilize Humphrey as much as possible as an informal lobbyist for its programs, policies, and appropriations requests.

Humphrey is most clearly suited to the modern Vice Presidency in the realm of foreign relations. He likes to travel overseas, is effective in face-to-face contacts with foreign leaders, and as several State Department officers have said, has a natural talent for communicating the best possible image of the United States to the opinion leaders *and* the average citizens of other nations. (In 1963 he won the affection of a few hundred Danes while he was touring the crowded Tivoli Gardens amusement area in Copenhagen with Lord Mayor Urban Hanson and American Ambassador to Denmark William Blair. He coaxed the dignified Danish leader and the Ambassador into a jolting ride in a concession of "bumper cars" (sometimes called "Dodge 'em" cars in American amusement parks); Hanson, Blair, and Danish witnesses were delighted. As Vice President, Humphrey must be somewhat more formal in his conduct abroad, but it is not likely that he will ever become stuffy

or lose his exuberant and contagious spirit of fun, which simply
makes friends no matter how great the language barrier.

He enjoys presiding over ceremonial occasions (greeting a foreign parliamentary leader, presenting a scroll to the winners of a
national student contest, or pinning a medal on an outstanding
government worker), and he likes to dress in a tuxedo or even
white tie and tails. The Vice Presidency provides many opportunities for ceremony and pomp.

Finally, the title and position themselves—no matter how
modest in actual authority—are a source of immense pride for
Humphrey. In the 1930's he never really expected to achieve any
higher status than pharmacist, small businessman, and, perhaps, a
member of the South Dakota state legislature. After his losing
campaigns for higher national office in 1956 and 1960, he concluded, at least intellectually, that he would remain a Senator
from Minnesota for the rest of his political life. He does not feel
himself very far away, in time, from the realities of life as an
apprentice pharmacist in the drought-torn Dakotas or as a political
amateur who could not get past the reception desk of the Democratic National Committee on his second visit to Washington in
1943. In 1964, the twenty-first year of his career as a politician, he
reached full national political maturity. He had been elected to
one of only two political offices filled by the votes of *all* the American people. On October 29, 1964, Chalmers M. Roberts wrote in
The Washington Post that "Humphrey has become a major political figure in his own right."

Despite the appeal of higher status and the increased responsibilities of the office, Humphrey as Vice President must inevitably
suffer in the relative silence of his new role. His natural instinct is
to develop and perfect his proposals in the stimulating atmosphere
of an extemporaneous public speech; as Vice President he must
suggest them in the privacy of a memorandum, phone call, or
conversation with the President. He is accustomed to speaking
openly when he does not like the nature or direction of an Administration policy; now he must keep quiet or cautiously voice his
criticism to the President. He has trained himself to learn the best
methods for winning attention and praise from the press; as Vice
President he generally gets only those headlines or editorial pats
on the back (or slaps in the face) which the President decides he

should get. In any public utterance or action he must consider the President's views and wishes first, and defer to them if there is any doubt. He is, except to his family, his personal staff and old friends, "number two."

A few weeks before the convening of the Democratic National Convention which nominated him, Humphrey was working in his comfortable Majority Whip office just above the Senate chamber when a friend asked, "Will you be at all sorry about leaving the Senate if you get the Vice Presidency? After all, you'll be giving up a good chance of earning a reputation as one of the greatest Senators and the reality of real, day-to-day influence on national policy." Humphrey, the Senator, smiled softly and almost wistfully as he thought of his career and life in the Senate. "Oh, sure, I'll be sorry if I have to leave the Senate. I don't know why I want to be Vice President, really. Who knows what motivates a man in politics?"

He was not being evasive or tight-lipped about his own yearnings. He is not an introspective or reflective man, and when he is questioned directly about his political ambitions or philosophy of public service, he can become embarrassed or tongue-tied.

Why did he give up the sure influence, seniority, and power he had taken sixteen years to build in the Senate? Why did he give up the good chance of moving into some "number one" position in the Senate in another few years? Why did he leave the probable lifetime security and the high prospects for fame in the Senate for a position which—despite its recently increased stature and responsibilities—remains "a hollow shell of an office"?

There can be only three sound reasons for a man of his talent, ambition, and relative youth to accept or want the Vice Presidency.

The first is simply a sense of duty. A man who is a conscientious public servant and a patriotic American cannot easily reject the request of the President of the United States to become his Vice President.

The second reason for a willingness to become Vice President is an urge to strengthen a high and honorable public office which has been neglected and mocked. Humphrey became Mayor of Minneapolis because he believed that he could add force to that legally limited and largely ceremonial position. He did so. He is confident that he can do the same for the Vice Presidency, partly through his own effort and partly because of the positive attitude of the President toward the office and the respect of Lyndon Johnson for Hubert Humphrey.

The third reason, which without doubt provided the major basis for Humphrey's *desire* to be Vice President, is the ultimate and unrelenting ambition of a national politician to become President of the United States.

The cold statistics of the history of the American Presidency grant to a Vice President fair odds for achieving the highest office in the land. Eleven out of thirty-six American Presidents—almost one in three—first served as Vice President. Eight of them succeeded to the Presidency on the death of the incumbent. The other three first served full terms as Vice President and then were elected President.

The odds have risen in this century. Since 1900 four out of twelve Presidents (Theodore Roosevelt, Calvin Coolidge, Harry Truman, and Lyndon Johnson) succeeded from the Vice Presidency, an even ratio of one in three.

The odds can be boosted if the Vice President is a relatively young man and the change in public attitude toward the Vice Presidency itself is considered. Since the nomination of Vice President Richard Nixon for the Presidency by the Republicans in 1960, the public has been more inclined to regard the "number two" office as a reasonably good qualification and training period for the Presidency.

In 1964, President Lyndon B. Johnson was responsibly aware of the possibility of his death in office. On the night he accepted the Presidential nomination, he celebrated his fifty-sixth birthday. He had made a remarkably complete recovery from, but could not forget, the serious heart attack he suffered in 1955. As he named his choice for the Vice Presidency, he said:

"I think in all my life that I have never taken any decision more seriously than picking Humphrey . . . I picked Humphrey because, in my judgment, and after checking with leaders all over the country, I was convinced that he would be the best man to be President if anything happened to me."

Even without the possibility of the death in office of President Johnson, Hubert Humphrey can expect to be a leading possibility to become the thirty-seventh President of the United States by a normal political process. Nationally the Vice Presidency will give him far more stature than the position of Senator from Minnesota. With President Johnson's continued sharing of responsibilities with him, his experience for the highest office will be broadened. With luck, his talents, energies, and skills will continue to be demonstrated in the office of the Vice Presidency and noted in the press. With time, he will be able to minimize the old anti-liberal antagonisms of such groups as businessmen and rank-and-file Southern voters. His abilities and record, even by 1964, had been demonstrated sufficiently to merit the praise of such traditionally nonliberal publications as *The Saturday Evening Post* and *Forbes* magazine. *The New York Times* editorialized just before the 1964 election, "Humphrey has the capacity and broad outlook needed in a Chief Executive." In 1968, the year of the next Presidential election, he will be fifty-seven. In 1972, when Lyndon Johnson would be constitutionally ineligible to run for re-election, he will be sixty-one. Both ages are within the commonly accepted limit for a Presidential candidate.

It is axiomatic in American politics that no man who has been "bitten by the Presidential bug" ever gives up his aspirations for the office. Hubert Humphrey wanted to be President in 1960. Even after he was solidly trounced by John F. Kennedy in the Wisconsin and West Virginia primaries, the Presidential fever did not completely leave him. Less than a year and a half after the 1960 election he spoke of his unsuccessful bid for the nomination in a CBS television interview:

"I never really felt that my chances were better than, let's say, one to ten. I didn't delude myself about the opportunities or the chances that I had. I went into it knowing that I was running an uphill fight . . ."

Interviewer Paul Niven then caught him somewhat off guard by asking, "Will you ever run again, Senator?" Even with the wounds of his 1960 defeat fresh and sensitive, Humphrey answered, "I have no such plans, but I have no plans to say I wouldn't."

A year later a staff assistant asked him the same question. He furrowed his brow and acknowledged that, as of early 1963, it was not likely he would ever get the chance to be nominated for either the Presidency or the Vice Presidency. After a moment's pause he added, "It's an unpredictable world. Who knows? I'm still young."

Humphrey is a politician who takes one step at a time, who believes that his duty is to do the best job he can in whatever position he has at any moment in his life, and who thinks that if his abilities for leadership are demonstrated that "perhaps the time will come when I'll be accepted for leadership." He has been accepted for leadership, but he hardly dares to admit, even to himself, that his ultimate ambition reaches higher than the Vice Presidency. In an address on "The Presidency" at Princeton University on October 9, 1964, he quoted Woodrow Wilson's credo of leadership:

"A great nation is not led by a man who simply repeats the talk of the street corners or the opinions of the newspapers. A nation is led by a man who hears more than those things; or who, rather, hearing those things, understands them better, unites them, puts them into a common meaning; speaks, not the rumors of the street, but a new principle for a new age; a man [to whom] the voices of the nation . . . unite in a single meaning and reveal to him a single vision, so that he can speak what no man else knows, the common meaning of the common voice. Such is the man who leads a great, free democratic nation."

And such is the kind of man Hubert Humphrey aspires to be. He wants to be President.

21

The Presidency

Six major forces beyond his own faith, will, and conviction have clearly and directly influenced Hubert Humphrey's life and political career: his father, his rural community experience, the depression, the pattern of progressive reform running from William Jennings Bryan to Franklin Delano Roosevelt, the people of Minnesota, and the institution of the United States Senate.

A seventh force, its effect subtler but today more powerful than any of the others, continues to shape him: the Presidency.

A man's political personality is conditioned, at least in part, by his own image of what he would like to be and by what those closest to him tell him he should be. For all his awareness of the apparently dim prospects, Humphrey wanted to be President for at least ten years before he achieved the nation's second-highest office. In the mid-1930's his wife believed that he "might be President someday." As early as 1948 some influential national figures were suggesting that he be considered for the Presidency. From the mid-1950's on, many friends and liberal leaders told him that he was qualified for the office, that he had a reasonable chance of achieving it, and that he would make a "great President someday." Such talk and speculation inevitably conditioned the way he thought, talked, and acted in public.

He has never had, however, a precise plan, and has never employed ruthless tactics to achieve the Presidency. He does not even consciously regard the office as the clear goal of his political life; he is always too preoccupied with his job and his tasks of the moment to plan or calculate for the distant future. He has never been willing to sacrifice a personal commitment to conscience or conviction to enhance his prospects for the Presidency. There have been times, even in the midst of the 1960 campaign, when he bluntly questioned his own qualifications for seeking his party's nomination. The Presidency, for him, has simply been the position of power to which any persistent and successful American politician should logically aspire. (And there is his natural instinct to climb, to rise, to reach the top. He had always responded to it, even as a boy in Doland, South Dakota, "where there was this big water stand, about a hundred feet high. I'd climb that, even though everybody told me I couldn't, or shouldn't. I liked to climb it. At the top you could see for such a long way, above the flatness . . .")

Until the 1960's, Humphrey was often awed by the office and the men who held it. Woodrow Wilson was his political hero. He idolized Franklin D. Roosevelt. Even after he had studied the office and dealt with it personally during the Administration of Harry Truman, he approached the Presidency with humility and deference. This attitude, at times, was reflected even in his relationships with men who formally campaigned for the highest office in the land. In the mid-1950's, when he was in his own right a figure of national influence, he was almost meek in the presence of Presidents, Presidential candidates, and even White House assistants. An aide once asked him why he spoke with such supercourtesy to Senator Estes Kefauver. He answered, as though any explanation were unnecessary, "Why, he's running for President!" During the eight years of Eisenhower's Presidency he was depressed by what he considered to be a waste of the tools of national leadership in the White House, but he rarely identified Eisenhower by name ("He's a good man, really") or used the term "the President" in public criticisms of the Administration. Instead he spoke of "those Republicans" or aimed his liberal indignation at such targets as Secretary of Agriculture Ezra Taft Benson or Secretary of State John Foster Dulles.

An attitude of awe toward the Presidency is somewhat justified. No political position in the free world commands greater power or influence. The legal authority of the President is far-reaching. He, more than any other man, can create events and shape the history of the strongest nation on earth. In a world of fast change and sudden crisis, his decisions are critical. He combines in one office several roles which are split among different men in many other nations: Chief of State, Chief Executive, Commander in Chief of the Armed Forces, head of his political party, top finance officer (with a budget in the mid-1960's of about a hundred billion dollars annually), and in a sense, chief educator or propagandist in the nation. His words are heard and his actions are watched almost constantly by most American citizens and most of the leaders of nations throughout the world. In his Inaugural Address in January 1961, John F. Kennedy said, "Man holds in his mortal hands the power to abolish all forms of human poverty and all forms of human life." No man has a greater share of that power than the President of the United States.

The President is not, however, politically omnipotent; the Constitution, the Congress, the press, and a free people limit his powers. The ingrained habits of the federal bureaucracy inhibit his ability to establish new policies or change old programs. Most of the people under him are awed by the powers of the Presidency; the President himself is usually most aware of the restrictions on his power, flexibility, and freedom to act.

As Humphrey came into closer personal contact with the Presidency during the Kennedy-Johnson Administration, his awe of the office was modified by an understanding of the limitation of its powers and by friendships with the men in the White House. From 1961 on, when he was in almost daily contact with the White House, he was no longer intimidated by the Presidency. He was still impressed with its immense powers, and sometimes boyishly excited by his participation in the drama of White House conferences, dinners, and strategy meetings, but his attitude was no longer dominated by deference. He looks at the Presidency today with respect, not humility. The White House is a familiar place into which he is welcomed for the highest policy discussions.

He also sees the White House as the noble symbol of the continuing strength and greatness of the United States. On a July night in 1963, while he was going home by way of Pennsylvania Avenue, he suddenly ordered his car halted when it reached a point between the White House grounds and Lafayette Park. Looking toward the north side of the White House, he said to his driver, "Graham, stop. I want to get out here for a minute."

The driver pulled the big car to the curb, and Humphrey eagerly hopped out. It was about 10:30 P.M., the night was balmy, and a dozen or so tourists strolled the wide sidewalk next to the

high iron fence at the edge of the White House grounds. An il-
luminated fountain sparkled in the middle of the north lawn.
Beyond the darkness of the grounds the White House gleamed
brightly. Humphrey stood quietly for a few moments, looking
through the fence. Then he turned to an assistant, David Gartner,
and said, "Isn't that beautiful? Isn't that just one of the most
beautiful sights you've ever seen?"

In the darkness of the sidewalk most of the tourists did not
recognize Humphrey. He chatted with a few of them, mostly
about the beauty of the White House and the fine weather that
evening. For fifteen minutes he and his assistant unobtrusively
paced the sidewalk and looked in toward the President's home.
Several times he stepped by himself to the fence and without
comment gazed at the splendid scene.

He was not being melodramatic or wistful. He was relaxed, and
he simply enjoyed an awareness of the majesty of the White House
as a symbol of the nation's history of representative democracy.

Finally, as he was about to leave, a guard at the northwest gate
recognized him and asked, "Senator, do you want to go inside?"
Humphrey was slightly embarrassed. "No, I'm just being a tourist
tonight." Then the guard offered to give him a personal tour
through the house and grounds, and he accepted. They spent an
hour wandering through the famous rooms, the guard explaining
details of design and history and telling about the project of the
First Lady, Jacqueline Kennedy, to replace long-lost furniture to
the public and private areas of the house. They stepped down to
the swimming pool area, walked through the East Room, the Red
Room, and the Main Dining Room, and peered into corners not
usually seen by the public or by Congressional leaders visiting he
White House on business. "Humphrey was as excited as a little
boy," Gartner remembers. "He would race from an antique table
to a Presidential portrait, to some old artifact dating from the
colonial period, all the time firing questions at the guard and
making such comments as: 'Look at that thing. Just imagine. It
was Andy Jackson's!' "

At the end of an hour, just before leaving, they walked out to
the Rose Garden behind the President's office. Humphrey paused
for a long moment of reflection. "This is the first time I've ever
really seen this place," he finally said. "I've been here hundreds of
times, but I've always been too busy to look."

Beginning in January 1961, with the election of John F. Kennedy, Humphrey was in the White House at least once a week for the regular Tuesday-morning breakfast meetings of legislative leaders with the President, and for innumerable informal and private discussions with Presidents Kennedy and Johnson. By 1962, according to White House Assistant Larry O'Brien, he "seemed like part of the family." His relationships with Kennedy and Johnson affected him and his career as much as or more than his general attitude toward the office of the Presidency.

In some ways he was closer to Kennedy than he could ever be with Johnson. One politician who has known all three men well says, "Humphrey has to feel that the President really listens to him. He is not greatly upset if the President disagrees with his ideas or says 'No' to a suggestion—as long as he feels he has been heard and understood. Kennedy was a great listener. You always felt that he grasped your point quickly and weighed it carefully. Johnson—at least in his first year as President—sometimes seemed too full of himself to be a good listener. Sometimes you sensed that although he looked right at you as you spoke, his mind was off somewhere else. That frustrates a man like Humphrey."

Both Presidents, however, needed Humphrey, for a variety of reasons. From 1961 through 1964 no man was more loyal to Presidents Kennedy and Johnson. He respected their office and enthusiastically and effectively supported almost all of their policies. In private conversations he was neither subservient to nor afraid of them. He was not at all reluctant to tell either Kennedy or Johnson things which each man needed to know but which he would not be particularly pleased to hear. Humphrey had never been a "yes man," and often at White House meetings he said, "I'm sorry, Mr. President, I think you're wrong." In a protected world of awed visitors and deferential advisers, the President of the United States needs to be challenged by men he respects. Both Kennedy and Johnson respected Humphrey's honesty as much as his political and legislative skills.

For Kennedy in particular, Humphrey's sense of humor and spirit of fun were important. The President is surrounded by people and problems of high seriousness and gravity; he needs to laugh. Humphrey could, with grace and good taste, kid Kennedy about something he had done or said. It was a sign of Kennedy's maturity and emotional balance that he could laugh at himself

and enjoy Humphrey's jibes. And in the pleasant banter of conversation after a formal White House meeting, Kennedy could
tease Humphrey without maliciousness and Humphrey could
laugh. The two men had far more than a political alliance based
on trust; they had a warm and convivial friendship.

The murder of President Kennedy on November 22, 1963,
grieved Humphrey and—as it did to millions of other Americans—
jolted him into full realization of his appreciation for the man. He
struggled for some element of reality in the grim weekend following the incredibly sudden and brutal assassination in Dallas. On
November 23, the day after Kennedy died, he spent an hour alone
in his office, dictating his thoughts and trying to piece together his
reactions. He had not been requested to set down his ideas, and he
had no practical purpose when he spoke into the dictating machine. On that bleak Saturday of dark skies and brittle emotions in
Washington, he simply wanted to talk and "collect" his thoughts.
In so doing, he revealed much about himself.

He told of being at a luncheon in the Chilean Embassy when he
heard the first news that Kennedy had been shot and seriously
wounded. Another guest, White House Assistant Ralph Dungan,
left immediately. Humphrey went outside to his car, to listen to
radio reports from Dallas, which at that minute told of two priests
entering the hospital emergency room where Kennedy lay. He
returned to the Embassy to be with his wife . . .

"Immediately I received a telephone call, and it was Ralph
Dungan from the White House. He told me that the President
had died. I could hardly believe it. I stood by myself for several
minutes in the library room, where the telephone was located. A
great wave of emotion swept through my body and mind. I walked
into the hallway and stood alone, looking outside, and broke down
and sobbed with grief.

"I tried desperately to regain my composure, and when I
thought I had, I walked into the luncheon room [to tell the
others] that the President had died . . .

"Mrs. Humphrey and I then went to our car, where Mr.
Graham was waiting for us, and I asked him to drive me to the
White House, since Dungan had suggested that I should stop there
. . . As we drove down the streets toward the White House, you
could see that people were shocked; they couldn't believe it . . . I

find it difficult to properly express and translate my emotions during this unbelievable and incredible period of anxiety, sorrow, and tragedy. When I received that telephone message, there was a sudden emptiness. I felt as if a part of my life had left me. In thinking back over it I never quite realized how close I was to the President, or, should I say, how much he really meant to me. Of course, I knew him as a colleague in the Senate, as a friend, as our President, and as a political leader. But then when he was taken from us, it dawned on me all at once that I had lost more than a President and political leader—that a very warm and wonderful human being, who was very much a part of my daily life, was gone . . .

"All day long I kept wondering if it was really true, even though I knew it was. It is very difficult to accept these hard facts. I had such strange emotions of unbelievable sorrow, of sympathy for the family, and particularly for Jacqueline . . . of worry and concern about Lyndon . . . I knew that this would be a terrible blow for him, and I was deeply concerned lest it might literally overwhelm him.

"And then I couldn't help but reflect upon the hate that has been engendered in this country by the extremists of the right and of the left; and now we saw the product of that hate—the terrible culmination of emotional instability that had been aggravated and aroused by hate and bitterness. Like everyone else, I couldn't help but think of how Dallas, Texas, had become known as the city that had treated our public officials so terribly. First it was Vice President Johnson during the 1960 campaign. Then it was Adlai Stevenson on U. N. Day, just a little over a month ago. [Both had been jeered and spat upon in Dallas.] And now the terrible, incredible, dastardly act of assassination of President Kennedy.

"Then I felt sorry for Dallas and the good people of that city. Because as in every other community, it is only a handful . . . of people who bring a bad name to their community or their neighborhood. The people of Dallas do not deserve any unkind thoughts. They deserve our sympathy and understanding . . . It only took one fanatic to commit this unbelievable act . . .

"We have had an experience now that surely must be on the conscience of every citizen of this nation. I couldn't help but think of how ironical it was that in this great America, this great democracy that believes, as it says, in human dignity, that here an act of violence should take place that takes the life of our President. Here we are, preaching to the whole world, attempting to lead the free world, and we have within our borders this incredible act of violence and brutality.

"Oh, if only this nation will learn from this tragic lesson. If only we will repent and seek forgiveness for our transgressions, for our abuse of freedom. Because in a sense, we are all somewhat guilty. Freedom becomes license to some and freedom of expression has been perverted, and it has been abused, and it has been made the vehicle for vicious propaganda and hatred that inspires people to do such terrible things as happened in Dallas to our President.

"I stayed at the White House for better than an hour and a half. I walked around and talked to the police officers and the guards. I found them heartbroken—big, strong men with tears rolling down their faces. I saw right outside President Kennedy's office, hanging on the wall in the corridor, two Texas Ranger pistols that were buckled to a piece of Texas ranch fence. And there was a little sign above them that said 'The Texas Peacemakers.' What irony . . .

"I was interrupted at this point in my dictation by Pat Gray [his secretary] telling me that I must go immediately to the White House, where the leadership of the Congress is to join President Johnson and Mrs. Johnson to pay our respects to the late President Kennedy and to view the casket . . .

"I have done so and have now returned to my office. It was a moving experience. The casket was in the East Room, draped with an American flag. It was not open, and I was relieved that it wasn't because I want to remember President Kennedy as a vital, active, creative, living human being. I paused for a moment in front of the casket with my Senate colleague Senator [George] Smathers. I said a little silent prayer for the late President and his dear family.

"Then I went in and called on Larry O'Brien . . . I expressed to him my thanks for bringing me a little closer to the President. Poor Larry seems so lost . . . I mentioned what a fine team we had built under the President's leadership, and that the team was beginning to function well. And that the President had been in full command of his position and job, and that he had been enjoying his work . . .

"A little later I went on to Kenny O'Donnell . . . and I saw a strong, ordinarily a taciturn and cool and calm man break down into tears, as did I. I again thanked Ken O'Donnell for letting me know the President a little better . . .

"Now, returning [in his dictation] to yesterday, Friday . . .

"After leaving the White House, where I had been with Ralph Dungan, I joined Mrs. Humphrey, and we went out to Andrews Air Force Base, where we saw the President's plane come in. We saw Mrs. Kennedy . . . We saw the casket lowered into the ambulance, tenderly watched over by those three loyal friends of President Kennedy: Kenny O'Donnell, Larry O'Brien, and Dave Powers . . .

"From the airport the Congressional leaders flew [by helicopter] to the old Executive Office Building, where President Johnson had his offices as Vice President . . . It was a very intimate and private meeting. We discussed no legislation. The President asked for our help. He spoke to us as one friend to another. And we, each of us in turn, pledged our cooperation, our counsel, our assistance.

"I stayed back for just a moment and had a private word with President Johnson. I think of him as Lyndon, as a dear friend. I assured him of my desire to be of all possible assistance. He put his arm around me and said that he needed my help desperately. A little later Bill Moyers, who is close to Lyndon Johnson, told me that the President would need me very, very much. He thought even more so than President Kennedy had ever needed me, if that was the case. . . . I said I was ready to serve in any way.

"After all, we do have duties and responsibilities, those of us in this government. We cannot afford to let crisis or tragedy interrupt the responsibilities of this nation or the responsibilities of those of us who are entrusted with the authority and the power to govern. We must go ahead. In fact, it is my view that the finest memorial we could give to President Kennedy would be to complete his program, to undertake to fulfill the many dreams and hopes that he expressed so eloquently and articulately. This I shall try to do to the best of my ability . . .

"I went to my office at 1313 New Senate Office Building about 8:30 P.M. [he was alone in that hour], and I was surprised to receive many long-distance phone calls from Minnesota and other places throughout the nation—calls from people who merely wanted to tell me how sorry they were over the death of President Kennedy, calls from plain people who would weep on the telephone. I recall one particular phone call from a Minneapolis or St. Paul cab driver, who had just finished work, and he called to tell me that his whole family wanted to be remembered to Mrs. Kennedy and the children, and how sorry they were that they had lost their great friend, President Kennedy. This was characteristic of all the calls. Not a single one was anything but filled with sorrow and sympathy and understanding. How wonderful it is that the people of this country felt so close to their President. This is one of the great attributes and qualities of our system of government and of our freedom—a freedom which brings the President very close to the people—and maybe too close for his own safety at times. But after all, the people loved him. It was just a lunatic, one crazy man, one man who was filled with bitterness that destroyed this champion of our country and of our people. We cannot blame the system, nor can we retreat from its challenges and opportunities . . .

"There is something gone from Washington and the nation in the death of President Kennedy. It is difficult to identify except that one feels a vacuum, a void, a tragic loss. President Kennedy brought to this city a new intellectual vitality, a scholarly approach to the problems of our time, and a lofty articulation of both the problems and the solutions. I recall again his great Inaugural Address—its power, its meaning, its challenge, and its excitement. Oh, how we will miss this man who was so young at heart, so brave in spirit, so brilliant of mind and wise in judgment . . . As Muriel [Mrs. Humphrey] said to me, many people criticized him for being in a hurry and for his ambition, but wasn't it good that he was in a hurry, or he wouldn't have had an opportunity to tell us what he had in mind for America, what were his dreams, his hopes, his aspirations for this country. Like any man, he had shortcomings, to be sure, but he did enunciate and articulate a beautiful dream and vision of this nation. He gave young people inspiration and strength, and that is so desperately needed in these times . . ."

(President Kennedy was buried on Monday, November 25. On that day there seemed an almost perfect clarity to everything about Washington. The sky was clear, the people were silent, the sounds of the bell of St. John's Church across from the White House and the drums in front of the funeral caisson were distinct. Deep emotions found expression in simple words. After the funeral Humphrey returned to the solitude of his office and continued his dictation.)

"I shall never forget the funeral. Members of the Congressional leadership were invited to the White House, along with others . . . We gathered for the funeral procession to St. Matthew's Cathedral . . . The funeral mass was beautiful and not too elaborate. In a sense, it had the purity of simplicity . . .

"Following the mass we went to Arlington Cemetery. There must have been a million people along the route of the funeral procession. I have never seen so many people on any one occasion. We went to the area prepared for the President. And how beautiful is the site. I fail to find the words to adequately express it. But it seems to me as if he stands as a constant sentinel over the nation's capital. The President's grave is like an outpost for observation of the capital city.

"At the grave site were, of course, the family. And then there were Charles de Gaulle, President Eisenhower, President Truman, and others. I saw Eisenhower and Truman speaking with de Gaulle. Out of this tragic moment came a renewal of friendship between Truman and Eisenhower. They rode together and they spoke together, and they have been talking to one another since then. Out of sorrow came some good.

"I shall never forget the flight of planes over Arlington Cemetery, and then U. S. Air Force 1, the President's personal jet, flying over at a low level, paying its last respects. Nor shall I ever forget the blowing of taps. It was so clear and beautiful, and yet so final.

"Then we saw our President laid to rest. The sun was shining brightly. It seemed as if the whole nation was in tears; in fact, the world was in grief. There is no way to adequately describe what transpired, except to say that God made His light to shine upon us through the beautiful sunlit day. And each of us in a real sense re-examined our conscience and soul.

"I couldn't help but think again and again, Why did this happen? Why—oh, why—in America did we have to experience such evil, such hate, such lawlessness, such violence? Maybe it was one way of telling the American people . . . to be more concerned about spiritual values, moral principles, and human dignity. I think so, or at least I hope so . . ."

A full year after the assassination of the President it was evident that John Kennedy had made a deep and enduring impression on Humphrey. He quoted from Kennedy's statements often, even at the Democratic National Convention and in the 1964 election campaign, when the prevailing political strategy suggested an emphasis on the *Johnson* Administration. Kennedy's influence on Humphrey cannot be defined precisely or measured accurately, but it is strong, and it continues. With obvious emotion and a mixture of affection, pride, and pain, he sometimes tells of the last time he saw Kennedy. That was on November 20, 1963, after a Congressional leaders' meeting in the White House. As Humphrey started to leave, Kennedy called out, "Hubert, come walk with me. I want to talk to you." The two men walked past the Rose Garden and into the President's private office. As always, Humphrey used a few of the minutes to advance his own ideas and projects; he wanted support for a proposed research center for the upper Midwest, and he advocated first priority for the Civil Rights Bill in the legislative timetable. (The Administration had been dubious about the expense of the research facility, and Kennedy had announced top priority for his tax cut program just few days before.) Then, Humphrey remembers, "We kidded back and forth a lot. He was in a good mood, and looked great. I said, 'You were just down there in Miami, speaking to that businessmen's group. How about switching? Next time address the ADA.' The President laughed. We talked a bit about Congress, and he spoke of how eager he was for his trip [to Texas]. He was eager to get away from Washington and go out to be with the people in the country. That was two days before Dallas. That was the last time I saw him. And damnit, I still miss him."

Kennedy once said that a President needed to get away from Washington often, to meet with the people in their own cities and communities, and he added, "Out here one can sense the power, the strength, the resources of this nation." In the last weeks of 1963 and in 1964, Humphrey could sense the relentless exercise of the power, the strength, and the resources of the American government. As he had said, "We must go ahead . . . We have duties."

Far more than any other man, Lyndon Johnson realized that.

On the Sunday night before Kennedy's funeral the new President phoned Humphrey at his home to ask why Senate leaders planned to bring up for action on Tuesday an amendment sponsored by Karl Mundt of South Dakota restricting the sale of American products, including wheat, to the Soviet Union and other countries behind the Iron Curtain. "This is a poor time to bring it up," the President said. Humphrey explained that the Senate was bound to the schedule by an unanimous consent agreement made two weeks before. "All right then, can you beat it?" the President asked. "How many votes do you have?" Humphrey answered, "Well, I'm not sure." Johnson, half serious and half in jest, said, "That's the trouble with that place up there. You fellows just don't have the votes counted."

Humphrey realized that the President was again demonstrating his old habit of wanting to be sure of a roll call vote before bringing up a controversial bill. He understood the mood of the former Majority Leader. On Monday morning, the day of the funeral, Humphrey ordered Senate assistants to check with every member to determine in advance what the probable vote would be. By the end of the day he was able to tell the President that he expected Administration forces to defeat the Mundt proposal by a vote of 56 to 37. On Tuesday night, after the amendment had been rejected, Humphrey phoned Johnson. "I want to report your first victory as President. We have defeated the Mundt bill by a vote of fifty-seven to thirty-five. I'm sorry I misinformed you earlier by predicting the vote would be fifty-six to thirty-seven." President Johnson chuckled and said, "You are doing well. That's a good start. Keep it up." And then, assuming that no conscientious leader would have taken the time to eat dinner on such a busy day, he added, "Come on over and have something to eat. I want to talk to you."

Humphrey arrived at Johnson's home (the President had not yet moved into the White House) at 9:30 P.M. At the dinner table with his family and a few advisers and aides, the President called for the several drafts which had been prepared for his first address to Congress and the nation the next day. He read parts of them aloud and asked for comment. Humphrey was outspoken in his criticism or praise of the drafts and frank in his suggestions on what Johnson should say.

"I told him the speech ought to be short," Humphrey remembers, "and that it ought to place a strong emphasis upon President Kennedy and the Kennedy program, and that somewhere in the speech he ought to make it crystal-clear that he intended to follow through on those policies and programs of the late President." As they finished dinner, Johnson said, "Hubert, you and Abe Fortas [an attorney and long-time Johnson adviser] go ahead and redraft these speeches and get me one that will be suitable for tomorrow."

Humphrey and Fortas worked together, culling random paragraphs from the early drafts and dictating new ideas and language. Humphrey suggested the line "Let us continue." At 2 A.M., less than twelve hours before the President was due to address Congress, they finished the final draft. Johnson delivered it almost without change.

The new President was receptive to Humphrey's suggestions, and he encouraged a continuation of the relaxed and friendly relationship they had enjoyed for fifteen years. One week after the assassination, when Humphrey was in Flordia for a brief Thanksgiving weekend rest with his wife, the President phoned to ask for his ideas on the commission (headed by Chief Justice Earl Warren) to investigate and report on the assassination. They also talked about reaction to Johnson's first address to Congress. Humphrey thought that the public and press reaction to the speech was good. Johnson teased him. "Hubert, you seem to like the speeches that you write better than the ones you don't write."

"Don't worry about the government and the country," Humphrey said to a few staff assistants when he returned to his office after one meeting with the President in early December 1963. "We have a tough leader and taskmaster in the White House." Congress was then stalled on even the most vital appropriations measures. After one strategy meeting had ended, Johnson called Humphrey back and said, "I want you, Hubert, to see that these appropriations bills get out and are acted upon." Humphrey and others pushed, prodded, cajoled, and maneuvered Congress into action. The legislative impasse was broken, even though many leaders in both the Senate and House had said, "It can't be done." Johnson ignored the pessimistic predictions. Humphrey said again and again, "We've got to try." The two men were in contact several times a day in the final weeks of the session.

Humphrey saw a new and different Presidency as he watched and worked with Johnson in 1964. One regular participant at the weekly breakfast meeting of the President, White House aides and Congressional leaders has said:

"We start promptly at eight forty-five. The President has a long agenda. He proceeds at once with its consideration. There is a difference of operation between Kennedy and Johnson because they are very different personalities. They follow the same general format in the discussion, but it is a matter of emphasis and technique. President Johnson goes over the bills again and again, until it is driven home that he wants action. There is no once-over-lightly. The breakfast meetings are longer. Johnson is more persistent, more demanding, less subtle, and—it might be added—a little less considerate of the desires of the members present.

"He made it crystal-clear that he wanted prompt action on the tax bill, for example, and he pitched in himself to assure it by innumerable conferences with Senators, and particularly with his conference with Senator [Harry] Byrd. He has been able to work with the Southerners and get them to loosen up a bit . . . the Johnson technique is one of moving carefully and only after he has contacted and consulted practically anybody and everybody concerned."

After the formal meetings Johnson often asked Humphrey to linger for private conversations about legislative and political questions. Again and again the new President consulted Humphrey on a wide range of domestic and foreign problems. He and his wife frequently had dinner with the First Family, and Humphrey was usually present at White House social affairs. But, rather surprisingly, he was not as close personally to Johnson in 1964 as he had been to Kennedy in 1963.

Paradoxically, Johnson pulled Humphrey closer to the office and the institution of the Presidency. Kennedy had for three years given Humphrey innumerable formal and unofficial assignments, which he loyally fulfilled. But in 1964, Johnson put Humphrey to work almost full time with hundreds of informal chores and such major assignments as the floor leadership for the Administration's Civil Rights Bill.

On Thursday night, January 16, 1964, Humphrey and his wife attended a White House dinner for a large number of Senate couples. When the formal evening ended, the President and Mrs. Johnson asked the Humphreys, Senator and Mrs. Fulbright, and Larry O'Brien and his wife to join them in the private living quarters of the White House for a late visit. The four couples spent an hour and a half in pleasant and relaxed conversation. There was some serious talk about the foreign aid program. Humphrey contributed his ideas freely.

A few days later he commented, "I think these exchanges have been mighty helpful. I'm in basic agreement about what the President wants to do. I must say I believe [my] memoranda have been helpful to the President. He thanked me a couple of times that evening."

22

Power and Purpose

Politics in the United States, it sometimes seems, is the art of the superficial.

In an electronic age of opinion polls, market analysis, image-making techniques, and ten-second television spots, a man's face and tone of voice can become more important than his beliefs or the fact that he has no particular beliefs. In a country in which the people are drawn into a whirl of recreation and pleasant diversions, they have little time to grasp the complex or cope with the difficult. In a society confused by the conflicts between races and repelled by the issues of survival or annihilation, the average citizen prefers the comfort of the easy answer and the superficial judgment.

"Can you give us a one-paragraph comment on Red China's nuclear bomb?" a reporter asks a politician. "Tell us—in thirty seconds—your views on civil rights," a television interviewer asks a national leader. From the time he leaves school, the averge American is conditioned to respect brevity and demand quick summaries. The pattern can foster demagogues, men who are more glib than wise or more handsome than honest. The news reporters cannot be blamed; their editors want the incisive quote and the capsule comment. The editors cannot be blamed; the readers or viewers are busy people who become impatient with the tedious and terrible truths of the twentieth century. The people cannot be blamed; how can they be expected to fathom the force of hate in the hearts of white men and black men or the awesome power of a billion Asians whose leaders hold a nuclear bomb?

The urge to stereotype men is as strong as the desire to simplify the issues. Generally an American politician is quickly pegged as a "liberal" or "conservative." He seems "sincere" or he sounds "shady." In the good-guys-or-bad-guys perspective of Americans, first impressions are often final impressions. Through most of the phases of his career the politician is described as two-dimensional. The larger his audience, the smaller his image becomes in the spotlight of national attention. Only when he reaches or approaches the pinnacle of power, the Presidency, does his image become large or great. A thousand spotlights are then turned on every facet of his character and personality. He is re-examined, analyzed, and enlarged for the public view. As the press and the people gaze at him more intently, he becomes "complex." (What man is not?) In a nation which worships bigness, he also becomes bigger than life. Because Americans are a hopeful people, the President and the men who are close to the Presidency often become, in the public view, all-wise political supermen. Their images expand into even larger superficialities. Then when it is perhaps too late for rational judgment by the public, the leader becomes more myth than man and a book about him—with a subtitle such as "The Man Behind the Myth"—becomes a best seller.

America's political leaders are not as small or simple as their first public images usually suggest, nor are they bigger than life when they approach the Presidency. The best of them are still men, occasionally mean, jealous, petty, or selfish, and often wrong in their judgments about what is best for America. But they are not ordinary men; they are uncommonly dedicated, patriotic, and skilled political leaders who are capable of brilliance and courage.

Through much of his career Hubert Humphrey has been described in absolute and simple terms, partly because of his own inclination to use them, even when speaking about himself. Especially in the heat of an election campaign, when he becomes tired or angry, he can surrender to the pattern of superficiality in American politics and his speeches can revolve around clichés, platitudes, and slogans. He was once a practicing pharmacist; he still likes to prescribe precise formulas to the imprecise realm of political affairs. He has said a thousand times to millions of people, "I am a liberal. I am a politician." His tone of voice for such self-description is usually flat and final, as if nothing more needed to be known about him.

He is a liberal and a politician, in the broad and modern connotation of those terms. But to stop with that dual identification would be as misleading as to describe Lyndon Johnson only as a Democrat and a Texan, or to have described John Kennedy only as a moderate and a wit. In some substantive areas Humphrey is basically conservative; his policies for small business and agriculture, for example, would halt a natural tide toward consolidation, merger, and bigness. And at times he is even apolitical; when he roots for the New York Yankees—which he does publicly and enthusiastically—he risks his political standing among baseball fans in nine other major cities with American League teams. He cannot be described in absolute terms. Because he is, in part, a product of experiences ranging from abject failure to great triumph, his qualities of confidence and insecurity are relative, not precise. Because he has involved himself with so many causes and so many people, his viewpoints are complex and diverse. Because his traits and techniques have changed and will continue to change, he cannot be pinned down with enduringly accurate characterizations. He is practical and idealistic, pragmatic and visionary, ambitious and humble—and almost constantly shifting from one mood or perspective to another.

In an instant of tragedy or through the process of an election, Hubert Humphrey could become President of the United States. Because of that possibility it is important for the American people to penetrate the superficial images which still cling to him and to recognize his limitations and strengths *before* the bigger-than-life myths begin to evolve.

Hubert Humphrey would be an unusual President, would probably be a good President, and might—if national and international circumstances sufficiently challenged him—be marked by history as a great President.

He would take office with several troublesome but not necessarily crippling limitations.

One of his most appealing characteristics—his love of people—would in one sense be a Presidential weakness. Humphrey is almost incapable of saying "No" to the request of any human being, particularly when it is made personally and directly to him. He would have trouble, as he does now, turning down the marginally important or inconsequential requests for his time and effort. He would be, at least at first, reluctant to make decisions which would hurt or disappoint individuals or groups of people he knows. With him in the White House there would be some procrastination in the making of decisions to resolve irreconcilable conflicts among his "friends."

As President he would need to develop a respect for the press generally, instead of simply liking most individual reporters. Every President becomes dissatisfied or irritated with the errors or superficiality of many news media, but generally a President learns to keep his expressions of indignation private, or within reasonable bounds. Humphrey would have to give up the luxury of angry complaints to reporters or blanket condemnations of the press (which he stated publicly in the past) and begin to regard the press as a valuable if imperfect element of the democratic process. If not, he would be in for trouble.

He would have to improve a few of his work habits. A President can and should devote attention to detail, and not limit himself to lofty policy questions. Humphrey has an excellent executive talent for "follow-through" on his large decisions, but he also tends to waste time by dabbling in detail or immersing himself in trivia. It is impressive that he enjoys spending hours dictating answers to letters which could be competently handled by his staff, but not when critical problems are left unattended or when important requests for appointments go unanswered. As President he would also need to realize that the person or people in front of him are not necessarily the most important human beings in the world with the most pressing problems of the moment. (In 1960 he kept two large groups of influential leaders in Salt Lake City waiting for an extra twenty minutes—he was already an hour late—while he talked in a hotel lobby with the editor of a monthly newsletter with a total circulation of nineteen readers.)

It would require an almost revolutionary change in his habits, but Humphrey as President would have to force himself to be on time for appointments and conferences more often. It was amusing when, in 1936, he ran into the church in Huron, South Dakota, for his wedding and breathlessly shouted, "Great guns, I'm late!" And there is a certain drama and aura of excitement about his entrances into television studios only a few seconds before a live network program begins. But as President he would cause himself and his programs unnecessary trouble if he continued the habit.

Most important, he would need to control his restless compulsion for pure motion and activity and to reduce his dependence on the actual presence of other human beings. The Chief Executive's time and energy are too valuable to be wasted on frantic and directionless efforts with little more purpose than to sustain a mood of urgency. At least a small portion of the President's time should be reserved for quiet and lonely thought on the great substantive questions facing the nation.

These weaknesses would probably become apparent in the first months of a Humphrey Administration. But he has the discipline necessary to adapt to the demands of a new position, which would probably minimize their effect after he had been in the White House a year or so. One of the most significant qualities in Humphrey is also one of the most important qualifications for an effective President: a capacity for growth. Humphrey has talent in reserve, ability in depth, and untapped resources of energy and intelligence which the duties of the Presidency would require. Throughout his career even his critics have acknowledged that he has continued to grow in stature and skill. He has, at times, required an apprenticeship or a period of adjustment before he began to demonstrate effectiveness in a new position. But basically he has been able to step smoothly into new and different responsibilities and to learn from his mistakes.

He might make some whopping mistakes as President, primarily —and this is a strength—because of his eagerness to accept difficult tasks and his courage to act for what he believes is right. The Presidential responsibilities would undoubtedly make him more cautious than he has been in the past, but he would continue to speak candidly and act decisively. His courage is not a sort of rigid devotion to doctrine, exemplified to some extent by such men as William Jennings Bryan and Robert LaFollette; he is far more practical and politically sensitive than either of those progressives. He takes great risks only when great challenges or his basic convictions are involved. His courage is of the most impressive caliber. As a man with a great need to be liked, he is willing to stand alone, to endure the indifference of others to causes which command his attention, and to risk even the mockery of a prevailing public attitude. And as he proved with his civil rights speech at the 1948 Democratic Convention, he has the courage to advocate forcefully a position even when he fully understands the extent to which that advocacy will endanger his own popularity or political future.

As President, Humphrey would work as hard as or harder than any man who has ever occupied the office. It probably would require the initiative of Mrs. Humphrey, the cooperation of his staff, the orders of the White House physician, and the combined strength of the armed forces to get him to take anything more than a three- or four-day vacation for real rest and relaxation.

He would, however, enjoy most of the work of the Presidency, and—within the outer limits of dignity and restraint—bring a spirit of fun and a sense of humor to the White House. If the people regarded John Kennedy's sophisticated wit as amusing, they would probably consider Humphrey's earthy humor as hilarious. If the Secret Service worries about Lyndon Johnson's habit of shaking hands through the White House fence, its agents would begin to battle ulcers after a few years of protecting a President Humphrey. It is entirely possible that as President, Humphrey might walk down and across Pennsylvania Avenue from the White House to tend to a personal financial chore at Riggs National Bank, on the corner of Fifteenth Street. In the process he would probably shake a hundred hands and sign dozens of autographs. (Soon after he ascended to the Presidency, Harry Truman innocently ordered a car during a noon hour and went to his bank to make a deposit. He was, of course, recognized by hundreds of shoppers and office workers in downtown Washington, and a massive traffic jam resulted.)

The White House itself would probably be less formal than it has been since the time of Teddy Roosevelt. (Or possibly Andrew Jackson. In 1960, Presidential candidate Humphrey told some of his audiences, "If I'm elected, you come on down to Washington. We'll have an inaugural celebration that'll make Andy Jackson's look like a church picnic.") He would make the White House, even more than it is now, "the people's house." Mrs. Humphrey would be an able, confident, and unpretentious First Lady. She would be relatively unpolitical, but she would be active and influential in efforts for such programs as research and care for mentally retarded children. On the wishes of both Humphrey and Mrs. Humphrey, the White House would enthusiastically welcome visits by children, ranging from toddlers to college students.

Humphrey would seek out and tend to attract able and conscientious men for major and minor appointments to federal positions. He would, possibly, make an occasional hasty judgment, but generally the quality of public servants in Washington would rise under a Humphrey Administration.

The government's employee force and the scope of its activities would enlarge, but Humphrey would not be "socialistic," as his enemies would fear. He might try for several TVA-type conservation programs, but he would also surprise many conservatives by cutting back some government activities which he would feel could be handled efficiently and willingly by the states, local governments, or private enterprise.

As do all Presidents, he would have trouble with Congress, partly because he would ask for and sometimes demand legislation which Congress—in its more conservative and deliberative spirit— would be reluctant to approve. Generally, however, he would be reasonable and skilled in his relationships with Congress. His sixteen years of experience in the legislative branch and his understanding of its processes and prejudices would boost the prospects for approval of his programs.

He would be relatively well qualified by knowledge and experience to deal effectively and quickly with a wide range of national and international problems, with perhaps—at first—the single exception of military policy and strategy. He would probably place emphasis on positive efforts in these fields: education, civil rights, welfare, conservation, medical research, the United Nations and other international cooperative agencies, disarmament and arms control, world food needs and foreign aid programs patterned after the concept of the Alliance for Progress in Latin America—which is centered on loan programs instead of outright grants and depends in large measure on local initiative and pledges of democratic reform.

Favoring a brand of personal diplomacy, he would be eager to travel overseas. He would probably show a greater willingness to negotiate with, or at least talk to, actual or potential adversaries in the world. He would also be tough, and not at all naïve, about the designs and conspiracies of Russian or Chinese Communist leaders. In any grave international crisis or direct threat to United States security, he would act as carefully as possible, but as decisively as necessary. He fully understands and is almost constantly aware of the potentially devastating effects of nuclear war and the possibilities of small local conflicts "escalating" into total war involving the major powers. He would make continuous and positive efforts to minimize the chances of war; his Administration also would stress a theme of positive and practical programs for "an enduring and just peace for all nations."

He would probably be a controversial President. He would make demands of the government, challenge the people, call for sacrifice, fight special interests when he felt that they were acting contrary to the public interest, and freely express his thoughts on almost every domestic and international question, issue, or event. The American people and most of the world's leaders would know exactly what he thought on most issues; inevitably many of them would not like what they heard from him. He would not be content to act only as the protector of the status quo. He would advocate, initiate, and experiment; his would be a "strong" and creative Presidency.

Some of his programs would fall flat; others might become great and lasting achievements. Some of his new ideas would be ridiculed; others would be acclaimed and put into practice. But whatever the procedural failures or substantive successes of a Humphrey Administration, he would infuse a spirit of vitality and originality into the atmosphere of a goverment which has often been ponderously dull and bureaucratically unimaginative. He would seek to stimulate greater interest by the people in political affairs and a stronger sense of identification by the people with their government. He would expand the President's role as chief "educator" in the nation—seeking to instruct and showering his audiences with facts, statistics, and ideas. He would also plead with the people to accept and act on their "moral responsibilities," and would hope to educate them to the complex issues of the times. He would seek to avoid any implication of "going over the heads" of Congress, but he would "go to the people" often as President, either directly or via radio-television. Even without a period of sustained crisis such as depression or war, he would probably institute a series of "fireside chat"-type addresses. Generally he would be eloquent and effective in such efforts, but occasionally he would be criticized for "lecturing" to the people or of talking to excess.

In his formal Presidential responsibilities he would be practical and sophisticated, fully aware of the realities of domestic and international politics and properly respectful of the traditions of the nation and the Presidency. In the larger and less precise sphere of his relationship with the American people, he would be essentially idealistic and optimistic. There would be no cynicism in his efforts to identify himself with and speak to the people as a whole. Under a Humphrey Presidency more citizens would probably regard their government as a noble extension of the national will and as a legitimate instrument for the achievement of national aspirations. If he and the nation were lucky, the United States during a Humphrey Administration would probably have a greater sense of identity and purpose. A Humphrey Presidency could become known as a period of "the American Community," and it is possible that the people would be conditioned to care more about one another, to express more compassion about other peoples, and— perhaps— become happier in the process.

Whatever his political fate, Hubert Humphrey can be expected to remain influential and to continue to contribute his talents and energies to the nation for many years. One of Washington's most thoughtful and respected reporters says, "Humphrey is a remarkable human being. He is typical of the very best characteristics of the United States. He is enormously energetic, enormously optimistic, deeply idealistic, supremely resourceful, and never depressed or put off by the stupidity of the human race. These are not necessarily unique American characteristics, but they are American and they are the best that we have. Humphrey, better than anyone else, typifies them."

Humphrey's basic force as a man and his essential power as a political leader do not spring from legal authority, political position, or even skill in the craft of government. His force stems from the humanity of his convictions; his power is somehow generated from within him, through his faith, his optimism, and his identification with people.

Benjamin Disraeli wrote: ". . . All power is a trust . . . we are accountable for its exercise . . . from the people and for the people all springs, and all must exist."

Hubert Humphrey would probably be impatient with the abstract quality of those words, but they represent an attitude which is central to his concept of political power.

A veteran Senate reporter touched on the essence of Humphrey's purpose when he said, "It's a reporter's job to spot the crooks and the phonies. We have to be careful about judging a man's motivation, but generally we find that the politicians who really care about people are the most effective. Humphrey cares, intensely, about people."

Perhaps Hubert Humphrey stated his own essential purpose most clearly in an address to the American Food for Peace Council in San Francisco a few years ago. He ended that speech with this expression of hope:

"Sometime maybe we in this country will get over headline history and start to look back into the fine print of the chapter of human achievement. When that chapter is read—and the book is yet to be written—I am convinced and I am confident . . . it will say that the American people, who were gifted and privileged to have abundance at a time of human need, also had the goodness of heart and spirit to dedicate these great resources that came to them from a bountiful and divine Providence to the welfare of God's finest creation—people."

ABOUT THE PHOTOGRAPHS

Treaty signing: At the White House Ceremony were, left to right, Senator John Pastore, Ambassador Averill Harriman, Senator George Smathers, Senator William Fulbright, Secretary of State Dean Rusk, Senator George Aiken, Humphrey, Senator Everett Dirksen, Disarmament Agency Chief William Foster, Senator Howard W. Cannon, Senator Leverett Saltonstall, Senator Thomas Kuchel, and Vice President Lyndon Johnson.

Humphrey's speech: "Yes, this is a wonderful time in which to live. It challenges the best in us. It calls for doing the impossible—performing miracles. Mediocrity must give way to excellence; timidity to daring; fear to courage.

"We dream of sending a man to the moon in this decade. We know that dream will be fulfilled only with sacrifice, a commitment, a plan and program. But we shall do it.

"Our greater responsibility—an even more demanding challenge—is to achieve mankind's dream and hope of a better world through sacrifice, a commitment, a plan and a program.

"Our strength is not to be measured only by our military, our industry, our technology; the real strength of a free society is in its people—and their commitment to freedom and social justice.

"With such standards our nation will be known not for the power of our weapons, but for the power of our compassion, and the strength of our dedication to human welfare."

INDEX

Acheson, Dean, 186
ADA (see "Americans for Democratic Action")
Adams, John, 172, 173
Agronsky, Martin, 27
Albany, Oregon, 35
Albright, Robert, 206
Alexander, Holmes, 206
Alliance for Progress, 72, 323
Alsop, Joseph, 18
American Broadcasting Company, 27
Americans for Democratic Action, 147, 150, 152, 153, 154, 185, 221
Anderson, Clinton P., 172, 257, 259
Anderson, Elmer, 249
Anderson, Mrs. Eugenie, 147, 148-149, 154
Anderson, Dr. William A., 63, 68
Anti-Semitism, 114, 123-124
Arms Control and Disarmament Agency, U.S., 263-264
Arvey, Jake, 155

Bailey, Charles W. II, 25
Bailey, John, 154
Baltimore Sun, The, 241
Baker, Bobby, 225
Ball, Joseph, 160-161, 162, 163-165
Barkley, Alben, 157, 160, 293
Bemidji, Minnesota, 92
Benson, Ezra Taft, 302
Berryville, Virginia, 188
Biemiller, Andrew J., 152, 153-154, 155, 156, 159
Birmingham, Alabama, 278
Bismarck, Otto von, 79
Bjornson, Val, 219

Blatnik, John A., 240
Blough, Roger, 239
Bowles, Chester, 128
Bradley, Judge Charles C., 56-57
Bridges, Styles, 185
Brown, William S., 107
Bryan, William Jennings, 44, 47, 65, 301
Buck, Muriel (see Mrs. Hubert H. Humphrey)
Bundy, McGeorge, 30
Burke, Edmund, 86
Burr, Aaron, 171
Byrd, Harry F., 187, 188-194, 196, 225, 236

Cahn, Julius, 233, 235
Calhoun, John C., 291
California Democratic Council, 83
Calver, Dr. George, 3
Catholic Church, Minnesota, 96
Catholic Issue in 1960 election, 18
Celler, Emanuel, 267
Christian Science Monitor, The, 241
Church, Frank, 237
Churchill, Winston, 145
Citadel, 188-189
Civil Rights, 42, 124, 150-160, 210, 276-285, 293, 323
Civil Rights Act of 1964, The, 177, 208, 217, 278-285
Clark, "Champ," 47
Clark, Joseph S., 237
Clay, Henry, 179
Collier, Tarleton, 129-130
Communications Satellite Act, 240, 267

Communism, 144, 145-149, 186, 221
Communist Control Act of 1954, The, 221-222
Connally, Tom, 184
Connelly, Matt, 182
Cook, Guy W., 40
Coolidge, Calvin, 51, 298
Cooper, John Sherman, 222
Corcoran, Patrick J., 107
Cosmos Club, The, 181
Cowles Publcations, 97
Cox, James M., 48
Crime, in Minneapolis, 106-107, 114-115
"Cross of Gold" Speech (Byran), 45

Daily Worker, The, 221
Dallas, Texas, 307
Davis, Charles, 198
De Gaulle, Charles, 311
Democratic Farmer-Labor Party, 98, 112, 113, 144, 146-149
Democratic National Convention, 1896, 47
Democratic National Convention, 1920, 47-48
Democratic National Convention, 1912, 47
Democratic National Convention, 1948, 150-160, 321-322
Democratic National Convention, 1956, 13, 242-243
Democratic National Convention, 1960, 247-248
Democratic National Convention, 1964, 8, 24-32, 91, 286-287
Democratic Party, 47, 89, 110, 111-112, 241
Denver College of Pharmacy, 55
Depression, The, 50-62, 301
Detroit News, The, 184
De Voto, Bernard, 100
Dewey, Thomas, 141, 162
Dirksen, Everett M., 171, 172, 204, 205, 206, 225, 226, 265-266, 279-285
Disarmament, 259-266, 293, 323
Disraeli, Benjamin, 79, 325
Dodd, Thomas J., 29, 264-265
Doland, South Dakota, 35, 36, 37, 38, 39, 40-41, 44, 48-49, 51, 55, 60

Donnely, Ignatius, 93
Douglas, Paul H., 159, 172, 192-193, 199, 200, 202-203, 206, 213, 237, 278, 284
Douglas, William O., 150
Driscoll, Joseph, 181
Drought, 50-62
Dudley, Massachusetts, 34
Dulles, John Foster, 186, 234, 235, 261, 302
Dungan, Ralph, 306, 309
Dust Storms, 52, 55, 57, 60, 61

Eastland, James O., 189
Eastern Establishment, 102-103
Edward VII, King, 45-46
Eel River, Minnesota, 34
Eisenhower, Dwight D., 72, 150, 185, 201, 208, 234, 235, 245, 260, 261, 262, 275, 293, 302, 311
Ellender, Allen J., 25
Emerson, Ralph Waldo, 236
Engle, Clair, 283
Estes, Billie Sol, 204
Evers, Medgar, 278

Farley, James, 10
Farmer-Labor Party, 94, 110-111, 112
Farr, George, 98
Federal Bureau of Investigation, The, 118, 125
FEPC, 124
First Congregational Church, Minneapolis, 41
Flynn, Ed, 155
Food For Peace, 272-274
Forbes Magazine, 299
Ford, Henry, 50
Ford, Henry II, 14
Fortas, Abe, 314
Fosdick, Harry Emerson, 44
Franklin, Benjamin, 169
Freeman, Orville, 99, 147, 148-149, 240, 241, 249
Fulbright, J. William, 225, 265, 266, 288, 316
Funston, Keith, 239

Gale, Samuel C., 124
Gallagher, William, 113
Garner, John Nance, 291

Gartner, David, 304
Gates, Frederick J., 126-128
George, Walter, 191, 197, 199, 200-201, 214
George Washington University, 59
Gilbey, Herb, 38
Goetz, Betty (Mrs. Arthur Lal), 260-261
Goldwater, Barry, 103, 204, 213, 275, 289-290
Grain Terminal Association, 272
Grange, The, 93
Gray, Mrs. Pat, 28, 29, 308
Gridiron Club, 14
Gromyko, Andrei, 233, 265
Grothe, Peter, 275
Gruening, Ernest, 237
Guest, Edgar A., 44
Guilford, Howard, 107
Gunther, John, 128

Hagerty, James, 27
Halleck, Charles, 204
Harding, Warren G., 7, 48
Harriman, Averell, 265, 266
Hart, The Rev. Albert, 41
Hart, Julian, 40
Hart, Philip A., 237
Hartke, Vance, 237
Heaney, Gerald, 240
Hemenway, Ray, 10, 98, 148, 240, 241
Henderson, Leon, 128
Hendrickson, Robert C., 183
Henry, Patrick, 170
Herman, Minnesota, 270
Herther, Irvin, 40
Hiss, Alger, 186
Hitler, Adolf, 46, 67, 74
Hoey, Clyde, 236
Hofstadter, Richard, 185
Holland, Spessard L., 189
Home, Alec Douglas-, 265
Homestead Act, The, 92
Hoover, Herbert, 51, 102
House of Lords, The, 178
House of Representatives, The, 174, 177
Houston, Sam, 173
Howard University, 12-13
Howes, Cecil, 111
Hughes, Richard, 26

Humphrey, Douglas, 28, 70, 206, 297
Humphrey, Elijah, 34
Humphrey, Fern, 42
Humphrey, Frances (Mrs. Frances Howard), 42, 59, 297
Humphrey, Hubert Horatio Sr., 34-35, 36, 37, 38-39, 41, 43-45, 51, 53, 54, 55, 56, 57, 58, 59, 60, 61, 153, 159, 182-183, 186-187, 301
Humphrey, Mrs. Hubert H. Sr., 35, 36, 42-43, 51, 61, 182-183
Humphrey, Hubert Horatio Jr., birth, 34; childhood, 35-48; marriage, 60; during Depression, 51-62; during World War II, 73, 112-113; campaigns for Mayor of Minneapolis, 105-108, 113-115; as Mayor, 115-130; campaigns for U.S. Senate, 160-165, 218, 219, 248-249; campaign for President in 1960, 17-23, 138-139, 241-247, 299; campaign for Vice Presidency, 24-33, 286, 289-291, 297-298; as Vice President, 4-5, 287, 293-300; and the Presidency, 301-305, 315, 319-325
Humphrey, Mrs. Hubert H. Jr. (Muriel), 19, 20, 21, 25, 30, 31, 58, 59, 60-61, 64, 65, 66-67, 68-70, 109, 182, 183, 186, 233, 241, 297, 306, 310, 315, 322
Humphrey, Hubert Horatio III, 70, 297
Humphrey, John, 34
Humphrey, Nancy (Mrs. C. Bruce Solomonson), 65, 70, 297
Humphrey, Ralph, 42, 297
Humphrey, Robert, 70, 285, 297
Hunt, Lester C., 183, 213
Huron, South Dakota, 54, 55, 58, 59, 60, 61

Influenza Epidemic, 1918, 37-38
Inside U.S.A., 128

Jackson, Andrew, 102, 304, 322
James, Henry, 181
Javits, Jacob K., 237
Jefferson, Thomas, 291
Jenkins, Walter, 26, 29, 289
Jenner, William, 171

Jensen, George M., 124
Johnson, Edwin C., 183
Johnson, Glenn, 98
Johnson, Lyndon B., 24-25, 26, 27, 29, 30, 31, 70, 72, 102, 133-134, 177, 183, 204, 206, 211-216, 222, 228, 236, 242, 244, 247, 249, 250, 261, 283, 285, 286, 289, 293-294, 295, 298-299, 305, 307, 308, 309, 312-316, 319, 322
Johnston, Olin D., 28, 209, 220
Joint Committee on the Reduction of Nonessential Federal Expenditures, 187, 189-194
Joseph, Mrs. Burton (Geri), 19, 20, 21
Judd, Walter, 99

Kampelman, Max, 146, 147, 149, 196, 198, 242
Karth, Joseph E., 240
Kasherman, Arthur, 114-115
Katzenbach, Nicholas, 281, 282
Keating, Kenneth B., 205
Keevan, Alice, 40
Kefauver, Estes, 98, 222, 242-243, 302
Kelly, Ed, 155, 159
Kennedy, John F., 11, 17, 18, 19, 23, 24, 72, 86-87, 101-102, 138, 188, 204, 242-243, 244-250, 263, 265-266, 276, 278, 293, 303, 305-312, 315, 319, 322
Kennedy, Mrs. John F., 304, 307, 309
Kennedy, Robert F., 20, 24, 247, 281, 282, 285
Kenny, Sister, 122, 123
Kenworthy, E. W., 204, 290-291
Kerr, Robert, 177, 183, 199-200, 258
Khrushchev, Nikita, 86, 233-236, 240, 249, 289
Kilgore, Harley, 220
King, Cyril, 277-278
Kirk, Russell, 271
Kirkpatrick, Dr. Evron, 68, 71, 106, 107, 110, 114
Kline, Marvin, 109, 114, 115
Knowland, William, 184
Kozlov, Frol, 233
Kristiansand, Norway, 35
Kubicek, William, 146, 149
Kuchel, Thomas H., 279-280, 285

LaFollette, Robert, 94, 179
Langer, William "Wild Bill," 94, 222
Laos, 85
Lawrence, David, 155
Lawrence, William H., 32
League of Nations, 48, 175, 265
Lehman, Herbert, 213, 220
Le Mars, Iowa, 56
Lenin (Vladimir Ilich Ulyanov), 46
Lewis, Sinclair, 39-40, 48
Liberals, in the Senate, 213, 215, 228, 237, 239-240
Liberalism, 65, 96-97, 185, 228, 237, 238-240, 241
Life Magazine, 236
Liggett, Walter, 107
Lily, South Dakota, 35
Lindbergh, Charles A., 50
Lippmann, Walter, 103
Lodge, Henry Cabot, 184, 230, 250
Long, Huey, 67
Long, Russell B., 67, 225
Look Magazine, 239
Louisiana State University, 66-67
Louisville Courier-Journal, The, 129
Lucas, Scott, 151, 152, 184, 200
Lutherans, Minnesota, 96-97

McCarran-Walter Immigration Act, The, 186
McCarthy, Eugene J., 27, 28, 88, 99, 237, 240, 241
McCarthy, Joseph P., 97, 171, 219-223, 237
McCarthyism, 186, 219-223
McFarland, Ernest, 200, 212-213
McGee, Gale W., 237
McGovern, George, 9, 273
McNamara, Robert S., 30
McWilliams, Carey, 123
Macalester College, 74, 112
MacArthur, Douglas, 218
Maclay, William, 171
Madison, James, 174
Madison, Wisconsin, 13
Magnuson, Warren G., 225
Main Street, 39
Malone, George "Molly," 172
Mansfield, Mike, 225, 226, 236, 250, 257, 280, 288
Marshall, Burke, 282

Marshall, George C., 149
Marshall Plan, The, 161, 162, 184
Marshall, Thomas R., 291
Mayo Clinic, 91, 137, 216
"Medicare," 258
"Meet the Press," 27, 279
Methodist Church, 41, 58
Metropolitan Club, The, 181-182
Mikoyan, Anastas, 233, 235
Millikin, Eugene, 160, 197-198, 199, 200-203
Minneapolis, Minnesota, 37, 44, 58, 60, 126
Minneapolis *Star* and *Tribune*, The, 97, 109, 114, 150
Minnesota, 66, 91-100
Mintener, Bradshaw, 118, 124
Mitchell, Wallace, 150
Mondale, Walter F., 99
Moody, Blair, 184
Morgan, J. P., 46
Morse, Wayne, 225
Morgenthau, Henry, 191
Morrison, Bradley L., 124-125
Moss, Frank E., 237
Moyers, Bill, 309
Mundt, Karl E., 288, 313
Murray, James, 184, 213-214
Murrow, Edward R., 183
Muskie, Edmund S., 237
Myers, Francis, 151, 156

Naftalin, Arthur, 106, 107, 110, 114, 147, 149
National Association for the Advancement of Colored People, 241
National Farm Bureau Federation, 56
National Foundation, The, 122, 123
Nelson, Gaylord, 137
Neuberger, Richard, 275
New Deal, The, 55, 58, 185, 241
New Orleans, Louisiana, 67
New York Times, The, 9, 70, 204, 290-291, 299
New York Times Magazine, The, 240
New York World, The, 46-47
New York Yankees, The, 50, 319
Niebuhr, Dr. Reinhold, 241
Niven, Paul, 209, 299
Nixon, Richard M., 22, 188, 249, 261, 275, 293, 298

Non-Partisan League, The, 94, 164
Norris, George, 179
Nuclear Test Ban Treaty, 5, 261, 262, 264-266

O'Brien, Lawrence, 87, 305, 308, 309, 316
O'Donnell, Kenneth, 26, 87, 308-309
Olson, Floyd B., 94, 99, 110, 164
O'Neal, Edward A., 56
O'Neill, Thomas, 241

Pageant Magazine, 8
Pastore, John O., 179, 225, 226
Peace Corps, The, 80, 81, 275-276
Pearson, Drew, 183
Peterson, P. Kenneth, 248
Phi Beta Kappa, 64
Pierce, Franklin, 7
Platt, Orville, 170
Polio Epidemic, 1946, 122-123
Political Power, 131-135
Politics, definitions of, 79, 81-83
Populism, 46-47, 66, 93, 94, 239
Powers, Dave, 309
Presidency, The, 301-305, 315, 319-325
Prohibition, 50
Proxmire, William, 237

Rauh, Joseph, 19, 147, 152, 153, 155
Rayburn, Sam, 25, 154, 156, 159
Republican Party, Minnesota, 109, 218, 219
Reuss, Henry S., 275
Reuther, Walter, 128
Ridder Publications, 132
Ridder, Walter, 8
Roberts, Chalmers M., 296
Robinson, Jackie, 241
Rochester, Minnesota, 91
Rolvaag, Karl, 137, 216
Roosevelt, Mrs. Eleanor, 128, 147, 243
Roosevelt, Franklin D., 48, 54, 55, 57, 58, 63, 65, 67, 72, 74, 113, 185, 239, 245, 301, 302
Roosevelt, Franklin D. Jr., 18
Roosevelt, Theodore, 17, 46, 47, 175-176, 229, 298, 322
Rossiter, Clinton, 291
Rowe, James, 19, 27, 140, 246

Rusk, Dean, 30
Russell, Richard B., 160, 177, 209, 225, 226, 279-285, 288
Ryan, Ed, 107, 115, 117-119, 120, 127

Sacco and Vanzetti, 50
Salinger, Pierre, 25
Sannes, Andrew, 35, 49
Saturday Evening Post, The, 8, 299
Sauk Centre, Minnesota, 39
Schlesinger, Arthur M. Jr., 87
Scott, Hugh, 237
Secret Service, 5, 322
Seeley, Sir John Robert, 79
Senate Committee on Finance, 199
Senate Committee on Foreign Relations, 5, 214, 224, 229
Senate Disarmament Subcommittee, 260-261
Senate, The United States, 169-180
Seymour, Gideon, 109
Shaffer, Samuel, 240
Sherman, Norman, 137, 217
Sherwood, "Doc," 40
Shipstead, Henrik, 94
Shriver, Sargent, 276
Simms, William, 108, 114, 120, 183
Smathers, George A., 308
Smith, Alfred E., 45, 155
Smith, Gerald L. K., 118
Solomonson, C. Bruce, 26, 29, 297
Sorensen, Theodore, 87
South Dakota, 34, 45, 51, 52, 54, 62
Southerners, in the Senate, 187, 188, 189, 208-210
Soviet Union, 232-236
Sparkman, John, 222
St. Cloud, Minnesota, 8
St. Louis Post-Dispatch, The, 181
St. Paul Dispatch, 37
Stassen, Harold, 99, 109, 160, 260
Stennis, John, 189
Stevenson, Adlai E., 13, 98, 137, 242, 243, 247, 248, 249, 261, 307
Stewart, John G., 259
Strout, Richard, 241
Symington, Stuart, 244, 250

Taft-Hartley Act, The, 150, 160, 162, 164, 186
Taft, Robert A., 160

Taft, William Howard, 46, 47
Talmadge, Herman E., 208
Tammany Hall, 83
Tax Bill debates of 1950-51, 197-201
Thompson, Mayor "Big Bill," 50
Thurmond, J. Strom, 150, 151, 159-160, 162, 173, 237
Thye, Edward, 183
Time Magazine, 181, 227
Toffler, Al, 8
Tocqueville, Alexis de, 103-104
Troyanovsky, Oleg, 233
Truman, Harry S., 72, 102, 132, 141, 149-150, 151, 154, 156, 160, 161-162, 182-183, 185, 186, 218-219, 259, 293, 298, 302, 311
Tugwell, Rexford, 54

Union Lakes, Minnesota, 34
United Nations, 84, 230, 323
University of Minnesota, 53, 61, 63, 64, 65-66, 67-68, 95-96, 97, 120
Unruh, Jesse, 132

Valeo, Francis, 260
Vandenberg, Arthur, 184
Vice Presidency, The, 132, 177, 286-287, 291-300
Viet Nam, 85-86

Walker, Frank, 111-112
Walker, Mayor Jimmy, 50
Wallace, Henry, 162
Wallace, South Dakota, 34, 35, 40, 48, 49, 55
Wall Street, 46, 65, 101, 239
Walsh, David I., 170
War Manpower Commission, 73
Warren, Earl, 314
Washington, D.C., 59, 181-182, 187-188, 194-195
Washington, George, 175
Washington Post, The, 9, 11, 206, 296
Waters, Herbert J., 19, 22, 23, 31, 249
Watkins, Arthur, 222
Waverly, Minnesota, 4, 100, 250
Webster, Daniel, 177
West Berlin, 72, 150
West Virginia, 1960 primary election, 17-23, 27, 138, 246-247
Wheeler, Burton K., 94, 179

Wherry, Kenneth, 184
White House, The, 182-183, 263, 303-304, 322
White, William S., 188-189
Williams, Harrison A., 237
Williams, Violet, 23
Wilson, Alfred, 124
Wilson, Woodrow, 44, 46, 47, 48, 175, 176, 179, 229, 265, 291, 300, 302
Winton, David J., 124

Wisconsin, 1960 primary election, 17, 138, 245-246
Wolford, Jimmy, 22-23
Works Progress Administration, 60, 68, 73
World War I, 46, 48, 53
World War II, 67, 74, 119

Yarborough, Ralph, 173
Youngdahl, Luther, 218-219